Understanding and Treating the Aggression of Children

1040 July -
Jun

Understanding and Treating the Aggression of Children

Fawns in Gorilla Suits

David A. Crenshaw and
John B. Mordock

JASON ARONSON
Lanham • Boulder • New York • Toronto • Plymouth, UK

Published in the United States of America
by Jason Aronson
An imprint of Rowman & Littlefield Publishers, Inc.

A wholly owned subsidiary of
The Rowman & Littlefield Publishing Group, Inc.
4501 Forbes Boulevard, Suite 200, Lanham, Maryland 20706
www.rowmanlittlefield.com

Estover Road
Plymouth PL6 7PY
United Kingdom

British Library Cataloguing in Publication Information Available

The hardback edition of this book was previously catalogued by the Library of Congress
as follows:

Crenshaw, David A.
   Understanding and treating the aggression of children : fawns in gorilla suits / David A.
 Crenshaw and John B. Mordock.
   p. cm.
   Includes bibliographical references and index.
   1. Aggressiveness in children.   I. Mordock, John B.   II. Title.
RJ506.A35C74 2005
155.4'18—dc22   2004026070

   ISBN-13: 978-0-7657-0034-6 (cloth : alk. paper)
   ISBN-10: 0-7657-0034-4 (cloth : alk. paper)
   ISBN-13: 978-0-7657-0561-7 (pbk. : alk. paper)
   ISBN-10: 0-7657-0561-3 (pbk. : alk. paper)

Printed in the United States of America

⊗™ The paper used in this publication meets the minimum requirements of
American National Standard for Information Sciences—Permanence of Paper
for Printed Library Materials, ANSI/NISO Z39.48-1992.

Understanding and Treating the Aggression of Children is dedicated to the following:

Christine Foreacre
Elizabeth Gorman
Jack Grogan
Barbara Langdon
Nancy McCormack
George Mora

For devoting their entire clinical careers to working with parents and children in gorilla suits. They and many others of our colleagues are our unsung heroes and heroines along with the fawns in gorilla suits they have so ably served.

Contents

Preface

$\mathcal{E}$arlier versions of some of the material, including case material, appeared in the following professional journals and books: *Journal of Clinical Psychiatry and Human Development, Residential Treatment for Children and Youth, The Pointer, Crisis Counseling of Children and Adolescents: A Guide for the Nonprofessional,* and *Bereavement: Counseling the Grieving throughout the Life Cycle.* Included among the clinical vignettes in chapter 9 were those contributed by Christine Oberrieth, William Van Ornum, Barbara Peelor, and Christopher Brown, all former staff members at the Astor Day Treatment Center; and Marilyn McGaulley and Mary Yeck, both with the Dutchess County Board of Cooperative Educational Services. We are grateful to all our dedicated former colleagues and interns at the Astor Home for Children, who greatly enriched our clinical experience and knowledge.

David A. Crenshaw is especially grateful to Kenneth V. Hardy, Ph.D., director of the Eikenberg Institute for Relationships, whose ideas, encouragement, and support have been a great inspiration for the writing of this book. A tremendous intellectual debt is owed to James Garbarino, whose writings on violent youth have been both enlightening and inspiring. The late Walter Bonime, M.D., senior training analyst at New York Medical College, provided me with private supervision from 1980 to 1992, and his wisdom and compassion guide and inform all of my clinical work and writing. Dr. Ray Craddick, my graduate school mentor, has remained a dear friend and source of support and encouragement throughout my career, and I will always be extremely grateful to him. It has been an immense pleasure and mutually stimulating learning experience to collaborate with my longtime and much admired colleague, John B. Mordock, in the writing of these two volumes, *Understanding and Treating the Aggression of Children* and *A Handbook of Play Therapy with Aggressive Children.*

We agree that neither of us could have undertaken such a project alone. In addition, we are extremely grateful to Dr. Jason Aronson, whose enthusiasm, kindness, and support for this project from beginning to end were energizing to both authors. Finally, to all the fawns in gorilla suits and their families we have been privileged to know and honored to accompany, at least briefly, in their arduous journey through life, you will always occupy a special place in our hearts.

1

Fawns in Gorilla Suits

A fawn at the edge of the woods watches with a wary eye. Any sudden movement startles it and sends it scurrying into the woods. If, however, the woodsman remains still and does not approach it, the fawn may, ever so cautiously, move a step closer to him. The metaphor of "fawns in gorilla suits" is introduced, the reasons children put on "gorilla suits" are presented, and the invisible wounds of the suit wearers are discussed. This introductory chapter explains the extreme vulnerability of these children and their need to put on "armor," or a "gorilla suit," or to hide behind a "brick wall of detachment" to protect that tender core.

Peter, a nine-year-old boy in a residential treatment center, chases a ball on the center's playground. He trips over a ball glove left behind by another child and falls hard to the ground, leaving a nasty scrape on his knee. A staff member, concerned that Peter might be hurt, approaches him with concern. Before the adult can get close, however, Peter picks himself up, grabs the discarded glove, and throws it as hard as he can toward the face of the would-be helper. He then screams a torrent of profanities and runs into the woods surrounding the ball field. Peter's reaction to pain, but perhaps more to the feeling of humiliation, is typical of children who put on gorilla suits. They are children who hurt deep inside from invisible but very real wounds, and they distrust the efforts of adults who seek to help. Fearing and anticipating the pain of rejection and humiliation, but dimly aware that others can offer protection and affection, these children don't dare seek care from others until certain that the care won't add to their existing pain. Never having felt secure, safe, and trusting, they have learned to function, albeit rigidly, without these feelings.

Although provided enough physical care to survive, children who don gorilla suits were never consistently loved, protected, and nurtured. They responded to their rejection with aggression, transforming from vulnerable fawns into vicious gorillas not to be reckoned with. The gorilla suit keeps

1

perceived foes at a distance. "If I attack people, I won't be vulnerable to the pain they can cause!" Deeply hurting from their profound losses, they adopt the stance that "I will hurt, reject, or abandon others before they can hurt, reject, or abandon me!"

Aggression and violence among young children have become a major national problem. The December 15, 2003, issue of *Time*, a widely read news magazine, contained an article about the problem entitled, "Does Kindergarten Need Cops?" (Wallis 2003). It discussed the behavior of five- and six-year-olds who were throwing objects at teachers, cursing them, and biting them "so hard they left teeth marks." Included in the article were statistics kept by the Philadelphia City School System. At the time the article was written, the system, which serves more than 200,000 children, had already reported nineteen instances of weapons possession and forty-two assaults by children in kindergarten or first grade in 2003. In one elementary school alone, twenty-one assaults were reported in the first two months of school.

In another nationally reported incident, Josh Belluardo, age thirteen, a student at E. T. Booth Middle School in Woodstock, Georgia, was killed when getting off the bus on November 2, 1998, when he was "struck in the back of the head, kicked in the stomach and hit in the face by a 15-year-old who had [apparently] been taunting him during the bus ride home" (National School Safety Center 2004). It is chilling to think that a child could violently beat another child to death immediately after getting off a school bus. Children as young as five have been given antidepressant drugs to combat the depression behind their aggression, and when the medications fail, they are being hospitalized at alarming rates. One young child in a foster home was hospitalized following uncontrollable crying for her natural mother. Her mother, who regained custody shortly thereafter, said,

> I never heard of medicating because of love. I didn't even know there was such a thing as a mental hospital for five-year-olds. I really have a problem with that. . . . Those medications are not supposed to be given to five-year-olds.

Some gorilla-suit wearers never experienced love, while others experienced it only fleetingly—the love was dispensed inconsistently and unpredictably, interspersed with indifference or even anger. Those with substance-abusing parents may have experienced both love and rejection, depending on whether the parent was high or sober. In violent and abusive families, the suit wearer may have been exposed to a range of parental responses, depending on the parents' mood swings and the tensions within the family. Billy, when nine years old, recalled, "I could always tell whether we were going to be beaten that night by the way my father drove his truck up the driveway after work. If he was weaving from side to side, I knew we were in for it."

Other children benefited from love early in their lives, only to have their sense of trust and safety shattered by a series of traumas at later points in their development. Divorce, death, unemployment, and physical and/or sexual abuse are some of the stressors that can devastate a child's sense of trust. Having once experienced the well-being that results from "good-enough parenting" (Winnicott 1965), these children find the loss is enormous.

Finally, for a small group of children in gorilla suits, life has been horrific! These are the repeatedly abused, often deprived, and severely traumatized children who undergo multiple out-of-home placements. Some never developed a sense of trust while others had it shattered in toddlerhood. These suit wearers are rejected even by other gorilla-suit wearers. Such children typically make up the population of special education classrooms, day treatment centers, and residential treatment facilities. These are the children both of us have treated during our many years serving seriously troubled children. For these children, risking even a modicum of closeness, even with warm and friendly adults, is monumental. Appreciating what is at stake for these children makes it easier to understand the extreme actions that result from their underlying emotions. Shirley Hoxter (1983), working with children of similar backgrounds at the Tavistock Clinic in London, states,

> The injured child's capacity for feeling love and the need for love is so fraught with vulnerability that it is no wonder that his communications abound with images such as armored vehicles, brick walls, ice walls or hedgehog spikes and snails' shells and similar means of warding off exposure to the pain of contact. (p. 130)

The vulnerable tender core that the children seek to protect from further pain led Dr. Crenshaw to the metaphor of "fawns in gorilla suits" (Crenshaw and Hardy in press). At the same time as the children slip on their gorilla suits, they also become emotionally detached. They become apathetic about their condition, actually numbed by the wounds to both their body and their spirit, and they adopt a second protective shield. They hide behind a brick wall of detachment and vow never to let anyone get close enough to betray them again. The primitive defenses they employ against the anxiety aroused by fears of rejection, humiliation, helplessness, and powerlessness also deprive them of emotional nourishment. Living within a context of cumulative emotional deprivation, fearing closeness, and at the same time longing for it result in their repeating earlier rejections. Mental health professionals call the phenomenon the *repetition compulsion*. But C. S. Lewis (1960), in *The Four Loves*, puts it more eloquently when he writes, "They seal off the very fountain for which they are thirsty" (p. 65).

Ronnie was a nine-year-old boy placed in residential treatment for his violent rages. He put on his gorilla suit when protesting his sorry state and hid behind a brick wall when giving in to his despair. One year, he received a birthday card from his biological mother, who had made no effort to contact him in more than six years. Hopelessly drug addicted, she had surrendered her legal rights to Ronnie when he was three. Because of a series of unfortunate events, followed by behavior problems, Ronnie was never successfully adopted, moved from foster family to foster family, and eventually ended up in residential treatment. In the card was a $20 bill. Ordinarily, Ronnie would immediately spend the small amount he earned for completing his chores. The evening child-care worker reported that when he made bedtime checks, Ronnie was fast sleep, tightly clutching the $20 bill, the only tangible gift he had ever received from his mother, but more important, the intangible but longed-for connection to a mother he never had.

Dr. Crenshaw vividly recalls an eleven-year-old Hispanic boy named Miguel, whom Dr. Crenshaw treated early in his career and who had a nightmarish personal history. Along with his understandable rage, fear, and pain, he had a warm, engagingly infectious smile. A goodness in the core of his being often emerged when he was kind, and he enjoyed being helpful. Staff members were heartbroken when word came that a social worker from the city where Miguel grew up would be arriving shortly to return him to his home. The night before, he had broken a chair over the heads of two of his dorm mates, resulting in lacerations requiring medical treatment, the last in a series of violent episodes that the staff could not prevent. There was no other choice but to return him to his home state, where he would be placed in a more secure facility.

Upon hearing this news, he ran out of the office and deep into the surrounding woods. Dr. Crenshaw pursued, got to within one hundred feet of him, and stopped, not wanting to drive him farther into the woods. Dr. Crenshaw stood behind a large tree but watched intently and yelled to him, "Miguel, you have to go back home!" Miguel yelled back, "Don't you understand? This is my home—the only home I have ever had! Please don't send me away!"

This episode occurred more than thirty years ago. Over those years, staff wondered what happened to Miguel and whether their efforts, had they been able to continue, would have turned his life around. The answer will never be known. But Miguel taught us a lesson that cannot be forgotten—a lesson in humility. Not every fawn in a gorilla suit can be helped. Efforts to help them will result in a number of heartbreaking failures. But wouldn't it be wonderful if Miguel knew, wherever he is today, that his warm smile and kind heart inspired Dr. Crenshaw to devote his career to helping children who don gorilla suits? Miguel was one of the first of many fawns in gorilla suits that we have been privileged to meet along our way.

In completing a follow-up study of children treated in the Astor Home for Children, a residential treatment facility where both of us worked, we experienced some interesting revelations about attachment feelings (Mordock 1978). Perhaps the most illustrative example was the response of a man who had spent most of his life in prisons and was serving a life term for murder. He was confined in California and could not be interviewed, but he agreed to complete a questionnaire mailed to him. He wrote on the form that whenever he felt depressed and suicidal, he conjured up images of the happy times he had while in the Astor Home and that these images kept him sane, much like the images of home that have helped war captives to tolerate torture.

When we checked his clinical record, we learned that he lived at the home for only six months, wasn't well liked by staff, was seen as a "loner" by peers, and spent lots of time in the time-out room. In fact, the event that led to his transfer to a more secure facility was his smuggling a crowbar into the time-out room and, when placed there following a planned tantrum, using the implement to rip the room apart. But for him, "The home was the best place I had ever lived in my life."

THEIR INVISIBLE WOUNDS

Hardy (1998) emphasizes that society directs considerable attention to treating visible wounds. When one is severely injured, burned, or scarred, the wounds are treated with concern, support, and empathy. Invisible wounds—those that result from living with devaluation, oppression, domination, degradation, abuse (physical, sexual, or emotional), poverty, or neglect—are rarely recognized or acknowledged. If devaluation is experienced early on, as a result of invisible disabilities, such as temperamental differences, learning disorders, developmental disabilities, and vulnerability to mood disorders, or if one is born female or of color, the resulting wounds rarely receive any attention. In fact, such wounds are usually unrecognized, and calling attention to them carries with it an element of risk, as numerous civil rights leaders can attest.

Hardy (1998) describes the dynamics of oppression that lead to "losing one's voice." He views therapy as a process of helping clients suffering from invisible wounds to "find their voice." The process is complicated by the stigma and shame that accompany their wounds. As we will point out in the next chapter, shame silences many who suffer from invisible wounds. In fact, the wounds themselves are devalued and trivialized, even by the well intended. Those who fail to appreciate that the rage displayed by many disenfranchised individuals follows from their suffering and who respond to them with their own rage create a cycle of violence difficult to interrupt. Hardy (2003) observes the difficulty of seeing beyond the reprehensible behavior of violent youth and appreciating their invisible, neglected, and in many cases dishonored wounds.

Children living with the invisible wounds of learning disorders can suffer repeated academic failure and a resulting humiliation that kills their spirit to continue trying. Sadly, not only is their suffering often unrecognized, but their redeeming qualities, strengths, and talents are also ignored. Continued academic failure can result in children's feeling utterly helpless and demoralized, on top of losing self-respect and hopefulness about future opportunities.

Dr. Mordock's wife, Melody, formerly a principal in a nationally recognized day treatment program for seriously disturbed children, was working as a substance abuse counselor in a public high school when a special education student, mainstreamed in regular classes, became extremely disruptive in the hallway and began screaming obscenities. Educational staff, hearing the commotion, stepped out of their classrooms, holding their arms out as if they were protecting children seated in their classrooms, and watched while the youth screamed, "You don't give a f— about me or my problems!" Melody happened to be in the hallway, waved off the staff, and whispered to the boy, "Your throat must be very dry after all that hollering! Would you like to come to my office for a glass of juice?"

"You don't even know me," the boy screamed.

"But I know when somebody's likely to be thirsty," she replied. When he agreed to come, she said, "You see that crowd down there? We will have to get past them without any trouble. Do you think you could do that with me?" He nodded affirmatively.

The distraught boy entered the room and gradually became calm enough to talk. He said that he had just been informed by guidance staff that he had failed all his subjects, but that he still had to attend all his classes until June—three months away. He vented his frustration at never having succeeded in school and was tired of trying and failing. While he wiped his tears, the principal, accompanied by two policemen, entered the office and told the boy he had to leave with the police and that he could never again set foot in the building. Melody asked if she could escort him from the grounds so he could leave with some dignity, but the principal refused.

Later, Melody felt incomplete about the situation, wishing the boy could have finished his long and undistinguished school life in a more dignified manner, saying good-bye to those he cared about and being affirmed for his past efforts. She was about to broach this topic at a meeting when, instead of receiving praise for her skills at crisis resolution, she was criticized for not calling the police—after all, she could have been hurt! The meeting focused more on "The boy is a closed chapter" than on how staff could more meaningfully engage him during the last three months of school or create more meaningful closure to his academic life. From such attitudes, it isn't really very hard to theorize why school shootings occur. Melody reports that about 90 percent of the youth she counseled in the high school got into trouble after being told that they had failed one or more subjects but still had to attend these classes anyway.

In this light, it isn't surprising that many school failures take the short step to walking with like-minded disenfranchised peers and joining in antisocial behavior that includes aggression and violence, substance abuse, reflexive sexuality, and other high-risk behavior. If additional wounds from poverty, racism, gender bias, bias against one's sexual orientation, absence of one's father or mother, or violence in the home or neighborhood are added to academic frustration, a scarred spirit or soul can be the result.

ENVIRONMENTAL TRIGGERS

Gorilla-suit wearers are especially sensitive to the larger environment. Left unsupervised for large parts of the day, they have unlimited access to television and sometimes to the Internet. Our culture has an ambivalent relationship with violence. We deplore and denounce it, but at the same time, we are magnetized by it: note the popularity of violent video games, action films, and television shows, not to mention the violent lyrics in the music that appeals to many youth. The prevalence of violence must have its origins within us. What is seen in the society at large is the projection, on a wide screen, of the human capacity for violence and destructiveness. Until this painful reality is faced and ways are found to transcend it, major changes will not occur in society as a whole or in the children who are raised in it.

Especially violent acts, such as school shootings, rarely result from a single pressing factor. Typically they were preceded by a long road cluttered with

trauma and exposure to violence, disrupted family and community life, bullying or taunting, failed romantic relationships, and in some cases neurobiological factors. Mulvey and Cauffman (2001) state,

> Previous research has shown that these events do not occur in a vacuum
> and that there are numerous rationales for and pathways to the violent
> act. Identification based only on the characteristics of an individual neg-
> lects these highly salient social and transaction aspects of school violence.
> (p. 799)

School shooters tend to be captivated by firearms or bombs and fascinated
with death or Satanism and to display psychological problems involving depression, impulse control, or sadism (Leary et al. 2003). Traditional male socialization, early victimization, and peer support from the Internet have combined to influence school shooters to externalize their hostilities, targeting
those they perceive to be bullies who humiliate and shame them (Markward
et al. 2001). The Internet offers isolated, alienated, and enraged victimized male
adolescents a new form of socialization and a source of support.

The National School Safety Center's Report on School Associated Violent Deaths (2004) reports, in its summary of violent school deaths from 1992
to 2004, that 263 resulted from shootings, 47 from knife wounds, and 18 from
physical assaults. Of the victims, 270 were males and 77 were females; 233 were
in high school, 55 were in junior high school, and 37 were in elementary
school; and 81 killings occurred on school grounds, with an equal number taking place near a school.

Internet access is also related to sexual abuse among elementary school
children. Janet Stanley, author of *In the Firing Line*, reported on the Fox evening
news program *The O'Reilly Factor* on January 7, 2004, that in her study of Australian children, every child under ten years of age who had sexually abused another child had Internet access to pornography.

Treating gorilla-suit wearers who have sexually abused or tormented
other children is no easy feat until one realizes that underneath the children's
rough exterior is emotional pain. If help givers can see past the armor and get
in touch with this pain, they can encourage the enraged children to discard
their gorilla suits and come out from behind their brick walls of detachment.
When caregivers do so, they will discover in each child a deeply wounded and
vulnerable core. In chapters 2, 3, and 4, we review some of the circumstances
that produce violent children and that bear on our treatment approach. Others in the field have reviewed the existing data on conduct disorders and the
relation between maternal and childhood depression, and readers are referred
to these works for more information (Bloomquist and Schnell 2002; Connor

2002; Gilligan 1996; Goodman and Gotleib 2002; Hill and Maughan 2001; Quinsey et al. 2004; Reid, Patterson, and Snyder 2002).

In the remaining chapters, and in *A Handbook of Play Therapy with Aggressive Children*, we discuss a number of techniques to help suit wearers remove their suits—first by taking them off partially, second by keeping them readily available, and finally by discarding them altogether. We also present techniques to help those in apathy and despair to come out from behind their brick walls—first by enabling them to peer over their wall, second by assisting them to sit on the top, third by helping them to venture out occasionally, and finally by helping them to tear their wall down. In between, there are times when we join the children behind the wall to assist them with their suffering.

Persistent aggressive behavior can lead to more serious and violent behavior in adolescence and adult life. Aggression and its more serious manifestation, violence, defined as inflicting serious bodily harm on others, are inextricably linked unless separated by successful interventions. The onset of aggression later in development is often a temporary response to frustration, usually to the developmental stresses and pressures of adolescence and, therefore, more easily reversible with brief interventions. When unusual aggression is observed in young children, intervention should begin immediately. A "wait and see" attitude is never helpful. If the child is referred for treatment and an assessment reveals a well-adjusted child, no harm has been done. The goal is to deliver treatment that addresses a traumatized child's losses and invisible wounds before they lead to further losses and traumas and to the spiral from childhood aggression to adolescent and adult violence.

There are no shortcuts or quick fixes to the problem of violence. Although training violent men to better manage their anger ("anger management training") has become a popular method for addressing the problem, it does not reach the real problems of violent youth. In many cases the anger of youth is justified. How would you feel if you were robbed of your necessities, beaten, humiliated, and then told you needed to manage your anger better? The training might help you to moderate your revengeful actions temporarily and keep you out of further trouble, but if your goods weren't replaced or your self-esteem wasn't restored, the results would be short lived.

The causes of violence are multiple and interwoven in a complex matrix. Violence can be eliminated only by efforts that are multimodal and multisystemic and that take place at multiple levels, with special emphasis on in-depth, emotionally focused work, which is increasingly rare in today's world of quick-fix approaches to complex problems. Many services are needed to assist violent youth. Our two volumes discuss the mental health component of those services. Effective mental health services are relatively lengthy, but their length is dictated, not by the needs of the therapist, but by the needs of the client. We believe there is no substitute for the intensive, empathy-based, affective work we describe in *Understanding and Treating the Aggression of Children* and *A Handbook of Play Therapy with Aggressive Children.*

2

Developmental Failures and
Invisible Wounds

The predisposing and precipitating factors that produce extremely aggressive responses to frustration are reviewed, with special attention given to the roles of trust, shame, unsolvable fear, and learned voicelessness. These factors are placed in the context of Erik Erikson's stages of human development. Gorilla-suit wearers, because of early traumas, many resulting from poor care and inadequate supervision, fail to master the first stage, trust versus mistrust, and this failure prevents them from mastering any of the stages to follow. Many suffer from a harsh and primitive conscience and seek punishment as often as they inflict it on others.

Unfortunately, children in gorilla suits lock horns with society. Unable to appreciate the reasons society puts limits on their behavior, they disregard hazards, fail to differentiate reality from fantasy, and respond to dangers no one else sees. Minor frustrations cause panic, and panic is followed by attacks on peers or even adults. Eventually, the children are labeled "aggressive" and referred to mental health clinics. If they are young, they are usually diagnosed with oppositional-defiant disorder or, if older, with one of the adjustment reactions. Rarely are they diagnosed with conduct disorder; they are too young to have committed the habitual delinquent acts necessary to receive this label, but follow-up studies reveal that many receive this diagnosis later in life or one even more severe—antisocial personality disorder.

In this chapter, we expand on the encapsulated view of gorilla-suit wearers we present in chapter 1 and take an in-depth look at the backgrounds of children who reluctantly put on gorilla suits. We also place their problems in a developmental context, using Erik Erikson's theories (1963) of child development.

Although childhood experiences should be no excuse for violent acts, overwhelming evidence indicates that most children who respond with serious aggression to seemingly minor frustrations grew up in rejecting, neglectful, abusive households with periodic abandonment by at least one caregiver (Bloomquist and Schnell 2002; Connor 2002). Evans and Rey (2001) identify the following risk factors for juvenile violent behavior: family variables, such as poor parental supervision or neglect, family disruption, and parental violence (81 percent of traumatic abuse in childhood is inflicted by parents and 10 percent by other relatives [van der Kolk 1999]); individual variables, including early aggressive behavior, poor social and cognitive processing skills, and developmental deficits such as hostile attributes and hyperactivity; social variables, which include sibling or peer delinquency or gang membership; and environmental variables, such as living in a dangerous neighborhood or an economically deprived and disorganized community. Aggressive behavior in children has been related not only to poor parenting but also to the parents' own maltreatment in childhood (Egeland, Stroufe and Erickson 1983).

A study of more than 400 delinquent youth remanded to the Office of Children and Family Services in New York for assault, sexual assault, robbery, or homicide revealed that losses were common in their lives (Crimmins et al. 2000). Drug use was frequent, as was self-medication. In fact, programs designed to help aggressive children can also be viewed as drug prevention (Strand 2002) and suicide prevention programs (Conner et al. 2001; Johnson et al. 2002). In addition, those charged with homicide have often witnessed stabbings, shootings, or killings within the family (Crimmins et al. 2000). Factors mitigating against violence include a healthy parental attachment, careful parental supervision, and high involvement of caregivers. Of lesser importance are family harmony, father involvement, and school bondedness (Evans and Rey 2001).

Most gorilla-suit wearers have limited opportunities to identify with the controls of nurturing and protective adults and, as a result, are poorly socialized. The struggles faced by these children become clearer when they are conceptualized within Erik Erikson's stages in human development (1963, 1968, 1982).

TRUST VERSUS MISTRUST

Children rejected from birth have never mastered Erik Erikson's first nuclear conflict of trust versus mistrust. Those who move forward with a basic sense of trust in others do so with "a sense of identity which will later combine with a sense of being 'all right,' of being oneself, and of becoming what other people trust one will become." Erikson states,

> Parents must not only have certain ways of guiding by prohibition and permission; they must also be able to represent to the child a deep, almost so-

matic conviction that there is meaning to what they are doing. Ultimately children become neurotic not from frustrations, but from the lack or loss of societal meaning in these frustrations.

Alfred Adler, the great individual psychologist, put it similarly. The child whose parents meet his basic needs for affection will develop a bond with society. The child will actualize his potential in ways that will promote society. In contrast, those who feel rejected will strive for superiority over others at the expense of society. Those well parented will develop mutual interdependence with society; those poorly parented see society as their enemy and act accordingly.

The child arrested at this first stage of development displays almost no internal controls, emoting anger at the slightest provocation. Omnipotent needs for control and unreasonable demands of others get the child into serious trouble. Often, the child shows minimal overt fantasy expression, and when fantasy is displayed, the content is predominantly aggressive. The child demonstrates primitive identifications, such as behaving like vicious animals or supervillains. No concern is shown for others, nor does the child expect concern when hurt. In fact, concern is often rebuffed.

For example, Main and George (1985) observe that when children were distressed, about half of their unabused peers showed sadness, concern, and empathic responses. No such behavior was displayed by the abused children studied. In fact, some of the abused children slapped, hit, or kicked their distressed peer, perhaps reflecting their treatment by their parents. In fact, uncontrollable crying is a significant contributor to child abuse by parents. Children in gorilla suits have not been adequately nurtured or protected. They lack prideful experiences of pleasing and being pleased. Those who were intimidated become intimidating, displaying aggression to cope with their ever-present sense of danger and their pseudoautonomy, which results in intense loneliness. As a result, moral standards are never internalized. In fact, depressed mothers, whose offspring can be labeled aggressive as early as age two (Zahn-Waxler and Radke-Yarrow 1990), often show diminished responsiveness to pleasant stimuli, decreasing the opportunity for children to be seen as pleasing (Sloan, Strauss, and Wisner 2001).

The relationship between maternal and child depression is remarkable (Goodman and Gotleib 2002). Clinicians can demonstrate the relationship in their own settings. For example, in an unpublished doctoral dissertation by Richard Carlson, performed in consultation with Dr. Mordock, preschool and kindergarten children's scores on a teacher rating scale of childhood depression could be predicted with 80 percent accuracy by the parent score on the Beck Depression Inventory.

Feeling neglected, abandoned, and unloved, children react with rage. Observe a baby crying because it has some unmet need. Observe further that, if the need is not met, the crying turns into angry shrieks. The prototype for anger as a response to frustration is set early. Children who experience the death of a loving parent often display anger during one stage of the grieving process, but children whose parents are rejecting have experienced the greatest loss of all—never to have been loved—and many respond to this loss in maladaptive ways.

EARLY SEPARATIONS

Many gorilla-suit wearers are separated from their parents and placed in foster care, where little time, if any, is spent helping them to deal with separation from their natural parents or from the community in which they lived (Crenshaw and Foreacre 2001). The parents may visit the child, promising a speedy return to their care, but time passes and reunions become frustrating experiences because, following each visit, the child experiences another loss. And if the child does return home, the parenting received is frequently not much better than it was before removal. Often the care is not as good as the child received in foster care, and so another loss is experienced, but one the child rarely verbalizes or admits to feeling. The child with intermitting parenting never successfully grieves the loss of parental affection.

Children in foster care rarely experience recognized losses. Torn from their natural parents, they also suffer from broken relationships with other key attachment figures (Crenshaw 2002). Disruptions in natural parenting are accompanied by disruptions in the network of extended connections around friends, sports, school, and activities, all of which are major social influences in the child's life. Rarely does a child remain in the same school, or even in the same community, when moved from one foster home to another.

Often children are removed from foster families through no fault of their own, such as the divorce or relocation of the foster parents, but the children can experience self-blame following the disruption and be less willing to relate to the next set of foster parents or to an outreaching teacher. These disruptions typically result in feeling unwanted, feelings that lead to anger and ultimately to rage, and it is the rage that usually brings the children into treatment.

More important, the meaning of each loss to the child in foster care is rarely understood. "Moreover, the children have no one in their life who can remember the cute things they did when they were younger, tell stories about the times when they were especially funny, or remind them of the people who were there early in their life to love and care for them" (Crenshaw 2002, p. 296). These are the stories of attachment that children love to hear again and again. These stories remind them, and reinforce in their minds, that they were much loved, valued, and wanted.

But let's not blame the foster care system for the children's problems; many troubled children placed in foster care who remain in the system throughout their youth display adequate adult adjustment (Mordock 1978). In addition, many children who remain in rejecting homes display aggressive and troublesome behavior that brings them to the attention of the justice system. They have lost what every child expects—loving and caring parents—and many mask these feelings with violent behavior. Those who don't have usually found substitute parents elsewhere, spending time with the parents of friends or relatives, seeking out teachers or youth center staff, or latching on to a boss at a job. These are the resilient children, but they are few and far between.

UNSOLVABLE FEAR

One aspect of nurturing and protective attachments is that fears are mitigated by the relationship. The frightened child is calmed by doting parents and learns to seek them out when injured or frightened. In sharp contrast, the neglected infant is not calmed by caring parents. In fact, crying can lead to abuse. But even worse, when the child is regularly and seriously frightened by the care-givers themselves, the child becomes at risk for "unsolvable fear," in which organized attachment responses to fear are impossible (Cassidy and Mohr 2001). When these children are hurt or frightened, extremely disorganized behavior occurs, followed by active flight from caregivers. Panic reactions are common among trauma victims, not only during the trauma, but well after it (Bryant and Panasetis 2001). Imagine how unnerving such attacks are for children with unsolvable fear. In fact, insecure attachments are a stronger predictor of the intensity of post-traumatic stress disorder symptoms than is trauma severity (Dieperink et al. 2001).

Some children not only receive no comfort from their parents, but also live in fear of them. Daily papers are filled with examples. In one year in the City of Poughkeepsie, in Dutchess County, New York, where both authors live, known killings included a seven-year-old who fell from the seventh floor in a high-rise apartment building. Three years later his mother was arrested for shoplifting and confessed to pushing him out of the window. A six-year-old was killed by his father, and the County Department of Social Services, as is often the case, was blamed for not putting him in foster care following earlier reports of abuse. A five-year-old was stabbed to death by his mother.

Diane Odel, who made the headlines in 2003 after the discovery of the mummified bodies of her three newborns, was brutalized and raped by her father as a child and lived in fear of her mother, who prostituted Diane to pay off the mother's debt to a loan shark and who allegedly influenced Diane to kill her three newborns (Yakin 2003). Diane describes her early experiences:

> My father never hit me when he was drunk. He would always hit me when he was sober. I don't know why, but . . . I was the whipping boy. He would grab my hair and pound my head, throw me down the hallway in our house between the staircase, against the wall. I was hit with a cat o' nine tails, thrown out of a chair, thrown through a door. Just about anything you can name . . . I couldn't understand at that time why she (her mother) would allow him to do the things that he did. And her comment to me was, "He's your father." (p. 2)

AUTONOMY VERSUS SHAME AND DOUBT

Already weakened by distrustfulness and disconnectedness, the child may then be denied the gradual and well-guided experience of making choices. As a child learns to "stand on his own two feet," protection from experiences of shame and self-doubt need to be provided. If not, then the child never resolves Erikson's second major stage, autonomy versus shame and doubt. As a result, the child gains power by stubborn control over minute portions of life. The shamed child is one who wants to go unnoticed: "Don't notice my exposure." As Erikson states, "He would like to destroy the eyes of the world. Instead, he must wish for his own invisibility." Too much shaming leads, at best, to a determination to get away with things or, at worst, to defiant shamelessness. Doubt is the brother of shame. Doubt comes from the pervasive feeling that nothing can ever be accomplished: "I can never do anything right" or "I can't do that."

During the stage of autonomy versus shame and doubt, the child unconsciously decides how much to cooperate, how much to resist, how much to express, and how much to repress. The child who feels control over life develops feelings of goodwill and pride. The child who feels controlled develops a propensity for doubt and shame. Some children receive relatively adequate parenting up until this stage. Then, either because of an inability to tolerate the child's developing autonomy or the parents' own temporary incapacity, the child is not supported in developing autonomy.

Many adolescents are relatively adequate parents until the child says "No," and then power struggles begin from which parent and child never free themselves. Children arrested at this stage of development display variable controls, characterized by marked changes in attachments to caregivers, both loving and hating the same caregiver depending on whether the caregiver satisfies or frustrates their needs. Global self-condemnation occurs—the result of having both internalized parental rejection and externalized the bad parts the parent rejects about the child.

Because the child has at an early age (twenty-four to thirty-six months) experienced an abrupt, sustained loss of closeness to and ability to please adults, the child also shows the following characteristics: ambivalence about the need for close contact; violent alienation from the baby-self and a mimicry of adult talk; lightning-swift, unpredictable changes in behavior; and a struggle to be good that is often a fear of the consequences of being bad, but with some desire to please adults.

THE ROLE OF SHAME

The continual failure of parents to respond with admiration, approval, or empathic understanding to a child's prideful behaviors results in narcissistic injury. The child responds with shame and humiliation, followed by rage and fantasies of revenge. The result is an impoverished and fragmented self vulnerable to interpersonal injury (Kohut 1971). While shame is internalized, there is always an observer present in the child's mind as a memory, a fantasy, or reality (York et al. 1990). Often when a child responds with anger to a humiliation, the anger is directed at a mental image (a scolding or rejecting parent figure), although the anger can be experienced as directed at others. Shame is a signal for repression and defenses to ward off anticipated humiliation or helpless exposure. Tangney and Dearing (2002) state,

> In brief, shame is an extremely painful and ugly feeling that has a negative impact on interpersonal behavior. Shame-prone individuals appear relatively more likely to blame others (as well as themselves) for negative events, more prone to a seething, bitter, resentful kind of anger and hostility, and less able to empathize with others in general. (p. 3)

James Gilligan (1996), who has written extensively about the role of shame in violence, states, "The prison inmates I work with have told me repeatedly when I asked them why they had assaulted someone, that it was because he 'disrespected me,' or he 'disrespected my visit' (meaning 'visitor')" (p. 10). Disrespect is so central in the vocabulary, moral value system, and psychodynamics of these chronically violent men that they have abbreviated it into a slang term: he *dissed* me. Gilligan writes,

> I have yet to see a serious act of violence that was not provoked by the experience of feeling shamed and humiliated, disrespected and ridiculed, and that did not represent the attempt to prevent or undo this "loss of face" no matter how severe the punishment, even if it includes death. For we misunderstand these men at our peril, if we do not realize they mean it literally when they say they would rather kill or mutilate others, be killed or mutilated themselves, than live without pride, dignity, and self-respect. (p. 10)

Kenneth Hardy (2003) adds that, in his experience, many violent youth would rather die than be dissed. Gilligan postulates that shame hides behind every act of violence, the purpose of which, whether directed toward individuals or entire populations, is to diminish the intensity of shame and replace it with pride. Gilligan reminds us, however, that most people do not commit violent acts, even though shame is experienced throughout the life cycle. Socialized individuals employ nonviolent methods to protect themselves from shame and to restore their wounded self-esteem. Most people feel empathy toward others and anticipate the guilt that would follow from an aggressive act. Empathy and anticipated guilt prevent them from committing violent acts, except under the most dire and threatening circumstances. Thus, those who commit violence when experiencing shame lack the capacity, at least in that moment, of feeling the empathy and anticipated guilt that ordinarily inhibit such behaviors. Nevertheless, Gilligan (1996) reminds us that even the most violent people in prison populations are not violent most of the time.

> [Violence] only happens when an incident occurs that intensifies their feelings of being humiliated, disrespected, or dishonored to the point that it threatens the coherence of the self, or when they find themselves in a specific situation when they feel they cannot withdraw nonviolently except by "losing face" to a catastrophic degree. (p. 114)

Spiegel and Alpert (2000) explore the relationship between shame and rage in the famous Columbine High School shootings. Shame, defined as a wound to one's self-esteem and a painful sense of degradation, was identified as a crucial element in the psyches of both killers. The relationship between shame and rage and the volatile combination it makes in some adolescents, along with the defenses activated by the pain of shame, were considered pivotal intrapsychic factors in the shootings.

The high school student we present in chapter 1 clearly felt ashamed by his long history of school failure, but school staff not only failed to recognize his strong feelings but also demeaned him further by the way they handled his response to his shame. In a study of fifteen school shootings, both acute or chronic rejection, taking the form of ostracism, bullying, or romantic rejection, some of which was experienced on school grounds, was a factor in all but two incidents (Leary et al. 2003). In addition, the shooters were preoccupied with firearms, fascinated with death or Satanism, were somewhat sadistic, and suffered from depression and loss of impulse control. The National School Safety Center's report, "School-Associated Violent Deaths," lists, among others, the following school killings apparently related to bullying or teasing (National School Safety Center 2004):

- Barry Loukitas, sixteen, shot and killed students Manuel Vela (fourteen) and Arnold F. Fitz and teacher Leona D. Caires and wounded student Natalie Hintz (thirteen) on February 2, 1996, at Frontier Junior High School in Moses Lake, Washington. The report indicates that Loukitas, who made straight A's and was called a "nerd," was reported to have been "relentlessly teased by Vela" and other students. Loukitas was "quoted as telling friends it would be 'cool' to go on a killing spree like the characters in the movie *Natural Born Killers*."
- At Valley View Junior High School in Simi Valley, California, Phillip Hernandez, fourteen, stabbed classmate Chad Patrick Hubbard, also fourteen, in the heart with a knife on February 1, 1994. Hernandez allegedly had been bullied by Hubbard.
- On May 24, 1993, at Upper Perkiomen High School in Red Hill, Pennsylvania, a town with a population of 1,794, Jason Michael Smith, fifteen, used a 9 mm automatic to shoot Michael Swan, sixteen, in the head. The report states Swan had bullied Smith.
- Michael Carneal, fourteen, started shooting at a prayer group meeting before classes at Heath High School in West Paducah, Kentucky, on December 2, 1997. He killed students Jessica James, seventeen; Kayce Steger, fifteen; and Nichole Hadley, fourteen, and wounded five others out of some forty gathered in the school lobby. Carneal used a .22-caliber handgun. According to the report, he may have been teased by some of the group as well as by some school football players.

While our two volumes focus on aggression directed at others, some of the aggression and violence of young people is self-directed. The children respond to shame with self-punishment. Numerous studies have identified the role of parental rejection in young people's suicidal behaviors (Wagner, Silverman, and Martin 2003). Although suicidal gestures have been related to parent–child attachment difficulties, completed suicides occur more often in families with a history of suicides, acrimonious separations and divorce, and alcohol and substance abuse, all situations characterizing the lives of children in gorilla suits.

A recent report (Galley 2003), titled "Student Self-Harm: Silent School Crisis," noted that school counselors are overloaded with kids referred following self-injury. This behavior is estimated to manifest itself in at least 4 percent of adolescents in the United States (Galley 2003). Secrecy and shame enshroud the problem, leading researchers to suspect underreporting. Girls are more likely than boys to cut or burn themselves, the two most frequent forms of self-harming, but self-harm occurs in boys as well (Alderman 1997). These children are not usually suicidal, but treatment begins with a comprehensive assessment to evaluate for intentions. Nevertheless, even when intentions are not lethal, if the cutting severs the wrong blood vessels, it can be extremely dangerous or even lethal. Alderman notes that the vast majority of these youngsters have suffered some physical, sexual, or emotional abuse.

Many adolescents don't experience the full impact of the pain they inflict on themselves because they dissociate. In addition, in response to injury, the body releases endorphins that have effects similar to morphine (Alderman 1997). After cutting, the adolescent often feels calm and relief, leading to a repetitive cycle of self-abuse. The wounds are hidden because of the stigma attached to self-mutilation. The most common excuse adolescents give when asked about the cuts or scars is "My cat did it" (Conterio and Lader 1998).

Levenkron (1998) advocates redirecting the focus to the underlying emotional issues. He views cutting as a compulsive act intended to relieve unbearable emotional pain, and he regards eating disorders as a way of seizing control. He distinguishes cutting from body piercing or tattooing, quite popular and trendy today in the world of adolescents. In Levenkron's view, self-inflicted injuries, like addictions, can be exchanges of physical for emotional pain.

Suicide is another solution children use to manage emotional pain. A recent review reports that from 55 to 85 percent of self-mutilators have made at least one suicide attempt (Stanley et al. 2001). The National School Safety Center's report, "School-Associated Violent Deaths," lists fifty-eight known deaths by suicide and six deaths of unknown causes during the period from 1992 to 2003.

INITIATIVE VERSUS GUILT

When a child moves into the stage of initiative versus guilt without having mastered the earlier two stages, failures cannot be forgotten quickly. True initiative does not develop. The child will be unable to attack problems playfully and with zest and enthusiasm. Lacking initiative, many children fail the early grades in school or, if larger than their peers, are socially promoted or referred for special education.

The child arrested at this stage of development feels the need for aggressive powers to cope with his sense of unsafety, pseudoautonomy, and sense of aloneness. The longing for a reunion with caregivers is now blunted by a need to save face. This need leads to overt defiance of external directions and control and, even worse, to more intensive efforts at revenge. Because of repeated humiliations in a dependency relationship, the child becomes entrenched in a state of pseudoindependence, which includes a self-image as a bad child. In reaction to anxiety about the self-image, self-willed protests of independence and defiance occur. Because wishes remain those of a younger child, a primitive sense of guilt develops over the wishes. Erikson states,

> One of the deepest conflicts in life is the hate for a parent who served as the model and the executor of the superego, but who (in some form) was found trying to get away with the very transgressions which the child can no longer tolerate in himself.

MUTUALITY VERSUS ALIENATION

Blatt and Blass (1990), based on Bowlby's work (1969) on attachment and on the British school of object relations (Fairbairn 1962; Winnicott 1965), have interposed, between Erikson's stages of initiative versus guilt and industry versus inferiority, a stage they call mutuality versus alienation. In this stage, because of the human capacity to form stable, enduring, and mutually satisfying interpersonal relationships, the child normally bonds with others. If mutually satisfying relationships have not developed, than the child becomes alienated from others. Instead of experiencing gratifying involvement, the child experiences isolating alienation.

The bonded child expands the self system to include a "we" dimension—the self is experienced with the other or the "we," and empathy becomes highly developed. Feelings about the self that arise within relationships gradually become internalized aspects of the self, and "relatedness" becomes a major dimension by which developmental progress is measured. Gorilla-suit wearers almost never master this stage, and their alienation underlies much of their rage.

INDUSTRY VERSUS INFERIORITY

In the stage of industry versus inferiority, the child now begins to "handle the utensils, the tools, and the weapons used by big people." The child's danger, at this stage, lies in feeling inadequate and inferior. Erikson writes, "If he despairs of his tools and skills or of his status among his tool partners, he may be discouraged from identification with them and with a section of the tool world." If the child loses hope of participating in the "industrial" world, he or she will remain fixed in earlier worlds, feeling doomed to mediocrity or inadequacy. "What's the use; no matter what I do, it's never right." Failure in school escalates as the child gets older and the academic tasks become more challenging, and special education becomes a "holding tank" rather than a place for progress. Studies of children placed in special education for behavior disorders reveal that about half are arrested within their first two years after "graduation" (Wagner et al. 1992).

LEARNED VOICELESSNESS

Another useful concept in understanding the effects of trauma and violence is learned voicelessness in response to an overwhelming sense of powerlessness (Hardy 1998). One aim of therapy is to help children to regain their voice. Alice Miller (1997) emphasizes that trauma victims have a pressing need to share their pain with someone they trust. Hardy (1998) cautions, however, that when children regain their voice, the degree of rage, pain, and deep sorrow they experience will threaten to overwhelm both the child and the therapist. We discuss this phenomenon more fully in *A Handbook of Play Therapy with Aggressive Children.*

3

Profound and Unacknowledged Losses

Children in gorilla suits have typically experienced a plethora of major losses in their short lives, often more than most people will endure in a lifetime. This chapter explores the concepts of disenfranchised grief, tangible and intangible losses, acknowledged and unacknowledged losses, and dehumanized loss, which play a pivotal role in the development of youth aggression and violence.

Children who experience the death of a loving parent often display anger during one stage of the grieving process, but children whose parents are rejecting have experienced the greatest loss of all—never to have been loved—and many respond to this loss in maladaptive ways. The child with intermitting parenting never gets to successfully grieve and mourn the loss of parental affection.

DISENFRANCHISED GRIEF

The profound loss of "good-enough parenting" (Winnicott 1965), experienced by many gorilla-suit wearers, is rarely recognized or mourned. Their unresolved grief is consistent with the concept of disenfranchised grief, defined by Kenneth Doka (1989) as "the grief that persons experience when they incur a loss that is not or cannot be openly acknowledged, publicly mourned or socially supported" (p. 4). Not only does the child fail to receive recognition, support, and facilitation for grief, but social sanctions for the loss are conspicuously absent. At best, the child's losses are unacknowledged. At worst, they are devalued and trivialized. For example, when a foster parent, or a friend of a foster parent, admonishes a foster child for not showing appreciation for the better care received in the foster home, the result is a de-valuing of the child's loss of the natural parent.

Children in foster care face special problems in having their losses recognized, and we address these problems in chapter 7. Foster children not only are separated from their biological parents but, typically, have experienced numerous broken relationships with key attachment figures as a result of failed placements in multiple foster homes (Crenshaw 2002).

We can remember a period early on in our residential treatment experience when children would show up for admission dragging their belongings behind them in a plastic garbage bag. This was a message of devaluation that was outrageous! Many years ago Steven Holzman, the director of operations at the Astor Home for Children, saw to it that on arrival every child was immediately given a suitcase and a teddy bear, a practice that continues to this day. It should come as no surprise that Steve is much loved by the children of the Astor Home.

THE COMPLICATED GRIEF OF RELUCTANT MOURNERS

A crucial buffering and protective element in facing any stressful life event is a close, stable, and confiding relationship with at least one other person. Compared with adult grief, the emotional responses in bereaved children are less pervasive, more intermittent, and more situation specific (Kranzler et al. 1990). Consequently, grieving occurs over a longer period of time (Crenshaw 1990b, 1994). One crucial factor on the road to recovery is the ability to maintain meaningful connections with others. If a grieving child, because of pain, poor social skills, or unusual circumstances surrounding a loss, becomes isolated from others, then grief reactions are compounded by loneliness and alienation. Children may withdraw from others because of their inability to tolerate the painful grief displayed by those around them, as well as their own, and avoid talking about the loss.

Young children, particularly preschoolers, are unable to express their grief in words and must do so in play. Those who do not play out their grief reactions will usually suffer, as will older children who cannot talk about them. When a parent dies and a child repeatedly puts a doll in a box and hides it, the surviving parent must support these actions rather than restrict them, as some suffering survivors may do because they feel worse when witnessing such actions. Even adolescents, particularly those with poor verbal skills, can experience difficulty putting their grief into words.

To some degree, all children are reluctant mourners, but children of multiple loss and trauma are especially adept at avoiding open expressions of grief

(Crenshaw 1992). Developmental capacity and environmental media contribute to successful mourning. Even preschool children can do a significant amount of grief work when properly encouraged. When caregivers model the expression of grief and respond favorably to the child's expressions, the child's mourning will advance through the appropriate stages. While sadness is adaptive, fear and anger as predominant affects are associated with emotional disturbance (Kranzler et al. 1990). The absence of sadness in the grieving child can reflect repression of associated feelings and can be partially responsible for behavioral disturbances.

Children of compounded loss and trauma can exhibit a limited capacity to grieve due to the pervasive impact of repeated trauma on cognitive and emotional development (Crenshaw 1992). Typically, these children also receive less favorable environmental facilitation for their grieving. Consequently, their grief can be reflected in behavioral disturbance, most often in anger and unusual fears. Poorly developed internal resources result in the child's feeling overwhelmed by intense sadness, anger at abandoning caregivers, longing for departed ones, guilt over his or her perceived contribution to the separation, and fear of making new attachments. New relationships can lead to future separation and loss and are, therefore, avoided.

Many children in foster care have lost parents to chemical dependency. During periods of recovery, such as following completion of a drug rehabilitation program, a parent may again become available to a child (Crenshaw and Hardy in press; Crenshaw 2002). Unfortunately, these reappearances can be brief and unsustained. The parent relapses and disappears again for long periods. Nevertheless, the child longs for the parent's reappearance and for the parent to be magically cured. And if the parent does actually return, and displays better caregiving skills, the care the child longs for is no longer age-appropriate care, and conflicts with the parent over the child's regressed behavior become commonplace.

LOYALTY CONFLICTS

Gorilla-suit wearers experience intense loyalty conflicts. They remain loyal to their natural parent regardless of how disappointing or hurtful their relationships with the parent have been. Often their loyalty is to an idealized image of the parent, and they repress their memories of neglect and abuse and maintain a fantasy image of receiving loving care even though they rarely, if ever, experienced such care. This fantasy is tenacious, a phenomenon referred to elsewhere as a *sustaining fiction* (Van Ornum and Mordock 1990). This sustaining fiction is maintained by the intermitting parenting the children receive from natural parents, whether the parents reside with the children or come in and out of the children's lives. In chapter 7, we discuss the special problems of treating children in foster homes.

In most cases, the sustaining fiction fails to protect the reluctant mourner from experiencing the pain that accompanies losses. The next disappearance of a parent who briefly reentered the child's life is a crushing blow accompanied by anger, sadness, and depression. And if the longed-for parent never returns, the idealized parental image is relinquished only with extreme reluctance. Lots of adults are in treatment because they still seek care from a neglectful parent. These are the healthier ones. Others are out wreaking havoc on society because they never received the care they felt they deserved.

DELAYED OR DISTORTED GRIEF REACTIONS

The consequences of unacknowledged and unresolved grief persist throughout life. Grief cannot be skirted; it must be felt and allowed to run its course to be resolved. Skipping, avoiding, or interrupting the grieving process puts the individual at risk for manifesting either delayed or distorted grief reactions (Crenshaw 1990b). In delayed reactions, the bereaved may show little or no outward signs of mourning at the time of the actual loss, only to react with profound grief at a later time in response to a less significant loss.

For example, when President John F. Kennedy was shot, studies of grieving adolescents revealed a number whose grief reactions were out of proportion to the loss. Background checks revealed earlier losses in their lives (Wolfenstein and Kliman 1965). In cases of distorted grief, the bereaved show few signs of intense grief at the time of loss, but later they develop psychosomatic symptoms, such as migraines or dizzy spells, or become irritable and angry at others, which often leads to serious interpersonal conflicts.

When unwilling or unable to mourn losses, children run a high risk for distorted or delayed grief reactions. Sooner or later an event occurs that brings the unresolved grief into focus, sometimes with startling intensity. That event is the "final straw" (Krueger 1978). The final straw can be any subsequent loss, such as change in placement, divorce of parents, loss of friendships, change of schools, relocation, or even graduation. Whatever the precipitating event, the child's intense reaction is partly in response to the present situation but resonates with earlier unresolved grief.

Dr. Crenshaw treated a sixteen-year-old girl whose life was replete with traumatic loss. She had witnessed her father and mother in a violent fight that ended when the father plunged a kitchen knife into her mother's chest, killing her instantly. She was eight years old at the time and was screaming at her drunken father to stop and then froze in utter shock and terror when he picked up the knife and stabbed her mother before her eyes. Her father went to prison for seven years, and she and her two younger sisters and older brother were placed in foster homes.

The incident, "the final straw," that brought her into treatment was a dinner held at her father's house after his release. She and her sisters, then living with an aunt and uncle, were gathered at the father's house for dinner on Mother's Day. What became intolerable for this teen was the unspeakable tragedy—that the family was gathered together around the table, all aware that it was Mother's Day, but no one uttered a word acknowledging the past horrific event. She described to the author how she could not eat her dinner because she felt the powerful urge to scream as loud as she could, "Don't you realize that this is Mother's Day and my Dad cooked this meal in the kitchen where he killed our mother?"

Over the years, the girl had used amphetamines and alcohol to numb the feelings, but the pain became unbearable, and her long-avoided grief could no longer be denied. After the dinner, she made a serious suicide attempt, mixing Valium with alcohol. She was in critical condition for several days after she was rushed to the hospital by her aunt, who found her unconscious in her room.

The author's first visit with her was in the hospital. She was confused and disoriented. She told him, in a dissociated state, that her brother had committed suicide two years before and that her dad had two children by a previous marriage whom he had not seen in more than twenty years. The legacy of traumatic loss in this family was beyond belief. These revelations, made during her confused mental state, were not brought up again until after several months of therapy, when she had gathered sufficient inner strength to talk about these and other losses in a drug-free state.

Intensive therapy with this young woman extended over a three-year period, with many crises and setbacks along the way. She and Dr. Crenshaw correspond periodically, and she always drops by to see him when in the area for family visits. She now lives on the West Coast, is married, has two young children, and works as a grief counselor for a nonprofit agency serving inner-city children.

Not all challenging clients experience such happy endings. We do not claim unusual or exceptional therapy skills, and we have had our share of heartbreaking failures. Therapists battle formidable odds when helping children who have had such bad starts in life, particularly if their continuing life experiences are harsh, depriving, and traumatic. The lion's share of the credit belongs to this remarkable woman, whose courage, strength, and determination were inspiring. Her loving aunt and uncle, who provided a stable home for her and her two younger sisters, should also be credited for the pivotal role they played in the transformation from her traumatic early life.

Dr. Mordock saw a teenage boy in supportive therapy for several years. He had been in several child-care institutions, a residential treatment center, and several foster homes. Outwardly, he appeared well adjusted, had a best friend with whom he hung out, was passing all his high school subjects, and was the county's best cross-country runner. When the foster parents divorced, plans were made to move him to another foster home in another county. Not wanting him to leave the community where he seemed so well adjusted, Dr. Mordock, who lived in the same school district as the divorcing foster parents, agreed to house him until he completed high school.

He spent two more years in the school, graduated, joined the air force, was stationed abroad, and served in the military police. One morning, they found him at his post with his head blown off. No evidence of foul play was found, and suicide was ruled out because he had just become assistant scout-master at the base troop and showed no signs of depression. It was ruled an accidental death. Nevertheless, alone at his post in the dead of night, it may have struck home that no one really cared about him in the way he deserved, and perhaps he put the gun to his throat and shot himself. The beneficiary of his military life insurance was Dr. Mordock's wife, the last "mother" he knew. His real mother attended his funeral and sobbed profusely. Yet she had abandoned him on the doorstep of an institution when he was an infant and never saw him again.

THE CRISIS OF CONNECTION

Earlier, we emphasized that children who don gorilla suits or hide behind brick walls of detachment long for closeness with others and at the same time find it threatening and disorganizing. Closeness challenges and undermines the defensive system they develop to feel safe from emotional pain. When an opportunity arises for gorilla-suit wearers to become close to someone, a profound crisis develops. They experience what is called conflicted dependency. Dramatic increases in acting-out behavior, intensification of symptoms, or even running away can occur (Crenshaw 1995). The warmth of others raises their anxiety. Never underestimate the degree of anxiety the prospect of closeness evokes in some children, even though their hunger for connection is intense. Children in residential treatment continually ask the therapist, whom they see in the hallway, "When are you going to take me?" But when it is time for therapy, the demands they place on the therapist result in limit-setting behavior and further feelings of rejection (see *A Handbook of Play Therapy with Aggressive Children*, chapters 3 and 4). This is the paradox encountered repeatedly by those working daily with aggressive youngsters in foster care and residential treatment settings. Miller and Stiver (1997) remark,

> Serious or repeated disconnections . . . lead people to create restricted and distorted images of the possibilities of relationships between themselves and others, and to construct meanings that disparage and condemn themselves. These images and meanings then further limit their ability to act within connections, to know their own experience, and to build a sense of worthiness. (p. 82–83)

Miller and Stiver also emphasize that the responses of youth to sexual and physical abuse represent an extreme, but all too frequent, illustration of disconnection. Their defenses and strategies of disconnection insulate them from attachment, connection, and intimacy, but when closeness becomes possible, they become lost and confused. These children sadly live without affection because their defenses, so necessary for survival, cut them off from the emotional sustenance vital for their well-being—the human connection, which terrifies them but which they so deeply crave.

DEHUMANIZED LOSS

Repeated losses, which are unrecognized and unmourned, become dehumanized, and the resulting rage, if not redirected, leads to revenge. Revenge is not on the path leading to successful mourning; it fails to ameliorate the underlying pain of loss. It does serve as a balm for the wound, but it doesn't lead to healing. Hardy (2003) makes an important distinction between anger and rage. Anger is reactive to a situation that is frustrating while rage is ongoing and deeper and related to an injury to the spirit or soul of the child, referred to by Shengold (1989) as "soul murder."

The ultimate manifestation of dehumanized loss is the alarming and disturbing symptom of cruelty to animals. Many gorilla-suit wearers display this symptom. The connection between childhood animal abuse and later violence toward humans is well established (Wright and Hensley 2003; Merz-Perez, Heide, and Silverman 2001; Felthous and Kellert 1987; Kellert and Felthous 1985; Wax and Haddox 1974a, 1974b). Duncan and Miller (2002) concluded from their review of the literature, however, that an abusive family context may be a better predictor of adult violence than childhood animal cruelty itself.

Hallern (2002) points out the irony that, for centuries, children were treated legally as chattel, property of their fathers. Because the father worked to support his children, he was free to do with them as he saw fit, including abuse. It was not until the late nineteenth century that society objected to such behavior, as attested by the first successful prosecution of a case of child abuse, which was based on a cruelty-to-animals statute because there was no such law relating to children.

Cruelty to animals may mark a subgroup of behavior-disordered children who have a poor prognosis (Luk et al. 1999), although the frequency and degree of cruelty are both important factors. Flynn's study (1999) of undergraduate students revealed that a number of seemingly well-adjusted men had committed animal cruelty in childhood or adolescence. Nevertheless, those who did so were physically punished more frequently by their fathers, both as preteens and teenagers, than males who did not abuse animals. Over half of the male teenagers in this sample who were hit by their fathers had abused animals. The relationship did not hold for males who were spanked by their mothers or for females who were spanked by either parent. Gender differences in response to family violence will be discussed in the next chapter. The association between a father's corporal punishment and a son's childhood animal cruelty persisted after controlling for other factors, such as child abuse, father to mother violence, and father's education.

The rage the child feels is displaced onto objects, animals, peers, other adults, and even onto the parents to some degree. In extreme cases, children have been known to kill their parents, some in angry outbursts and others in a carefully planned manner. When losses become dehumanized, the capacity to feel is lost. Because the losses are not recognized or addressed, a self-protective mechanism develops whereby the losses are "numbed off," and empathic feelings for the losses of others are absent. The loss of the capacity to feel the pain of others is viewed as a crucial ingredient in the escalating cycle of violence in children. The losses themselves have become dehumanized (Hardy 2003). This is the point when children and adolescents become a menace or threat to society. Since they are unable to feel their own pain, they are unable to feel the pain they inflict on others.

Dr. Crenshaw vividly remembers a shocking and frightening event from his childhood. On a Sunday afternoon in Gower, a small, rural Missouri hamlet of about 250 people, where Dr. Crenshaw grew up, a boy of fourteen was arrested. He was found walking around town in a "daze." In all likelihood, he was in a dissociated state. He had killed both his parents and all his siblings earlier that day in their home, in the village of St. Joseph, and was found wandering around in the author's tiny hometown, about fifteen miles south of St. Joseph. Such an event shattered the relatively sheltered and uneventful life of this small, usually quiet farming community. It is hard to imagine the kind of anger and rage that would lead a fourteen-year-old to kill his entire family, but such events are becoming less rare, forcing us to examine our own potential for rage and violence. If violence exists in our society, it must also exist in us, and our best line of prevention is to openly and honestly confront our own capacity for anger, rage, and violence.

4

New Findings from Neuroscience: Implications for Treatment

In the past decade, findings from neuroscience have attracted great interest among clinicians. One interesting finding is that the brain is use-dependent, implying that the brain is shaped and developed by the nature of its exposure to favorable or unfavorable experiences. Children who are exposed to extreme and repeated violence and trauma may develop brain and neurophysiological systems that are persistently set in an alarm state.

$\mathcal{A}$cts of violence have become part of the landscape of contemporary life in America. Technology has perfected instruments of violence to the point that loss of civilian life can occur on an unprecedented and devastating scale. Throughout history, military losses have exacted an enormous toll, with suffering by both combatants and their families. Now, as we discovered on September 11, 2001, thousands of unsuspecting people can be obliterated by simply going to work on a beautiful September morning. Millions of children around the world, often overlooked as victims of violence, saw the towers attacked repeatedly over television.

Violence disrupts homes, schools, neighborhoods, and communities. Although national rates of youth violence have declined in recent years, an unacceptably large number of young people still remain both victims and perpetrators of violence (Flannery et al. 2003; Dahlberg 1998; Mercy and Potter 1996; Sickmund, Snyder and Poe-Yamagata 1997; Snyder and Sickmund 1999; Tolan, Guerra, and Kendall 1995). Homicide rates among males aged fifteen to twenty-one doubled between 1950 and 1991 and were ten times higher than Canada's and twenty-eight times higher than France's or Germany's (Centers for Disease Control and Prevention 1996; World Health Organization 1994). In fact, youth between the ages of twelve and fifteen are the victims of more violent acts than any other age group (Snyder and Sickmund 1999).

Violence often results in a domino effect of negative life events, drastically altered daily routines, and altered community values (Joshi and O'Donnell 2003). These stresses, combined with losses, can impact children's brains, minds, and bodies in a systemic way, appreciated only by understanding the whole child in the sociocultural context in which the child lives. While a review of the negative effects of living in violent neighborhoods is beyond the scope of this book, being exposed to firearms, associating with violent peers, viewing violent television, and playing violent video games all contribute to children's violent behaviors, as do witnessing and experiencing domestic abuse (Anderson and Dill 2000; Attar, Guerra, and Tolan 1994; Buka et al. 2001; Cicchetti and Lynch 1993; Cooley-Quille, Turner, and Beidel 1995, Dill and Dill 1998; Duncan 1996; Fitzpatrick and Boldizar 1993; Garbarino 1995; Garbarino and Bedard 2001; Gorman-Smith and Tolan 1998; Huston and Wright 1998; Jenkins and Bell 1997; Lynch and Cicchetti 1998; Miller et al. 1999; Osofsky 1995a, 1995b; Price, Merrill and Clause 1992; Schwab-Stone et al. 1995; Slovack and Singer 2001; Taylor et al. 1994).

The typical American child watches twenty-eight hours of television per week and by age eighteen will have seen 16,000 simulated murders and 200,000 acts of violence. Commercial television for children is fifty to sixty times more violent than prime-time television, and cartoons average eighty violent acts per hour (American Psychiatric Association 1998).

Living in communities where violence is common can increase domestic violence (Forehand and Jones 2003). Surrounding violence can negatively affect children's social and academic development even when they are not directly exposed to violent activity (American Psychological Association Commission on Violence and Youth 1993; Swartz and Gorman 2003), often because the parents are forced to use harsh disciplinary techniques to protect their children (Deater-Deckard et al. 1996). Controlling parental practices create their own set of problems (Barber 2002). High levels of parental involvement can buffer the detrimental effect of violent neighborhoods on girls' aggressive behaviors but are less effective for boys (Forehand and Jones 2003).

However, domestic violence, the violence of concern in this book, is the greatest stimulus to children putting on gorilla suits (American Psychological Association 1996; Brandwein 1999; Carlson 1984; Chalk and King 1998; Edleson 1999a; Fantuzzo et al. 1997; Jaffe, Wolfe, and Wilson 1990; Jouriles 2004; Holden, Geffner, and Jouriles 1998; Ornduff, Kelsey, and O'Leary 2001; McNeal and Amato 1989; Margolin 1998; Spaccarelli, Sandier, and Roosa 1994). Ulman and Straus (2003) demonstrate that children who strike their mothers are more often those who witnessed parent violence, regardless of whether the violence was husband to wife, wife to husband, or corporal punishment and physical abuse inflicted on the children themselves. Children learn to use violence to resolve conflicts, especially in interpersonal relationships (Emery and Laumann-Billings 1998). Between 1.6 and 1.8 million American women are severely beaten by their intimate partners each year, and each year over 29 million children commit an act of violence against a sibling (Ulman and Strauss; Straus and Gelles 1990; Tjaden and Thoennes 1998).

Some 25 to 30 percent of women are beaten at least once in an intimate relationship (Plichta 1992, Straus and Gelles 1988, 1990), and in 50 to 60 percent of the families where women are battered, the children also are battered (Edleson 1999b; Fantuzzo et al. 1997). Two studies contributing to these statistics examined the medical records of children whose mothers came to the hospital for medical treatment following battering (Stark and Fitcraft 1988; McKibben, DeVos, and Newberger 1989). Ross (1996) reports that among husbands who are first-time wife abusers, 23 percent abuse their children as well, but each additional act of violence toward the wife increases the odds of the husband's abusing the child by 12 percent, demonstrating that cumulative marital stress increases child abuse (Margolin and Gordis 2003). Battered women are also twice as likely to abuse their own children as are other mothers (Straus and Gelles 1990), and teenage mothers have the highest abuse rates and infant homicides (Overpeck et al. 1998). Eighty percent of women in shelters for battered women are accompanied by one or more children. In fact, 50 percent of the residents in these shelters are children (Osofsky 1995a, 1995b), and shelter life can create its own set of stressors (Jenkins 1995). Overall, about three million children per year are abused by family members (English 1998).

What must be stressed is that domestic violence is not only an environmental influence; neurological and physiological changes that accompany abusive and traumatic experiences can result in elevated levels of aggression. In general, abused children have difficulty managing their emotions, maintaining a cognitive-emotional balance, and inhibiting their aggression (Gorman-Smith and Tolan 1998; Williams, Lochman, and Phillips 2003). Maternal abuse has been related to emotional dyscontrol and paternal abuse to impulsive aggression (Chang et al. 2003). Abused infants show disorganized attachments, often approaching their mothers backwards and then suddenly freezing and staring off into space. When separated from their abusive mothers, they show conflicted and fearful behavior upon reunion (Karr-Morse and Wiley 1997). As a result, children abused before fourteen years of age have more difficulties modulating anger and display more self-destructive and suicidal behaviors than do older victims of abuse (van der Kolk 1996), and as we mention in chapter 2, the earlier the abuse, the greater the maladjustments. Thus, early trauma has more debilitating consequences and speaks to the compelling need for prevention and early intervention, a topic we discuss in more detail in the last chapter.

Bruce Perry (2003) stresses that

> Ironically, many violent behaviors are the result of a defensive response to
> perceived aggression. The neurobiology of fear, therefore, holds as many im-
> portant clues to prevention and treatment interventions related to violence
> as the neurobiology of aggression. (p. 1)

THE BRAIN IS EXPERIENCE DEPENDENT

Perry (2003) observes that factors such as chronic traumatic stress, elevated
testosterone level, or unregulated serotonin or norepinephrine systems (systems
that increase the activity of the brain stem or decrease the moderating capacity of the limbic or cortical areas) will increase a child's aggression, impulsiveness, and capacity for violence.

> Deprivation of key developmental experiences (which leads to underdevel-
> opment of cortical, sub-cortical, and limbic areas) will necessarily result in
> persistence of primitive, immature behavioral reactivity, and, thereby, predis-
> pose an individual to violent behavior. (p. 2)

As the higher cortical areas become more organized, they modulate and
control the more primitive lower portions of the brain (midbrain and brain
stem). Children who have experienced early neglect and trauma develop sen-
sitized brain stem systems. Neglect, for example, decreases the moderating capacity of the limbic or cortical areas, which remain disorganized as a result of
chaotic developmental experiences (Perry 2003). As part of the human adaption to exposure to violence, threat activates the brain's stress-response neurobiology (Perry 2001; Perry, Pollard, Blakley, et al. 1995). This activation, particularly if chronic, affects the development of the brain (Lauder 1988; McAllister
et al. 1999; Perry 2001). Children raised around violence are more likely to be
violent (Loeber et al. 1993; Lewis, Mallough, and Webb 1989; Koop and Lundberg 1992; Hickey 1991; Halperin et al. 1995).

CONSTANT ALARM STATE

While learning theorists use modeling to explain disruptive behavior, Perry
(2001) writes that violence can also be understood, in part, by the persistence
of the hyperarousal (alarm) state and by extreme cognitive distortions that accompany persistent states of fear. If, for example, children are hypervigilant to

threat and danger, they can overreact to rough horseplay or accidental contact by perceiving malicious intent when none was intended, a behavior often displayed by children with serious behavior disorders and a phenomenon we address in *A Handbook of Play Therapy with Aggressive Children.*

The neurophysiology of the child repeatedly exposed to traumatic experiences, including violence, is one of hyperarousal. The child is constantly in an alarm state. The internal regulating capabilities of the cortex are negated, and the midbrain and brain stem mechanism predominate. As a result, nonreflective acts, impulsive responses, and reactive aggression to perceived threats become the child's modus operandi. Living in a constant state of fear and threat leads to hypervigilance and to cognitive distortions that can turn lethal should the child find a weapon available, which perhaps explains why some children kill for no apparent reason (Shenken 1964). In addition, the high rate of substance abuse in conduct-disordered youth may result from efforts to modulate the hyperaroused state or to offset the emotional numbing that often follows being continually aroused (Weems et al. 2003).

Alan Schore (1996) has identified the key role played by the orbitofrontal cortex, demonstrating that the connections between the cortex and subcortex are regulated by the orbitofrontal area. Like Perry, Schore emphasizes that maturation of the orbitofrontal system is experience dependent. The system is directly influenced by the nature of the attachment relationship. Consequently, Schore sees this region of the brain as playing a vital role in both infant attachment and emotional regulation, and dysfunction of this area can increase the risk of impulsive violence. Schore and others (DeBellis, Baum, et al. 1999; DeBellis, Keshavan, et al. 1999; Pynoos et al. 1997; van der Kolk 1996) conclude that negative early relationships can lead to lifelong inability, particularly when under stress, to regulate the emotional states of rage, terror, and shame.

EMOTIONAL MEMORY

LeDoux (1996, 1998) emphasizes the pivotal role played by the amygdala and hippocampus, both in the limbic region of the brain, in emotional memory, a nonverbal phenomenon. Events experienced before the development of language, especially when accompanied by strong emotion, can remain active influences throughout our lives. Thus, emotional memories of intensely experienced incidents that occurred in preverbal stages of development can be activated by environmental triggers such as sounds, sights, and smells, and the individuals affected, and those around them, will be surprised by the affected individual's sudden display of fear, panic, aggression, or violence.

This phenomenon is frequently observed in children in gorilla suits. A boy will be running around excitedly on the playground, apparently enjoying himself, and suddenly display an outburst of aggression. If it is true that a certain level of heightened excitement or physiological arousal can trigger a dramatic change in behavior, then this truth supports a view we present in chapter 11, that staff should spend less time trying to get children to find the reasons for their disruptions and more time helping them to develop calming and mood-altering behaviors.

VIOLENCE EXPOSURE, BRAIN ABNORMALITIES, AND BODY CHEMISTRY

While a detailed review of the brain-behavior relationship in abused, traumatized, and aggressive children is beyond our scope, we will mention some general findings. EEG studies of abused children suggest they have abnormalities in the hippocampal/limbic region and the cortical area of the brain (Teicher et al. 1997). Aggressive children display higher heart-rate increases under threat and more hostile attributes than matched control subjects do, and higher heart rate and increased hostile attributes are associated with higher levels of aggression (Williams et al. 2003). In adult women abused as children, abnormal cortisol levels have been associated with stress (Bremner, Vythilingam, Vermetten, et al. 2003), as might be expected, but they have also been related to certain periods of the day (Bremner, Vythilingam, Anderson, et al. 2003). Exposure to uncontrollable stress can reduce the levels of neuropeptides that mediate responses to stress (Morgan and Rasmusson 2003). Because social support and affiliation can buffer the effect of stress on the body, some suggest that stress can limit the production of oxytocin, a neuropeptide known to promote social behavior (DeVries, Glasper, and Detellion 2003). Even more disturbing is that changes in intracellular chemical concentrations correlate with high anxiety and dependency. For example, the functional levels of natural killer cells are markedly reduced in grieving clients, suggesting impairment in the immune system (Gerra, Monti, and Panerai 2003).

Perry (2001), after synthesizing the research findings, suggests that exposure to violence in childhood alters brain development and that the resulting abnormalities are more prominent if the traumatic exposure is early in life and if it is severe and chronic. Perry (2003) cautions,

> As we search for solutions to the plagues of violence in our society, it will be imperative that we avoid the False God of Simple Solutions. The neurobiology of complex, heterogeneous behaviors is complex and heterogeneous. In

the end, paying attention to the neurobiological impact of developmental experiences—traumatic or nurturing—will yield great insight for prevention and therapeutic interventions. (p. 2)

IMPORTANT GENDER DIFFERENCES

Major differences exist between the responses of boys and girls to violent situations. Any child consistently exposed to intrafamilial violence will develop a chronic fear/alarm response, but there are marked gender differences in the response (Perry 1997; Perry, Pollard, Baker, et al. 1995; Perry, Pollard, Blakley, et al. 1995).

Females are more likely to exhibit increased internalizing symptoms, such as anxiety, depression, and eating disorders, and females tend to exhibit normal heart rates or mild tachycardia when exposed to trauma. Furthermore, their heart rates decrease during interviews about the trauma events. Males are more likely to show externalizing symptoms, such as impulsive, unreflective, reactive, and hyperactive behaviors (George and Main 1979). Perry (1997) views this sex difference as resulting partly from the chronic physiological hyperarousal and hyperactivity state that exists at much higher levels in boys than in girls. In addition, marked cognitive distortions are concomitant with the hyperaroused physiological state.

In other words, male youth, in a persistent "fight or flight" state, are highly prone to misinterpret cues and distort events, will be more reactive, and will respond more readily in an impulsive and violent manner than girls will. The originally adaptive "flight or fight" response of animals to stress has been reversed in aggressive boys. First they fight, and then they flee. And fighting not only gets them into trouble with authority figures and into special education classrooms and treatment programs; it can also get them injured or killed on the streets. This quickness to respond aggressively is dramatically exaggerated by the influence of alcohol and drugs (Shupe 1954; Lindqvist 1986; Cordilla 1985). Some attribute the biological differences between boys and girls to evolution, suggesting that the two sexes have evolved by handling stress differently (see Pitman 2003).

In a group of boys living in a residential treatment center whose past experiences included exposure to severe and prolonged domestic violence, a subset of the hyperaroused, reactive boys developed predatory, aggressive behaviors (Perry 1997). A chilling finding from following this subset of boys into early adolescence was their decrease in heart rate when asked to discuss specific violent acts in which they had been involved. Perry (1997) states, "Some of these youth described a soothing, calming feeling when they began 'stalking' a potential victim" (p. 137–138). Particularly troublesome was Perry's following observation:

> The detached, calm, dissociated (and reinforcing) feeling these boys felt is reminiscent of the feelings described by borderline adolescent girls who cut themselves and may be related to an endogenous opioid release similar to that seen in various dissociative states. (p. 138)

In summarizing this research, Perry (1997) states,

> Unfortunately, the emotional emptiness resulting from neglect can only be filled by the temporary pleasure that an exogenous euphoriant (e.g., heroin, cocaine) can provide. Similarly, a young man may find the only escape from the distress and pain caused by the anxiety of a persisting fear response is with alcohol. It is often the intoxicating agents that allow expression of the neurodevelopmentally determined predisposition for violence. (p. 139)

Larson and Lochman (2002), discussing their Anger Coping Program, an anger management program based on a cognitive-behavioral model, note that in literally all the research on the program's effectiveness, the participants were boys. They explain that boys are enrolled in the program because they are higher risks, as a gender, for externalizing behavior problems and the associated mental health and legal difficulties that accompany them. Numerous studies suggest that girls express anger and aggression in a somewhat different manner than boys (Crick 1997; Crick and Bigbee 1998; Crick and Werner 1998).

In contrast to boys, girls more often display what has been called relational aggression, a nonphysical form of aggression characterized by rumor spreading, rejection and social exclusion, and mean-spirited teasing as a means of retaliation. For this reason, they lock horns less with society and are not often referred to anger management programs.

How do you prevent or treat the relational aggression displayed by girls? We suspect it can be treated with the methods we present in *A Handbook of Play Therapy with Aggressive Children* since aggression, no matter what form it takes, is still a response to frustration or a symptom of an underlying problem. Nevertheless, not including girls in quasi-prevention efforts or even in treatment programs until they externalize their symptoms at a much older age does a disservice to girls, who suffer no less than boys from invisible wounds. Sadly, it reveals the persistence of male privilege in our culture. The girls whose invisible wounds are more likely to gain attention are the girls who act like boys. In fact, Larson and Lochman (2002) state, in spite of the absence of research on using the Anger Coping Program with girls,

There is no reason that practitioners should not use the program with girls who are demonstrating anger control problems, particularly if such problems are manifested as reactive physical aggression. In other words, the more the girls' anger resembles the boys' anger, the higher the likelihood that the Anger Control Program will be an appropriate intervention. (p. 131)

What these two clinicians are inadvertently saying is that girls should receive treatment when they externalize their symptoms. They usually don't, however, until they experience their growth spurt during preadolescence. Consequently, boys as young as four, usually those enrolled in Head Start programs that partner with mental health agencies, can receive interventions for aggressive behavior, but girls have to wait until they are twelve or thirteen or even older (Not all girls become aggressive even at preadolescence). In fact, the majority of girls who do come to the attention of mental health agencies are those who harm themselves or become suicidal in adolescence. In essence, the treatment needs of the majority of girls, those who suffer silently for long periods, are being seriously shortchanged by society.

Both boys and girls may manifest dissociative states, but girls are more likely to internalize and inflict self-harm while boys are more likely to inflict harm on others. The crucial point, however, is that the sexes respond differently to stress, but the stressors can be the same. Both boys and girls suffer enormously from invisible wounds, and the findings from neuroscience argue for a need for very early interventions and even earlier prevention efforts with both sexes.

IMPLICATIONS FOR THERAPY

In recent discussions of trauma, van der Kolk (2003) emphasizes a need to reset the bodily state at the time of trauma to a position of safety and control and suggests that verbal processing alone may be inadequate to accomplish this task. He points out the potential value of action-oriented therapeutic approaches, such as body movement therapies, massage, exercise, and Eye Movement Desensitization and Reprocessing, that address what he considers to be the core of post-traumatic stress disorder (PTSD): *frozen inaction*. He believes the more action-oriented therapies address the helplessness and powerlessness that result from the inhibition of effective action at the time of the trauma. The victim is so overwhelmed by fear and terror that actions are frozen. When the body state is set in the alarm position, manifested by physiological hyperarousal, the higher order cortical brain apparently goes "off-line." As a consequence, van der Kolk believes, verbal processing alone may not engage the subcortical regions of the brain, where memories of the trauma events are stored.

Academic researchers have not embraced van der Kolk's suggestions that unconventional therapies may help trauma victims (Wylie 2004). He has been heavily criticized by some trauma researchers for his support of nonmainstream therapies, which, in their view, lack empirical support (see discussion in Wylie 2004, p. 41). Others in the trauma field admire van der Kolk for his bold ventures into new frontiers and his openness to new ideas.

There has always been, and continues to be, heated debate over the role of "scientific evidence" versus the "clinical observation." When therapists "know" something works, they don't wait for science to prove them right (Wylie 2004). The science-based researchers are concerned that unproven therapies, especially those they consider esoteric, may waste clients' invaluable time and, in the worst case, may cause harm. Practicing clinicians point out, however, that most so-called evidence-based therapies have been "proven" largely on the basis of treatment of university-based, homogeneous client populations and through the use of manual-based treatment protocols. Consequently, these evidence-based therapies don't reflect the realities of the clinical world, where clinicians are called on to treat patients whose complex and often multiple clinical conditions would rule out their use as subjects in empirical studies.

Van der Kolk points out that researchers "ruthlessly screen out any confounding variables. But 'confounding variables' are the stuff of ordinary therapy" (quoted in Wylie 2004, p. 67). Very few fawns in gorilla suits would be selected for inclusion in evidence-based studies because most display comorbid conditions, and complex and multidetermined sociocultural and neurobiological factors contribute to their problems.

Although this controversy is far from resolved, the therapies embraced by van der Kolk have been used primarily with adults. But if frozen inaction is indeed the core of unresolved PTSD, then play therapy (the subject of *A Handbook of Play Therapy with Aggressive Children*), because it involves action and is built on the principal of transforming experiences passively endured into those actively mastered, may help to "unfreeze" the frozen child.

In addition to frozen inaction, memories or reminders of the trauma can immediately activate the alarm-state physiology referred to earlier, leading to shutdown of the higher cortical centers. This shutdown leaves individuals on a ship besieged by an affective storm and piloted by the midbrain and brain stem—the primitive control centers of the brain. Enabling patients to safely return to shore should be the first priority of therapeutic interventions.

A number of clinicians, including both of us, addressed this issue long before the effects of trauma on the brain were recognized. Dolan (1991) emphasizes the need for safety when treating adult sexual trauma survivors, especially when they get caught in the "undertow" of intensively reliving the original terror associated with the trauma. She describes helpful techniques, developed from a combination of solution-focused therapy and Ericksonian embedded hypnotic techniques, that enable a trauma survivor to anchor in the present when flooded or overwhelmed with painful memories and affect from the past. Mills and Crowley (1986), also drawing on an Ericksonian framework, describe similar strategies for use with children, including drawing techniques, metaphors, and stories to enable children to approach the painful material without being overwhelmed or retraumatized. We have incorporated some of these techniques in the play therapy procedures we present in *A Handbook of Play Therapy with Aggressive Children* (see chapters 13–16, 18–19, and 21).

SOCIAL SKILLS TRAINING

A recent literature review reveals that young children who hit, kick, verbally insult, and threaten others are more likely to assault others in adolescence (Flannery et al. 2003). These early aggressive behaviors need to be targeted in prevention programs in elementary schools because they escalate interpersonal conflict into violence.

Training children in social skills, including appropriate self-assertion, is one approach to the problem. But social skills training, delivered in isolation from other assistance, especially if it is narrowly focused as in anger management training, does not address the complex emotional underpinnings of aggression and violence in youth (Hardy 2003; Skarlew et al. 2002). Nevertheless, social skills training can enhance a child's prospects for successful adjustment. Children with better social skills have a greater chance of forming meaningful relationships. The research on resilience suggests that the availability of at least one trusting relationship can buffer depression and stress-related mental health disorders. Good relationships with peers can also serve as a buffer against peer victimization (Swartz et al. 2000).

The development of pro-social skills, especially the ability to empathize, is crucial in efforts to interrupt the cycle of violence (Fraiberg et al. 1965; Hardy 2003). Because early abuse can disrupt cognitive functioning (Reider and Cicchetti 1989), a number of cognitive behavioral programs are available to teach social skills. Several are widely used in both individual and group formats. We cite some of them in chapter 5 of *A Handbook of Play Therapy with Aggressive Children* when discussing the coping approach to treatment of traumatized children.

Studies also suggest that aggressive behavior can be reduced by altering the social environment at school (Dahlberg 1998; Flannery et al. 2003; Englander-Golden et al. 1989; Reid et al. 1999; Stoolmiller et al. 2000; Tremblay et al. 1991), especially by rewarding and praising pro-social behaviors (Walker et al. 1995) and by facilitating social competence (Hawkins et al. 1999). Social skills instruction with eight- to ten-year-old children resulted in lasting decreases in both disruptive behaviors in the classroom and negative social interactions on the playground (Lane et al. 2003). The children in the latter study were all at risk for antisocial behavior and unresponsive to a schoolwide primary intervention program.

Using data from the Seattle Social Development Project, a recent study (Herrenkohl et al. 2003) examined protective factors that reduce the likelihood of violent behavior at later ages. The youth studied were those who received high teacher ratings for aggression at age ten. Youth who showed less violence at age eighteen were those who regularly attended church, were raised in relatively well-structured families, and had bonded to school staff by age fifteen. Those who became violent lived in a more disorganized neighborhood and had greater involvement with antisocial peers at age fifteen.

Social skills training programs need to be culturally sensitive. It is a disservice to teach inner-city children skills that are based on a suburban, middle-class value system and then send them back, more vulnerable, into the streets and neighborhoods where they live (Hardy 2003). Therapists must appreciate the survival orientation required to function in high-crime and violent communities. The children typically know more about the rules of survival on the street than does the middle-class therapist who has lived a relatively sheltered life. A therapeutic goal is to provide the child with options to aggressive behavior, help the child choose among a number of alternative actions, and teach the child to use the defensive strategy of disconnection in more flexible and discerning ways (Hardy 2003; Miller and Stiver 1997).

THE CRUCIAL CAPACITY FOR EMPATHY

Empathy, as defined by Epley, Savitsky, and Gilovich (2002), is a multidimensional concept (Feshbach 1978), consisting of both cognitive and emotional components (Davis 1983). It includes concern for others, sympathy (Cialdini et al. 1997), personal distress (Mikulincer et al. 2001), and perspective taking (Chartrand and Bargh 1999). Empathy has been a key ingredient in effective therapies ranging from those of humanistic therapists, like Carl Rogers, to those of psychoanalysts, like Heinz Kohut (Wang et al. 2003). Empathy is one of the key antecedents and precursors of pro-social behavior and a sense of justice (Hoffman 2000). Empathy deficits have long been associated with interpersonal aggression (Miller and Eisenberg 1988). Throughout our two volumes, we emphasize the essential role of empathy in interrupting the cycle of violence. This is an area where the child and family therapist can make the most meaningful contribution. In *A Handbook of Play Therapy with Aggressive Children,* chapter 14 is devoted to specific techniques and strategies to develop the capacity for empathy. Bruce Perry (1997) presents an ominous story about the lack of empathy in violent youth.

> A fifteen-year-old boy sees some fancy sneakers he wants. Another child is wearing them, so he pulls out a gun and demands them. The younger child, at gunpoint, takes off his shoes and surrenders them. The fifteen-year-old puts the gun to the child's head, smiles, and pulls the trigger. When he is arrested, the officers are chilled by his apparent lack of remorse. Asked later whether, if he could turn back the clock, he would do anything differently, he thinks and replies, "I would have cleaned my shoes." (p.132)

Perry explains later that bloody shoes led to the boy's arrest. This empty boy was unable to show any empathy, any connection to the pain caused his victim or the victim's family, a family that lost a child to senseless violence. Perry describes this child murderer as "emotionally retarded." The boy's background revealed neglect and humiliation by his primary caregivers. Perry suggests that the part of his brain that enables one to feel connected to the pain of others, empathy, simply didn't develop. Perry states,

> The abilities to feel remorse, to be empathetic, to be sympathetic are all experience-based capabilities. If a child feels no emotional attachment to any human being, then one cannot expect any more remorse from him or her after killing a human than one would expect from someone who ran over a squirrel. (p. 133)

In their classic paper, "Ghosts in the Nursery," Fraiberg and colleagues emphasize that until people can confront and feel their own pain, they will not have the capacity to feel for the pain of others (Fraiberg, Adelson, and Shapiro 1965). Shectman's study (2003) of cognitive and affective empathy in aggressive boys revealed that aggressive boys showed a lower level of affective empathy, although they did not differ in cognitive empathy from boys in the comparison group. In fact, the measure of affective empathy among the nonaggressive boys in the comparison group was twice as high as that of boys in the aggressive group.

Blair's literature review (2003) suggests that children with psychopathic tendencies have difficulty recognizing sad and fearful facial expressions. The study by Blair and colleagues (Blair et al. 2002) also demonstrated that children with psychopathic tendencies display impaired recognition of fearful vocal affect. Children, and adults, with psychopathic tendencies apparently experience difficulty appreciating the sad and fearful feelings of others and recognizing others' fearful and sad facial expressions and their voiced feelings.

Blair and colleagues (Blair et al. 2002) state, "Psychopathy is a disorder characterized in part by emotional traits such as callousness, a diminished capacity for remorse, and superficial charm, as well as impulsivity and poor behavioral controls" (p. 682).

LACK OF EMPATHY FOR THE SELF

Observing children in gorilla suits who injure themselves is an eye-opening phenomenon. They can hit their heads, bruise their knees, or even break their arms and never ask for assistance, attend to the injuries, or accept help from others. Sometimes they don't even show pain. Earlier, we emphasized that many parents of gorilla-suit wearers were rarely solicitous toward their children's injuries. In fact, when they noticed their child's injury, some even resented having to stop ongoing activities to attend to the child. Often when an abused child comes to the attention of medical specialists, examination reveals earlier injuries that were never attended to. Having no attentive adults with whom to identify or imitate, the children adopt a noncaring attitude toward themselves. They don't expect injuries to be attended to by others, nor do they themselves attend to the injuries. They continue their ongoing activities, bleeding all over themselves and others or onto the ground. In short, they lack self-empathy.

Self-empathy is neglected in the clinical literature, but it is a crucial deficit of aggressive and violent children. A girl treated by Dr. Crenshaw, presented in *A Handbook of Play Therapy with Aggressive Children*, chapter 17, illustrates how the lack of self-empathy was tied to the traumatic events of her life.

The girl's lack of self-empathy was emotionally rooted in the details of her traumatic experiences, some involving sadistic abuse from her uncle. Until she could reveal the original details of her abuse, including the feelings of terror, rage, disgust, and self-hatred that accompanied it, she was unable to let go of her self-loathing and contempt, let alone empathize with the pain of others.

We view the therapist's empathy, persistence, and ability to contain strong feelings of the child as the keys to the healing process. Myers (2003), when emphasizing the pivotal role of the therapeutic relationship, and especially the role of empathy, observes that when clients have "known" and experienced empathy, acceptance, and understanding from their therapist, they report increased self-acceptance and self-empathy. As a result, the therapeutic relationship becomes a powerful agent of change and emerges as a model for relationships with self and others.

SOME EMPATHY TRAINING PROGRAMS

Helping nonempathic children to develop empathy is absolutely essential to break the transmission of violence from one generation to another. There are no shortcuts to developing empathy. If lacking, the skill can be learned only after a long period of in-depth, emotionally focused therapeutic interventions. In *A Handbook of Play Therapy with Aggressive Children*, we present examples of the Affect Recognition Picture and Story Series and the Empathy Picture and Story Series (Crenshaw and Garritt 2004), both clinical tools to help children develop their affect recognition skills and their capacities for empathy. This therapeutic task is not easy, and the results are not consistent. In contrast, efforts to facilitate the development of empathy and other interpersonal skills earlier in life are more fruitful and less costly.

ROOTS OF EMPATHY

A program called Roots of Empathy, developed by educator Mary Gordon, is a classroom-based social competence promotion program for elementary school children widely used in schools in Canada (Schonert-Reichl, Smith, and Zaidman-Zait 2003) and is being piloted in Japan. The program fosters the development of empathy in elementary school children. It is founded on the belief, backed by empirical evidence, that an inverse relationship exists between empathy and violence. Violence decreases as levels of empathy rise. When children understand and respect the feelings and points of view of others, they are less likely to bully or intimidate peers. It is hoped that program graduates will engage in less family and societal violence in the future. An innovative feature of this program is class visits by an infant, one of the infant's parents, and a program-certified instructor from the local community. Empathy skills are learned partly through interactions and observations with the baby. In the 2003–2004 school year, 20,000 children in classrooms across Canada received the program. Program participants in grades one through three in the 2000–2001 school year showed significant gains in knowledge of emotions, social understanding, and pro-social behaviors with peers. Participants also displayed decreased aggression in interactions with peers and decreased teasing and bullying. Eighty-eight percent of those participants who displayed some form of proactive aggression (e.g., bullying) on preprogram measures showed less proactive aggression after the program. In contrast, 50 percent of nonparticipants who displayed proactive aggression on preprogram measures showed increased aggression after the program.

THE SECOND STEP PROGRAM

The Second Step Program is a primary prevention program designed to deter aggression and facilitate the social competence of children from preschool through grade nine. Three areas are stressed in the curriculum: empathy, social problem solving, and anger management. Participants have shown favorable gains in the targeted skills (Frey, Hirschstein, and Guzzo 2000).

THE DINA DINOSAUR PROGRAM

A third promising program is the Dina Dinosaur Social, Emotional, and Problem Solving Child Training Program. This program has been developed for preschool and early-school-age children with early onset conduct problems, in keeping with the research demonstrating that programs designed to reduce aggression and conduct problems are more effective when delivered to children before age eight. This program teaches emotional understanding, empathy, perspective taking, friendship development skills, communication skills, anger management, and interpersonal problem-solving skills. Initial findings have been encouraging, and a long-term program evaluation study is in place (Webster-Stratton and Reid 2003).

CONCLUSION

Bruce Perry (2003), whom we quoted at the beginning of this chapter, writes that individual violence results from several factors and can take many forms:

> Some violence is due to impulsive behavior, some due to disinhibition by drugs or alcohol, some due to serious mental illness, some to hate, revenge, or retribution. How any individual comes to kill is a complex combination of circumstances, and it is almost impossible to know exactly "why" for any given act of violence. (p. 1)

To keep things in perspective, clinicians should remember that the majority of persons who are emotionally neglected in childhood do not grow into violent individuals. Many suffer in other ways, and the more resilient may not suffer at all. As Perry (1997) observes,

> These victims carry their scars in other ways, usually in a profound emptiness, or in emotionally destructive relationships, moving through life disconnected from others and robbed of some of their humanity. The effects of emotional neglect in childhood predispose to violence by decreasing the strength of the subcortical and cortical impulse-modulating capacity, and by decreasing the value of other humans due to an incapacity to empathize or sympathize with them. (p. 133)

Greenwald, on the staff of the Mount Sinai Traumatic Stress Studies Program, views trauma, in association with other contributing neurobiological and sociocultural factors, as a key to understanding the development and persistence of conduct disorder. Greenwald notes that trauma histories are ubiquitous in the conduct-disordered population and that trauma effects can help clinicians to understand many features of conduct disorder, including lack of empathy, impulsiveness, anger, acting out, and resistance to treatment. Greenwald argues that the current standard of care fails to fully address trauma, which may partially account for the low success rate of current treatment approaches with conduct-disordered youth.

Our experience supports the notion that many of the most aggressive and violent children seen in clinical settings, especially those placed in residential treatment centers, are those who have been traumatized by exposure to violence, abuse, and other social toxins. Caregivers and helpers need to recognize the traumatized children behind the gorilla suits. Until the child can undertake emotionally focused work involving the integration of past traumatic experiences, empathy for the self or for others will not develop.

But we also must remember that not all children traumatized by violence become aggressive and not all children are traumatized by violence, especially those buffered by involved and supportive parents, schools, and pockets within violent communities (Bernard 1991; Prevatt 2003). Jerome Kagan, who has studied child development for more than four decades, recently stated in an interview (2000),

> The development of a human being is extraordinarily complicated. Many things go into it. Yes, kindness and love and consistency of care in the first two years of life make a small contribution. It's not that they have no influence whatsoever. Therefore, parents should love, tend to, talk to their young infants, and that's what most parents do. That's correct. So it does make a

difference if you abuse your child or love your child, that does make a difference . . . but that's not the whole story, that's just the beginning of the
trail of development. (p. 8)

I would say short of being abused, half the time from birth to age two, I
mean seriously abused, I would be willing to acknowledge that if [serious
abuse] happened to you, you might be permanently harmed and that recovery would be difficult or impossible. But over 95 percent of children
around the world do not experience that, and for those, there is a great capacity for change. (p. 10)

Kagan (1998) also reminds us that we must be careful with the language
we choose when discussing development. In this book, we take great care to
describe factors contributing to, but not causing particular developmental outcomes. Kagan (1998) has been particularly critical of the notion of *infantile determinism*—the belief that early life phenomena are the most potent forces in
shaping a life. He emphasizes that the evidence for such a thesis is simply not
compelling (see Kagan 1998, pp. 83–150). In a presentation titled "How We
Become Who We Are," Kagan (1998) describes a tapestry of four threads interwoven in an incredibly complex way:

1. Our biology, which includes our temperament;
2. Our social relations, which include our family;
3. The culture in which we live and the values we learn;
4. The historical moment in time in which we live.

Kagan also talks about children "in full sentences." It is not accurate, he
says, to talk about aggressive or fearful children but rather about children who,
under certain conditions and in a specific context, may act aggressive or fearful. These specific circumstances and situational factors need to be delineated
in order to accurately describe the child. Unless a context is provided, these de-
scriptors have no meaning. No child is aggressive or violent all the time. Children who are aggressive at school may not be aggressive at home. In addition,
the children may be aggressive at school only when they feel demeaned or devalued, such as when another pupil calls them "stupid" or when school staff
members treat them disrespectfully. Delineating the conditions under which a
child will become anxious, fearful, and aggressive is part of any comprehensive
plan, and such planning must precede the effort to provide play therapy.

The Psychodynamics of Gorilla-Suit Wearers

Children in gorilla suits, having failed to master Erickson's early stages of development, are empty and seek possessions, suffer from primitive guilt, and seek punishment. The chapter concludes with a discussion of the stress experienced by therapists working with them.

Children who have failed to master Erikson's early developmental stages struggle with three basic issues: hunger, shame, and helplessness. They feel weak, small, and unable to control events. Consumed with anguish, unsolvable fear, and grief, and feeling disconnected, they struggle with demands they are ill equipped to meet. Abraham Maslow (1954, 1971) emphasized, in his theory of need hierarchies, that children whose basic needs are unmet have little energy left to address higher order needs, such as self-development and self-actualization, needs that motivate school achievement. The children still struggle with concrete issues, such as relating to parents and peers or even survival on the street. Consequently, facing other struggles, especially those involving abstract concepts, as academic subjects do, seems meaningless to them. Bombarded by a hostile and depriving world, and constantly in an alert state, they respond in kind, and the cycle of violence they create is difficult to halt.

When parents harbor hateful feelings toward their child, a false sense of safety is established by both identifying with their power and displacing the omnipresent fear of their actions into an imaginary world. If the parents are extremely hostile, the child's imaginary world will be full of "creatures bent on destroying children." When the parents' hostilities are less intense, these creatures become the allies of the child (like the parents who love the child when the child meets their needs and who hate the child otherwise). The child also depersonalizes the self and endows objects with displaced or projected feelings (e.g., one toy car is consistently used to smash other toys or objects), or the illusion is created that the child is all powerful (he or she becomes Super Boy or Super Girl).

At the same time, in order to feel loved, the child becomes convinced that the rejection experienced results from being imperfect, represses knowledge of the parents' angry feelings, and searches for defects within. He or she is a "monster." But such a self-perception creates feelings of shame. To counteract these feelings, the child develops an exaggerated posture of perfection. "There is nothing wrong with me!" Consequently, the child develops inordinate sensitivity to criticism—a protective pattern of anticipating blame, accusation, or punishment. Criticism is forestalled by projecting threats to adults and acting as if threatened by others. The result is a child who avoids simple challenges, is a master at self-deception, and represses all but angry feelings. If faults were acknowledged, shame would be revealed, but what is more important, anger at parents would be exposed. With acknowledgment of this anger comes awareness of its cause—parental rejection.

Children who have experienced multiple losses, children Garbarino (1999) calls "Lost Boys," need intensive help with loss. Nor should the needs of girls be overlooked. Hardy (2003) points out, as noted before, that in our culture, girls who receive clinical attention are those who act out like boys. Girls who suffer from profound losses by internalizing their pain and becoming quiet, withdrawn, and depressed may be viewed as simply "good girls." Yet their pains are no different from those felt by aggressive and violent males. Girls are just as needful of intensive intervention as boys.

Sadly, abused and neglected girls often suffer silently with anxiety disorders, eating problems, and depression and don't receive help until they develop more serious internalizing symptoms, such as hysterical seizures (Goodwin, Simms, and Bergman 1979), multiple personality disorders (Bowman, Blix, and Coons 1985), become involved with drugs (Jacobsen, Southwick, and Kosten 2001), or inflict harm on themselves with cutting, suicidal gestures, or actual attempts (Carr 2002; Gratz 2003; King et al. 2001; Johnson et al. 2002). Suicide is the fourth leading cause of death in youth between ten and fourteen years of age. Girls make more suicidal gestures than boys, but almost four times as many boys than girls actually kill themselves (Brent 2002), probably because the methods they use are more lethal. David Schaeffer, of the University of Columbia, reports (Associated Press 2004) that 1,883 ten- to nineteen-year-olds killed themselves in 2002 and some 1.8 million teenagers attempted suicide that year, with more than a fourth of them requiring medical attention.

When their growth spurt makes girls bigger than boys (Quinsey et al. 2004), they can become equally aggressive, as well as sexually promiscuous (Woodward and Fergusson 1999; Yampolskaya, Brown, and Greenbaum 2002; Zoccolillo, Myers, and Assiter 1997). Studies also suggest that as family stressors increase, girls develop more externalizing disorders (Gaylord and Kitzman 2003). Sexual acting out can be part of a girl's abortive mourning process, a process we discuss in *A Handbook of Play Therapy with Aggressive Children*, chapter 14, but just as often it is an attempt to actively master sexual traumas that were passively experienced. Unfortunately, these attempts are usually unsuccessful, especially for those who have been sexually abused (Noll, Horowitz, and Bonanno 2003), and many later become prostitutes (Della 2003; Widom and Kuhns 1996).

Grieving associated with intangible losses can be difficult work. The complexity results from the wounds' being unacknowledged by others, and sometimes by the child, who has buried the losses deep inside, where they have scarred the soul. Unattended wounds usually result in serious complications. The most devastating wounds are those resulting from devaluation, or being stripped of one's humanity (Hardy 2003). The result is shame, loss of dignity, anger, and ultimately rage. Additional crushing blows include loss of vision, loss of hope, and loss of dreams. Take away a person's dreams and you destroy the soul (Hardy 2003). The humorist Mark Twain said, "Don't part with your illusions. When they are gone you may still exist, but you have ceased to live" (Columbia World of Quotations 1996a). Emily Dickinson wrote, "Hope is the thing with feathers—that perches in the soul—and sings the tunes without the words—and never stops at all" (Columbia World of Quotations 1996b). Bonanno (2004) argues that we underestimate the resilience of people in coping with adversity in life. He discusses the trait of hardiness, which helps to buffer exposure to extreme stress. Citing Kobasa, Maddi, and Kahn (1982), he writes that hardiness consists of three dimensions: being committed to finding a meaningful purpose to life, the belief that one can influence one's surroundings and the outcome of events (internal locus of control), and the belief that one can learn and grow from both positive and negative life experiences. Buffered by these beliefs, "hardy individuals" appraise potentially stressful situations as less threatening than do others, thus minimizing the experience of distress. They also are more confident and better able to use positive coping mechanisms, such as problem solving, and to find support, thus helping them to deal with the distress they do experience (Florian, Mikulincer, and Taubman 1995).

Bonanno (2004) believes that clinicians who provide critical incident debriefing and grief work in the aftermath of exposure to a potentially traumatic event ignore the hardiness in individuals. Providing services is not usually necessary and, in some cases, can have a deleterious effect, at least for those capable of normal bereavement. Bonanno (2004) cites the research of Neimeyer (2000), who found in a meta-analytic study of grief therapies that 38 percent more participants got worse following treatment, compared with no-treatment controls. Clear benefits were seen, however, when services were provided to bereaved persons experiencing chronic grief.

We have no quarrel with Bonanno's assertions. The wholesale application of critical incident debriefing, grief therapy, or any form of treatment should follow thorough assessments of the clinical needs of exposed individuals. Providing unnecessary treatment can pathologize normal reactions to loss and trauma and fail to respect the natural coping mechanisms that exist in many people. Bonanno (2004) makes the point that chronic post-traumatic stress disorder is of great concern but stresses that "the vast majority of individuals exposed to violent or life-threatening events do not go on to develop the disorder" (p. 24).

We agree that a "cottage industry" seems to have developed around grief counseling and trauma debriefing, and the wholesale application of these interventions, without careful consideration of individual needs, may in some cases lead to negative outcomes. Throughout our two volumes, we emphasize a strengths-based approach to treatment and have urged clinicians to avoid "pouncing on pathology." Not all stressful experiences are traumatizing. Searching for pathology while ignoring healthy responses to adversity is an ill-advised practice.

Nevertheless, children in gorilla suits have been exposed to repeated loss and have received little or no assistance with grieving these losses. In many cases, their losses have gone unrecognized. We have stressed that their losses are buried deep inside themselves, cut off from their feelings, and their need to grieve is not recognized even by them. Yet their aggressive and sometimes violent behavior bespeaks the depth of their rage, profound sorrow, fear, pain, and emptiness. Bonanno's writings bring a more balanced view to the topic, but they should not cloud our vision about those suffering from invisible wounds, wounds that devastate the spirit and soul and require intensive treatment to heal. It would be a sad mistake if the concept of resilience is taken to mean that everyone can be resilient or hardy or, even worse, if every child is expected to be resilient. This belief would set many kids up to fail. Politicians, for example, could decide it was unnecessary to fund programs for economically deprived children, reasoning that these kids could be resilient if they really wanted to be. It is important to remember the prospective studies of youth who grow up in crime-ridden and violent inner-city neighborhoods. None of the children followed met the stated criteria for resilience (see chapter 14).

If children get a good start in life, have positive temperaments, and have the support of the family, schools, and larger community, and then something horrendous happens to them, observers may be amazed at the ability of most to cope with stress. Some of the children may even find positive meaning in the experience, and beneficial consequences may result, such as greater appreciation of how fragile and precious life is. In sharp contrast, fawns in gorilla suits are exposed to few if any of these buffering, or protective, factors. In addition, they experience repeated traumas, such as living every day in socially toxic communities and catching the nightly news to learn if any family members were shot. They are the children who need intensive clinical interventions and the ones our two volumes address.

EMPTINESS AND THE QUEST FOR POSSESSIONS

Most neglected children feel they never get enough love. They feel empty. In response, they can become obsessed with acquiring symbolic equivalents. For some the symbolic equivalent may be food, and for others it may be things. They often steal and hoard possessions. "I cannot depend on others to meet my need—self-reliance is my only safe course." Many demand things from adults, especially a therapist, or attempt to take things from others or from the therapy room. When adults deny these requests, even for simple objects, like a blank sheet of paper or a paper clip, the child will call them stingy and uncaring. But to accede to these demands for things, no matter how insignificant they may be, distracts from treatment and undermines the treatment process. The child's emptiness is also filled with fruitless efforts at self-love. Cockiness, selfishness, and unwillingness to admit faults are all efforts at self-love that further alienate others. Most of these children are difficult to like. Inwardly, however, the question of who shall love the child becomes intolerably compelling to the therapist.

TROUBLED BY A PRIMITIVE CONSCIENCE

There is a general misunderstanding of the undersocialized child's conscience development. It is often said that the child who is overly aggressive has no conscience—that the child does not feel guilty. From material presented in chapter 2, we can see that this statement is only partially true. Like all children, the undersocialized child's morality begins with internal self-criticism. But it stops there. Because this self-criticism is not softened by self-praise, the child suffers from intensive self-criticism that threatens the sense of well-being. Consequently, protection from this criticism is managed by both externalizing the "bad" parts of the self and projecting punishable impulses onto others. (Externalization and projection are defined and discussed in chapter 11.) As a result, the child becomes extremely intolerant of others, and when guilt is aroused, indignation increases.

All children have a harsh and primitive conscience at one stage in their moral development. Piaget refers to this stage as one in which the child believes in retributive justice and particularly in expiatory punishment, or that misbehavior is punished to set things right. The punishment is arbitrary, and no relationship exists between the content of the misbehavior and the nature of the punishment. The child is spanked, hit, or sent to bed early for misbehavior. Painful coercion is used to produce guilt. Later, as the child matures, he or she realizes that adults and peers punish by reciprocity. They use natural consequences, such as excluding the child from those he or she disrupts, depriving the child of the object misused, doing to the child what he or she did to others, or asking for restitution.

Undersocialized children rarely develop beyond the notion of expiatory justice. While the normal child will give back two punches for the two he received, the undersocialized child will seek revenge well beyond "eye for eye, tooth for tooth." He will want to "kill" the other child. In addition, the child believes in the superiority of punishment over equality of treatment long after other children's moral development has moved from concepts of retributive justice to those of distributive or egalitarian justice. The child continues to believe that disobedience is a breach of normal relations between parent and child and that some reparation is necessary. To accept punishment is the most natural form of reparation, and the child will seek it until he or she gets it. In contrast, other children come to realize that forgiveness is necessary. They do not seek revenge because there is no end to revenge. They learn to understand the psychology of situations and to make judgments according to norms of a higher moral type.

For example, if told a story about a boy who is given a piece of bread and then loses it overboard while playing around, most normal children will say that the boy should be given another one because little children are clumsy and not very clever. They will say that while he should have known better, he did not do it on purpose and, therefore, should not have to go hungry simply because he was not careful. In contrast, the undersocialized child never advances to this stage. He thinks the child should be punished and go hungry. "He was naughty—his mother isn't pleased—he must not get any more." The child is unable to take into consideration the circumstances of the individual, in this case that the child was small or clumsy. Egalitarian ideals of justice are learned from caring adults and grow out of the child's movement from unilateral respect for adults to mutual respect and cooperation. The child with arrested moral development is one who has responded to the punishing adult with either an inner submission or a sustained revolt.

Because the child's moral development is arrested at the concept of retributive justice, disgust and repulsion toward the destruction of people and

their belongings—attitudes necessary for the preservation of human values—
never develop. Some of the children we saw in play therapy in the residential
treatment center where we both worked physically attacked or threw a chair
at the therapist. In the days after the session was terminated and the child
placed in a crisis room, the child would ask the therapist, without emotion, for
something when passing the therapist in the hallway. When new to the center,
we thought the requests were an effort to ensure continued acceptance following the transgression, but experience taught us otherwise. "Out of sight is
out of mind" was the real reason. The children never reflected on the attack.
In fact, the children were incapable of such reflection.

Undersocialized aggressive children who don gorilla suits need treatment
designed to enhance their attachment to and identification with adults who
hold altruistic values. Such attachments take considerable time to develop.
Only when the child desires to please a caregiver or other adult and is capable
of realizing that he or she has let the adult down in some way will guilt and
empathy develop. In addition, the attachments should be maintained throughout the child's renewed efforts to move through the developmental stages never
mastered.

SEEKERS OF PUNISHMENT

A child with so much retaliatory anger toward his or her parents needs to con-
ceal this hate from both the self and the parents in order to survive, feeling that
"without my parents, I have nobody. I will be all alone. I will die." Disappointment in parents, shame at feeling ignorant, and hateful envy of siblings are
all intolerable feelings that a harsh primitive conscience will not allow the child
to acknowledge. Punishment is sought from others whenever those feelings in-
trude into consciousness. Provocative behavior typically results in the punishment needed to silence the conscience. Such a child seeks punishment not only
from caregivers but also from his or her psychotherapist. To respond with limits is mandatory; to respond with anger or punishment is antitherapeutic.

THE THERAPIST'S NEEDS

Because of the particular psychodynamics of children in gorilla suits, as well as
their families, they present a difficult challenge for therapists. Their aggressive
behaviors require firmness, and their attachment difficulties require constant
maintenance of firm boundaries. Clinicians can become emotionally exhausted

fending off the children's aggression day after day and can begin to distance from the clients to defend against these onslaughts. In addition, the ambiguous material they present in session after session can reduce the enjoyment of therapy, especially in therapists who tend to be perfectionists (Wittenberg and Norcross 2001). And therapists must be able to tolerate long periods of boredom, often having to combat empty treatment sessions with a degree of enthusiasm akin to that of the creative kindergarten teacher.

The authors suggest that therapists make a copy of Misch's article (2000), "Great Expectations: Mistaken Beliefs of Beginning Psychodynamic Therapists," and refer to it often in times of turmoil. Koltler (1991) writes,

> If at sometime every week (or every day in some cases), therapists do not feel stuck, at a loss as to how to proceed, confused and unsure about what is happening with clients, then they are probably neither very honest with themselves nor very open to confronting the limits of their capabilities. (p. 196)

Studies of clinicians working with aggressive clients reveal the presence of secondary stress disorders in 25 to 31 percent of therapists (Bell 2003; Lucero 2003). Those who cope best with such clients are those who maintain a healthy balance between work and private life, enjoy leisure time activities, create clear personal boundaries and role definitions in their work, do not define themselves by their career, and are optimistic, but remain objective and able to differentiate between what can and what cannot be accomplished (Lucero 2003; Pegel 2003). They also possess buffering personal beliefs, task-oriented coping strategies, and a strong sense of personal competence, have resolved their own personal traumas, have good control over their own emotions, experience the support of their families, and draw heavily on their early experiences with positive role models (Bell 2003).

Adults working with children in gorilla suits often get into conflicts about what is best for the children. Simon Wilkinson (2001) writes that "some people who choose the helping professions can get caught in their own compulsive caregiving strategy—a strategy which can have developed on a background of relative neglect, a depressed mother in early childhood, for example" (p. 326). Intrastaff conflicts, or even interagency conflicts that arise around the children's needs, can relate to the various rescuing strategies driven by the compulsive rescuing behavior of professionals. Dr. Mordock recalls working with a mother whose son was earning points toward a bicycle. The probation officer working with the child, who had discretionary funds available to use to prevent placement, bought the boy a bike, completely disrupting the treatment strategy in progress, of which the probation officer had been fully apprised.

In residential treatment, conflicts also arise over when a child is ready to return home. Sometimes the conflicts are between agency staff and child protective workers, but other times they arise within the agency, such as between the child-care workers, the therapist, and the direct-care staff or between the direct-care staff and the social workers responsible for family treatment.

Over the course of our residential treatment experience, we have worked with some clinicians who couldn't manage either the children or the conflicts between staff and who were counseled to pursue work with other clinical populations. Not everyone is suited to work with children whose psychodynamics can bring out the worst in people. Balancing firmness with tenderness is no easy task. "Tough Love," while an overrated child-rearing attitude, is needed to help the children, and tolerance is needed to manage the conflicts between staff. Those not stimulated by the task of curbing aggressive behavior or by resolving inter- and intra-agency staff conflicts, but instead continually made uncomfortable by both tasks, should use their talents to help other types of children.

Gorilla-suit wearers have a remarkable ability to touch the raw, sensitive, and vulnerable parts within the therapist, so much so that some therapists, especially when feeling helpless and wanting to "do something" for the child, engage in unprofessional behaviors that can lead to loss of their jobs and sometimes even their licenses to practice. The children also are skillful at eliciting reactions from adults that justify the children's own anger at and mistrust of adults. Gorilla-suit wearers use distancing and disconnection because these defenses have insured their survival. When adult caregivers take the bait, the caregivers feel demoralized for responding in such an antitherapeutic way, and their guilt and shame can tempt them to avoid or distance from the child.

The emotionally taxing work of trying to heal fawns in gorilla suits burns out an inordinate number of young, idealistic people who, with good intentions and heart, approach this work hoping to make a difference. Those who last are therapists with a realistic appreciation of their limitations and, especially, an ability to refocus on the children without being overwhelmed by failures or the inability to help some children overcome the hurdles facing them.

Therapists need to constantly remind themselves, as Bonime (1983) points out, that when they feel impotent, hopeless, helpless, enraged, frustrated, or depressed, all occupational hazards in work with aggressive children and their families, their feelings don't begin to match the degree of impotence, hopelessness, helplessness, rage, frustration, and depression the children and their families are feeling. Furthermore, not all reactions produced in the therapist by a client contaminate therapy. Some can be viewed as projective communications (see chapter 11), communications that allow the therapist, in modulated intensity, to feel what the client feels. These communications are important windows into the inner life of the child. The only way to distinguish between projective communications and unhealthy contaminations is for the therapist to continually examine his or her reactions every day. The therapist's own personal therapy can greatly assist in that effort. As Hoxter (1983) states,

> We can never observe emotional injury; we can only observe the adaptations and maladaptations which each individual utilizes in attempts to cope with pain. The pain remains unseen; our only perceptual organ for it is the most sensitive of instruments, our own capacity for emotional response. By maintaining our sensitivity without being overwhelmed or resorting to withdrawal or attribution of blame, we may then be better able to provide the answer which brings relief: the experience of a relationship with someone who can be relied upon to attend to suffering with both receptivity and strength. (pp. 131–132)

Those who work with fawns in gorilla suits and their families need close supervision, especially regarding the attachment issues that arise when working with this population, and collegial consultation and support.

work at this —

6

Risk Factors When Treating the Traumatized Child

Six problems can occur in the treatment of traumatized children: arousal of strong emotions, diversion from more pressing problems, increase of self-blame, cementing of a deviant self-image, failure to appreciate the nature of the relationship between a male therapist and a female child, and some issues experienced by therapists.

The upsurge in interest in treating traumatized children, particularly those sexually abused, has led to a plethora of recently developed, but largely untested, interview and play therapy techniques to treat this population, both in individual and in group therapy. The belief (also largely untested) that the child needs to disclose the details of the abuse in order to be fully adjusted has led to the use of specific structured procedures to help the child disclose, although this view has been challenged (Seligson 1993).

Many of these procedures were developed to get the child to disclose for investigatory rather than for therapeutic purposes (Hindman 1987; Seman-Haynes and Baumgarten 1994; White et al. 1986), but they have been adapted for therapy as well. In fact, without the use of these techniques, children in outpatient treatment rarely, if ever, play out or discuss their sexual abuse (Mordock 1996b). Interviewing techniques also have to be modified when children come from disorganized and relatively nonverbal homes (Mordock 2001). Nevertheless, the question of harm done to some children by the use of such techniques has not been adequately addressed. While a formal study of sexually abused children in treatment suggested that therapist structure for disclosure caused the children no harm (Mordock 1996b), cases have been reported in which children got worse following efforts to address a child's past abuse (Mordock 1999b).

Many therapists believe that therapy is without risk. Nevertheless, evidence, both empirical and observational, indicates that therapy can sometimes be harmful (Ackerman and Neubauer 1948; Mordock 1999b; Siegel 1991; Silverman 1977; Stuart 1970; Strupp 1994). In fact, Clarizio and McCoy (1983) write that mental health interventions with delinquent adolescents, many of whom are gorilla-suit wearers, "risk damaging those they are designed to assist" (p. 338). Frances and Clarkin (1981) conclude, "the psychotherapies, like drugs, can produce addictions, side effects, complications and overdosage if prescribed in an unselective fashion" (p. 552). Sometimes no treatment is the best treatment choice (Frances and Clarkin; Mordock 1999b). The Play Therapy Decision Grid, presented in *A Handbook of Play Therapy with Aggressive Children*, chapter 5, discusses when abusive and traumatic events can be explored.

Therapeutic efforts for disclosure of abuse or other traumatic experiences can cause four basic problems: arousal of strong emotions in the child, serious disruption of the family equilibrium, reinforcement of a negative self-image, and neglect of other, more serious issues.

AROUSAL OF STRONG EMOTIONS

Arousal of strong emotions can make a client worse. Recent studies suggest that many clients with post-traumatic stress disorder (PTSD) can benefit from both systematic desensitization and flooding techniques, that those few who get worse during treatment do so only temporarily, and that their outcomes do not differ from others' (Foa et al. 2002). Most of these adult clients, however, were not victims of childhood traumas or even of horrific traumas. Studies of holocaust victims indicate the need for some individuals to completely repress their horrifying experiences (Bergmann and Jucovy 1982).

Clinical experience reveals that some children with repressed traumatic experiences need a very controlled environment to handle the behaviors they display when they begin to reexperience the feelings connected with their abuse. Extreme anger, loss of impulse control, and marked depression can accompany the working-through process (Crenshaw, Boswell, et al. 1986; Crenshaw, Rudy, et al. 1986). Working with clients who have experienced traumatic stress must involve a thorough assessment of their ego strengths. Expression of strong feelings is beneficial only when the feelings can be integrated and understood by the child. If they lead to ego disorganization, their expression can be harmful, as the vignettes below reveal.

A noncommunicative girl, referred for school behavior problems, including the expression of suicidal ideation, displayed considerable clinical evidence that suggested she had been abused, but she would not discuss the topic. She did agree, however, to let the clinic psychiatrist hypnotize her. The message given to her under hypnosis was that it would be all right to tell her therapist her feelings. Within a day, she became markedly depressed, was hospitalized, and displayed markedly regressed behavior in the hospital and remained so after a precipitous discharge.

A boy placed in a day treatment setting had begun to make progress but rapidly deteriorated following his assignment to a therapist. Once he established a relationship with the therapist, he spontaneously began to talk about some traumatic experiences. The therapist wrote, "His behavior and affect deteriorated, he became increasingly self-injurious, and suicidal. He was hospitalized twice and eventually placed in residential treatment. I'm not exactly sure if I did anything specific, but I do know that once he had a relationship with me he began to deteriorate."

A nine-year-old girl refused to see Dr. Mordock after her first session, in which she spontaneously played out a scene with puppets in which a parent was beating a child for wetting the bed. (With hindsight, one can see the play should have been interrupted as it was too revealing for an initial session.)

Dr. Mordock once received an angry call from the single mother of a young boy who had just left an uneventful play therapy session in which Dr. Mordock had mentioned only neutral topics and had said very little. The mother demanded to know what had been said to the boy about his father because he had flooded her with questions following the interview that she could not and would not answer, and his behavior had worsened. She never returned the child to therapy.

St. John (1968) describes a session with a fifteen-year-old girl in residential treatment who had experienced a series of foster home placements before placement in the center. St. John said to the girl, "You must have felt very lonely and unwanted as a child." He reported that the child began to sob bitterly and cried for the rest of the interview. The next week she refused to speak to him and sat in lonely silence. In the cottage, she regressed until she had to be hospitalized. In retrospect, St. John realized that the girl was too fragile to deal with such strong emotions. When he first noticed her tearful reaction, he should have changed the subject to a pleasant topic or to a topic she had used defensively in earlier sessions. We would suggest that he should have switched to a coping approach, a topic we discuss in *A Handbook of Play Therapy with Aggressive Children*, chapter 5.

Dr. Crenshaw had a similar experience after his first session with Melissa, a nine-year-old. Her father and mother divorced, and the father, to whom she was very attached, had remarried and moved to a distant city. The "last straw" came when her father failed to acknowledge her recent birthday. When the author began to explore what that experience was like for her, she began to sob in a heart-rending way.

When the time for Melissa's second appointment arrived, her mother called to express her distress. Melissa had become hysterical and had refused to get in the car. Melissa also refused to come to the phone to talk with the author. The author asked Melissa's mother to relay the message that he very much wanted to meet with her and to schedule a new appointment for her. The message included telling her that he was sorry that he had asked her to talk about upsetting things. He realized that it was too soon and should have given her more time to work up to talking about something that is so hard for her.

She refused to get in the car when the time for her second appointment arrived, only this time she was willing to come to the phone. She said very little, but she was willing to listen. The author told her that he was sorry that their last session had been so hard for her and that he had made a mistake. He told her to think about and write down the topics she felt ready to talk about, and he promised that she would be able to pick one of those topics. When she came in for her appointment, he told her that when she felt ready, she could add topics to her list. The author was backpedaling to try to create the "safe place" that Havens (1989) describes as essential for therapy to take place. In the initial session, Dr. Crenshaw mistakenly assumed she needed, and was ready, to express her grief and loss. She needed to start treatment on a coping track, requiring some ego strengthening before facing emotionally painful issues. She should have been redirected to a less emotionally loaded topic.

Antonio, a case we present in *A Handbook of Play Therapy with Aggressive Children*, chapter 1, got temporarily worse after he disclosed his early abuse, but he was in a treatment center, where his behaviors could be therapeutically addressed. Not all clinicians will be able to modify their treatment plans for children when the children get worse. Dr. Mordock, in a study of the effectiveness of a treatment continuum, which included data on the frequency of placement decisions, emphasized that many clinicians may choose placement over the more difficult job of modifying treatment plans so that a child can remain in the community (Mordock 1997b). The following vignettes illustrate how traumatized children can be overwhelmed by even spurious events that trigger a memory of a traumatic event.

Rebecca was celebrating her ninth birthday by going out to lunch with her therapist. Just as she was getting ready to sit down at a table in the restaurant, which was located in front of a large picture window, a look of terror suddenly appeared on her face, and her body posture froze. Her therapist asked her what was wrong, but several minutes passed before Rebecca could explain that she had seen, through the window, a blue Ford that looked like a car that her father once drove. Her father had severely abused her before her placement. Although she was well aware that her father was in jail at the time, the appearance of this blue Ford, resembling the car that her father drove, triggered a panic reaction.

Charlotte, eleven years old, experienced a wave of panic whenever she saw a Coca-Cola sign. Later, staff learned she had been sexually abused in an ice-skating rink where Coca-Cola signs were posted throughout. Just the sight of the sign activated painful memories of her abuse.

Michael, age seven, set fire to a shed in a wooded area behind his house the night before his parents were going to bring him to Dr. Crenshaw's office to discuss being sexually abused.

Nevertheless, even children unwilling to experience the strong emotions that accompany discussing the details of their abuse can be helped if the abuse situation is addressed in other ways:

Termination of therapy was requested by a girl who had dealt with other issues but who had avoided discussing her sexual abuse. The therapist remarked to her that before she left therapy, she should write a letter to her dad asking him to apologize for his sexual abuse. She did so, but she was not satisfied with his repetitious "I'm sorry" in his apology letter. The therapist wrote the dad's therapist and asked if the dad would include a description of what he did to the girl, why he chose her as the victim rather than her sisters, and what he learned from the experience. The dad did what was asked, and the girl verbalized her satisfaction with the result. She wanted five copies made—one for her, her father, her father's therapist, her mother, and her clinical record. Nevertheless, she never discussed the actual abuse experience itself.

Children experiencing multiple placements in foster care must usually be handled differently from the child referred to a clinic for suspected abuse. Most often foster children's abuse took place years earlier, and the experiences are buried in their memories, even though they act out daily the effects of their abuse. Often their abuse had been ongoing before placement, and they need a period of quiet reintegration before being able to discuss it openly. Most multiply-placed children have experienced additional traumas, including neglect, frequent losses and separations, abandonment anxiety, and chronic academic failure. Issues related to these traumas usually preoccupy them more than their abuse. Nevertheless, abuse. Nevertheless, much of their inappropriate behavior stems from their early abusive experiences. Many blame themselves, not only for their own abuse, but also for their parents' problems, such as substance abuse. Instead of experiencing a discrete or isolated trauma, they lead lives characterized by multiple and ongoing stresses. Gil (1995) reports that one of the insidious effects of out-of-home placement is that 97 percent of the children in foster care believe they were placed because "they were bad."

As a consequence, the treatment of children who have been repeatedly abused requires an ego-strengthening, or coping, approach, discussed in *A Handbook of Play Therapy with Aggressive Children*, chapter 5, before abusive experiences can be worked on openly. Most often the children need a milieu treatment plan, in either a therapeutic group home or a residential treatment center, that includes intensive individual therapy; speech and language development; expressive art, music, or dance therapy; and staff working closely together to accomplish some very basic tasks. Major objectives of treatment include helping the children to feel empowered, respecting their need for privacy, making them feel safe and creating safety nets, building and supporting their defenses, facilitating their mastery of concrete skills, building true self-esteem, and facilitating contained and controlled reenactments. Techniques to meet these objectives are discussed in later chapters. With children who continue to face ongoing trauma and multiple stressors that make them unsafe, attempting uncovering therapy can make them worse. All treatment plans should also include helping parents replace their abusive behavior with appropriate child-rearing practices, and we discuss service strategies for parents in chapter 8.

In some cases, clinical staff members believe that a child's ego development is so arrested that certain traumatic experiences should be left repressed until the child has matured and considerable developmental advancement has occurred. Unfortunately, many children who shed their gorilla suits do not seek therapy when they are adults. A child who hid under the table and watched his mother knife to death his three siblings made substantial progress while in residential treatment. His aggressive behavior diminished, he began to learn in school, and he made friends with both staff and peers. Nevertheless, at no time did any material surface related to the stabbing incident. In play therapy, dreams, or words, he never revealed feelings about this early event and, after considerable debate among clinical staff, it was decided not to probe this issue in therapy. His suppression of his memories of the event was so successful that he didn't even experience night terrors or sleeping problems.

Nevertheless, when he was nineteen, he walked into a bar and picked a fight with a known knife wielder and was killed by the man's knife. Did he engage this dangerous felon out of survivor's guilt, or was it a fatal reenactment of his earlier trauma? Trauma victims are known to return to the scene of their victimization or to similar circumstances, and when asked why, they respond in ways that suggest they are attempting to master the anxiety connected with the experience and to feel in control of their lives: "I ought to be able to walk on this street no matter what happened to me here in the past!"

DIVERSION FROM MORE PRESSING PROBLEMS

Concentrating on disclosure of abuse may divert the therapist from dealing with the real motivation for certain sexual behavior and with a child's other serious problems. For example, Bader (2003) believes that being rejected by parents is far more devastating than being sexually abused, especially by pedophiles, whom children often are attracted to because they feel rejected at home. Concentrating on the sexual abuse and neglecting the child's rejection would be a serious mistake. Sexual behavior, although it can be a reenactment of an abuse experience, also can reflect needs for peer approval, anger, rebellion, escape, a cry for help, self-destruction, search for love, or delayed mourning. Borgman (1984) reports that some girl victims protected their mothers and siblings from outbursts of violence by offering themselves sexually to the mother's mate. The girls "perceived their mothers, often accurately, as having a need to maintain their relationships with the offenders, and the girls did not want to interfere with that" (p. 184). Therapist failure to recognize this protective behavior and acknowledge its positive intentions could make the youth worse.

We emphasize in chapters 2 and 3 the issues that need to be addressed in the treatment of children who wear gorilla suits. Their unrecognized losses, their voicelessness, their sense of shame, and their underlying rage are all where the therapist should begin. Abrams (1990) states, "What happens earliest may not be the most formidable because of effects of subsequent plateaus of development" (p. 414). We can't imagine how Antonio would have responded had Dr. Crenshaw tried to get him to reveal his abuse early in treatment. But sooner or later a child must come to grips with early experiences. While holocaust victims may be able to suppress their horrible experiences, there is evidence that even their grandchildren suffer from fears that can be explained only by their grandparents' abuse experiences (Bergmann and Jucovy 1982).

When sexual abuse first became identified as a major contributor to psychopathology, some therapists hopped on the bandwagon and began to attribute everything to sexual abuse. Dr. Mordock once attended a workshop in which the presenter claimed, "Show me a bulemic or an anorexic child, and I will show you an incest victim." Male therapists in the audience whose daughters had suffered or were suffering from either problem cringed. The reprehensible practice of mother blaming, popular for years in clinical work, switched to father blaming! Even worse, of course, such thinking diverts therapists from looking at the real causes of these two disorders and alienates both the girls' families and the girls themselves.

INCREASING SELF-BLAME

Second, the child who remains in the home following an abuse disclosure can experience both self-blame and blame from other family members for the consequences to the family that follow the disclosure. Negative parental reactions after the report can not only aggravate the child's trauma (Kendall-Tucker, Williams, and Finkelhor 1993), but they can be even more traumatic than the abuse itself. By law in most states, a therapist has to report child abuse when it is suspected. In New York state, for example, all mandated reporters must complete a state-approved training course in recognizing and reporting child abuse, the assumption being that reporting abuse is always in a child's best interests. Nevertheless, children are often rejected by their mother and even by their siblings if their father is reported for abuse. Sauzier (1989) reports that 24 percent of child victims treated at a family crisis program showed more psychopathology at follow-up than at intake, and 19 percent of adolescents regretted their disclosures. In addition, substantial numbers felt the disclosure had a harmful impact on the child and on the family (45 percent and 43 percent, respectively). No wonder so many children recant their abuse (Rieser 1991) and resist therapy (Haugaard 1992). In addition, once disclosed, the feelings associated with the disclosure cannot be worked through because the therapist has to report it.

If the child remains in the home after the report, the therapist's chances of helping the child are diminished, even if the child remains in therapy. About one-third of identified sexually abused children are sexually abused again (Arata 2002), and 22 percent of fathers who sexually abused their daughters are cited for physical abuse within five years of the sexual abuse report (Rice and Harris 2002). And if the child is placed in foster care and allowed to remain in treatment, placement further traumatizes the child and becomes the dominant issue with which the child struggles, perhaps blaming herself even more for the abuse. The child is not likely to deal successfully with either issue in therapy because the consequences of the report are associated with, if not attributed to, the therapeutic experience, and distrust of the therapist results. No matter how much the therapist emphasizes the protective role of therapy, the child no longer believes it nor is likely to believe it in the immediate future. Nevertheless, not reporting strong suspicions of abuse leaves the child in an equally traumatic situation. The therapist faces a double-edged sword!

In the end, we would strongly assert that, in spite of system failures, therapists must not wittingly communicate that the children would be better off if they remained silent. We would be returning to an era, not too far in our past, when abuse was not reported or disclosed, and if it was, it was not believed. Dr. Crenshaw spent 1962, his freshman year in college, working as a ward attendant at a state psychiatric hospital in the Midwest. At that time, sexual abuse was not a spoken topic in our culture. Working in one of the chronic psychiatric patient wards of this hospital, primitive by today's standards, the author read a chart that was shocking. The woman in question was sixty-two years old and had been admitted to the state hospital at the age of thirteen. She had resided at the hospital for forty-nine years! She was admitted in 1913 after accusing her father of incest. Her family insisted she was crazy, and they found a psychiatrist who diagnosed her as psychotic, probably because dissociative experiences were considered hallucinations at the time. She had not received a family visit in many years. We cringe when thinking that this young girl's courageous and honest report of incest was declared crazy by both the family and the mental health system at that time. She was forever forsaken and forgotten by the family and left to spend the next forty-nine years of her life in a degrading institution. While her body was still alive, the human spark, the spark that makes one fully alive, had left this woman long ago, and it was impossible to make meaningful contact with her.

In *A Handbook of Play Therapy with Aggressive Children*, chapter 5, we present a young incest victim who was hospitalized following dissociative reactions, diagnosed as schizophrenic, and for eighteen months was given an antipsychotic medication that is now known to cause serious and permanent health problems, most of which the woman experienced throughout her rather unhealthy life. There is no telling how many other young girls who were sexually abused suffered from similar circumstances. In the pre-1975 psychoanalytic literature in which the treatment of adolescent girls and young women is described, many of the symptoms discussed could have easily resulted from sexual abuse. Instead, the therapist attributed them to fantasies.

While a rich fantasy life, including sexual fantasies, characterizes adolescence, any fantasy of an abuse experience should be checked against reality and not merely dismissed as the product of a rich imagination. It would seem the ignorance and repression of the past are not really so remote. Despite its many limitations, the present system of reporting child abuse is at least a step in the right direction.

CEMENTING A DEVIANT SELF-IMAGE

Therapeutic interest in a child's sexual abuse experiences can contribute to cementing the child's image of himself or herself as a sex object, deviant person, or helpless victim (Borgman 1984; Seligson 1993; Weinbach and Curtis 1986). Parental misconceptions and fears can perpetuate the effect of a sexual assault on a child. Overt or covert references to the assault can give the impression that something irreversible has occurred that can cause immeasurable emotional harm to the victim. This view is emphasized by Seligson (1993). Children will deny being abused because the experiences are unacceptable to their self-image or their image of the abuser. For example, one latency-age girl who failed to disclose her abuse, in spite of maternal support, reluctantly disclosed after hearing the taped confession of her father. Yet later, when the therapist reviewed the confession, the girl denied one behavior of the father, stating "He never did that." In addition, the brother, who was also abused, but attached to the father, found reason to dismiss his father's confession as false.

In addition, children who see themselves as helpless victims may be less able to prevent future abuse, perhaps one reason, in addition to reenactment, for the high revictimization many children experience, even after removal from home. The therapist's task is to help children deal with the self-blame they often experience after abuse because they failed to prevent or resist the abuse or because they enjoyed parts of it, such as when eating sweets, fondling, and caressing are involved in sexual abuse. Nevertheless, to maintain that they were merely helpless victims can help cement the helpless image. Efforts should be made to help children prevent future abuse, at the same time emphasizing that prevention may not always succeed. Without this caveat, the training program can set the child up for future guilt. A young girl, for example, who was sexually abused in her adolescence had also been raped in her early school years. She did her best to fight off her second attacker and immediately reported the assault. While this youngster had learned multiple ways to protect herself since the first molestation, it was still not possible to prevent the later traumatic incident. It would be grossly unfair to this adolescent to leave the impression that she must have done something wrong or else she would have been able to prevent the rape.

Gorilla-suit wearers already have an unacceptable self-image. They are deathly afraid that, if someone gets to know them, the anguish they experience over others' negative judgments will overwhelm them. They constantly twist embarrassment into anger—scream, punch, topple board games, or threaten to break objects—to have something else disintegrate instead of them. A positive sense of self needs to be encouraged to blossom, to become strong, and eventually to replace the deviant self-image they hold dearly but also abhor. The process is a long one and can't be hurried. Nor can efforts to help children reveal their sexual abuse.

Complicating treatment is the reality that some children were not just helpless victims of abuse but actively participated in it. Dr. Mordock worked with a child who, along with a group of other children, was repeatedly molested by a pedophile. Not only was the man probably perceived as kind; he was perhaps kinder than the child's neglectful parents. In addition, the pedophile gave the children money and gifts their parents couldn't afford or thought were unnecessary. In fact, the first child molested persuaded others to join him at the molester's home, a small "after school club" was formed, and a child pornography ring developed.

One of the boys was placed in residential treatment and was seen in group therapy by Dr. Mordock, who, along with the boy's individual therapist, was unaware of the past involvement with the molester. During group therapy, the boy uttered anal curse words, dressed up in women's clothes, and flaunted his buttock in an effort to be seductive. In fact, his sexualized behavior and blunt overtures toward the other children caused them to regress and required his removal from the group. Consultation with his individual therapist, a woman, revealed that although he displayed feminine interests, he rarely engaged in sexualized behaviors in her presence and that her efforts to get at the root of his sexualized behavior in the presence of others were unsuccessful. She had hoped the group milieu would help to change his seemingly feminine identity to a more masculine one.

Several years after the boy's discharge, a policeman visited the center and showed part of a compromising photograph of the boy to staff in the hope of identifying him and finding the perpetrator. In light of what we learned from the police, his behavior became understandable. Had we known these facts when he was in treatment, we would have structured treatment differently. But we would have needed to acknowledge his active involvement in his abuse and the attention, pleasure, and power he got from it.

THE MALE THERAPIST AND THE FEMALE VICTIM

Helping children to deal with their own sexual arousal is one of the most difficult tasks in the treatment of sexually abused children, especially when the therapist is male and the child is female. Only a small body of literature exists on male therapists treating female clients, especially clients who are sexually preoccupied, as are many abused girls, but we recommend that male therapists read the following citations, even though some of them are almost thirty-five years old: Fox and Carey (1999), Jones and Gehman (1971), Kernberg (2000),

Kraft (1990), MacVicar (1979), Mann (1989), Mattsson (1970), Simon (1989), Tyson (1980), and Silverman (1977). These readings can be supplemented by readings on sexual boundary issues in treatment: see Dalenberg (2000), Gabbard (1996), Gabbard and Lester (1995), Harper and Steadman (2003), Schetky (1995), and Swartz and Olds (2002).

Some professionals believe a female sexual abuse victim should never have a male therapist. Nevertheless, matching the sex of clients and therapists is not always possible, nor is it always necessary. While most sexually abused children have been abused by men, a number have been abused by women as well. In addition, as in the case of Antonio, women have sometimes been willing participants in their child's sexual abuse, and female therapists can elicit as much, if not more, anxiety than male therapists can in such cases.

Others believe that treatment by a male therapist can be helpful because the female victim expects revictimization and is helped to heal when it doesn't recur. For six years, Dr. Mordock was the primary therapist in a residential treatment unit for girls between the ages of seven and thirteen. Sexual material not only came up, but so did sexual advances. The sexual advances were responded to first with limits and later with clarifications:

> THERAPIST: Pull your skirt down over your knees and sit up like a lady. I'm your therapist and not a possible boyfriend. You're too young to have a real boyfriend, even if you might like to. But I will never think of you in that way.
> CHILD: You don't think I'm pretty.
> THERAPIST: "Pretty" is nice, but it seems that you're more interested in being pretty than in being other things. Why don't you draw yourself doing something that has nothing to do with being pretty?

The male therapist who doesn't acknowledge that his affectionate feelings for the girls he treats can have sexual undertones—and we are sure this also applies to gay therapists who treat older boys—is headed for trouble. For three years at the Devereux Foundation, Dr. Mordock benefited by treating adolescent girls while he was under the supervision of a female psychoanalyst who wouldn't let him forget for a minute both the covert and overt seductive behavior of the girls or his responses to it, both acknowledged and unacknowledged. He was surprised to learn that with prepubescent girls, however, the feelings, though more subtle, are no less present. When he found himself seeking out a particular girl on his visits to the living units or thinking about becoming a foster parent for a young female client, he sought regular consultation with a female colleague.

On one occasion, on the advice of his female colleague, Dr. Mordock saw an eleven-year-old sexually abused, but not sexualized, girl in the gym in an effort to ease the girl's heightened anxiety in the close quarters of the play therapy room. He taught her to play basketball while they talked about some of her worries. The girl became quite a good player, and when she was placed in a foster home, she joined the school basketball team, displaying skill for which she was greatly admired. While Dr. Mordock never addressed her early sexual abuse, she made a substantial adjustment in the community and years later is still trouble free.

Van de Putte (1995) describes three types of sexualized play observed during play therapy with sexually abused children and suggests guidelines for coping with the children. The three types are (1) abuse-reactive play, (2) reenactment play, and (3) symbolic sexualized play. Van de Putte, describing the dilemma therapists face when confronted with sexualized behavior, states,

> Therapists who set limits that are too rigid and consequences that are too threatening may only succeed in scaring the child into further silence regarding his/her sexual abuse experiences. A therapist who is too tolerant of repeated sexualized behavior runs the risk that the child client may interpret his/her lack of intervention as a desire on the part of the therapist to see the child perform sexually. (p. 28)

Van de Putte recommends that therapists seek a balance between allowing children to express experiences of sexual abuse and imposing structure and setting limits. The children need help to channel expressions of sexual experiences into more developmentally appropriate and socially accepted behaviors. The therapist's reactions to a child's sexual provocations help to achieve this balance. Dr. Mordock tells his clients that they can hug or fondle the doll but not him and remarks inquisitively, "I wonder why you want to fondle the doll in this way?" If a child's sexual behavior frightens or disgusts a therapist or if the therapist becomes sexually aroused, both the child and the therapist can become even more confused and troubled.

> THERAPIST: You are developing into quite an attractive girl, but just because I notice your development doesn't mean I will ever respond to you as if you were my girlfriend.

Dr. Mordock sometimes became aroused by the sexual provocations of older adolescent girls whose histories suggested that they manipulated adults with sexual behaviors. His response usually went something like this:

> THERAPIST: You have learned to flirt with boys and men, even offering yourself as a sexual object to some, but I will not let you continue to degrade yourself by behaving in this fashion with me. If you cannot stop your sexual teasing, we will have to terminate the session for today. And

when you come for your session tomorrow, we can talk about your sexual feelings, and matter related to them, if you choose to, but we cannot
act upon them.

GIRL: Come on, Doc, I know you find me attractive.

THERAPIST: Of course. You're well aware of your effect on boys and even
older men, but I believe there is more to you than you think. Perhaps you
need help to discover another you—one that can be more of a person
than just a sex object.

When treating sexualized children with histories of sexual abuse, high-
quality supervision is essential, especially for young and inexperienced therapists, and ongoing consultation with colleagues is imperative for seasoned clinicians. When negative emotions are aroused in the therapist by a child's sexual
preoccupations, they sometimes serve as distractions from the therapist's own
issues about sexuality. Many therapists will need to undergo their own personal
therapy in order to help sexually abused children who continually manifest
sexualized behaviors during therapy sessions.

In terms of limit setting, some therapists take an extreme position on this
issue, clarifying early on with sexual-abuse survivors that sexual behavior will
not be tolerated (Jones 1986). The intent is to communicate, right from the
get-go, that therapy is safe place where the relationship with the therapist will
not be a reenactment of their earlier relationships with perpetrators (Jones
1986; Van de Putte 1995). At the first sign of sexualized behavior, or any attempt a child makes to disrobe, even removal of socks, the session is terminated
(Haugaard and Repucci 1988).

In contrast, Van de Putte (1995) advocates a discerning and flexible approach. He emphasizes that not all sexualized behavior during therapy sessions
is "sexual acting out" and believes it naive to adopt a "one size fits all" approach
to its expression. Instead, he insists that each of the three categories of sexualized play he delineates requires different interventions.

ABUSE-REACTIVE PLAY

Abuse-reactive sexualized play is defined by Van de Putte (1995) as "when a
sexually abused child, perceiving he/she is at risk to be abused, begins displaying sexual behavior similar to what occurred when he/she was abused"
(p. 32). We would expand this category to include behavior the child has
learned to use to control or manipulate others. Sexual victimization is reenacted, but the child now controls the situation. The child has become the se-
ducer instead of the one seduced. What has been passively experienced is

now actively mastered. The seductive girl is no longer the helpless victim. Instead, she is the powerful seductress. Such behavior usually appears in the early stages of therapy, reflecting both the child's expectations that the therapy relationship will be a repetition of past sexualized relationships and the anxiety the child associates with such expectations. Van de Putte (1995) recommends that abuse-reactive sexualized behavior be met with clear limits, such as "I do not want you to be sexual in here with me" or "I want this to be a safe place for you and I want you to know that I will not be sexual with you or do anything to hurt you." If the child persists, it may be necessary to terminate the session in order to make the limits clear and nonnegotiable.

REENACTMENT PLAY

The second category of sexualized play described by Van de Putte (1995) is reenactment (see Allan 1988). Van de Putte describes reenactment play as follows: "The child client re-creates and re-experiences the abuse he/she suffered in the presence of the therapist, using toys, dolls, and other play props, in combination with his/her own body, to depict details of his/her molestation experiences" (pp. 34–35). Van de Putte notes that distinguishing between reenactment and abuse-reactive play can be difficult. Reenactment play usually occurs in the middle phases of therapy, after the child has developed sufficient trust in the therapist, as well as a strong alliance. The child becomes willing to risk disclosing the details of abusive experiences through play. Nevertheless, the intensity of such play can lead a therapist to misjudge the play and view it as abuse-reactive behavior, especially if the child tries to involve the therapist in seductive play. If that mistake is made, the child may feel rejected, concluding that the therapist can't handle witnessing his/her traumatic sexual experiences. When the therapist is in doubt, Van de Putte recommends assuming that the child is reenacting past abuse. If the child focuses a reenactment directly on the therapist, however, clear limits need to be set. Van de Putte emphasizes that when a child displays reenactment behavior, the therapist needs to bear witness to the event and affirm that the event belongs to the child—that the child now controls the event and can choose to share it as is, alter its expression so that it is less threatening, or back off and not share it.

Maria, an eight-year-old treated by Dr. Crenshaw, had been encouraged to stay up with her father to watch a movie or program on television. Her mother would go to bed. The father would suggest that Maria lie down on the couch next to him, and then he would put a blanket over her. He began touching her and fondling her genitals, and even though she felt extremely uncomfortable and anxious, she couldn't help but feel some sexual pleasure from the touching. Her mother interrupted this activity on one occasion and became enraged at Maria.

> MARIA: [*Plays out a scene in which the little girl doll was being yelled at by her mother because she had been doing "dirty things" with her father at night.*]
>
> THERAPIST: [*The therapist suggests that perhaps there was a wise older person that she could talk to about this very upsetting experience. Maria agreed that this was a good idea and chose the "wise old owl" puppet. The therapist, in the role of the wise old owl, began to ask reality-based questions.*] Whose idea was it for your father to touch you in the private parts of your body? Who is the adult here? How old did you say you were? Only eight! How can you be responsible for an adult's actions? Let me tell you something. This is very important! I didn't get to be a "wise old owl" for nothing. You catch my drift? If you don't remember anything else from the wise old owl, I want you to remember this: Anytime an adult does something sexual to a child, it is the adult's responsibility, not the child's! And I don't care if you enjoyed or liked some parts of it, it is not your fault! Sometimes our bodies respond in ways we can't help, just like when you peel an onion, you can't help but cry. Now I want you to repeat after me, and in fact let's make a chant out of it: "No matter what anybody says, when an adult does something sexual to a child, it is the adult's fault, not the child's!" One more time, "It's not my fault!" [*The wise old owl and the girl doll repeat the chant several times with increasing intensity and conviction.*]

SYMBOLIC SEXUAL PLAY

The final category of sexualized play is symbolic sexualized play. "Symbolic sexualized play occurs when the child behaves sexually in the context of thematic play in an apparent attempt to build upon and come to some new understanding of his/her sexual abuse experiences" (Van de Putte 1995, p. 37). All therapists hope to reach a point in therapy when the child attempts to understand and to make sense out of his/her sexually traumatic experiences, when the child tries to comprehend, to find meaning and purpose, and to reach a new perspective about his or her experiences of sexual exploitation by others. This category of play usually occurs in the later stages of therapy. Van de Putte (1995), when describing the role of symbolic sexualized play in recovery, writes that the play "is helping the child to develop a reality-based understanding of how his/her sexual abuse makes sense in the context of the larger world" (p. 38). Dr. Mordock often responds to this behavior with the following remarks:

> THERAPIST: [*In response to a girl's efforts to give him a big hug.*] Sometimes I'm so proud of you that I also would like to give you a big hug, but it's never been my job to give you physical comfort.
> CHILD: But I hug my dad!
> THERAPIST: Yes, but I'm not your dad, even though you've sometimes wished I were, and while you've learned that hugs from male staff members are signs of their affection for you rather than of sexual interest, helping you to distinguish affectionate feelings from sexual feelings, it's never been my job to hug you, but rather to help you to learn more about yourself so you can obtain genuine affection from others rather than the indiscriminate hugs and the inappropriate touching you always sought in the past.
>
> Remember, when you first came to therapy, how you were more concerned about being pretty than about other aspects of yourself? You thought men liked girls just because they were pretty and could do things to make men, and sometimes themselves, feel good. Now you know that sexual activities are adult activities and that adults who involve children in sexual activities are wrong to do so.

During symbolic sexualized play, the therapist looks for opportunities in the course of the play to introduce meaning, perspective, and an altered understanding of the trauma events that can be conveyed to the child in a convincing way, sometimes through the metaphor of the play or through direct verbal exchange using the play sequences as a springboard for discussion of these issues.

Van de Putte's paper is well worth reading because he presents many caveats and cautions, as well as possible missteps in treatment when therapists deal with specific forms of sexualized behavior.

OVERIDENTIFICATION WITH THE CHILD

Those working with abused children, particularly in out-of-home placement settings, such as a residential treatment center, need to guard against "adoption dynamics," a situation in which the therapist or other staff member feels he or she can provide better care for the child than the parents can. This attitude stems from overidentification with the child, a common countertransference issue in child treatment. Even when the desire to adopt is unstated, children sense the devaluing of their parents in such an attitude. Since the child remains loyal to the parents, even if maltreated by them, the attitude alienates the child from the therapist. As we stress in chapters 8 and 9, therapists should seek out the strengths in each child's parents and ally with these strengths.

Overidentification can take many forms, some subtle and some not so subtle, but blurred boundaries are one result. One intern in psychology baked cookies for the children, and when told that her role as a therapist precluded such behavior, she accused the clinical staff of being rigid and uncaring. Needless to say, she was asked to leave the training program. Another intern was discovered late at night, long after his workday had ended, sitting at the bedside of a child. He argued that the child was lonely and needed his company. A young social worker in a day treatment center became so allied with a child that she left her job so the child could move in with her. The young girl met the social worker's need by calling her "Mom." Later the mother moved in with her as well, and the worker mothered them both. She is now working as a therapist with elderly clients. A psychologist in a residential treatment center became so attached to several boys he treated that he started taking them home over holidays and then on weekends. His boundaries and his role became so blurred that his employment was terminated.

The art of healing a fawn in a gorilla suit begins with making an attachment, a connection with the disconnected, in spite of the child's determined efforts to resist or discourage the would-be healer. The next step entails being able to contain the powerful negative emotions of the child until the child is strong enough to own them and to work through them. The ultimate goal, as Henry (1983) states, "is related to what Melanie Klein (1957) referred to as the basic source of inner strength—the internalization of 'a good object' . . . which loves and protects the self and is loved and protected by the self" (p. 188). In the meantime, the healer should never take personally either the child's hostility, often verbal but sometimes physical, or the child's affection, especially the child's sexualized affection. Instead, the therapist must set appropriate limits and view the child's behaviors as manifestations of the traumatized child hidden within the gorilla suit.

But the therapeutic task that requires emotional strength and stamina is the ability to listen to the child when traumas are revealed in detail. This is no easy task. Some of the experiences children have suffered are horrendous, akin to experiences suffered by the Jews under Nazi persecution. Statements written by victims of Nazi medical experiments created such emotions in the six staff processing their claims for retribution that two of the staff quit their jobs (Neumeister 2003). Therapists can experience similar, if not stronger, emotions because the child reexperiences the pain in the therapist's presence. When treating a relatively full caseload of trauma victims, even well-trained therapists can experience "compassion fatigue" (Figley 2002) and even secondary, or vicarious, traumas, which can produce a loss of boundaries (Rand 2003). But if the pain can be tolerated by both parties, the end result is worth the turmoil created by the process.

7

Some Special Considerations When Treating Children in Foster Care

The treatment of gorilla-suit wearers placed in foster care presents a host of unique challenges. They include helping the children to work through stages of protest, despair, denial, and apathy; correcting misconceptions about reasons for separations; resolving loyalty conflicts; minimizing splitting; managing the exaggerated importance placed on material goods; emphasizing the positive qualities of the natural parents; and managing reunions with natural parents. Often these issues take precedence over efforts to uncover and reconstruct traumatic memories. Therapists need to examine their own attitudes about foster care, especially their rescue and adoption fantasies.

*F*oster care is any out-of-home care for a child that is financed by county and state departments of social service. The care can be provided in a single-family home, called a foster home, where the child may reside with other foster children as well as with the foster parents' natural children; therapeutic foster care, in which the foster parents receive a special stipend and adjunct mental health services are provided to the child, with ongoing consultation with the foster parents; group-home care; therapeutic group-home care; and institutional care, in either a normal child-care institution or a residential treatment center.

Children who enter foster care experience unrecognized traumas of unfulfilled expectations. While in care, their all-absorbing wish is to return home. They feel like "forgotten orphans" (Zimmerman 2003). Dr. Mordock once asked all sixty-eight children in a residential treatment center, many of whom had been abused by parents, the following question: "If you could have three wishes granted, what would they be?" All but two said their first wish was to go home. Older children expect their placement to improve their family situation—when they return home they will receive the love and attention they missed. When they are discharged from foster care, many discover that their

79

family remains relatively unchanged and that problems still abound. Their dreams are shattered.

PROTEST, DESPAIR, DENIAL, AND APATHY

Children in placement move through four stages after being placed: protest, despair, denial, and apathy. Those under age four, either chronologically or emotionally, become extremely upset, regardless of the reasons for their placement, and they react in predictable ways. First, they strongly display their distress. When the natural parents visit during this initial stage, the children release a flood of tears and demand to be returned home. Their protests verge on panic and are followed by outbursts of anger, often displaced onto the foster parents when visiting parents leave. These outbursts often precipitate requests from the caregivers in the foster home that social service terminate parent visiting. "Their visits stir things up. The child is calmer without them."

Older children also panic after being placed. They control these feelings, however, by preoccupying themselves with thoughts of home or by displaying fantasies of being omnipotent and all-powerful. They brag or boast of their accomplishments, or they make some up. Time between parental visits seems endless. But they still move through the stages of protest, despair, denial, and apathy. Most mask the stages by a variety of defenses and behavioral symptoms. Witness the plight of Antonio, the case presented in *A Handbook of Play Therapy with Aggressive Children*, chapter 1.

Older children who have some attachment to the natural parent when they enter foster care usually cry, often alone and unobserved. While their sorrow expresses their pain and loss, it is also a cry for the lost parent, a last-ditch plea for reunion. When their cries go unanswered, they actively protest their placement with rage and indignation. Children who feel abandoned are prone to defiance and acts of physical aggression, and they need help to play out and eventually verbalize their frustrations.

> THERAPIST: You're really angry at having to leave home. And you're not even sure who you're angry at—your parents for sending you away, yourself for not pleasing them, or the folks who have taken you in. Probably you're angry at everybody!
> THERAPIST: It's hard to express your anger at your parents for sending you away because you might worry that they'll never take you back. It's easier to get angry at your foster parents because you never wanted to be with them in the first place.

THERAPIST: We know you're really upset and angry at having to leave home. It's all right to be angry, but you need to talk about your angry feelings. It's not all right to smash things and hit people. No one can let you do that.

If these interventions are effective, the child's protests become more verbally controlled, more communicative, and less physical. When the anger cannot be worked through, the emptiness that accompanies despair causes greater distress than anger because the anger implies at least the hope of reunion. Nevertheless, when the child's protests fail to ensure the parents' ongoing presence, increasing helplessness is displayed. The child will become withdrawn and apathetic and manifest eating and sleeping disorders. When the mother visits, her attention is no longer demanded. Untrained foster parents often believe that the distress has finally lessened.

Many young children, especially those who blame themselves for their abuse, view their placement as punishment for wrongdoing. They often focus concern on the intactness of their bodies, becoming distressed at even minor injuries, insisting on bandages for the tiniest cuts. Without their mothers, regardless of the care they are provided, the children feel unprotected and vulnerable to injury. Their placements occur during a period in their young lives when anxieties are fed by fantasies of bodily harm and mutilation. Unsure when they will return home, they exaggerate how long it will be until they see their parents again. Only the mother's actual presence can alleviate the anxiety of a child four years old or younger or the child whose emotional development is arrested at this age, as is the case with many children in gorilla suits.

The third stage is denial. The children show interest in their surroundings and appear sociable. When the parent, most often the mother, comes to visit, the children act as if they don't know her and no longer cry when she leaves. Some feel so numb that visits are unenjoyable, even taxing. In response, the natural parent may feel unneeded and restrict visiting, believing "The child is better off in placement." If parents continue visiting, they often bring other offspring with them and have picnic lunches on the agency lawn, seemingly oblivious to the child in placement, who constantly wanders away from them. Child-care workers who have their own adoption fantasies complain about such behavior, citing it as evidence that the parents don't care about the child.

To ward off emptiness, loss, and despair, most foster children resist discussing their home or parents because those topics evoke too much pain. Foster children can also avoid reenactment play. Playing scenes of home or discussing family life when they're not a part of it adds insult to injury. But some effort to help clarify their feelings, as well as reality, is a necessary step in their treatment. Sometimes the clarifications occur within the metaphor of the child's play or drawings, but often they are directly stated.

> THERAPIST: Remember when you first came here? How angry you used to be? We talked about your anger at your parents, at us, at yourself.
> CHILD: I don't care.
> THERAPIST: That's just it. We think you care very much, but your anger didn't get your parents back. Have you given up hope? Do you think you'll never get home?
> CHILD: I don't care.
> THERAPIST: Maybe your parents won't be able to take care of you every day. Maybe visits will be your only contact for some time. I don't know. But others care about you, too—your foster parents, your teachers, your friends.
> CHILD: They do not! They do it for money.
> THERAPIST: Yes, they get paid for taking care of you. [*Says no more.*]
> CHILD: Yeah, but not much, I'll bet.

Children in foster care often harbor feelings of revenge. Many of those old enough to write to their families are reluctant to do so, particularly when they aren't written to. Sometimes, the child receives a regular phone call from the parents and sees no reason to write. They should be encouraged to write during therapy. It keeps alive issues that have contributed to their placement and allows feelings to surface that can be discussed in therapy. Their refusal to write can also be addressed in therapy sessions.

> THERAPIST: You won't write your parents because they haven't called or written you. You think they should write you first. You're the one away. I can understand that feeling, but it's important for you to tell your parents that. Maybe they think you're happier here! Sometimes parents get discouraged, too, and feel they're no good, that their child is better off without them.

Denial is followed by apathy, characterized by listless effort at routine tasks and withdrawal from people and activities. Some children even pretend their parents are dead. In this condition, the children are more manageable, and their "calmness" can be viewed positively. Be wary. With feelings hidden and a frozen smile on the face, the child follows the daily routine, but no progress— no growth—is taking place. Some believe the child has finally accepted separation from parents. They are mistaken. Clarification of feelings in therapy may keep children from reaching this stage, but the therapist must be prepared to tolerate long periods of despair and apathy.

On the other hand, some children are secretly relieved to be in foster care. Living in an unpredictable family situation is extremely stressful, and safety and support at another home can be a blessing. Some children's best days are their days away from home, and they know it but will never admit it. Friendships with foster parents, child-care workers, teachers, and therapists, along with weekend visits to parents, who are often on their best behavior, can be a better life for some children. Most parents intend to do the right thing, but intentions aren't always enough. Children who are away from a disorganized, overwhelmed, and rejecting home are free from the daily ridicule, criticism, and unpredictability discussed in chapter 2. Rarely, however, will these feelings be conscious because of the intense loyalty conflicts they experience. Neither of us has ever suggested to a child that he or she prefers being away from home.

Some older children resist foster or institutional care because their behavior is more restricted in such settings. They desire to return home, not because they suffer from severed ties with loved ones, but because they get their way there more often. When living at home, they stay out until it suits them, go to bed when they want, and have no responsibilities. In short, they are unsupervised and omnipotent. Often these children are referred to institutions. While a structured and routine program is good for them, they resist it.

MISCONCEPTIONS ABOUT SEPARATION

Children's age at placement often determines their attitudes about separation. Children with a sibling born shortly before their placement may conclude that their anger toward their mother and her "new baby" was the reason they were sent away. Children placed as infants and never returned home may later decide that their mother placed them because they cried too much or were too messy. Children placed in special education may think their academic failures so shame their parents that they no longer want them. All these young children may conclude they are "no good." Self-blamers have more negative self-images than other abused children, regardless of the frequency of the abuse the others receive (Grant and Vartanian 2003).

Older children can also feel responsible for being placed. Both age groups need help to clarify their feelings and to remove distortions. Children in foster care expect rejection. Sometimes their wait for the rejection is so intolerable that they bring it on themselves: "There, now I can relax. The worst is over." Children often blame themselves for their placement because active blaming is preferred to helplessness: "I caused it." Is it not better to be a strong and bad somebody than a weak and good nobody? It is difficult to work with children who are convinced they are monsters.

THERAPIST: Perhaps you think your mother didn't keep you at home because there was something terribly wrong with you or terribly wrong with her?

THERAPIST: You think you must have done something pretty bad for your mother to give you up?

LOYALTY CONFLICTS

Most children experience loyalty conflicts when placed and draw adults into these conflicts. Young children express great ambivalence toward foster parents. Some fantasize about returning home but, at the same time, hope their foster parents will replace their real parents. Foster parents need to understand that they and their friends should avoid telling the defiant child, "You've never had it so good" or "Your real mother is irresponsible" or "You should be more appreciative—you're lucky to be in a home such as ours." Such comments contribute to feelings of worthlessness. To feel worthwhile, children need to feel loved by their parents or someone in their past. When they hear their parents criticized, the children feel criticized. If their parents are no good, then they are no good. It isn't a big jump from that idea to "If my mother does not love me, then I'm unlovable." We are so much a part of our parents that when they are attacked, we ourselves are vilified. For a child to admit to neglect is to affirm that he or she is worthy of neglect. To want to be other than like the parent is to aspire to be nobody at all.

Weitzman (1985) presents a case of a nine-year-old boy who set his therapist's car on fire because he thought his treatment team was too critical of his depressed mother. Children are not merely reactors to a distressed family system; they act on the system as well, sometimes destructively, even after parents start improving.

A boy, experiencing positive feelings for his foster mother, tells the therapist how wonderfully his parents treat him at home. He states, "I'm only in this awful foster home because my parents are not well and cannot take care of me." This fabrication is not a lie. It is what the boy needs to believe in order to keep alive a positive image of his parents. This is his sustaining fiction (Van Ornum and Mordock 1990). To admit that his parents are neglectful is to affirm that he is worthy of neglect. When children are allowed to express positive feelings about real parents, and they are not challenged (the fabrications and sustaining fictions are accepted as real), more mature feelings will be expressed eventually, and the therapist can help the children to integrate both the positive and the negative feelings held about parents and parent substitutes, including the therapist. Foster children often "split off" an image of their own mother as a good mother, one of the primitive defenses discussed in chapter 11. They develop an idealistic view of her and try to make their foster mother into the bad mother.

SPLITTING

For foster children, love and hate are intensified. Hate of the natural parents is fueled by the additional resentment of being placed. The desire to love and be loved by parents grows because it is unsatisfied. As these two opposing forces become stronger, their resolution becomes increasingly difficult, making the children more anxious, uncomfortable, and guilty. The children can't reconcile the two opposing sets of feelings they have for the same parent, so they devise a way to sidestep the whole conflict. They split the feelings into separate parts and attach each feeling to a different adult. The children now feel only one way about each of the two mothers (or fathers) in their lives. Therapists should not attempt to undo the split unless the child's ego strengths are sufficient to be on the invitational track of therapy, discussed in *A Handbook of Play Therapy with Aggressive Children*, chapter 5, a track requiring a stable placement and support available in the immediate environment.

What happens most often is that love is felt for the lost parents, to the point of overidealizing them, and hate is expressed toward their present caregivers. This process can be accelerated if caregivers make negative comments about the natural parents or overly positive comments about the foster parents. In working with foster children, adults should communicate to the children how disappointed the children must feel to live in someone else's home, or in an institution, and how they must miss their real mother or father.

> CHILD: When I go home, my mom lets me stay up to eleven o'clock. And she's not always telling me to pick up my clothes.
>
> THERAPIST: [*Knowing that the natural mother provides no structure whatsoever, mostly because she is preoccupied with meeting her own needs, replies*] Your mom has different rules. It must be tough to follow two sets of rules. You probably feel we treat you unfairly, but remember that my own children follow the same rules as you do. When they grow up, and when you grow up, you can make your own rules too.
>
> CHILD: I like it a lot better at home. I wish I were home instead of here— I hate it here.
>
> THERAPIST: It's hard living away from home. We all wish you could have what you want, too.
>
> CHILD: My mom says she's taking me home next week.

THERAPIST: Wouldn't that be something if she could! I'll bet she sure wants to. She feels bad not being able to care for you.
CHILD: She really is!
THERAPIST: When I hear from your social worker, we can both pack your bag. I'll miss you when you go.

By having their feelings reflected, children in foster care can be freed to accept the foster parent or a child-care worker as a "not-so-bad person." If told how "good" the foster parent is, they automatically defend their own parent. This reaction can produce further splitting and jeopardize their placement.

EXAGGERATED IMPORTANCE

Foster children often seem greedy. Acquiring and possessing things becomes important—an endless quest because they never have enough, and what they do acquire, they often break in anger because its acquisition didn't meet their real, but repressed, need. A little girl got angry because her ill foster mother would not give her candy from the bedside table. The girl snatched a cloth napkin, ran away, and cut it up. Such behavior is not unusual for children in foster care. Material possessions become equated with love. Sometimes when foster children are unable to satisfy a need, the pain of being unable to feel close to their natural parents rears its ugly head. Getting things, collecting things, squirreling things away become an obsession. Sometimes foster children take, or ask for, relatively useless objects.

One little girl in a day treatment program asked for nearly everything in the offices and classrooms. While the child was not allowed to take things from the therapy room, her treatment plan included encouraging her to collect discarded objects, such as dried-up pens, paper clips on the floor, fallen thumbtacks, old memos and flyers from the bulletin boards, or worthless items like bottle caps and twigs from the playground. The foster mother was alerted, and she agreed to proudly examine the girl's daily scavenges after school each afternoon.

The constant demand for things reflects not only cravings but also hope for better things. Mitchell (1993) notes that within psychoanalytic theory there have been two fundamentally different approaches to hope. Within classical or traditional theories, the hope initially displayed by the patient is seen as reflecting the desire to cling to wishes for the gratification of infantile impulses, which have to be renounced in favor of a higher process of thinking more in line with the reality principle. From this perspective, hope serves as an obstacle to therapeutic progress:

The waiting required by hope suffocates the possibility for the spark of desire and its fulfillment. The actual object is never the right object; the time is never now. Real satisfaction is always sacrificed in the hope of eventual fulfillment at some future time. (p. 205)

A contrasting view of hope sees hope not as a suffocating agent but as part of the search for a particular psychological experience in which a genuine sense of desire may actually become possible, in which the self can begin to experience a new beginning. This contrasting tradition was imbedded in the works of Winnicott (1965) and Kohut (1977), for example.

Ghent (1992) discusses the paradox between the urgent wish to express true needs and the appearance of demanding, sometimes vengeful neediness that acts as a noisy distraction from the more genuine longings for human warmth and responsiveness. In particular, Ghent wrote,

> In the course of analytic work we often find ourselves welcoming the beginning appearance of such dark forces as envy, greed, hatred, especially as they seem to be heralding the (re)vitalization of some genuine need. We may have to hold for a long period the paradoxical meaning of these intense feelings: in one moment, defensive and constrictive and, in the next, progressive and vital. (pp. 142–143)

Pizer (1992) illustrates the crucial importance of negotiating paradox in the treatment process when presenting his treatment of a man profoundly in need of a father. His client needed to grieve not only the early loss of his father but also the loss of a potential future that his father's presence might have allowed him to achieve—a paradox experienced by all gorilla-suit wearers regardless of their sex. The therapist could not be his client's father, not only because it wouldn't be real, but also because the man's mourning needed to proceed without denial. Yet paradoxically, for the treatment to proceed, the client had to become, over time,

> like a son to whom, in my own countertransference, I could feel like a father. I could not recognize this paradox before I had overcome my own resistance to giving . . . the guidance [my patient] requested, which was a kind of parenting the patient had missed. (p. 231)

The parental feelings described by Pizer are identical to those felt by therapists treating children in gorilla suits. One aspect of treatment is conceptualized as providing children with a "new paternal object," an object desperately needed by those whose parents rejected them—the reason why so many feel like "psychological orphans." Children in foster care can incessantly complain about the care they receive in placement, and when the therapist attends to these complaints, a "transference erotic" can be established—a transformation through which, metaphorically, the therapist assumes, in the child's view, the character of the "rescuing angel" (Benjamin 1994). For example, there are instances when a child's vehement criticisms of foster care appear to be a call for the therapist "to go to war on his behalf," to become his "avenging angel" (Zimmerman 2003). The complaints are also desperate pleas for the therapist to validate the worth of the complaints, to confer on the child a sense of recognition and self-validation, wanting the therapist to act as the avenging angel, to add a sense of legitimacy to perceptions and complaints, and to enact rectifications for the child.

Such a transference puts therapists in a difficult dilemma. Some of the child's complaints are valid. Foster parents and child-care workers are not perfect. There are times when therapists, especially at treatment-team meetings, can take actions to modify specific aspects of a child's milieu. There are other times, however, when acting concretely on a child's life can make things worse for the child. Most therapists struggle with this dilemma by "sometimes intervening and sometimes not," but always struggling with ambiguity and uncertainty about whether their decisions to intervene will actually be helpful (Zimmerman 2003). In addition, hindsight becomes unsettling because therapists are troubled by uncertainty about whether more helpful actions could have been taken. Consequently, it is important that therapists be aware of countertransference issues, particularly the degree of rescue or adoption fantasies they hold. No one should treat children in gorilla suits without ongoing supervision or regular consultation from well-trained colleagues.

EMPHASIZE THE POSITIVE QUALITIES OF NATURAL PARENTS

Children in foster care need help to find positive qualities in their natural parents or other relatives so that they can experience these qualities in themselves. If the parents are seen as losers, the children view themselves as losers. Paradoxically, better relationships with foster parents will occur when positive qualities are found in natural parents. Children say to themselves, "If my parents have some lovable qualities, then I'm lovable, and if I'm lovable, I can be loved by the foster parents and other adults." Thus, they open themselves up to their foster parents.

Often untrained foster parents shudder when children in their care express love and admiration for their natural parents because the foster parents fear the children will become just like the natural parents. A six-year-old's expressing admiration for his father's strength (a father who used his strength to rob people and is in prison) doesn't mean the boy will grow up to be a mugger. Or when a preteen girl, whose mother is a prostitute, goes "boy crazy," it doesn't mean she will end up like her mother. Untrained adults often fear that foster children will become like the "bad parts" of their parents. Consequently, they are reluctant to tell the children good things about the parents because they fear encouraging identification with the parents' bad qualities as well. These fears are unfounded and prevent foster children from meeting a fundamental need—the need to discover who they are. Two examples of positive statements to these children are

> THERAPIST: You're getting to be strong, just like your dad. He was a good athlete, both at football and baseball. Maybe if you practice a lot, you can get to be a good player, just like him.
> THERAPIST: You have pretty eyes, just like your mom.

The importance of such statements cannot be overstated. Most foster children fail to identify with adequate adult models in their immediate environment because they have not let go of their parents. Until these children can relinquish the past, they cannot take from the present or the future. This does not mean that children must be helped to "forget" their parents. On the contrary, they must be helped to remember, know, and ultimately accept their parents for who they were and who they are. They must be helped to a new and different love for their parents, not one that rises out of unfulfilled needs and deprivation, but one that expresses compassion and acceptance. This partly means they must come to see their parents as unable to care for them, not as unloving. Children's identification with parents includes identification with their attitudes. If parents feel helpless, hopeless, and desperate, children need help to see things differently. The problems and confusing behaviors of their parents must be made understandable:

> THERAPIST: It's really hard to want to be close to your mom and not have her close to you. How awful you must have felt, and still feel, being unloved by your mom. But she had many problems and couldn't express her feelings for you.
> THERAPIST: How frightening it must be to live with parents who can't always show their love. You must want to run away, but that would be scary 'cause you'd feel terribly alone. Other people don't easily replace the ones we love, and sometimes we won't let them.

Foster children need help to discover positive qualities in themselves. It is difficult for them to feel self-confident when they feel demoralized. They make many disparaging comments about others and eventually about themselves.

THERAPIST: You feel really discouraged about yourself today.
THERAPIST: You've seemed pretty hopeless about yourself lately.

Remember that therapy is not a social relationship. Statements made to children must be empathic. It does not help a young boy who is mad at himself for poor drawings to tell him, "You can do better if you try harder," a typical caregiver response to a child's failure. When his discouraged feelings are reflected, he can look at himself more objectively and realize that he's not so bad after all. Then the therapist can reply, "Perhaps you'd like some help with that," or "Try again. Maybe with a few suggestions from me, you can make it better." When children feel discouraged, it further alienates them to hear "You did okay yesterday." In their hopelessness, they want to feel understood, to be in communication with someone, to feel connected. When they perceive their real message being received, they feel less hopeless, will judge themselves less harshly, and will try a task again.

Therapy is also not giving false praise. Often children make scribbles on a piece of paper, and well-meaning adults will praise them for their wonderful production. Therapists should know better, but both of us have supervised trained therapists who do not. While such praise might be appropriate for three-year-olds, it certainly isn't appropriate for older children whose scribbles result from minimal effort. During a visit with a foster parent, the parent was shocked when the foster child, about eight years old and not in therapy, showed hastily made scribbles to Dr. Mordock, who replied, "That's not a good drawing, and you know it. Come on in the kitchen, and I'll help you to make some good ones." The child initially resisted but then complied, and for months after continued to ask her foster mother, "When is Dr. Mordock going to visit me again? I want to draw with him." Most children know when they have really tried and when they haven't. They will accept praise even when it is hollow—but they won't grow from it.

Therapists should praise children's efforts rather than their results. Sometimes when praised by adults, children fear they won't produce the same result again, and their motivation wanes. Praise is helpful only when it is sincere, Praise benefits motivation when it encourages performance attributes that are related to controllable causes, promotes autonomy, enhances competence without reliance on social comparison, and conveys attainable standards and expectations (Henderlong and Lepper 2002).

THERAPIST: Mark, you put a lot of work into that English assignment. We appreciate such effort. Keep it up, even though we know it's hard. You can send it to your mom.

VISITATIONS: ANXIOUS REUNIONS

Most children in foster care display problem behavior before or after a visit with their natural family (Haight, Kagle, and Black 2003). Teachers may experience frenzied, chaotic behavior from foster children on afternoons before a visit or in mornings after a visit. Unfortunately, teachers rarely meet with social service staff or get informed about the upcoming events in foster children's lives, sometimes because social service staff members are too busy to speak with teachers, but also because some think such information is confidential. The therapist needs to take the initiative to find out when visits occur and inform those who need to know.

Generally, there are three types of visiting arrangements for children in foster care: parental visits to the foster home, supervised visits in the office of the social worker, and visitation in the home of the natural family. The last type can be one-day visits, overnight visits, or weekend visits. Equipped with this knowledge, caregivers can adjust their expectations of children before and after the visit. If children are visiting their parents on Friday and become highly anxious in anticipation, fewer demands can be placed on them. On the day after a visit, knowing they will be edgy, staff can modify the children's activities accordingly.

When Dr. Mordock was a trainee in psychological appraisals at the Little Flower Children Center in Long Island, New York, he compared the projective test responses of a child he had just tested with the results of the child's previous test results, completed within the last two months. On the Rorschach, a projective test rarely used with children today, the child saw numerous storm clouds on the ink blots and a "big spider" on Card VII, often called the "Mother Card," because lots of children see "Two women dancing." His previous responses were more benign. He had seen two women on Card VII. Dr. Mordock's supervisor, Joseph Bannichek, who had tested thousands of children during his twenty years at the center, felt the present test responses probably reflected the child's concerns about an upcoming home visit—the dark clouds reflecting his stormy feelings, or anger at his mother, and the "big spider" his perception of the devouring mother. (Carl Jung identified the spider as a universal symbol for mother in his cross-cultural studies.) Fresh from graduate school, where the Rorschach had been derided, Dr. Mordock was extremely skeptical. He was told by Joe to check the visiting schedule to see if he was right and, sure enough, the child had a visit scheduled on the upcoming weekend.

Why is visiting so traumatic? Primarily because it creates fantasies about reunion. Reunion holds forth the expectation that the loss will be undone.

"Mom will love me better than she did in the past" or "I will behave better than I did before" or "My visit home will put things right." In the child's mind during the time away from home, parents become idealized, imbued with magical curative powers. Visits shatter this illusion. Reunions reveal reality. The children discover that their parents still have problems. Mom will have changed too much or too little. Mom will be reminded of how "bad" the child was—that he or she didn't live up to her expectations. Dad is even more critical. Or the children fear they will do all the wrong things and never be able to go home for good. Children in treatment centers can be criticized for not progressing fast enough—"You've been in that center for three months and you still talk back!"

Visitations make parents and children aware that they may be growing apart. They are no longer sure how to relate to each other. Intimate communication between parents and children is nourished by togetherness and diminished during separation. The mother now undervalues her importance. What exists is an altered state of togetherness. Both parents and children have the same apprehensions and expectations about reunion. Child-care workers, foster mothers, and even therapists have witnessed this altered state on numerous occasions and have wrongly attributed it to bad parenting. "The mother doesn't really care; she only comes up here for a trip to the country. Look how she ignores Tammy and talks to others." As we mentioned earlier, she is not ignoring the child, and she really does care. But she is uncomfortable, and she doesn't know how to reach her child.

Reunions serve as painful reminders of past rejections and contribute to feelings of self-doubt. Both parents and children can be reluctant to reach out to one another for fear of rejection. The children's attachments to surrogate parents warp the quality of their reunion. Concrete changes threaten foster children—a new sibling, a mother's new boyfriend, or a remarriage. Issues from the past are compounded by issues in the present.

Children need help to stay grounded in the facts, as their intensely experienced ideas may become confused with reality. When caught up in the past, children have a distorted view of the present. They need help to understand and to accept the past—to relinquish what was, or what might have been, and to affirm what is.

ATTITUDES ABOUT FOSTER PARENTS

People become foster parents for different reasons. Some become foster parents for altruistic reasons, a genuine desire to help children. Others want another child to add to their own fulfillment or to keep their natural child company. Another group, called kinship foster parents, are relatives of the children sought out by social services and asked to care for the child. Most agree to do so and are paid a nominal fee. Still others need the extra income that comes with taking in a foster child. Whatever the reason, good foster parents can produce positive changes in children's functioning regardless of the level of the child's entering pathology (Barber and Delfabbro 2003; Coco 1998). In our experience, adults who see foster parenting as a job, but who also have confidence in their parenting skills, provide the best homes for children who maintain ties with natural parents. Unfortunately, foster parents with financial motives are judged harshly by other people in the children's lives: "They're just doing it for the buck!" Many altruistic foster parents become quickly disillusioned when they discover that their love does not significantly change the child. They fail to see the fruits of their labor and give up quickly.

Evidence suggests that adoptive parents who have their own attachment problems are less effective caregivers of previously maltreated children (Steel et al. 2003). There is no reason to believe that this same relationship doesn't exist for foster parents as well. More than 25 percent of kinship foster parents, sometimes called "other mothers," screen positively for depression (Smith 2003), and we have already stressed how depression can adversely affect mothering.

In addition, children actively rejected at birth show more attachment problems in adoptive homes than other maltreated children, the adoptive parents found it more difficult to relate to them in a warm and responsive manner, and the situation worsened by the end of the first year (Rushton, Mayes, and Dance 2003).

Foster parents whose initial motive is financial approach the tasks as would a professional and are able to manage the child in spite of "not getting much back," as often happens before children become adjusted to the home. Therapists need to examine their own judgments about people who take in children. They need to show empathy for the foster mother, who will go through some rough testing from the child.

Foster children need firm controls. Most children are placed because of difficulties with parents. Many are unmanageable and need a home with supervision, support, and controls. Typically, children learn to control themselves by wanting to please a loved adult. Normal children, not wanting to lose the parent's love, learn to control their impulses. When children enter foster care, they are unsure whether anybody really loves them. They find themselves in a new home with strangers, people they have no desire to please. Many of these youngsters behave worse soon after placement.

When foster parents are firm and the child's behavior becomes compliant, the child becomes more receptive to love and affection. These controls can seem unusually strict to outside observers who unfairly criticize foster parents. Children in placement may try hard to discredit their foster parents so they can return to their natural parents. They will take advantage of judgments they sense others hold about the foster parents. During this testing period, they try to align other adults against the foster parents. They may tell the therapist that their foster mother does not feed them, or they may put on old, dirty clothes to make it appear as if they are not being cared for.

When this happens, unsuspecting adults can make hasty judgments about the foster family without checking things out. Some youngsters are adept at orchestrating teachers, staff members of social service agencies, and even therapists against foster parents. One eleven-year-old boy in foster care announced to his teachers and classmates, "You know, I have to eat in the basement." Everyone became concerned, and a call was made to the caseworker to further investigate the boy's claim. It turned out that the family had remodeled the basement as a living area for everyone in the family, the rooms upstairs being used as a showcase when they entertained company. Another child took his dirty underclothes out of the soiled laundry, tore them up, put them on, and then arranged for an accident so the school nurse could see the way he was dressed, knowing she would complain to his social worker about the poor care he received at the foster home.

Foster parents should be treated with respect and their point of view listened to carefully. If they are involved in the work for financial remuneration (as is the therapist), they should be treated as professionals who, in most cases, will do a good job with the children. Foster parents sometimes take abuse from natural parents who feel guilty that they can't take care of the child or fear losing their child's love. Consequently, they try to demean the foster parents in the child's eyes: "You don't have to listen to her. She's not your mother." They will criticize the foster parents in front of the child with comments such as (from an abusive mother) "You've been beating my child. I'm going to sue you!" or "I don't like her dressed in blue. I never liked blue on her" or "What right have you to cut my child's hair? I want him to have long hair, not short hair." Foster parents need support so as not to return such anger and to feel appreciated for their work.

Unfortunately, caregivers can become abusive at times, especially when pushed to the limit by aggressive or seductive behavior. The repetition compulsion displayed by gorilla-suit wearers can result in adults' treating them in kind. Or the seductive behavior of sexually abused children can result in their further sexual abuse. While children's complaints about caregivers can be grossly exaggerated or have no basis in reality, they can also be true. The careful therapist will unobtrusively investigate all allegations, unless abuse is actually suspected, and, in that case, reporting the suspicions is mandatory.

Clinicians working with foster parents must help them relate to the child's natural parents as positively as they do to the child and encourage them to support the natural parent's growth. Eventually, the child will return home. If the foster parents become a resource for the natural parents rather than protagonists, the child's transition home will go more smoothly. Unfortunately, the very traits that make one a good foster parent can interfere with one's working closely with natural parents. As a group, foster parents, compared to natural parents of normal children, see foster care as more desirable for the abused child than the child's natural home, want the child to have limited contact with natural parents, and have higher standards for the parental behaviors required before the child can return home (Corsen and Furnell 1992). Natural parents often find that their visiting plans are not supported by foster parents (Barber and Delfabbro 2003), a problem that interferes with the formation of a collaborative partnership.

A CAUTION ABOUT THERAPY WITH CHILDREN IN FOSTER HOMES

The behaviors of many foster children result in their referral for therapy. The problem, however, is that therapy can dilute the relationship with a foster mother. Now another adult is added to the child's life! Theoretically, a therapist is a neutral figure who helps children sort out their feelings about the parent figures in their lives. What sometimes happens is that the therapist, especially a therapist with strong rescue fantasies—one who desires to take children out of their dilemma—becomes an additional parent figure, and the children's confusion multiplies. Teachers, child-care workers, and nurses have more clearly defined roles. Although children may be attached to them, these professionals work with many other children, and children know they are not going to be taken into their homes. But the therapist sees them alone, planting the seed for the fantasy. If the therapist has not worked with foster children before, he or she may not know that such fantasies exist, and in that case the "therapy" will not be therapy at all but simply fuel for confusion.

Strengthening Relationships with Parents: Identifying the Parents' Struggles

The personal struggles of parents of children in gorilla suits are presented. They struggle with unfulfilled dependency needs, poor self-concept, bonding failure, disturbed identity formation, cognitive immaturity, chaotic lifestyles, denied affects, and social isolation, all of which interfere with their ability to effectively parent their children.

*E*normous amounts of time and effort are needed to make an impact on parents whose children wear gorilla suits, some of whom abuse the suit wearer. The common reaction of staff at school and social service agencies is to want, indeed demand, that change come immediately. To witness suffering, especially in innocent and vulnerable children, is draining—but even more draining is harboring false expectations that interventions will instantly rectify the situation. Staff of most child protective agencies, with whom psychotherapists work most closely, are overburdened, and turnover is high. Typically, new hires are untrained, and by the time they have learned from their mistakes, they are burned out and resign. Usually, abused and neglected children are placed in foster homes for short periods, and clinic therapists are relied on to provide the intensive, long-term clinical support necessary to treat the children and their families. Unfortunately, often the children are returned to the natural parents before the treatment is completed or are switched to another foster home, a placement that brings with it a new set of problems.

Nevertheless, little progress can be made in the treatment of children wearing gorilla suits without working with their natural parents. In the past decade, social scientists have become increasingly interested in the concept of resilience. Unfortunately, when studying resilience in children, most investigators equate resilience with protective factors, or factors that buffer the child from negative influences. Abusing parents do not display these buffering child-rearing practices. To the contrary, they add to the stress the child faces in the larger community. In fact, the child-rearing strategies they use render the child more vulnerable to other stressors.

Trauma researchers have examined individuals who have not only coped effectively with trauma but used the traumatic experience as a catalyst for growth (O'Leary 1998). These individuals become resilient (Masten 2001) or achieve "transformational coping" (Aldwin 1994) or posttraumatic growth (Tedeschi and Calhoun 1996). "In the face of these losses and the confusion they cause, some people rebuild a life that they experience as superior to the old one in important ways" (Tedeschi and Calhoun, p. 2). Consequently, most trauma researchers apply the term *resilience* to survivors of trauma who show no ill effects and who may have actually grown from the traumatic experience, suggesting that future traumas will be less devastating as a result of the growth following the earlier trauma. In the case of child abuse and neglect, however, few resilient individuals have been described in the literature. Early traumas make the child vulnerable to later traumas, and eventually the child either dons a gorilla suit or becomes seriously maladjusted.

Bryon Egeland, project director of the Mother-Child Project at the University of Minnesota's Institute for Human Development, and his colleagues have followed a sample of maltreated children living in impoverished environments from birth to young adulthood, and they all show ill effects of their early maltreatment (Aguilar et al. 2000; Egeland 1997; Egeland et al. 2002; Yates, Egeland, and Sroufe 2003). There were no "resilient" or "hardy" children in the project's sample, suggesting that unless neglectful and abusive parents can change their child-rearing tactics and parent-child relationship patterns, their children will continue to suffer. But more than changes in parenting are required. The situations that created the poor parenting have to be addressed. Background factors in the lives of high-risk mothers explain close to 75 percent of the variance in maternal sensitivity and positive responsiveness toward their toddlers. Other research suggests that the more stressors experienced by families, the more poorly their children function. What is worse is that the family effects are not offset by the children's coping strategies (Gaylord and Kitzman 2003).

Garbarino (1999), in *Lost Boys*, points out that "Resilience is not absolute; some settings overwhelm human capacities" (p. 116). Garbarino cites Tolan's research (1996) aimed at answering the question, "What percent of fifteen-year-old African American kids living in disruptive families and growing up in the most violent and dangerous neighborhoods of Chicago are resilient? Tolan's measure of resilience was being no more than one year behind in school, requiring no remedial education, and no mental health or developmental problems sufficient to require professional intervention to recover. Over a two-year period, Tolan followed these inner-city youth. Sadly, the answer to the question was zero. Not a single one of the fifteen-year-olds was resilient, as measured by escaping both significant academic deficits and mental health disorders. Garbarino (1999) summarizes the findings by stating, "The relentless pressure imposed on children exposed to the lethal combination of community violence, family disruption, racism, and personal experience of trauma is uniformly overwhelming. The accumulation of threat is too much for any of them to bear" (p. 116).

Consequently, short-term treatment approaches are not satisfactory. Even intensive long-term treatment may not allay the powerful cultural and personal factors that contribute to family characteristics producing vulnerable children (Repetti, Taylor, and Seeman 2002).

It generally takes at least a year for a neglectful or abusive parent to develop a working relationship with a treatment agency. One organization that makes an impact on abusing parents is Parents Anonymous, a self-help group similar in organization and philosophy to Alcoholics Anonymous. Yet even this very effective organization reaches only a few parents—those who decide to join and to commit themselves to the group. Change requires a period of support and encouragement and may end up being only minimal. As one abusing parent said, "Since I joined Parents Anonymous, I don't beat my kid anymore, but I still don't like playing with her. Every time I say we have to stop, she carries on and cries, and I wish I hadn't started playing with her in the first place."

It is easy to become angry at the parents. A normal response is to want the children taken from them. Unfortunately, acting on these angry impulses does little to help either the abused children or their families. The therapist must consider the world of the abusing parents, and while this should go without saying, both of us have worked with therapists who were themselves abused as children, and they often show an unhealthy identification with the child at the expense of the parents. Not only have many of the parents been abused as children, but they have often been displaced from their homes by urban renewal projects without much thought given to their needs (Mordock 1971). Therapists can quickly identify with parents by accompanying them to the local social welfare office where they apply for benefits and pick up their welfare checks. If the therapist doesn't walk out of the office angry, then the welfare office must be an atypical one. Recipients are treated rudely and with contempt by staff at the centers. And if the visit doesn't result in anger, ask to read the mother's latest letter from the welfare office threatening to cut off her child-support payments if she doesn't keep the office informed of her ex-husband's latest address. Chances are the mother has never received a single support check from the welfare office because her husband never sent any. And how about the mother who was told that if she didn't have her promiscuous thirteen-year-old daughter's "tubes tied," she would lose her Medicaid privileges. The daughter

was a girl we suspect was sexually abused when younger. When the mother resisted the surgery, she was investigated for Medicaid fraud.

HOW THE NATURAL PARENTS FEEL

Different factors interact to produce abuse. Frequently, abusing parents are
poor; poverty breeds frustration. Many were themselves abused as children and
put on gorilla suits in response (Serbin and Karp 2003; Thornberry, Freeman-
Gallant, and Lizotte 2003). They suffered the same violence, humiliation, and
despair that their children suffer and that accompany poverty in our society.
They, like their children, feel unable to meet life's daily demands. More children with developmental difficulties are born in impoverished environments,
especially to teenage mothers (Rogers, People-Sheps, and Suchindran 1996).

Raising a child with developmental difficulties, such as premature birth,
mental retardation, physical disabilities, congenital malformations, and subtle
neurological difficulties, is a difficult task, especially when supports are lacking.
These disabilities cause increased stress in parents and, therefore, are ever present in abused populations. Vulnerability in the infant, such as low birth weight
or colicky behavior, can be heightened by a separation from the mother after
birth. The mother herself may be poorly nourished and experiencing significant stress in her marriage. She may also be experiencing poor health, a variable that has been related to parent-child attachment difficulties (Kaufman and
Uhlenberg 1998).

Many abusing parents lead lives in which their own needs for safety and
love are not met and never have been. "Wanting" characterizes their lives. Most
have lost significant others early in life. An early death of a parent or a difficult
divorce chokes emotional fulfillment during childhood and takes an even
greater toll years later. Abusing parents grow up with unmet needs and look to
their own children to satisfy their emotional deprivations. Instead of wanting
to give, they expect to receive: "I have never really felt loved all my life. When
the baby was born, I thought he would love me. But when he cried all the
time, it meant he didn't love me, so I hit him."

Parents who abuse misunderstand the basic nature of children. When they
were growing up, they lacked a positive role model of parenting. To be good
at parenting, parents must express love, show tolerance, and serve as examples.
Most parents who abuse were raised without seeing these qualities in practice,
and many were abused themselves (Ornduff, Kelsey, and O'Leary 2001). One
father whose severe disciplining included forcing his son to kneel on carpet
tacks explained, "It may seem cruel to you, but as children this is the type of

punishment we received, my wife and I. We were just using the same type of punishment. If we did not care about him, we would not do this."

No matter how poor, how deprived, or how overwhelmed, most parents would rather not abuse their children. They become frustrated, they can't control their frustration, and they take it out on their offspring. Shame and guilt follow, but the parents can't seem to help themselves and may lack empathic skills. Many child abusers report "going through hell," claiming to have a vision of how powerful their anger can be, a concept of where their anger will take them if pushed too far, and a constant dread that they will be pushed too far. One parent stated, "We don't like being child abusers any more than society likes the problem of child abuse."

Some parents feel so stressed that they would like their children in foster care or even adopted. Unfortunately, their relatives pressure them to keep the children without supporting them. Giving up the children means loss of the meager love they receive from their extended family. As one grandmother said to her daughter, "You give away my grandson and you're not welcome in my house anymore." Other statements are less direct but convey the same message, such as "Anyone who would put their child in foster care is an unfit parent." Consequently, they keep the child in an effort to please their parents, but they find themselves continually criticized for mishandling the child. The unconscious wishes of one mother to give up her child were displayed following a therapy session with Dr. Mordock. In the next session she vented her anger. "I told my mother that 'Dr. Mordock wants me to give up my child. Boy, Mom, did that suggestion make me angry.' How could you possibly think I would do that?" Not once, however, had the topic of foster care come up in the treatment session.

On another occasion, following a flood of complaints about her child's misbehavior, Dr. Mordock asked a mother how the children related to her husband. She replied, without emotion, that "he worked long hours six days a week and played golf on Sunday," an activity she supported because he needed to relax from the pressures at work. "No," she emphasized, "it is my job to care for the children, regardless of the difficulties, and his job to bring home the bacon." About a week later, she called the author's supervisor and complained that her husband had been criticized for not being a good father, that Dr. Mordock was a terrible therapist, and that she would not come back to the clinic until he was fired. Yet the only mention of her husband in the treatment session was the one question above. After she had answered as quoted above, discussion switched to another topic. Within a month, her most troubled child was placed in a residential treatment center, and she left her husband.

When seen in initial data-gathering sessions in mental health clinics, parents typically voice a variety of complaints against the referred child. The therapist who wishes to remove the child from the negative spotlight may respond with, "Mom and Dad sure have lots of complaints about you. I'll bet you feel discouraged, perhaps even unloved." This technique can backfire if the therapist has failed to empathize with the parent's discouraged feelings. Such empathy shown to the child early in treatment can result in the child's feeling justified in his or her behavior. Even when empathy is directed at the parents by remarking, "You must feel overwhelmed by your son's behaviors," parents can perceive this statement as implying parental incompetence. In response, they become defensive and escalate their inappropriate parental behaviors in an effort to regain self-esteem.

Many abused and neglected children are raised by single mothers (Olson, Ceballo, and Park 2002). In chapter 1 we present some brief background information on a mother who was arrested after killing her three newborns. Another report in the popular press described a mother who was charged with criminal neglect when her son committed suicide after repeatedly being bullied at school. She was working sixty hours a week in a department store to make ends meet, a contributing factor to her son's neglect. But what about the fathers involved in these two cases, or in other similar cases? Their neglect by abandonment is never even mentioned. They get off scot free. Remember this fact when working with mothers of gorilla-suit wearers.

In this chapter, our goal is not just to help clinicians understand how parents actually spur their children to put on gorilla suits, but also to empathize with the reasons they do so. Our friend and professional colleague John Haverlick, a trainer of family therapists, left the Astor Home to devote himself to private practice. About five years later, he turned his practice over to his partners and returned to the field of child welfare. When asked why, he replied, "I grew tried of helping couples where the chief problem was a distant husband who'd rather play golf on weekends than go shopping with his pursuing wife. I missed working with people with significant troubles." This feeling is shared by both authors. Treating disenfranchised families is difficult, but the rewards are great. When families with children in gorilla suits make even small changes, the changes can significantly improve their lives.

Although we have just described some of the general characteristics of abusing families, we will now make an effort to synthesize these characteristics, organize them around key issues, and cite the relevant literature in support of the issues. Remember, however, that in spite of the problems we review below, all parents have some strengths that can be used as building blocks to successful treatment (Bell 2003). In the next chapter, we describe what is required to restructure family patterns so that aggression is no longer the child's habitual response to stress or the only means of achieving desired ends.

When we discuss characteristics that many parents of gorilla-suit wearers have in common, we identify only the characteristics that led the children to put on gorilla suits. Almost all of their parents, no matter what their life circumstances, have strengths that can be mobilized to change their behavior. It is the therapist's job to help parents to identify these strengths and to put them to use. Keep in mind that parents living in communities or families characterized by constant violence may have experienced traumas that have interfered with their abilities to be effective parents. They may need help with issues related to these traumas before they can make changes in child rearing (Lewis 1996), particularly mothers who have been abused by their partners, many of whom were gorilla-suit wearers as children (Ehrensaft et al. 2003). Battered women are twice as likely to abuse their children than are other women, some doing so shortly after their own abuse (Straus and Gelles 1990). And a significant percentage of husbands who abuse their wives also abuse their children (Edleson 1999b). In fact, each additional act of violence against their wives increases the odds of their abusing their child by about 12 percent (Ross 1996).

Child rearing in violent communities is no easy task (Garbarino and Bedard 2001). The task has been equated with raising children in a war zone (Dubrow and Garbarino 1989). Fearing for both their own and their children's safety, parents can become overprotective and overcontrolling, actually intrusive, producing the negative consequences associated with that parenting style (Barber 2002). Feeling unable to ensure their children's safety (Osofsky and Jackson 1993/1994), some can deny their children opportunities to master normal developmental transitions; some also resort to harsh physical punishment to enforce rules they think will keep their children safe (Osofsky and Fenichel 1993/1994). These tactics can increase their children's feelings of insecurity and distrust (Zeanah and Scheeringa 1996). Other parents, in order to feel less anxious, minimize their perception of the violence around them and, as a result, may be oblivious to their child's problems (Fick, Osofsky, and Lewis 1997). And still others have themselves been traumatized and are numbed, frightened, and depressed, with less energy to devote to parenting. Parents need help with their own problems and with structuring their children's lives. They need to establish routines that make children feel cared for, set firm limits rather than physically punish, interact positively with their children when not disciplining them, and find safe havens for their children in the community so they can decrease their rigid efforts at control.

Many of the parents have spent part of their own youth in foster care, have experienced academic failure as students, and have been involved with child protective service agencies. As a result, they feel anxious and uncomfortable in bureaucratic settings, and when anxious and uncomfortable, they can become blaming and angry. As a consequence, they can be viewed by the staff of

schools, social service agencies, and even mental health centers as uncoopera-
tive, antagonistic, and neglectful, leading to further feelings of rejection. Common characteristics displayed by the parents include unfulfilled dependency
needs, low self-esteem, bonding failure, disturbed identity formation, cognitive
immaturity, denied affects, chaotic lifestyles, and social isolation.

UNFULFILLED DEPENDENCY NEEDS: I LONG TO BE LOVED

Generational Patterns

Most parents of children wearing gorilla suits were themselves raised in families that failed to meet their needs. They came from broken families, those
characterized by loss, and from incomplete families, those characterized by lack
of attainment (McKinney 1970). Failure to buffer their children from strong
emotions is bad enough, but when the parents' strong emotions also become
the source of a child's overwhelming fears, the child's emotional development
is arrested. Since the gorilla-suit wearer's parents were raised similarly to the
way they are raising their children, everybody in the family suffers from arrested emotional development. Just as the gorilla-suit wearer becomes the object of parental anger, the parents were the helpless victims of the grandparents'
rage and disillusionment with life. Loving and angry feelings were never clearly
distinguished. Angry love is the norm—and angry love is what the parents feel
and display toward their children.

Need for Nurturing

Typically, the parents' need for nurturing is stronger than their need to be good
parents. This need is manifested in numerous ways. First, they retain a strong
desire for approval from their own parents and become angry when such approval is not forthcoming (Galdston 1975). Their parents related to them
through scolding, directing, and advice giving. These dependency-producing
interactions created conflict but also familiarity. When the parents resisted their
own parents' advice, both parties suffered. The offspring's newly won achievements were gained at the cost of losing a familiar relationship. As children, the
parents couldn't stand such a loss because it also meant giving up identification
with their parents, whom they perceived as lost and anxious without them. As
a result, strong ambivalent feelings exist about their own parents, and struggling, but not coping, with these feelings absorbs much of their energy.

Second, they expect their spouse to take care of them (Justice and Justice
1976). Such expectations result in the spouse's feeling controlled. Both parents,

then, expect to be taken care of by the other even though they feel controlled by the other rather than fulfilled. The resulting marital discord evokes painful memories of their own deprived childhood, engendering frustration and rage toward the spouse and often toward the child, regarded either as a rival for the spouse's attention or as the cause of the spouse's unavailability.

Marital Discord and Triangles

All marriages progress through the stages of idealization, disappointment, disenchantment, redefinition, and productivity (Nadelson, Polonsky, and Matthews 1984). The marriages we are referring to are arrested at the stage of disenchantment. Power and control in such relationships are not shared by mutual negotiation. Each partner pushes the other to accept his or her view of reality, arguments ensue, and battering sometimes follows. Courts may order some of the fathers to undergo anger management training. Although such training can be effective (DiGuiseppe and Tafrate 2003), it rarely addresses the communication problems that lead to battering and child abuse (Cahn and Lloyd 1996; Heyman and Neidig 1997) or the unique features of violence in intimate relationships (Gelles and Straus 1988). The parents' different views of reality result in their blaming each other for their child's problems and placement in treatment, often accompanied by a placement in special education, to which one or both parents object. The parents rarely assume joint responsibility for the problem or its resolution. If the child progresses, the denying parent dismisses the progress by claiming the child never belonged in treatment in the first place. If the child fails, the failure is blamed on the treatment center and on the parent in favor of the treatment.

In all marriages, each partner's past problems are brought forward and resurrected in the present. When these problems are serious ones, intense marital frictions develop. To maintain marital stability, the parents regularly triangle the child into the parent's problems. When the intensity of emotions between a twosome becomes too great, the pair will predictably and automatically involve a vulnerable third person in the emotional issue. With involvement of the third person, the tension between the twosome decreases (Bowen 1978). The child becomes not only the scapegoat for marital difficulties but also the spokesperson for the parents' feelings—"Dad hates you"—resulting in the accused spouse's retaliating against the child. Other parents openly state, "Your father and I got along better before you were born!"

Flight from Stress

As stress mounts, the parents experience a strong desire to flee from family responsibilities. Many respond to stress with avoidance strategies, resigning themselves to their fate and displaying periodic emotional outbursts, especially if they themselves were traumatized in early childhood (Grantz 2003). Dissatisfactions with parenting contribute to their flight (Mammen, Kolko, and Pilkonis 2003). Often, they seek out similar-minded parents and spend time expressing mutual complaints about their partners and their children. While "gathering and talking" may seem like a good strategy for coping with stress, studies suggest that spending more time in leisure activities is a superior one (Gaurilovie et al. 2003). Thoughts about fleeing from parental responsibilities are shared by many parents of normal children, but they are rarely acted on or blamed on the child. In the families we are discussing, actual flights from parenthood occur, and the children are often blamed. Such flights are soundly criticized by the child's grandparents, as well as by educators and others working with the family. Such criticism serves only to intensify wishes to flee. Battered women often flee their homes, most taking their children with them, but many return, primarily because they lack financial resources (46 percent), have no place to go (28 percent), or lack police support (14 percent) (Anderson et al. 2003).

POOR SELF-CONCEPT: I AM PLAGUED BY SELF-DOUBTS

Because the child's parents have faced years of criticism in their angry love relationships with their own parents, their spouses, and school authority figures, the parents' self-images are extremely low (Herrenkohl et al. 1984; Webster-Stratton 1985). For this reason, many never leave their spouses, believing that no one else would ever have them—"I'd rather fight than be alone." In addition, the mothers have a predilection for "mean men" (Galdston 1981). The men's meanness provides an acceptable target for the mother's lifetime of anger and keeps her anger directed outward rather than inward. Directing anger at nice men burdens her with guilt. Husband-hate or child-hate is more tolerable than guilt and self-hate.

Marked Feelings of Incompetence

A lifetime of criticism results in severe self-doubts—the parents never feel competent. They doubt their ability to do minimally acceptable jobs and, when their anxiety is high, they feel incapable of performing even simple tasks (Steele 1975), especially those related to child care (Greene et al. 2002). Yet the intentions are there; they share the same values as other parents. They want to obtain a good education for their children, to live in stable homes, to be good parents, and to have significant job opportunities. Because of past frustrations in meeting these goals, however, they are unwilling to risk further involvements, which

can lead to additional failure. Yet, even their immobile behavior meets with criticism: "How come you don't look for a better job or a better apartment?" and
"How come you didn't go to Open House at your son's school?" The guilt they
experience over not being better parents and the sorrow they feel for mistreat-
ing their child cannot be mobilized to change behavior as long as energies are
directed at facing and defending against constant criticism.

Their Child Is a Challenge to Their Ideal Self-Concept

The normally assertive and demanding behavior of children is felt as a challenge to the parents' already poor self-images. Because of their own parents'
unrealistic expectations for them, their ideal images are too high. Consequently, they are prone to self-criticism, followed by self-hate, denial, and anger
at others. Their children develop similarly, as each subsequent generation re-
produces the patterns of the previous generation. The children, encouraged to
grow up too soon, also become unreasonably angry over their own failures,
but, like their parents, they quickly displace their anger onto others. Punishment by others is often preferable to harsh self-blame.

Self-Hate and Child-Hate

If we like ourselves, we like extensions of ourselves—we like our own children.
If we don't like ourselves, we are much less likely to like extensions of ourselves
unless they live up to our every expectation of them, which most children
don't. And those who do only do so until they lash out in anger against such
subjugation (Shenken 1964). If we view ourselves as bad, we view our children
as bad (Galdston 1975, 1981). Consequently, many of the child-rearing actions
of parents with extremely low self-esteem are related more to their own internal stress states than to the child's actions. To the child, his or her parents' behavior is capricious and incomprehensible and creates feelings of helplessness.
This leads not only to anger to combat helplessness but also to a deficit in the
child's awareness of his or her impingement on others, a deficit that the child's
parents also display because of the similar parenting they received. When they
storm in angrily, accusing school teachers or others of mismanaging a situation,
they are rarely aware that their anger may be frightening to professional staff.
The parents' capricious behavior may also contribute to the impaired verbal
ability noted in abused children (Burke et al. 1986).

Children Seen as Monsters

When children escalate their anger, they further solidify their parents' view
that they, the children, are bad and that their assertive and aggressive behav-

iors are willful assaults. Many of these parents refer to their children as monsters (Galdston 1975). These negative perceptions of their child can be harmful if not dealt with during treatment (Herrenkohl and Herrenkohl 1979), particularly when the child's aggression is punished by educational or child-care staff rather than handled in an ego-supportive manner, a topic we address in another chapter.

Often a parent feels guilty after attacking the child and will hug the child to try to make up for the hurt. Frequently this is the only time the child experiences affection, and the child may learn to provoke parental abuse in order to receive tenderness. For aggressive children, anger, hurt, humiliation, and hugs are all interrelated. Patterns for what psychiatrists call sadomasochistic behavior can develop early.

They Punish Rather Than Prohibit

Although parents of aggressive children punish aggressive behavior, they never learn to prohibit such behavior. For example, a mother may repeatedly scream at her son for taking long showers and even hit him when he gets out, but she may never simply reach in and turn the water off. A daughter may be screamed at and physically punished for never cleaning her room, but no other consequences ever follow this misbehavior. The mother may regularly give her child money for candy and never realize she should withhold this money until the room is clean. The connection is never made because the money is given to absolve the mother's guilt about her own hostile behavior. A boy may hit his mother while she both screams at him to stop and retaliates in kind, but she never simply restrains the child from hitting her. Consequently, the boy never learns to handle his own aggression (and neither did the parent). The boy constantly aggresses and regresses. He pounds the table and sucks his thumb. He runs hard, but runs into a wall to stop himself. The parents also aggress and regress. They will come to the school and rant and rave at staff and then hole up in their rooms and talk to no one. Alcohol is another method used to control their anger—"Don't blame me; I was drunk."

BONDING FAILURE: I NEVER FELT CLOSE TO MY CHILD

Because of their extreme ambivalence toward becoming a parent, mothers often fail to seek adequate prenatal and postnatal care. High use of drugs and alcohol contributes to their problems. As a result, biological harm is often done to their children. This harm, although not causing obvious problems, can result in the parents' feeling estranged from their infants and the infants from the parents. Such strain can contribute to a host of developmental difficulties (Friedrich and Boriskin 1976; Mordock 1979) and to the parents' interpreting the children's behavior as rejection. For example, hyperactive children often squirm and struggle when hugged, and tactile-defensive children can cringe when hugged. Both behaviors can interfere with mother-child bonding, particularly in mothers with strong self-doubts and who personalize everything. In addition, infants and toddlers living in violent communities or exposed to domestic violence can regress in toileting and language; sleep poorly; show a limited range of emotions; and become restless, irritable, and hyperalert (Osofsky, Cohen, and Drell 1995; Zeanah and Scheeringa 1996), all behaviors that can interfere with making attachments.

DISTURBED IDENTITY FORMATION:
I DON'T KNOW WHO I AM

Because of their attachments to unstable parents, who responded to them as extensions of their own bad selves, parents of aggressive children often have internalized multiple identities. They view themselves as inconsistently as their parents behaved toward them. They become overwhelmed with self-hate and defend against these feelings in the only way they know—by denying their shortcomings and blaming others for their problems (Green 1979). Having no firm sense of who they are, they often fear harming their children, not sure that they can curb their anger. Often they need intervention from child protective service agencies. Although they will vehemently protest such treatment, they can also be relieved. Without stable self-identities, the parents fear loss of control, feel alienated from themselves, and experience feelings of depersonalization.

COGNITIVE IMMATURITY:
I AM THE CENTER OF ALL THINGS

Because parents of children in gorilla suits have no clear boundaries between self and others, they interpret most events in terms of themselves (Newberger and Cook 1983). Piaget uses the term *egocentrism* to describe such thinking ("Because I'm angry, others must be angry"). Egocentric parents describe their relationship to their child in terms of what they need rather than what the child needs ("I want my child to feel proud of me"). The parents discipline their child's actions not because of the actions themselves but because of the parents' own fears ("You must make them behave so they don't get on dope"). The young child, punished severely because he or she might get into trouble as an adolescent, never learns the specific objectives of the parents' disciplinary acts. There is no synchronization between the parents' actions and thoughts and the acts and feelings of the child (Newberger and Cook 1983).

Belief in Cultural Myths That Lead to Unrealistic Expectations ✓

Because of their cognitive limitations, egocentric parents are prone to share two major belief systems. First, they hold dearly to the cultural myths promulgated by society that lead to unrealistic expectations of children: the Gerber Baby is a bundle of joy; the Madonna Myth of Sacred Motherhood; good children keep their toys and clothes neat; children should be seen and not heard; children should not talk back; and boys should not learn silly games (Herrenkohl et al. 1984; Smith 1984). These myths have particular potency with certain groups. Single mothers are overrepresented among abusive and neglectful parents, and many of them are teenage parents, who abuse their children, as well as kill them, more often than older mothers (Overpeck et al. 1998).

From our knowledge of adolescent thinking, we recognize that most adolescents' thoughts center on themselves and that they can be irrational and impulsive. Teenage parents, partly from a desire for their child to grow up quickly so that the parents can get on with their own young lives, and partly out of ignorance, expect children to reach developmental milestones long before they are mature enough to do so. Consequently, adolescent parents have grossly unrealistic expectations for their infants. When their child doesn't respond in keeping with these expectations, the parents' feelings of inadequacy are aroused, and the child is blamed for these feelings. Fears that the child is abnormal begin early and are kept alive by special educational placements that occur many years later.

Surveys of adolescents reveal that most expect children to be toilet trained before they are able (as early as six months of age), to walk earlier than possible, and to talk before they are ready (Parks and Smeriglio 1983; Dallas, Wilson, and Salgado 2000; Ruchala and James 1997; Vukelich and Kliman 1985). When children don't reach these milestones as expected, some adolescent parents take it personally, particularly those who are troubled themselves ("This child is deliberately defying me!").

Adolescents have particular difficulty with an infant's demands. Most teenage mothers, because of their own unmet needs, have less energy to meet the needs of a growing child. Girls who have been sexually abused in childhood (Widom and Kuhns 1996), those with emotional and behavioral problems, and those hooked on drugs are high risks for unwanted pregnancies

(Yampolskaya, Brown, and Greenbaum 2002; Woodward and Fergusson 1999; Zoccolillo, Myers, and Assiter 1997). Usually the first unwanted child is followed within two years by another (Kalmus and Namerov 1994), and the likelihood of abuse increases as responsibilities rise.

When the twenty-five-year-old mother of three beats her youngest child, we often forget that it all began when her needs went unmet as a teenager, and in search of love, she became a young mother. One teenage mother thought her infant was deliberately disobeying her because the child repeatedly dropped objects from her high chair onto the floor. When adolescent parents try to accelerate the development of their children, the attempts are met with resistance, and interactions occur that can result in abuse. "I just couldn't stand his crying, and when he finally stopped I felt relief," a young mother admitted. The boy stopped crying because he was beaten unconscious.

Belief in Cultural Myths about Strong Punishment

Second, parents of aggressive children believe in strong punishment ("Children need to be punished to behave," "Children are bad and must be straightened out"), and these beliefs are strengthened by peer support. Such beliefs encourage compulsively self-righteous punishments that border on sadistic acts (Menninger, Mayman, and Pruyser 1963), perhaps the only acts for which the parents get approval from their own parents and from like-minded peers. The parents' cognitive immaturity also leads to a form of thinking mistakenly viewed as denial by professional helpers. Minuchin and his colleagues (1964), who worked with parents of boys enrolled at the Wiltwyck School for Boys in upstate New York, often heard parents say that, because they were unaware of their child's behavior, it was outside the boundaries of their ability to cope with it.

CHAOTIC LIFESTYLE: IF I CHANGE CIRCUMSTANCES, MY LIFE WILL IMPROVE

Because of cognitive immaturity and lack of clear boundaries between self and others, parents of aggressive children are unable to associate stress with the stressful event that causes it (Egeland, Breitenbucher, and Rosenberg 1980). The stress permeates all aspects of their functioning and adversely influences their responsiveness, empathy, and ability to nurture the child. Because they lack skill in problem solving, these parents often respond to stress by precipitating a crisis in the child so that they can seek help for the child and thereby calm themselves in the process.

Their cognitive immaturity also results in magical thinking about problem resolution. Frequent moves and job changes result from the fantasy, "I can start all over." These moves further disrupt their lives and those of their children. Their hope that "things" will make them feel better leaves them always short of money and pursued by creditors, causing additional crises in their lives and leaving little time for reciprocal relationship building with family members.

DENIED AFFECTS: NOTHING I DO IS FUN

In order to deal with disappointment, loss, poor self-image, and failure, affects connected with these feelings are strongly denied (Berkowitz 1977). Constant suppression of feelings occurs in order to ward off feelings of helplessness and self-hate. As a result, parents are unable to have fun. Often crises are precipitated when denial starts to fail; they can be alive only when things are happening ("Although my man may be mean, he's also exciting"). Pessimism and cynicism predominate their thinking ("Nothing will ever work").

SOCIALLY ISOLATED: I FEEL ALL ALONE

Adequate support systems are not available to assist multiproblem families. They cannot rely on help from their own parents, and when help is given, it comes with criticism ("Can't you manage your own problems?"). Consequently, parents of aggressive children are unable to break continuous contact with their children, and often they don't want to—their children are their only companions, albeit sometimes hated ones (Galdston 1971, 1981). The parents feel misunderstood and alone in the world (Polansky, Ammons, and Gaudin 1985). ("No one understands what it's like for me!") Many feel they lack a social support system to help them meet their own needs (Greene et al. 2002), and considering the attitude of their own parents and other relatives toward them, these feelings are not difficult to appreciate.

ELICITING THEIR COOPERATION

How do you ask parents who cannot nurture to do so? How can they be directed to solve conflicts if they have no capacity to manage disagreements? How can those who blame others for their child's failures be assisted when such blame falls just short of physical attacks on the therapist? But more important, how do you help parents who engage in the following thought process (Singer and Miller 1983)?

1. I'm an adult so I should be able to manage my life.
2. I can't, so I'm seeking help.
3. If I permit you to help, I'm confirming my incompetence to manage my life.
4. The only way to demonstrate my competence is to resist your help and advice.

In the next chapter, we attempt to answer this question.

9

Strengthening Relationships with Parents: Helping Parents to Be More Effective

This chapter presents eighteen therapeutic principles to apply when helping parents to put aside their struggles and to relate more appropriately to their children. Supporting parents to be more effective parents is viewed as a collaborative venture building on parental strengths. Unlike outpatient work, the therapist has to take advantage of "windows of opportunity" and, therefore, needs a flexible work schedule. Discussion focuses on the application of principles unique to each stage in the helping process.

In the last chapter, we described parents of children who don gorilla suits as having the following characteristics: unfulfilled dependency needs, poor self-concept, bonding failure, disturbed identity formation, cognitive immaturity, chaotic lifestyle, denied affects, and social isolation. Each characteristic needs to be addressed when engaging these parents in treatment designed to free children from enmeshment in their parents' problems. The child can then respond positively to his or her own treatment and education.

The problems of the parents of children in gorilla suits can easily overwhelm clinicians. Without guidelines to assist therapists in setting realistic goals for clients and for themselves, clinicians are subject to burnout, resulting in lowered self-concept, dehumanizing attitudes toward clients, and increasing inflexibility (Ecklwich and Brodsky 1980). Parents of gorilla-suit wearers rarely, if ever, give positive feedback to a therapist about their progress, a factor contributing heavily to therapist burnout (Kestenbaum 1984).

In addition to a general treatment philosophy, we present eighteen different principles to apply and some specific procedures to follow to optimize the engagement effort. The format is modeled after Stanton and Todd (1981), who set forth principles for engaging families of drug abusers. The material is divided into various content areas. Within each of these areas, one or more principles are set forth. These principles have emerged, after multiple failures, in one of New York State's first licensed day treatment programs for emotionally disturbed children—the Astor Day Treatment Center, first licensed by the New York State Department of Mental Health in 1976. Interagency discussions between day treatment staff and the staff of the Dutchess County Board of Cooperative Educational Services, which operates special education classes for aggressive children, suggest that these same principles can be applied in less intensive psychoeducational treatment settings.

STYLE OF INTERVENTION

First, clinicians, and those working with them, such as educators, crisis counselors, and child-care workers, need to be sensitive to the parents' needs for self-determination. These parents have had "advice" and direction from others all their lives. Their experiences of being in control are limited. A nonjudgmental, unintimidating attitude is essential in initial efforts to engage such parents. Thus engaging families in the treatment process requires sensitivity to the multicultural issues of class, race, gender, sexual orientation, geographical region, ethnicity, and nationality. Issues of economic oppression are major forces in the lives of many of these families. This brings us to our first principle.

Principle 1: Emphasize Collaboration

The parents are asked for their help in understanding the child and in helping school staff to attend to their child's needs. Feedback from parents indicates positive reception to helping efforts that are viewed as collaborative (Magura 1982). Ask for their help before and immediately on their child's enrollment in treatment. The closer the therapist's first contact with the parent is to the time of enrollment, the greater are the chances for involving the family, even when meaningful involvement may actually occur much later. Many children placed in special education classes for the seriously emotionally disturbed or behaviorally disordered are in crisis before placement. Once the placement has occurred, the family often feels the problem is resolved. Magical thinking prevails. If contact is delayed, the parent may think the agency is successfully handling the problem ("You're the experts. Why ask for my help now, after you've had my child for three months?").

Dr. Crenshaw participated in a consultation with Salvador Minuchin, an influential leader in the field of family therapy, and his associate Jorge Colapinto. Minuchin and Colapinto spent four days evaluating the Astor Home for Children, the residential treatment center where Dr. Crenshaw was employed. The two professionals interviewed the staff, the children, and the children's families with the goal of revising the center's intake, treatment planning, treatment services, and discharge planning to make them more "family friendly."

The first day of their four-day visit is the one Dr. Crenshaw will always remember. Minuchin met with management staff as the first activity of that day. He asked each of the administrators and department heads sitting around the table to tell him what they did and to explain the "nuts and bolts" of their part in the overall program. Minuchin listened patiently, asking only a few clarifying questions. When the remarks were finished, he became reflective and after a pregnant pause said, "Now you have told me all the ways you are competent. How about the ways you are incompetent?" Dr. Crenshaw looked around the table and saw that all his colleagues had the same surprised and bewildered expressions on their faces as he did. Minuchin explained, "If we are very competent, we don't really need the parents. We are the experts and can take care of everything. In that case the parents will not feel comfortable setting foot on our turf. They will simply leave their child in the care of the 'medical experts,' expecting the child to be 'fixed' and their role only showing up to take the child home." Minuchin explained further that it is not enough to think it "would be nice" to have the parents involved in the treatment program. Staff must convey that they desperately need the parents to be involved or else the staff will surely fail.

At the Astor Home for Children's Fiftieth Anniversary Conference, one of the most impressive presentations was a panel entitled "Building Ultimate Partnerships with Families." The panel was moderated by Joan DiBlasi and four parents who served as family advocates for the agency (Evans, Gonzales, Heringa, and Torres 2003). The key points made by panel members appear below:

- Put major emphasis on hope from day one!
- The therapist too often sees the family as the problem—we need to be invited in as collaborators!
- Parents who resist see agencies as a threat to take away their child!
- Listen to all family members—hear our stories.
- Give us lots of hope!

Principle 2: Be Accessible and Dependable

The therapist must pursue the child's parents regularly through home visits, phone calls, letters, and invitations to the treatment center or school (Green 1979; Stanton and Todd 1981; Wolfe 1984). Minuchin and Colapinto (1994) emphasize the difficulties in being a "family friendly" agency because most agencies and programs have procedures that are hierarchal. The contact must be personalized. Such parents are unforgettably impressed by particular incidents that appear beyond the call of duty. Birthday cards, get-well cards, and visits to parents when they are sick can help them feel that someone cares.

A rather dramatic example of personal involvement occurred when a child in treatment died and the child's therapist attended the child's funeral. A breakthrough in the family's resistance followed, and the therapist was able to help the parents deal with other problem children in the family. But don't expect gratitude for such efforts. Expressing grateful feelings interferes with the parents' need to express anger. This need will remain strong for some time. Otherwise, they will choke on their own rage.

INITIAL PHASES OF COUNSELING

Principle 3: Accept the Parents Where They Are

If the parents blame the clinician, the school, or the treatment center itself, these accusations should be taken seriously. The clinician shouldn't get defensive—such a response merely escalates parental anger or precipitates their flight. Listening to the parents is the first step. No one has listened long enough for them to feel understood and for their anger to subside. If they feel they have to keep saying it, then they feel they have not been heard or taken seriously. Take responsibility for their anger—"You're right; we should have been more careful with Jimmy. Maybe he was upset because we kept him from gym; perhaps that was a mistake on our part." Many of these parents have never heard anyone in their life acknowledge a mistake or apologize to them. Even if you didn't err, say you did. The same techniques that work with aggressive children work with aggressive parents (e.g., "I must have given you the wrong problems today, Bill; I'm sorry. Here, let's try these." [*Teacher substitutes easier problems for ones a child has angrily thrown to the floor.*] or "I'm sorry, Mrs. Jones, for the transportation problem; I must have relayed the wrong information to the transportation department.")

If the parents say the child is to blame, listen to that, too. Revenge begins early. The three-year-old whose father forgets to bring him a desired object from work retaliates by refusing to let his father carry him up to bed, stating, "I want Mommy to do it" (see Friedrich and Boriskin 1976 for a discussion of the role of the child in his or her own abuse). One mother laments that every night she makes a special dinner for her teenage son, turns back his bed, and lays out clean, ironed clothes for his next day. Yet her son repeatedly stays out late, often never comes home, and never acknowledges her for these efforts. Mike Tyson, once the heavyweight boxing champion of the world, talked of the degree of hatred and indifference between children and their mothers:

If a kid knew his mom was going out with money and didn't want to steal
it himself, he'd tell me where she was going, what time. I'd wait for her and
rob her, then we'd split it. (Smith 1988, p.74)

The parents' explanations for their child's problems should be accepted
and their difficulties in managing the child acknowledged—a first step toward
the parents' feeling understood. As Angyal (1965, p. 18) says, "We only come
to life by being understood and acknowledged by someone else. The worst
punishment is to be unnoticed by everyone."

A woman whose husband treated her like a child and who grew
up under extremely violent circumstances was enraged that her
preschool-aged son had been placed in day treatment following a
Child Protective Services report. She would call staff and rant and
rave to the secretary but would not speak to her assigned therapist.
The clinical director made a very low-key home visit, bringing
donuts and coffee. Following this visit, the mother called the clinic
and stated she was going to kill herself. The clinical director and
therapist talked to her on the phone together and then both went
out to the house. She was quite hostile, pacing and yelling that no
one ever listened to her. These episodes occurred about once per
month, so the therapist discussed premenstrual syndrome with her,
but she initially resisted the idea of a connection between her emotional outbursts to her son's behavior. The woman's husband came
to the center and requested counseling sessions with his wife, hoping that their sexual relationship would improve. At first they were
seen together, but because he simply rambled on, complaining about
his wife while she paced, they were seen separately. In these sessions,
the husband was helped to see that treating his wife more like a
woman and less like a child might help her to act more like a woman
and feel more sexual toward him. At the same time, the mother was
praised for getting help for her son, for ignoring her stepmother's
advice, and for being the strong one in her family.
  The mother was placed on medication, and when she got violent over the phone, she was told, "I'm not going to talk to you until you take your medication. Hang up and call back when you have
done so." Often during home visits, she became angry, went to the
door, opened it, and yelled, "You can leave now!" Nevertheless, her
child stopped hitting her. From material gathered during his therapy,
it became clear that the son actually liked his mother better than his
father, but "Since Dad hits Mom, I'll hit Mom to be like him."

The parents never went out because the mother feared their child might tie the babysitter to a chair. Consequently, the therapist trained a babysitter to sit with her son. The mother began to speak more calmly about her troubles; she spoke about viewing everything the child did as her fault. She focused more on her own family history and came to feel that she was the strong one in her family.

In residential treatment programs, Minuchin and Colapinto pointed out, if staff expects children and parents to meet high standards, the families can feel incompetent and inadequate. Seldom do families hear an SOS from residential treatment staff directed at them. It is a big mistake for professionals to present themselves as the experts who will take care of everything. Minuchin states strongly that parent visitation is an important component of the healing process and that under no circumstances should visitation be restricted because of a child's behavior, a decision made early in both Dr. Crenshaw's and Dr. Mordock's residential work (Mordock 2002a). An exception should be made only when a child cannot be transported safely to and from home because of unstable emotional functioning. Both of us can remember many agonizing treatment-team meetings focusing on this issue. Was it safe and prudent to transport a child who had been going through a turbulent period? Could the child and family safely manage the visit?" In most situations, it was decided that the risk was worth the child's need for family contact, and in most instances the family adequately coped with the visit.

Principle 4: Reduce Demands on Parents to Achieve Control of the Child

Achieving control of their child's aggression should be a long-term goal rather than a short-term goal for parents. Early efforts at control can result in stronger hostility toward the child. Behavior modification techniques suggested too soon can be used inappropriately on the child and then later rejected because "I've tried that already." In addition, their inappropriate use is experienced negatively by the child, who then escalates anger toward both the parents and the therapist, who the child knows instructed the parents to use the misused approach. Parental dissatisfaction contributes to children's aggression (Mammen, Kolko and Pilkonis 2003), and it isn't very satisfying being pressured to control the child. Instead, positive interactions should be encouraged, a topic we will discuss later in this chapter.

An important point must be made about boys growing up in single-parent families headed by the mother. Garbarino (1999) observes that many violent adolescent boys of single mothers felt that, when growing up, they needed to protect their moms against violent boyfriends and stepfathers. By the time these boys reach adolescence, the mothers have lost control over them. Garbarino also notes that, once these boys adopt the role of "protector of Mom," they will no longer relate to their mothers as authoritative figures and do not respect their mothers' attempts at discipline.

Principle 5: Avoid Initiating Family Interactions That Create Additional Conflict

Do not encourage expression of emotionally charged issues or conflict resolution between family members. Listen to their views about these conflicts, identify them as problems, but don't bring family members together in an effort to resolve these difficulties. Encouraging family members to interact around highly charged issues can release destructive behavior of intolerable proportions (Weitzman 1985). These families are not necessarily committed to working through conflict with one another for the sake of more adaptive family functioning. They are more likely seeking to regain a level of functioning they experienced in the past or to distance themselves from the problem. Bringing highly disorganized families together in traditional family therapy can result in hostile interchanges that continue long after a session has ended. Escalating the conflict further causes even more erosion of the equilibrium (Weitzman 1985). Few meet the criteria for inclusion in family therapy (see Mordock 1999a).

Planned and supervised child–parent interactions focusing on the parent-child relationship can be more beneficial than parent counseling (Ziegenhain et al. 2003), but we don't mean activities such as annual staff-family picnics, open houses, or awards days, which were designed for other purposes. Parents can be transported to the center to engage in art and craft projects, musical events, rhythmic activities, or simple table games, activities that they might later engage in at their own homes and that can enhance their relationships.

A colleague of Dr. Mordock developed a series of storytelling and puppet-play activities for families with a parent in addiction recovery (Cwiakala and Mordock 1997). Children were transported from foster homes, kinship homes, group homes, and children's institutions to the drug rehabilitation center where their parents were enrolled. Through the metaphor of play, the children and their parents processed issues related to substance abuse in a nonjudgmental and entertaining manner that made the parents feel closer to their children. The material was also used to structure psychoeducational groups for young children with a parent in addiction recovery (Cwiakala and Mordock 1996).

Principle 6: Respect Their Current Methods of
Maintaining Psychological Equilibrium

If the parent blames the child, the clinician can allow it but can also emphasize that it takes at least two to make a problem and at least two to solve it. Aggressive children are expert at eliciting anger from others and can keep a family in turmoil at the same time that they keep it connected (Kent and Pepler 2002). Emphasize this fact. Use a symptom-oriented approach and help organize the parents or other family members around the child's symptoms. Pittman (1982) remarks, "Therapists know better than to side with the battered child, since the battering parent already resents the love and sympathy given the child" (p. 366). Both the parents and the child are unduly sensitive to criticism. Because the child has internalized destructive aspects of the parent's personality, the child experiences both rage at family members and loyalty toward them. If the child feels staff members are blaming parents, the child is likely to try to defend the parents. Weitzman (1985) presents the case of a nine-year-old boy who set a therapist's car on fire because the boy thought his treatment team was too critical of his depressed parent. The children do not merely react to a distressed family system; they act on the system as well, sometimes destructively, even after parents start improving.

> A thirteen-year-old boy in special education lives with his stepfather and his mother. His father died of a stroke related to alcohol, and his mother subsequently married the father's brother. The boy remains at home, but his older sister goes back and forth between home and the paternal grandmother's house. Although the mother refuses to see the therapist either individually or in counseling sessions with her son, the boy talks more about his problems with his stepfather/uncle than about problems with his mother A home visit with the stepfather reveals that the boy is always on the phone with his sister or his girlfriend. The stepfather doesn't approve of the girlfriend because she is enrolled in another day treatment center. The stepfather threatens to throw the boy out and refuses to let him work to earn money for his own phone because he might get into trouble. The therapist takes the tack that the stepfather is right—that the child will probably lose any job he takes—because in the clinician's experience, most youths like the stepson fail in several jobs before they learn responsibility. He will also probably have several undesirable girlfriends before he settles down, but how will he learn if his stepfather won't give him a chance? This approach eventually leads to the stepfather's increased willingness to examine his own role in the child's behaviors.

Principle 7: Use Life Cycle Explanations to Reduce Self-Blame

Every family experiences stress at various stages in family life. Explain that their troubles result from these normal stresses. "It's no wonder that you have these problems, considering your son's approaching adolescence." "Your unemployment makes things difficult." "You never learned how to parent from your parents." "You expect too much from yourself at this time in your life." "Considering the adversity you have faced, you've done surpassingly well."

> A child enrolled in a Head Start program and was referred to day treatment primarily because the mother had violently resisted the parent advocate's outreach efforts. In addition, she would come to the Head Start center and scream at the staff. After enrollment, she screamed at day treatment staff and at the school bus driver if he came late. She called the teacher and yelled about the condition of her son when he came home. The therapist visited her home and let her ventilate her anger at staff without defending those charged. The mother removed her child from school, and after receiving a letter from the therapist simply stating that staff missed her son and hoped he would be back soon, she returned him to school. She also began to call the therapist to relay her anxiety about her own behavior toward her son. She began to talk about her family, and the therapist used this knowledge to explain reasons for her extreme reactions in terms of her life experiences. With the therapist's taking away some of her self-blame, she began to have less need to blame others around her and to vent anger at her son.

Minuchin and Colapinto, in the consultation sessions described earlier, underscored that the art of therapy includes the ability to convey to the family the attitude that they are responsible for the child's healing. The therapist must convince the parents that they are the therapist's partners in the treatment process without leaving them feeling responsible or blamed for pathology. This seems to be an art form that only the most skilled clinicians are able to accomplish. Minuchin and Colapinto also observed that if the staff members like a child, they will start to see the child as a victim to be protected from the family, and the family needs protection by the clinician from the staff's "adoption fantasies."

Principle 8: Confront the Unrealistic Self-Ideal

The cultural myths that unrealistically guide much of the parents' thinking, as well as the unrealistic expectations of their own parents, need to be thoroughly addressed. Their unrealistic beliefs about what their child "should" be doing and what they, as parents, "should" be accomplishing must be confronted gently. The "unrealistic self-ideal" contributes to feelings of failure, and the accomplishment of more realistic goals can contribute to an enhanced self-image. A parent can be given a simple task to do with the child, one that the therapist has already accomplished, such as playing a board game with the child, and its successful completion can be a starting point for improved parent-child relations.

Principle 9: Acknowledge Their Good Parenting Efforts

Even abusing parents have moments when they relate positively to their children or support their children some way. Therapists need to look for these moments and call them to the parents' attention: "It was a good parental decision to allow Jack to come to school here" or "You presented your views of Bobby well to members of the Committee on Special Education," for instance. Such comments help to build parents' feelings of self-confidence. Parents should be acknowledged for overcoming great odds. Their self-contempt and periodic self-denigration keep them locked in guilt feelings (feelings that are hidden because their expression is masked by anger). Praising parents' good efforts, no matter how small, helps to uncover buried assets and increase self-esteem. The parents can discover that they are seen, with all their shortcomings, as likable, worthwhile human beings.

Parents need help to remember the times when they were better parents. Efforts should be made to get them in touch with past memories of success. Parents also need to get in touch with the "Crucial Cs"—to connect, to feel capable, to feel as if I count, and to have courage (Shifron and Bettner 2003). Such efforts take a long time to bear fruit. Many individuals with low self-esteem turn any evidence of self-worth into the opposite because their self-contempt is so fundamental. Depression and low self-esteem go hand in hand. Unfortunately, when depression lifts, self-esteem can still remain low (McGrath and Repetti 2002).

During their consultation, Minuchin and Colapinto stressed to agency staff, "If you're a diagnostic center, you need to document pathology. If you are a change center, you need to prioritize strengths. It is a question of mind-set." The focus of family work in residential centers needs to be on what has to change for the child to return home. Minuchin and Colapinto urged residential treatment staff not to cling to a romantic view of families. Children will not return to conflict-free families. The two consultants challenged staff to consider whether the agency is an adoptive or a fostering agency. If fostering, the agency is a transitional one, and staff need to be satisfied with a partial job.

Staff members in residential treatment centers need to focus on finding the level of functioning that the family can capably handle and make sure that this standard is not surpassed, or else staff will never feel the family is ready for the child's return.

Principle 10: Encourage Self-Love and New Forms of Gratification

Because adequate self-esteem cannot be obtained in the daily lives of most parents of aggressive children, self-love must be developed and encouraged in practical ways. Newman and Martino (1973), for example, discussing their treatment of a fragile mother, describe a strategic point in treatment. They suggested that the woman take a short walk and buy herself something whenever she felt overcome with guilt and anxiety. She found this to be a meaningful way to give to herself at difficult moments. Many low-income families, especially single-parent families, lead a relatively sparse life devoid of interesting, fulfilling, and rewarding activities and social connections. Whenever the therapist can encourage the parent to join a support group, pursue a hobby, or cultivate a neglected friendship, it will benefit not only the parent but their children as well. If their gas tank is not always on empty, they will have more to give and share with their children.

MIDDLE-PHASE STRATEGIES

In the middle phases of treatment, the clinician becomes a source for the parenting the mother or father never experienced. A client's fear of intimacy is proportionate to the intimacy allowed with his or her own inner feelings and the feelings of intimacy experienced in prior relationships. Because many parents have been abandoned in past intimate relationships, increased feelings of intimacy in the therapeutic relationship become a threat to that relationship. Intimacy fears, combined with conflicts over primitive needs for nurturing, intensify the parents' struggles with their wish for gratification, their expectation of rejection, and their guilt over their relationships with their own parents. They will test the therapist and agency staff in ways designed to provoke rejection and resolve these conflicts. They will break appointments, make unreasonable demands, and withdraw from treatment, leading to the next principle.

Principle 11: Set Firm Limits on Their Behavior

Parents can sometimes be as demanding and belligerent as their children and need firm limits placed on their behavior, such as "I will talk to you when you calm down and stop shouting; call me back when you're calm." Such limits should be set only after a relationship has been established and the parent trusts that you are setting these limits for his or her own good ("I can't really understand you when you shout so loudly").

A single mother of a boy who had been in a day treatment program for more than three years resisted involvement with the first worker assigned because she fantasized that the worker, who lived in the same apartment complex as she did, told the neighbors about her problems. She also ignored the second worker's calls and letters. She insisted for three years that her son did not belong in the center. Her view was that "helpers" end up hurting you nine out of ten times. Her ex-husband constantly blamed the boy for the divorce ("I would have stayed with your mother if you weren't so bad"). In response to staff pressures, the boy was seen up to five times per week in individual therapy, but he continually acted out his anger toward his father by raging against the counselor. During this period, the educational staff felt that the therapist was not setting appropriate limits.

The therapist eventually confronted the mother, saying "We can't help your child until you come in and assist us to create consistency." During a conversation in the parking lot, the counselor stated, "I'm seeing your son five times a week, and you can't even come in once a month to assist me—you're letting us down." She became enraged and vented about all her responsibilities. The therapist responded, "Yes, it's one more thing in an impossible schedule, but we still need you to do it." She failed to respond. She was then called to a school meeting for a discussion of residential placement for her son. She cried about losing him but could see the rationale for the recommendation. Following the meeting, the therapist gave her his home phone number and told her to call him about her thoughts. She called him over the weekend and admitted her past refusal to cooperate. The therapist then drafted a written contract requiring her to make eight out of ten weekly sessions and daily phone contact; then the recommendation for residential placement would be tabled.

The son made immediate improvements following his mother's initial visits. When she ran herself down and criticized her fat body, she was helped to follow through on her good ideas in spite of her self-view as a bad parent. She decided to resign from her evening job so that she could spend more time with her son. The worker assisted her in obtaining social security income benefits and encouraged her to work a few hours "off the books" to supplement the benefits. One technique used by the therapist during sessions was speaking directly to different parts of the mother's self: "Let's talk to the bad mommy; let's explore and honor that part of yourself, remembering that you don't have to be that part but simply talk to it."

Principle 12: Change the Position of the Husband-Father in the Family

Numerous writers have stressed the importance of involving fathers in family treatment. Children who interact positively with fathers display less hyperactivity (Keown and Woodward 2002), less bullying (Flour and Budman 2003), and less involvement with deviant peers (Werner and Sibereison 2003). Yet surveys of clinicians reveal that most rarely involve fathers in their treatment efforts, even when treating relatively well-to-do families (Duhig, Phares, and Birkeland 2002). Engaging fathers in treatment is particularly difficult for inexperienced therapists (Shapiro and Budman 1973). L'Abate (1975) has suggested a number of ways to involve resistant fathers. In general, ignore statements by the mother that he won't let you see him; call him directly (Stanton and Todd 1981). Once he is involved, the chief task is to help him build bridges between the competent areas of his life, usually his work, but also his hobbies and interests, and his family functioning. Many of his work-related competencies include interpersonal, organizational, and problem-solving skills, which are in contrast to his inability to operate effectively as a husband and father within his family. The bridges that need to be built are those that translate work skills into his home life and help the family to accept these skills into their life (Tonti 1982).

Principle 13: Examine Biological Factors

While family and individual difficulties abound, many aggressive children also have subtle neurological problems, hyperactivity, mood disorders, temperamental difficulties (sometimes labeled "strong-willed child" or "mother killer," among other things), and mental illnesses. Although it may be difficult to determine which came first, the "chicken or the egg," we take the position, for treatment purposes, that the child contributes to the problem as child attributes can provoke or elicit harsh child-rearing practices (Shaw and Bell 1993). In addition, the presence of neurological or temperamental problems makes impulse control more difficult and takes away from the parent some of the blame for the child's difficulties. The parent may resist a neurological examination of the child for fear the child may be considered "crazy." Consequently, the parent will need education and training about subtle neurological problems, how they affect a child's behavior, and how discipline needs to be modified to cope with them.

A mother who saw nothing positive about her son and misused behavior modification suggestions made by the therapist eventually was reported to Child Protective Services (CPS) by the therapist for not fixing the boy meals and for parading around the house nude in an alcoholic stupor. After allowing her to vent anger about the report, the clinician insisted that the boy have a neurological examination (he hadn't had a physical examination in eight years). Because of the boy's disjointed talk and inability to follow his thoughts through to conclusions, the therapist thought he might be neurologically impaired. Unless such an exam were given, the child would be referred to a residential school. After the examination, wherein the physician identified minimal neurological problems and placed the child on Dexedrine, the mother admitted in relief that for years she had avoided taking her son to any doctors for fear that he would be found "crazy" like his father. The medication and the relief of the mother's fears resulted in an improvement in the child's impulse control. The mother, for the first time, began to see some positive qualities in her son. She remembered that he had once taken care of a stray dog and that she had bought him a pet. Later, she actually thanked the therapist for forcing her to deal with problems by reporting her to CPS and insisting on the neurological evaluation.

THE LATER PHASES

In this phase, parents have become more open about their backgrounds and more dependent on the therapist for assistance. At this time, the therapist should focus discussions on the parents' relationships with their own parents (Hunter and Kilstrom 1979).

Principle 14: Help Parents Sort Out Intergenerational Patterns and Conflicts

Parents need help to see their own parents' strengths and weaknesses and how the relationship with them resulted in current problems. They need to recognize their own parents' limitations and ways to improve relations with them. Parents can talk to their own parents using the "empty chair" technique. In fact, one study suggests that individuals who fully express unmet interpersonal needs to a significant other in the "empty chair" had treatment outcomes relatively independent from the treatment alliance formed with the therapist (Greenberg and Malcolm 2002). If the grandparents are still alive, the therapist can help the parent to move from empty-chair exercises to forgiving the grandparents for their transgressions. These exercises can occur only after the parents have developed a secure attachment to the child's therapist. Otherwise, parents may have more negative recollections of their own parents' caregiving (Woodhouse et al., 2003). Attachment research has demonstrated that memory for attachment-related content varies by attachment style (Crowell et al. 1996; Mikulincer and Orbach 1995).

In addition, studies suggest that over time, individuals whose original perceptions of their parental attachments, called attachment-related representations, modify their perceptions of parental interactions in keeping with their original parental images (Brook and Cassidy 2003). In other words, individuals who originally perceive their interactions with parents as negative will, over time, come to see the positive interactions they had with them more negatively. These individuals need to overcome this tendency in order to develop more positive relations with their parents, and parents of gorilla-suit wearers in particular need to do so to diminish the criticism they receive from their own parents and to break the cycle of generational abuse (Serbin and Karp 2003; Thornberry, Freeman-Gallant, and Lizotte 2003). Once the parent has begun to sort out the intergenerational patterns of conflict and distortion, education in basic parenting can begin. During such discussions, feelings previously experienced as not belonging to the self begin to be owned by the parent. Current emotions begin to be experienced in terms of attachments to past emotions, often referred to as "earlier similars" (Van Ornum and Mordock 1990).

Principle 15: Gradually Turn Over Executive Powers to the Parents

Parents need help to become firm with their children without being mean. Their concrete disciplinary efforts should be reviewed in detail so the clinician can see where they can improve. Teaching them approved and safe physical holding techniques can also be helpful. They should also be supported to make decisions about their child. Often parents defer to the "experts," but they need to be empowered as "experts" when it comes to making decisions about what is good for their child.

> The mother of a seven-year-old boy in day treatment, abandoned by her abusing husband, became completely dependent on her son, saying "There is no one in life but him." She would not admit that he

was out of control. Although she would call the school to say hello and give address changes, she would not commit to an appointment for thirteen months. She finally came to the center when her son was too disruptive to ride the school bus home. She was so distraught, however, that the clinical director arranged for her and her son to be admitted to a private psychiatric hospital in the local area. In the car on the way to the hospital, she admitted that she couldn't be away from her son. She was afraid of being alone, being abandoned, and facing failure as a person.

The therapist kept in contact with them in the hospital. Following their discharge (after a one-week stay), the mother started coming in for treatment. She has now taken responsibility for doing things on her own. She took her son for an intake assessment at the agency's residential program, something she wanted to do by herself. (Residential staff were quite critical that the therapist did not accompany her for the intake and were skeptical when informed that day treatment staff had encouraged such behavior; interagency rivalry exists even in the best of agencies!) Later she took her son to a psychiatric hospital where he was admitted and is currently receiving care.

Principle 16: Be Patient and Wait for a Trigger Event

Parents can resist involvement for long periods. Frequently a crisis will facilitate their cooperation. For example, a father who had resisted treatment efforts for several years sought help from school staff when his wife absconded with his children, and he was awarded custody on their return. He had never had to parent and admitted the need for help.

> Dr. Mordock, annoyed by a mother's angry outburst at a teacher, after which she dragged her child out of school and into her car, trailed her to the parking lot, stood in front of her car, and yelled to her, "Your temper is as bad as mine, but we care about James no matter what you think, and we'd care about you, too, if you let us. You can take him home now, but I expect to see both of you in my office first thing in the morning." The mother didn't appear, but James did, which was not the usual pattern as she had always kept him home for days after such actions, claiming she was going to "put him in another school." But she never again came to the school to remove him when angry with either him or us. She never sought help, at least from us, but she left us alone to do our job with James without any further interruptions.

On some occasions, progress might follow a parent's own willingness to "break the silence" about the parent's own past or present abuse. Parents' willingness to speak openly about the violent events in their own lives can reduce their sense of isolation, allowing them to begin their own healing and to relate more positively to their children. When a parent suddenly reveals a past trauma, therapists should respond in the same empathic manner as they respond to a traumatized child. The parent needs to tell the trauma story, and the therapist needs to listen. The revealing parent needs constancy, and the therapist needs to stay available. The parent needs to share, and the therapist needs to receive. The parent needs to describe the evil experienced, and the therapist must convey empathy and belief (Kinzie 2001). In short, the therapist must serve as a witness to the parent's own abuse and must be a container of the unnameable horror (LaMothe 2001). If spouse abuse is ongoing, the therapist must help the mother develop a plan of action to avoid the abuse. If this means leaving home and going to a battered women's shelter, then the therapist should support this action but not berate the mother should she decide to return home.

Much of what is referred to as resistance, lack of cooperation, or angry lashing out is a reflection of the family's sense of powerlessness and the lack of respect they have felt in their interactions with the staff of mental health, probation, and social service agencies. They feel that no one is interested in their stories or in appreciating the hardship of their lives. They feel humiliated and devalued when seeking help from community agencies, particularly in a society that values rugged individualism.

Dr. Crenshaw remembers a mother who initially refused to come to treatment-team meetings or to participate in family therapy sessions when her son was placed in residential treatment. When staff finally listened to her story, it all made perfect sense. She had gone to the local hospital because her son had become violent and was acting dangerously. After he was seen in the emergency room, she was told that hospital staff was placing him in a diagnostic center. She strongly objected, pleading that she simply was seeking help to control her son's behavior. The very reason she sought help was the reason hospital staff gave for removing her son from her home: "You are unable to control your son." After evaluation at the shelter, he was placed in the foster care system, and she had to temporarily surrender his custody to the commissioner of Social Services in order for him to receive help. Two years later, after a series of failures in foster family homes, he was placed in residential treatment. She had been fighting to get him back ever since his first placement.

Staff now understood her lack of trust, rage, and sense of powerlessness, as well as her justified view that no one ever listened to her. Staff did a lot of listening and, as a result, she shared more and more about her extremely difficult and painful life. It was clear that she loved her son and wanted him back with her. She started coming to treatment-team meetings and participating in family therapy. The team social worker spent considerable time in her home when her son returned for visits, coaching her on setting firm and clear limits and following through with realistic consequences. This story had a happy ending. After ten months in the residential program, and after the staff's vigorous advocating on the mother's behalf with Social Services, the boy was returned to his mother, with whom he remains to this day.

Principle 17: Be Prepared to Use Power Tactics to Reduce Ambivalence

Parents can reach a point at which their ambivalence is so strong as to block further progress, and the therapist and program staff may have to take a firm stand in order to overcome it, saying in effect, "Our only alternative is residential treatment" or "We can't continue to work with your child without your help. We are recommending discharge." The next case vignette illustrates this principle. It also illustrates that treatment includes helping parents find more appropriate treatment, at least at a given point in time.

> A nine-year-old boy, previously in public school classes for disturbed children, was enrolled in a day treatment center because of severe temper tantrums and ritualistic and stereotyped patterns of behavior. If he couldn't do his school work in the time period he wanted, he would throw temper tantrums for one hour or more. He was adopted, primarily because of his father's wishes for a child, and then the father died. His mother refused to come to the center to participate in her son's treatment, claiming that she was an old lady and didn't have a car. During the boy's first year in day treatment, she was seen on only two home visits. During this period, the boy refused to talk during his therapy sessions. In the classroom, his own need to establish a routine resulted in no peer interactions. The teaching staff thought he belonged in a psychiatric hospital. The mother said, "Why do you people want him out?" Staff were instructed not to discuss alternative care because the mother could not resolve her own ambivalence as long as she could fight our wishes.
>
> Eventually, the mother admitted that she couldn't handle the child at home either—particularly his fighting with his brother. The therapist asked for her help in finding a placement for him—a collaborative effort with a common goal of finding a hospital for him. The mother saw an advertisement in the newspaper for a private out-of-state hospital; she called the hospital, and the therapist pre-

pared an intake packet for the hospital admission team. The admission team reported that they could admit him in four to eight weeks, but their experience with New York state was that Medicaid would not pay for out-of-state placements. When the bed became available, the therapist came in on Sunday and called a number of New York state hospitals, taking the name of each admissions worker when the worker stated they had no vacancies. On Monday, he read the list of rejections to Medicaid officials and also told them of the opening at the out-of-state hospital. They approved the placement.

The therapist and another staff member drove to the hospital, met the mother and child there, and participated with her in the hospital intake process. After the hospital staff agreed to accept the child, contingent on the mother's coming for joint therapy sessions, she tried to back out, saying she couldn't get there or afford a motel. They offered her housing and submitted that she either come to the therapy sessions or take her son home. That ultimatum resulted in her agreement. Suddenly a mother who couldn't come into the day treatment center for sessions could take a train to another city and then transfer to a second train to the hospital.

After the child had been evaluated at the hospital for a month and placed on Thorazine, a tense discharge meeting took place at the hospital. The meeting was tense because the mother's reactions to the hospital's discharge recommendations were unpredictable. The therapist and the child's teacher were both in attendance. Hospital staff advised the therapist to discharge the boy from the day treatment program he had attended before hospitalization because the mother wouldn't come in for regular sessions. The mother agreed to attend sessions regularly, and the therapist arranged for a cab to bring her for weekly sessions. The cab company received payment from Medicaid. Sessions were divided between the therapist and the mother talking about situations the child felt were unfair and the mother and son playing together with the counselor. When the boy felt angry at home, he was instructed to call the therapist at home and discuss his problem. If he felt bad, he was asked what he could do for his mom in order to be forgiven.

At home, he was placed on three different point systems, but often he felt double-crossed by his mother when she failed to adhere to a system. The mother was instructed to step back and analyze what she could do instead of digging right in to solve a problem. Eventually, however, both mother and son regressed to horrible

physical fights with one another, and they both came to the therapist expressing their desires to separate until they could learn to get
along together. Residential treatment was jointly sought, with the
staff assisting them in their search efforts.

Principle 18: Set Realistic Goals Based on a
Thorough Ongoing Family Assessment

A number of families respond to the developmentally oriented, ego-supported
efforts just reviewed with less progress than hoped for. Consequently, families
must be periodically assessed in terms of three levels of goal attainability
(Terkelsen 1980). The highest level is full restoration. At this level, the family
recaptures its capacity to promote the need attainment of all its members. The
second level is supplementation. At this level, the family is not expected to at-
tain sufficiency in and of itself. The treatment plan deliberately includes creation of some more or less permanent attachment between the family and an
external helping agent (Lamb 1980). The family becomes semiautonomous;
involvement in self-help support groups or continual support by center staff
will always be required to preserve family stability.

The lowest level is replacement. Too much is missing in the family, resulting in the family's needing extensive supplementation to function adequately. One or more of its members will require periodic placement in foster
homes, group homes, or other institutions. These supplemental services should
be used in the context of the relationship established with the parent and with
awareness of the parent's needs for control. Although some staff may view the
use of such facilities as treatment failure, their use can create some family stability and enable the parent to better parent younger children. The parent
should participate in finding, planning, and using these services. Such planning
helps to promote the parent's growth, the ability to cope more effectively, and
the parent's self-esteem. Providing concrete services without parent participation only encourages strong regressive tendencies, and only temporary and
sporadic relief occurs (Newman and Martino 1973).

As illustrated in several of the case vignettes, the principles should be
applied even when referring a child to a more restrictive setting. Such settings clearly have a place in restoring and maintaining a family's stability.
Placing a child in one can be a step in successful treatment of the child.
Follow-up of studies of children in residential treatment revealed that those
provided ongoing care in agency-operated programs until their young adult
years showed more positive changes than those returned to one or both of
their biological parents (Prentice-Dunn, Wilson, and Lyman 1981; Mordock
1978).

EFFORTS TO CHANGE DISCIPLINARY PRACTICES

As we emphasize in chapter 2, numerous studies have provided reliable evidence that poor parental management strategies (such as lack of supervision and monitoring and harsh and inconsistent discipline) are related to troublesome child behavior. Consequently, therapists in children's mental health settings, even if seeing the child in play therapy, direct some efforts at helping parents to change disciplinary strategies with noncompliant children. If the child has been placed in foster care following abuse, the family court may require the parents to seek mental health treatment. Usually, clinicians focus on helping such parents to replace inappropriate disciplinary practices with appropriate ones. In fact, local departments of social services often pressure mental health clinics to offer "group child management classes" for abusive parents. Such groups often help relatively organized and well-structured families whose children, because of developmental problems such as mental retardation, speech and language delays, or hyperactivity, need special guidance.

Unfortunately, such groups rarely work for disorganized and unstructured families, many of which are led by single mothers. In addition, both operant conditioning studies, including those done at the Oregon Social Learning Center (Patterson, Reid, and Dishion 1992), and real-world experiences have demonstrated that when regularly scheduled reinforcers are withdrawn, children will rapidly increase the previously reinforced behavior in an effort to obtain the expected reinforcer.

This well-known phenomenon has led clinicians, as part of informed consent procedures, to alert parents that their child can get worse before getting better. Yet some clinicians, rarely having lived with a disturbed child in a marginally functioning family, fail to realize the stress the child's temporarily regressed behavior can cause when new disciplinary practices are tried that seem to backfire. From the work of Constantine (1987), Patterson (1983), and Patterson and Forgatch (1990), it would be predicted that the temporary escalation of misbehavior will elevate the level of stress a parent experiences, increase the parent's irritability, and thereby increase the parent's negative interaction with the child and cause further disengagement of the already undercontrolling parent. The family's precarious equilibrium remains shaky, and the child becomes worse; temporary now becomes permanent.

As stress increases, families are more likely to do more of what is already familiar to them. Consequently, the family can respond to the child's increased noncompliance by tightening their controls. The child can then display even more resistance, followed by the family's blaming the therapist for disrupting their precarious control over their child and withdrawing the child from treatment. While some families can reinstate the proper degree of control over their child, others cannot, and the child runs away or gets into more trouble in the school or community. The latter situation sometimes happens with disabled youth in the United States who receive counseling mandated by an Individual Education Plan (IEP) in the schools. Parents cannot immediately withdraw a child from such programs (a parent right under informed consent procedures in licensed clinics). The problem of the parent's withdrawing a child can be compounded in undersocialized children because their developing relationship with the therapist can exacerbate their relationship difficulties with a parent.

A second problem can occur when training parents to discipline differently. When problems are conceptualized as resulting from inappropriate parental practices, parents can perceive therapists as blaming and become discouraged even when the "blame" is subtle and couched in positive terms. Because many parents of abused children lack both sufficient ego strength and affective energy to challenge the therapist, their immediate response can be either stopping "wrong" but marginally effective practices or escalating practices suggested by the therapist. Such rapid changes in discipline can result in escalation of the child's symptoms. For example,

> A highly oppositional boy, who also seemed quite depressed, lived with his father and stepmother. His father, a military man, was very authoritarian, and his stepmother thought the child was evil. The boy longed for his real mother, whom he rarely saw, who was a substance abuser, and who was frequently in and out of jail. In addition to providing play therapy for the child, the therapist encouraged the stepmother and father to "catch the child doing something right" and to encourage him to play with peers instead of exposing him to endless groundings and other harsh punishments. Unfortunately, the boy saw the therapist's actions as blaming the parents, as did the parents, who began to withhold therapy whenever the boy was "bad." Eventually, his "badness" increased and they dropped out of treatment.

CONCLUSION

Children who put on gorilla suits awaken parents' own childhood conflicts, and these conflicts often interfere with their child-rearing efforts. The children threaten the parents' hopes and their trust in the future and become symbols of the parents' failure as parents. By the time they take their child for treatment, the problems have escalated to the point that small changes can go unnoticed (the space for new growth created by cutting a few trees from a dense forest is easily missed). Some parents fear that the child's progress will make them look bad as parents. They fear the therapist will discover major mistakes they made earlier in the child's life or mistakes they are currently making. The therapist's awareness of these fears and his or her empathy for the parents must precede efforts to help parents understand their child's needs. Support for overwhelmed parents can result in renewed support for their child.

To practice the principles listed above, clinicians must be permitted considerable flexibility in selecting working hours. Supervisors must remain available to help staff deal with the constant onslaught of angry feelings from parents in initial phases of treatment and the limit-testing behaviors in the middle phases. Staff members often respond to angry client behaviors with their own anger, withdrawal, boredom, compulsive activity (Kohut 1982), and, perhaps more crucial, their own feelings of abandonment (Kenemore and Peterson 1987). Therapists must be continually supported by supervisors who assist them in setting realistic goals and who arbitrate differences of opinion that occur between the clinical, child-care, and educational staff so that staff members representing each discipline feel supported and encouraged for their efforts.

10

Strengthening Relationships with Direct-Care and Instructional Staff

Direct-care staff, such as child-care workers, recreational staff, and teachers, are the backbone of special education, day, and residential treatment programs, programs largely populated by fawns in gorilla suits. If the treatment philosophy and mission adopted by administrators and clinicians are not accepted with conviction by the key "front-line" staff, the program not only becomes nontherapeutic but replicates the dysfunctional splits that many of these children have experienced in their original families. This chapter focuses on ways to include child-care and teaching staff in the therapeutic mission of the program and to value their contributions to the treatment process.

$\mathscr{B}$ecause the therapist attempts to understand the child and convey this understanding to others, the child is helped to both maintain and strengthen his relationships with important caregivers. These adults can be his natural parents, teachers, foster parents, or staff in group care settings. The therapist serves as the child's advocate. No matter how hard the child tries to hide his or her vulnerabilities in group situations, where the child is at the mercy of others, eventually the vulnerabilities are revealed in therapy. It is much easier to like and to enjoy children when one is in touch with their vulnerabilities than when they are disrupting a family, a classroom, or a recreational activity.

Caregivers almost always define a child's problems as misbehavior: anxiety attacks are defined as manipulations, not eating is viewed as not minding, and so on. The therapist's effort to get others to think about the child's behaviors differently, even though the plea often seems to fall on deaf ears, helps the child to form attachments with significant others. In return, these developing attachments motivate caregivers and teachers to continue struggling to help the child. Educating children in gorilla suits is not easy, and most workers need help and support from the child's therapist.

The abuse and trauma experienced by children in gorilla suits overwhelm them with anxiety. Those sent from foster family to foster family, or who have experienced parental death, divorce, or abandonment without adequate support, can deal with their losses and helplessness by becoming aggressive, needing to feel powerful to cope with their vulnerability and aloneness. And their aggression is usually responded to in kind. Over the years, the children internalize a view of adults as policemen/aggressors rather than as protectors/providers. They anticipate blame, accusation, and punishment and forestall them by extreme noncompliance when younger and by violent threats when older. To be controlled by others is to be humiliated. In response, they weave a protective cocoon, put on gorilla suits, and hide behind brick walls of detachment, all of which estrange them from others and halt their developmental advancement.

We have repeatedly made the point that, in the absence of nurturance, protection, and prideful experiences of pleasing and being pleased, children feel a sense of rage characteristic of earlier phases of their development. They scream and flail like two-year-olds, and they can be dangerous when doing so. Their rage also blocks the development of a mature conscience. Fear of punishment does not deter their misbehavior, and they are not easily socialized. Aggression is readily displaced onto others. When they hurt another, they show no sign of remorse, concern, or empathy with the victim since they do not expect like responses from others when they are hurt. Their fantasy is limited to the violent kind. Batman, Superman, and the Hulk are their models.

To progress developmentally, the children require a highly structured and controlled environment, provided by ensuring that certain needs are met that will stimulate growth. In chapter 12 we discuss the development of a therapeutic milieu for those placed in day or residential treatment centers, and in chapter 11 we discuss training staff to support each child's existing defenses while helping the child to acquire more adaptive ones. In this chapter we discuss more general needs.

More than fifty years ago, David Beres (1952) delineated the therapeutic needs of children who never mastered early developmental tasks. Their aggression must be treated by (1) promoting a stronger ego, one with more mature defenses against anxiety and with more adaptive capabilities; (2) removing sadomasochistic disturbances and promoting sublimation of drives; (3) promoting identification with positive caregivers; and (4) minimizing external factors that promote frustration. More recently, Gruber (1987) emphasized that treatment should concentrate on helping gorilla-suit wearers find positive inner images (locating the good object); helping them with differentiation; supporting their ego and its further development; promoting internalization of the therapist as an object; reconstructing their early experiences, particularly pre-verbal experiences; and helping them verbalize instead of act.

In our work with children wearing gorilla suits, we emphasize that the children need to have ten basic needs met in order to achieve emotional growth:

1. The need for dependable relationships that meet the child's need for nurturance and acceptance
2. The need to be protected and rescued from situations in which they feel frightened
3. The need to avoid experiences involving loss of face
4. The need for clear, consistent, and well-defined limits
5. The need to have punishments limited
6. The need to have prohibitions made predictable
7. The need to talk about frustrations
8. The need for a broadened horizon of "do's"
9. The need for recognition of strengths
10. The need to expand concrete skills

CREATING DEPENDABLE RELATIONSHIPS WITH OTHERS

The therapist's willingness to listen to others' frustrations with and complaints about the child helps draw off some of the counteraggression that it is natural to feel toward extremely noncompliant children but which further contributes to their loss of face and to escalating their aggression. All adults are influenced by the child as much as the child is influenced by them. Adults will be friendly toward friendly children, angry toward hostile children, and irritated by irritating children. The opportunity for caregivers to discuss the child with an empathetic adult can serve to rekindle their interest in the child. But since the therapist represents the child in their eyes during such interchanges, the therapist shouldn't be surprised if anger felt toward the child is displaced onto the therapist. Just remember, it is better these angry feelings get expressed toward the therapist than toward the child.

A follow-up study of a large group of emotionally disturbed children treated in the residential center with which both of us were affiliated reveals that many of the children who lived with their natural families following discharge were no longer enrolled in school. In contrast, those who, at the time of the follow-up study, were discharged to foster or group homes were still in school (Mordock 1978). We believe that the children in foster and group homes remained in school because they had a social worker assigned to them who went to the school to advocate for the child each time the child was threatened with suspension. Nevertheless, clinicians shouldn't be surprised when suggestions made to teachers are not always appreciated.

A somewhat intellectually limited preteen in a special class for behaviorally disordered youth developed a strong attachment to the teacher's aide. Whenever the aide was absent or assigned to another setting, the girl would experience considerable separation anxiety and become disruptive. She had taken to "stealing" small items from the aide. It was suggested to the aide that the child needed some belonging of the aide's to hold onto whenever the aide was assigned to another setting. Could the teacher give the child such an object whenever the aide was out? All agreed that this was a good idea. Several weeks later we asked if this suggestion was working. The teacher said it was not; the child had thrown the object on the floor, yelling "I don't want this!" What had worked was a lecture from the teacher that she would not tolerate this nonsense from the girl each time the aide left. The teacher neglected to mention that such lectures had never worked before and that the child always retrieved the object from the floor after her verbal tirade.

PROTECTION AND RESCUE

Adults may balk at the thought of protecting extremely defiant children, but protection is precisely what will help them to become less aggressive. Therapists need to constantly advocate for and support such actions. Gorilla-suit wearers usually start fights because they fear attacks from others. Initial rescue attempts can be as simple as breaking up fights without placing blame and administering to cuts and bruises, no matter how small, a point emphasized by King (1975) in his work with delinquent adolescents. Caregivers should be discouraged from making comments like "Don't make such a fuss. It's only a small cut," "Big boys don't cry," or "Don't be silly; a tough guy like you doesn't need a bandage for that tiny scratch!" They have already been rebuffed in that manner numerous times. Rarely did they receive solicitous responses to their cuts and bruises when they were young. Other mothers fuss over their young children with comments like "Did you get a boo-boo?" or "Come here and let mommy kiss it and make it all better." Instead, the mother ignored their hurts, chastised the child for the accidents that caused them, or, even worse, actually caused them herself. Caregivers should let them cry and give them a bandage! When adults impose limits on a child's aggressive behavior, they should at the same time verbalize that their goal is to help the child replace hitting behavior with talking behavior—in other words, to learn to talk about felt anger. Such assistance is much more productive than continually punishing the child.

AVOIDING LOSS OF FACE

Gorilla-suit wearers, defying adult directives, often get into verbal, and sometime physical, battles with staff. And, unwilling to share adult attention or their belongings, they are always fighting with their peers. Arguments with staff can be reduced by taking children aside to discuss their inappropriate behavior rather than admonishing them in front of their peers. Other nonhumiliating disciplinary options include rewarding the well-behaved child sitting next to the misbehaving one. But managing battles with peers consumes tremendous staff time. Staff members need to separate fighting children from potential audiences because fanfare adds fuel to the fire and can keep a fight going. In the classic musical *West Side Story*, two reluctant young gang members are literally pushed into a fight by one of their peers. Neither youth really wanted to fight, but someone in the crowd poked one of them, and a battle ensued. It is a common ploy of gangs to encircle potential contenders so that they cannot escape and a fight has to take place.

An audience usually heightens a child's anxiety. In any group activity or situation, one technique to prevent defiance from escalating to physical aggression is to handle the situation with as much privacy as possible. This helps dilute the intensity of feelings. Youngsters may need to save face for their audience, and this need can become their motivation to fight. A display of bravado might not be needed if they talk with an adult in privacy. Privacy also accentuates the relationship between adults and children, providing children with an external source of reassurance, guidance, and control.

In educational or treatment settings, staff members need a ready-made plan to separate children in conflict and to dispel audience effects whenever fights develop. One staff person can be designated to counsel the anxious and defiant youngster, and other individuals can disperse the onlookers. Only one adult should communicate with the defiant, upset youngster. Teachers, child-care workers, and nurses often ask, "Shouldn't we all work together to try to calm Peter down?" The answer is a clear No. If more than one adult talks at the same time, the child shuts everybody out and becomes even more belligerent and violent because the child fails to establish contact with any of them. When one-to-one contact is established with angry children, usually they will calm down, particularly if techniques are taught that will help them to do so. Through such personal contact, the children begin to view the interviewing adult as an ally who will help them control themselves—even though they often verbally abuse the interviewer in such situations. They follow the interviewer's cues—the demeanor, the passive physical gestures, the tone of voice—in regaining their composure.

THE USE OF I-MESSAGES

Angry children become angrier when they are ordered to do something. Orders or commands usually take the form of "Stop that!" or "You know better than to ... " or "You're acting like a baby!" or a hundred modifications of these admonitions. In contrast, I-messages are less apt to provoke resistance and rebellion. To let children know how their behavior affects another person is far less threatening than to suggest that there is something bad about the children. For example, a child who angrily storms off the playing field while menacingly swinging a bat can be told something like this:

> ADULT: I'm not happy about the possibility of getting hit on the head, but I'm willing to talk to you from here and see what made you so angry. You can keep your bat for now, but let's talk.

Personal I-messages often serve as an introduction to dialogue and discussion. One unruly youngster began to recklessly sort through all of the glassware assembled for the seventh-grade chemistry lab exam. A teacher's saying "Don't you do that!" might cause the student to be more careful, but more likely it will prompt the child to further flaunt his behavior and break the glass. If instead the teacher says, "Robert, please. I'm getting nervous. I'm afraid that somehow a glass will be broken," there is a good chance that the student will put the glass down. Almost paradoxically, I-messages often de-escalate a crisis. Both individuals are on an equal level of respect, and this in itself takes the edge off a potential confrontation.

Extremely defiant children should know that their violence elicits fear reactions in others. The adult can use I-messages as well as appropriate self-disclosure. Many ask, "Why should adults tell aggressive children that they make us afraid? If the children know this, they will act tougher and more aggressive." On the contrary, children often act tough to cover up their own fears of others. If adults feel fear but express something else, the children get tougher. Expressing fear in a noncombative stance takes away a child's need to be more aggressive.

Teachers can help children save face in a variety of small ways. For example, teachers need to realize that calling the parents to complain about their child's misbehavior is counterproductive. Instead, the teacher should be encouraged to send home notes when the child has been productive. This simple tactic can pay huge dividends. Parents, feeling defeated by their children's school-related problems, can resort to punitive disciplinary tactics when their children misbehave in school. Such notes improve parent-child relations. They interrupt the cycle of the parents' being embarrassed by the child's misbehavior and responding with inappropriate and often severe punishments, which increase the child's anger at the parents, which the child displaces onto the classroom teacher.

When this suggestion is made to teachers, some respond that they must keep the parents informed about their child's misbehavior, stating, "If I don't send such notes home, the parent will complain that they never knew their child was a problem until they learned that the administration is recommending the child's placement in special education. They need to know, well in advance, the reasons we are making such a recommendation." We can understand this attitude if the teacher realizes that the child needs a more structured setting, but notes home about misbehavior don't need to start until the teacher is convinced that the child will need placement. Few placements are made quickly. Until then, positive notes home are more helpful. Nevertheless, special education teachers, and even teachers in day treatment centers, who should know better, also send notes home or even call parents on the phone about a child's misbehavior. We think these efforts are actually counteraggressive ones and a sign that the teachers need in-service training or much more emotional support from clinical and administrative staff.

LIMITING PUNISHMENTS

Numerous studies have demonstrated that punishment does not change behavior. It can suppress behaviors, but only in the presence of the one punishing them. Nevertheless, many teachers and child-care workers, reflecting the views of society instead of their training, believe children should be punished for their misbehavior. Nearly forty years ago, Fritz Redl (1966) wrote that for punishment to work, six actions need to happen. First, when punished, the child has to get mad at himself or herself for the transgression rather than getting mad at the punisher. Second, the child's anger at himself or herself has to be constructive anger that leads to a corrective action plan and not to self-hate. We need go no further because no gorilla-suit wearers ever get beyond the first two actions.

Administering natural consequences, however, is another matter, even though natural consequences are more difficult to implement than punishment. If an angry boy punches a hole in the wall, he should help the maintenance man repair the hole. If the maintenance man is not particularly good with children, however, then a child-care worker has to supervise the repair work. If two children are constantly at each other's throats and damaging each other's personal belongings, then the two could be forced to spend more time together until they learn to tolerate or ignore each other. But some staff member has to take responsibility for supervising their time together. Time is money, and administering punishment is a lot quicker and easier and satisfies the natural desire for retaliation or revenge—but does nothing to curb a child's transgressions.

PHYSICAL INTERVENTIONS

Most children in regular schools rarely require physical intervention to keep them under control. Verbal interventions usually prevent a tantrum from escalating into a full-scale physical confrontation. Gorilla-suit wearers, referred from public schools to special settings—hospitals, special education classes, residential schools, or day treatment facilities—are seriously impaired in their ability to control themselves. They possess the capacity to harm. As a result, situations occur when verbal efforts to control aggression are inappropriate. When the children's primitive defenses break down and they throw objects or attack others, verbal intervention can be ineffective and can make the situation worse.

When using physical holding techniques, the following principles should be kept in mind: (1) the goal of the physical intervention is the care and treatment of the children, so the intervention must be therapeutic and not punitive; (2) staff must display safe restraining and carrying techniques that convey to the children that the adult is able to safely control them, and these techniques require special training, practice, and certification; (3) staff must be decisive and not show ambivalence when holding a child because children are extremely sensitive to cues and will often intensify their defiant behavior if they sense uncertainty; (4) once a physical intervention is begun, it must be carried through; (5) all intervenors should have a partner or a person available on call, or they should be part of a team in carrying out the intervention; and (6) intensive follow-up counseling should be provided: the children should talk with staff about what happened, and the adults must explain why physical holding was needed. The children need to be helped to find ways to handle frustration in a nonviolent manner in the future. The crisis should become a tool to teach children to be more effective in dealing with important life issues.

Unfortunately, the teaching and social service fields at large have adopted physical holding techniques to manage out-of-control children. Isolation rooms have been prohibited in many treatment centers. In New York, for example, when it was learned by the centralized training agency (a large state university approved by the state departments of Education, Mental Health, and Social Services to provide crisis intervention training) that injuries occurred during escorts (the term for removing the child to a quiet room), agency staff members were instructed, through state training updates, not to escort children anywhere but to simply hold them, usually face down on the floor, until the child could walk calmly to a quiet room or return to the ongoing activity.

Instead of taking a passive, nonaggressive posture when facing the child, many workers now actively prepare for physical contact, anticipating the need for a physical hold. The child responds accordingly, and when a hold follows, many children feel humiliated and overcontrolled and experience the hold as punishment or even as abuse. Some even have dissociative experiences and become more out of control. Often their aberrations are misinterpreted by workers as efforts to get a worker to release them.

Children are held in classrooms and in hallways where their cursing, yelling, and pleas to be released not only upset other children and disrupt their work but also stimulate acting-up behavior from the children watching these events. In addition, the acting-up child has an audience—an absolute no–no in crisis-resolution efforts. We believe that many children will push adults to the limit of their "punishments." If the children see the limit as a physical hold, then that's what the children will push for and what caregivers will quickly gravitate to when other interventions initially appear unsuccessful. Institutions nationwide experience countless numbers of physical holds per month, and children end up being held following noncompliant rather than out-of-control behavior.

Organizational amnesia sets in, and older knowledge is forgotten, replaced by ongoing quality assurance studies examining the frequency and the events surrounding physical hold occurrences, followed by retraining efforts in active listening intended to decrease the total number of holds to a figure below some arbitrary threshold. Both of us were involved in crisis intervention for many years before physical holds became the recommended intervention strategy for managing out-of-control children, and neither of us had to physically hold a child unless the child was hurting someone or significantly damaging property. And in such cases, the child was held only until safety was ensured and then let go and helped to become calm—a procedure any reasonable person would follow when witnessing children hurting themselves or others or seriously damaging property.

High-quality residential treatment programs have made a huge push in recent years, through intensified staff training, close monitoring, and supervision, to drastically reduce the number of physical holds. When staff members are trained to use other techniques to manage disruptive behavior, and their use regularly monitored, both the number of critical incidents and the use of physical holds decrease (Nunno, Holden, and Leidy 2003).

PREDICTABLE PROHIBITIONS

Setting limits, if done in a responsible and consistent manner, is an effective way to curtail crisis situations with violent children. When children are losing control of themselves, they look for someone to provide them with limits. Limits make them feel safe. They define what the children can and cannot do. We discuss limit setting in the therapy room in *A Handbook of Play Therapy with Aggressive Children*, chapters 3 and 4. One caution about limit setting needs to be mentioned: staff members need to be prepared to enforce the limits they set. Failure to do so will cancel the limits' potential effectiveness. The limits set must be enforceable and reasonable.

Many teachers make defiant children "sit minutes," either inside or outside the classroom: "If you don't finish your work, you'll have to sit for two minutes." This type of limit setting has three advantages. First, it specifies to the children what they can and cannot do. Second, it gives them private time to pull themselves together. Third, sitting minutes is no fun, and the children soon wish to return to the group activity, this time with improved behavior.

Effective teachers also provide alternatives. If defiant children are given the option to choose from among several alternatives, they will feel less confronted and ordered about. They feel they have some say-so in the decision. Often they choose one of the options, and the crisis is avoided. For example, an anxious, uneasy boy arrives in class and announces that he is not going to do any work that day. If the teacher responds, "Oh, yes you are! Sit down at that desk and do your math, right now!" the student may walk out the door. But if the teacher says, "You can do your math. Or maybe you'd rather do your language lesson first. Which of these would you like to choose?" Given these choices, the student may pick one of them, and a crisis will be defused. Choices should be kept simple for the child, with no more than two or three options offered. Most important, the child needs to know what the consequences will be if the choices offered are declined.

A WORD ABOUT BEHAVIOR MODIFICATION PROGRAMS

One of the advantages of behavior modification programs, in which a child earns points for displaying positive behaviors or loses points for displaying negative behaviors, is that they make prohibitions predictable. They also increase staff consistency and serve to limit punishments that are counterproductive. Loss of points for clearly defined behaviors is better than other punishments for these same behaviors. Nevertheless, both of us prefer programs that give rather than take away points because giving points implies that children can control their behavior. In addition, taking away points can activate traumatic losses from the past. For example, Tommy, a case example we present in chapter 17 of *A Handbook of Play Therapy with Aggressive Children*, was triggered into a severe rage episode just by falling behind in a game. Losing points, like being punished, will not change behavior, but getting points can create prideful feelings, and these feelings can stimulate meaningful internal changes. In points–lost systems, staff members can become angry and strip a child of so many points that both discouragement and resentment set in, and the child gives up efforts to earn new points. Children can also retaliate against the adult who took away the points, which results in more points lost, and the cycle of aggression escalates. In addition, children may feel that their misbehavior was caused by another child's attack, and when they lose points, they will protest the perceived unfairness until the cows come home.

HELPING CHILDREN TALK ABOUT THEIR FRUSTRATIONS

Training in the helping professions emphasizes that helpers should "get close" to persons being helped. The physical display of affection comes naturally when working with children. In the language of feelings, a sincere hug or pat on the shoulder can communicate more to the child than hundreds of words unless the child has been physically or sexually abused and consequently misinterprets signs of affection. When children are angry, however, touching them increases the likelihood that they will lash out physically.

First: Give Them Space

Angry children need their own space, an area to occupy by themselves, or at least a physical distance of several arms' lengths from others so that they don't feel encroached on. The research by ethologists suggests that all animals—even as sophisticated a species as we believe ourselves to be—will lash out with explosive power and energy when they feel trapped or cornered. Angry children often misperceive a friendly pat on the back or a touch to the arm as an aggressive act and respond accordingly. Feeling the pat was a shove, their reasoning goes, "They hit me first; now I'll hit them back." Staff need to be very careful about gestures made toward defiant children. Children in crisis generally feel a loss of security and control. If staff approaches them calmly, with a self-assurance that is not overpowering, angry children are reassured. A relaxed physical posture also communicates that the adult is there to talk with them and to understand them. One way to defuse defiant children's anger is to stand at least one arm's length, and preferably more, away from them so that their personal space is respected. They thus know the staff member will not become physically violent, and so they do not feel intimidated.

Most adults directly face those with whom they are talking. When gorilla-suit wearers become extremely defiant, this approach is likely to communicate that the interviewer is ready to square off. They should not be faced directly. The interviewer should stand near them at an angle, or sit down near them, in as relaxed a manner as possible. Standing at their level rather than towering over them communicates that the interviewer is there to spend time in constructive problem solving. Making a nonthreatening or conciliatory gesture invites the youngsters to respond in a similar way.

For example, when a child who has lost control is placed in a crisis room, the interviewing adult should enter the room shortly after placing the child there and sit quietly on the floor some distance from the child. Similarly, when a youngster threatens with a bat, the other children are quickly and quietly removed, and the interviewer takes a passive stance, well away from the potential bat swinger, and either goes down on one knee or places his or her hands in a jacket or pants pocket. This gives the youngster space to back down while saving face. It communicates that the adult does not intend to attack or take away the bat. The youngster is scared as well as angry; both feelings need to subside before the bat will be relinquished. Sometimes simply turning and walking toward the building, commenting, "Come on now, let's go inside," will induce the angry child to follow with the bat hung at his or her side.

Some judgment should be used, however, when assuming a passive position. Dr. Mordock once entered the time-out room and sat down on the floor to talk to a small and extremely bright seven-year-old. The boy had an explosive temper and had lost it. At first he remained distant, then he approached and realized that he towered over the reclining psychologist. A feeling of omnipotence overtook him, and he struck a brutal blow. Dr. Mordock did not know that this small boy had a history of taking advantage of the weaknesses of others. He had been referred for hitting his teachers and throwing chairs at adults, including his mother. Sitting on the floor actually invited attack from this little child. Dr. Mordock should have read the boy's record before interviewing him.

Second: Help Them Become Calm

Some clinicians, influenced by the writings of Fritz Redl (1959, 1966) and his followers (Bona [Northrup 1987]; Morse 1991; Wood and Long 1991), feel that clinical interviews with children who have lost control, called life space interviews, can assist the children to understand why they lost control and help them to avoid loss of control in similar circumstances. These interviews focus on discovering the what and why of the child's disruptive behavior. Others view a child's loss of control, and the ensuing crisis, as a signal of the need for critical incident stress debriefing (Dyregrov 1997, Stallard and Salter 2003). And another group sees the life space interview as an opportunity to connect with the child, to help the child create new meanings, and to share a dynamic in which a greater sense of personal trust is created (Mead and Hilton 2003). Consequently, when a child loses control, he or she is taken aside and interviewed. The therapist focuses the interview on trying to understand what led up to the incident, why it was so upsetting, and how the child can avoid future incidents. Answers are sought for various questions, such as whether the situation reminded the child of earlier traumas, did it stir up jealous feelings the child holds toward siblings, or did it remind the child of past humiliations. Then the interviewer tries to help the child think of other things to do when upset instead of losing self-control and lashing out at others or becoming self-destructive.

We hold a different view. We recommend delaying such interviews until after children have learned how to calm themselves when upset. When children first enter treatment, they precipitate a crisis nearly every day, if not every hour. Taking them aside for interviews takes them out of the milieu designed to meet their needs. When an upset child is asked to reconstruct what led to an upset, the child can quickly get "into the experience again" and get more upset rather than becoming calm. We recommend first teaching the child methods to use to become calm when upset and then returning the child to ongoing milieu activities as quickly as possible. It is the milieu that helps children grow and develop more adaptive defenses and coping skills, not crisis interviewing techniques. While staff may be enthused by the thought of conducting a creative interview after a crisis, the need for the interview is the staff member's and not the child's. Those who see the interview as an opportunity to make a meaningful connection with the child overestimate their significance and underestimate the value of the milieu. Workers with such attitudes are likely to burn out quickly (Mordock 1999c).

After children have developed self-calming skills, they can begin the more difficult task of understanding the whys of their behavior. The first step in helping children regain lost self-control is to get them to think about what they can do to calm themselves, not why they lost control in the first place.

Jerome Singer (1966, 1976) found that individuals who are practiced day-dreamers handle aggressive feelings by daydreaming of pleasant and enjoyable states. They obtain relief from negative affect following frustrating experiences by emoting fantasies that change their mood. Singer also discovered that individuals who rarely daydreamed tended to remain aggressive. In earlier chapters, we discuss that children in gorilla suits rarely daydream, have very primitive fantasies, and lack the ability to engage in fantasy play.

Consequently, we recommend that when children's aggression gets out of control, therapists teach them methods to change their mood into a calm one. We discuss some calming techniques in chapter 11, preferring those associated with finding a positive introject. Searching for positive introjects can be combined with helping the child develop mechanisms of restraint, also discussed in chapter 11. Once children have learned how to calm themselves, crisis intervention simply involves a routine of removing the child from the ongoing situation, escorting the child to the time-out room without saying anything, putting the child in the room, and sitting down on the floor at the doorway without facing the child. Remarks are restricted to reminding the children of activities to perform that will make them calm and informing them that return to ongoing activities will occur when they can prove to the worker that they are calm. Children whose anger is stronger than their ability to calm themselves are allowed to rant and rave, but most become calm within ten minutes to a half hour even without skill in instituting self-calming measures. Those who have learned calming strategies will become calm much sooner.

Some very primitive children or seriously traumatized children are unable to find symbolic activities or images that will calm them. When asked to visualize a "safe place" (see chapters 9 and 13 in *A Handbook of Play Therapy with Aggressive Children*), they can come up with none. They may visualize a place that starts out looking safe, but the place is quickly invaded by monsters and demons. Often these children need "alone time" in a particular place to calm themselves. They can be helped to find a quiet, dark place in the building (a safe place, for some the symbolic equivalent of the womb). They are accompanied to their chosen place and allowed to enter it. The adult stands nearby, keeping the child in sight, and waits for the child to say that he or she is calm and ready to return to the ongoing activity.

Children can also be made aware of the conflict cycle (Long 1991) and the stages of the typical temper tantrum (Trieschman 1969) and encouraged to utilize their calming techniques when faced with frustrating experiences in the milieu (cognitive behaviorists would embrace this technique). If calmed by internal images, the child can be instructed to conjure up the images when frustrated in the milieu. Usually this activity goes unnoticed by others. But if children require actual activities to calm themselves, often these activities cannot be used in the classroom.

Third: Talk to Them after They Have Made Progress in the Milieu

After children have made substantial progress in treatment and the crises they precipitate are infrequent and followed by guilt or loss of self-esteem (i.e., the children have now internalized the value of maintaining self-control and are disappointed in themselves for not dong so), they can be interviewed about their disruptive behavior. Children initially resist talking because they anticipate scolding by the interviewer. But after they have experienced a long history of simply being removed from crises, calming down, and returning to ongoing activities, empathic interviews can be helpful.

When the children are not in a crisis state, their bodily preoccupations can offer an occasion for establishing a relationship. As previously mentioned, sympathetic and genuine comments of concern about body scars, disfigurements, bandages (however small), and recent scrapes and bruises will often elicit a friendly acknowledgment from the youngsters and an entrée to a discussion.

GET TO THE ROOT OF THE PROBLEM

Direct-care staff need to be continually reminded that children are made angry by what they perceive as a problem. Problems typically render children helpless. They respond to helpless feelings with efforts to feel in charge, and often their take-charge methods result in conflicts with others. Although adults can compromise with children in gorilla suits, the children's need to feel all-powerful may override these efforts. Adults must help these children verbalize what is bothering them so that the cycle of defiance can be broken.

When under pressure, staff members often forget basic principles. The therapist's task is to remind staff that the goal is to understand children, to burrow beneath the surface talk and deal with their real problems. Children are adept at throwing up smoke screens when they are troubled about something. These diversions must be sidestepped and efforts made to get to the root of the problem. Empathy is essential. For example, if a child has just cursed a classmate over a seemingly trivial incident and the adult in charge says "Cursing is forbidden" or "Cursing is against the rules," then the adult has missed the boat. The real issue is not the cursing; it is the child's anger. The task is to find out what is bothering the child, but not in the middle of a major upset. After the child has calmed down, the adult can speak privately with the child, employing a puzzled and unknowing look and speaking in a quiet tone.

> ADULT: Gee, Mike, I'm concerned about your anger. I may be wrong, but it's over something that doesn't seem important to me. I wonder what you're really mad at. Could it be . . . ?

An empathic approach cuts through the angry words and threats and helps children become aware of the real reasons for their fury. Most children in gorilla suits are bewildered and confused. Their emotions surge up within them in a frightening way. Amid this jumble of conflicting emotions, they experience difficulty controlling themselves. When children can sort out their confusion and label the various feelings that contribute to their bewilderment, they can control themselves better.

When faced with screaming and cursing children, staff members need reminding that the anger is rarely the result of the momentary frustration experienced but is usually the result of deeper and entirely different issues. The anger is a displacement. When these children discover the real issue, they usually calm down. Often their discovery follows empathic remarks to them, but they will rarely acknowledge that their feelings were understood correctly. They go away silent, and staff wonder what the "exact thing" was they said that turned the tide. The children's only response is "I want to go back to class now." One child-care worker described how she penetrated a young girl's smoke screen of defiance:

> Shannon, a newcomer to the residence, was having difficulty feeling accepted by the other children. Just before Shannon entered the residence, her grandmother died, and Shannon had apparently never verbalized anything about this death. The pressure of withholding (not ventilating) these two issues surfaced during an incredible physical outburst when she threw things all over her room. This occurred after she was informed that she could not go on a field trip due to an incident that had occurred during school. She wanted me, I thought, to restrain her guilt at possible responsibility for her grandmother's death. We had discussed this before at great length in a team meeting, so I was aware of it.
>
> My partner took all the other children aside and I directed Shannon to her room. She kept yelling, "Let go of me!" even though I wasn't even touching her. You could tell that she was trying to set me up for a physical confrontation. Finally, Shannon broke down and started to cry. She embraced me and began weeping about how she loved her grandmother. This was totally unrelated to how the incident began—being refused permission to go on a field trip. This was her way of letting things out. Then she cried about how nobody liked her in the dorm, as well as how her grandmother

didn't really like her and that's why she left. During this incident, Dr. Mordock felt like he had provided a safe outlet for her.

Events leading up to angry explosions can sometimes be understood by examining the role of antecedents and consequences. Very few children explode in a vacuum, without connection to other people or events. When a "crisis situation" is over, staff members should be encouraged to sit down with other people who were involved in the situation and ask themselves some of the following questions:

• What was the chain of events that led to the child's defiance?
• What effect, positive or negative, did the intervention have on this process?
• Could something have been done differently?
• What were the core issues being expressed by the child in the torrent of angry words and actions?
• What approaches can be used in the future?

SOME PRACTICAL OBSTACLES

A significant number of teachers, and often they are good teachers, are reluctant to let the child perform concrete calming activities in place of academic work. Studies have demonstrated that teachers who are most effective at raising overall academic standards have a lower tolerance for students with special needs (Hocutt and Alberg 1994–1995). Meetings with teachers can be characterized by much debate, with the teacher insisting that the child will use the suggested calming techniques to avoid schoolwork or that other children will want to do the same or a similar activity instead of academic work. On their side is outcome data that demonstrate that the closer the child is to grade level at discharge from special educational programs, the more favorable the outcome. Good teachers are possessive of their children and want them in class as much as possible.

We have learned, however, that most troubled children urgently want to be successful with schoolwork, even to appear to others as doing their lessons; "looking busy" is their catchword when they can admit to their deficiencies. If the milieu values academic learning and if supports for academic achievement are in place throughout the milieu, most children will not misuse the techniques that calm them. But some teachers can never be convinced, even by their colleagues (especially by their colleagues); these are the teachers children must be prepared to face when they return to the classroom. Time spent with a crisis worker, particularly if the teacher perceives the time spent as a fun time for the child, will be perceived not only as unproductive time but as "coddling" the child.

Some teachers, even those employed in treatment centers, want the child to be reprimanded by the crisis worker for the behavior that led to the interruption of academic activity. They ask the crisis worker, "Did you speak to the child about the unacceptable behavior that led to the incident?" Some even ask their teaching assistant to take over the class while the teacher joins the crisis worker to discuss the situation, often hoping to get a quick apology and an immediate plan of action to avoid future disruptions.

These joint interviews can cause considerable problems for the worker whose goal for crisis intervention is calming the child and getting the child back into the ongoing milieu, particularly when the crisis worker employs a slow-moving, "ignorant interrogator" approach to discussing a situation with a child and the teacher wants to get to the heart of the matter immediately.

With teachers displaying this attitude, the child is guided to return to class in a manner most acceptable to each teacher. The child is helped to finish the work missed and told that the teacher was rightfully upset by his behavior; he or she should enter the class with the head down and take his or her seat quietly. Questions put to the child by the teacher can be answered with, "I did some things in the crisis room that would help me get back to work." Teachers were met with as often as possible to reinforce their good work with each child.

In contrast, most, but not all, child-care workers are pleased to have the child returned to them in a calm state and make fewer value judgments about the methods employed than teachers do. In addition, joint interviews with child-care workers are not as difficult as those with teachers. Child-care workers usually let the crisis worker take the lead in the joint interview, realizing that the child-care worker and the child are in conflict and appreciating a third person's assistance in resolving the conflict between them. But there are always staff members who want the child punished after a transgression, and these are the most difficult staff to work with.

BROADEN THE LIST OF "DO'S"

This need, so simple to emphasize, is neglected in many treatment settings. Lots of programs list all the things each child does wrong and then develop an individualized or group behavior modification program in an effort to eliminate them. Centers also list the rules all children are expected to follow, such as do not curse, do not run in the hallway, and do not leave class without permission.

In some centers, children earn points for following rules. In sharp contrast, how many times do we see a reminder in each child's room that they should say something nice to another child each day or that they will bake cookies at the end of the day? How much time is spent emphasizing the simple things the children can do?

Dr. Crenshaw spoke with Charles Appelstein (2003), a valued colleague, at the Astor Home's Fiftieth Anniversary Conference. Appelstein has conducted training sessions at a number of residential treatment centers, as well as public schools, on effective disciplinary strategies with behaviorally disruptive children. He related that he has been amazed with the results of recent efforts to get children to rehearse desirable behavior. Behavioral rehearsal is so simple a concept that it can easily be overlooked when bombarding children with the typical deluge of prohibitions. Appelstein was particularly excited about combining behavioral rehearsal with self-reminders of the desired behavior in the form of a song. Some children make up a rap song to make the reminder more indelible in the consciousness and memory. A child, along with Appelstein, might even dance to the rap reminder. Applestein demonstrated an example of one combination of "rap and self-instruction" by performing a rhythmic dance in the lobby of the hotel. The approach is appealing because youth love music and movement, and if new behaviors can be practiced in a playful context, favorable conditions have been created for change. Some treatment settings let children engage in positive activities only after they have behaved for a certain period of time. "You can dance after you have cleaned your room." Such arrangements are acceptable for normal children, but abused and neglected children should be allowed to dance and sing whether they clean their room or not.

RECOGNIZE STRENGTHS

When a clinician examines treatment plans developed in many settings, he or she discovers that most plans contain a list of the child's strengths (a requirement of most accrediting and licensing bodies) but that staff members make little use of these lists when planning treatment. Often, a child's "strengths" are not viewed as strengths at all and are overlooked. When a boy copies a book and tells others that he wrote it, he often is viewed as manipulative or as "cheating" rather than as having an interest in writing. If a girl displays disorganized behavior in the morning but shows more motivation later, rarely is it noted that she "works best at midmorning." More often she is noted for "taking a long time to settle in." Even when a child has an obvious interest in art, alerting the child's art teacher is often the only way the interest is woven into the treatment plan. How many times do the therapist, art teacher, classroom teacher, and gym teacher team up to help a child develop an art project that involves them all in the effort?

Usually clinical intervention is required to develop a plan in which individuals from different disciplines work cooperatively together. The social worker or psychologist who consults with teachers in special class settings, whether they work in public schools or in treatment settings, can help children by helping teachers utilize strength-oriented planning. Discovering the interests of children in gorilla suits is not an easy task. Untrained staff often misread the cues communicated by the child. For example, a boy may be humming quietly in class. Instead of sensing that he may have an interest in music, the teacher admonishes him for disrupting the class. Similarly, a girl may show a staff member a picture she made, but because it looks copied, the child is admonished instead of encouraged to draw.

Careful observations of the child are required to assess possible strengths. Keeping logs is extremely helpful. Often, however, logs become repetitive and stereotypical—a clue that staff members are no longer individualizing treatment planning efforts. Continual clinical monitoring is required for treatment plan development and implementation. In the two cases that follow, the educational plans are not elaborate; instead they are rather simple applications of the strength-based treatment planning principle. Recreational and child-care staff can also develop strength-oriented plans for each child, modeled on the method employed in the two cases illustrated. Other case examples appear in Mordock (1999a).

> Donald, age eleven, displays his poorest academic functioning in the morning and then improves gradually as the day progresses. Spelling tires him excessively, and his outbursts occur during this activity. He is extremely sensitive to marks he receives on his work and responds poorly to pressure. He enjoys art and music and is calmed by art activities. He also works best when standing up. His personal interests suggest that social studies could be used to increase his interest in learning.
>
> OBJECTIVES: (1) Donald will increase his spelling skills from 20 percent correct on a first-grade list to 60 percent correct on a similar list, (2) Donald will report feeling more successful at spelling, and (3) Donald will produce a series of picture books illustrating social studies lessons.
>
> TREATMENT PLANS: The most meaningful learning experiences will be given later in Donald's day. Artwork will follow and precede Donald's work on academic subjects. Spelling will be left until

just before lunch. Donald will do his math problems on a chalkboard, where his mistakes can be easily erased. Whenever possible, Donald will work standing at an adjusted easel placed by the wall. He can select activities to work on. If he does the selected activity well, he can select the next activity. He can write a book about himself and illustrate it. He will practice writing freely and, when doing so, will ignore spelling mistakes and legibility. When frustrated with new learning, he can copy his freely written work to improve his legibility.

In strength-based treatment planning, the child's current approach to learning and his or her learning styles are used to maximize learning. Donald's academic lessons are provided when he is at his best later in the day. His interest in art is interspersed between lessons, he is given a chalkboard to desensitize him to mistakes, and he is allowed to work standing up. In deficit-based planning, which is the typical approach in most treatment centers, goals would be developed to change Donald's tempo and style; for example: (1) Donald will be able to perform a greater portion of his academic work in the morning, (2) Donald will learn to switch assignments without requiring motivational encouragements, (3) Donald will learn to tolerate making mistakes, (4) Donald will learn to work in a seated position. While such goals may be appropriate later in Donald's treatment, to implement them early in his treatment is not consistent with a strength-based philosophy. Implementing deficit-oriented goals early in treatment is not in keeping with the larger goal of minimizing frustrations and can result in increasing rather than decreasing a child's primitive defenses.

Edward, age ten, arrives at school overstimulated and disorganized. At dismissal, he becomes anxious. He can maintain his attention to a task for only brief periods (six to seven minutes). He displays a compulsive need to be first in everything: first in line, first to get lunch, and so on. Praise and encouragement appear meaningless to him, and criticism or punishment destroys his learning efforts completely. Concrete reinforcers, such as food, work best. Edward enjoys musical activities. He can recognize letters only when they are written in uppercase, and he can read simple words written in uppercase. He is fascinated with clocks, and although he can recognize the numbers on them, he has no math skills.

OBJECTIVES: (1) Edward will work on academic material for five minutes without interruption, (2) Edward will read a preprimer and complete workbooks at that level, (3) Edward will learn basic math facts up to ten.

TREATMENT PLANS: All of Edward's serious academic work will be scheduled at midmorning. He will never work on new academic material independently. He will work for five-minute periods interspersed with games, taking a walk, eating, talking, and similar activities. Edward's need to be first should be used to introduce a sequential sense to learning. He will develop a calendar to structure his time. He will plant carrot and watermelon seeds and keep a "Carrot and Watermelon Diary" to teach and reinforce the concepts of time, learn the nutrients needed by a seed in order to grow, and assume responsibility for caring for plants. Art activities will include making social studies picture books, with extra art and music used as rewards for completed work. All his preprimer materials and workbooks will be retyped in uppercase print. After he has mastered a book, the same book will be presented in lowercase letters. Clocks will be used as motivators, incentives, and rewards; time-out from clocks will be used as a disciplinary activity.

Scheduling Edward's academic activities at midmorning allows Edward to maximize his efforts. The goal is not to help him learn in the morning. Scheduling short learning periods, interspersed with games, minimizes the disruption resulting from his inability to concentrate for longer periods. As he masters material, he will be less anxious, and his concentration skills will increase. The initial goal is not to increase his concentration span; this will occur naturally with increased knowledge and self-confidence. Edward's need to be first is not tackled head-on but is viewed as a cognitive deficit as well as a self-esteem issue. It is handled symbolically through his interest in food.

EXPANDING CONCRETE SKILLS

Most multiply abused children lack rudimentary social and recreational skills. Pressed into the service of adult sexual needs, sexually abused children can exhibit pseudomaturity. Nevertheless, they have missed out on many important experiences, such as initiating and maintaining meaningful conversations with others. Many cannot identify, label, or express basic feelings or appropriately assert themselves (see *A Handbook of Play Therapy with Aggressive Children*, chapter 15). Often they need to learn appropriate strategies of self-control and problem solving, as well as assistance with daily survival skills such as crossing streets and asking for help if they become lost. Typically, such issues are not addressed in traditional out-patient therapy, but they are essential topics in treatment of the severely abused child who has been denied many basic experiences and whose resulting deficiencies contribute to feelings of being externally controlled and personally ineffective. And they are essential ingredients of milieu treatments.

Meeting this need for developing concrete skills involves expanding each child's communication, self-help, leisure time, academic, and athletic skills, and it also includes improving each child's interpersonal skills. Five- and six-year-old children are particularly prone to eruptions of hostility that seem irrational or even incomprehensible. They are often incapable of judging why someone bumped or pushed against them. Often they perceive an accident as a personal affront or hostile attack. Children at this age are unable to form correct judgments of other people's motives unless they are assisted to do so. Older aggressive children, many of whom are emotionally arrested at preschool age levels, also misperceive the intentions of others. They respond to ambiguous situations with aggression, not because they don't understand another's motives, but because they attribute hostile reactions to others (Dodge 1993; Mayes and Cohen 1993): "Because I'm always angry, others are always angry at me."

CLARIFYING INTENTION AND MOTIVATION

Mediating conflicts between the children should include a thorough discussion of the difference between an accidental and a deliberate act, with reference to the child's own pervasive anger:

> ADULT: David, just because you're angry at other kids doesn't mean they're always angry at you. Sam wasn't even thinking about you when he ran into you in the pool. He was thinking about swimming and didn't even see you.

Offending children should also be included in the discussion to communicate to angry youngsters that the other child's intent was not hostile. Those approaching adolescence know the difference between accidental and intentional behaviors, but they are quick to see interchanges as challenges. They interpret others' remarks as belittling even if the others were only boasting or insisting on their own viewpoint in a discussion. Their pride is at stake, and they feel called on to repeatedly prove themselves. The incidents that spark violent attacks often are trivial. When the children are angry, they aim to hurt others with little regard for the consequences, but later they realize that fighting can get them into serious trouble. In such situations adults have to back off quickly or swiftly remove other children who are the targets of the aggression.

ADULT: I realize you feel Patrick insulted you and you'd like to hurt him for it. But consider the source—it's only Patrick. To hit him might make him look like he's right, and you know he probably didn't mean anything by it anyway. It was just a thoughtless remark.

GETTING ASSISTANCE

Any caregiver working with children in gorilla suits needs a backup person. Rather than a sign of defeat or failure, it is a sign of strength to know when help is needed. No one can handle repeated aggressive outbursts of children without being affected. Many people in the teaching and helping professions feel both a need to help others and a need to set exacting, demanding standards for their own performance. Yet even with the best intentions and crisis intervention skills, caregivers' encounters with gorilla-suit wearers don't always work out the way one wants or expects them to. Sometimes a situation gets out of control—by definition, that's a crisis! Asking someone to step in to help at a time of weariness or frustration can benefit the situation. Often a neutral person, one not embroiled in the conflict, can diffuse a conflict, and both the staff member and the child can then resume their ongoing activity.

Sometimes, especially with newly hired staff, when one of us, in a position of leadership, stepped in to remove a child from a conflict situation, the direct-care staff felt one of two ways. First, they wondered what unseen skills we had that made the child calm down. This was easily explained: we were not part of the conflict and offered the child a way to both save face and retreat from the conflict rather than further alienating the worker. Second, direct-care workers felt that their efforts to calm the child were interrupted and that the interruption undermined the worker's authority.

This second attitude is dealt with by explaining that the worker's efforts were being perceived by the child as confrontations, as dressing-downs, and that such confrontations are never helpful. Children witnessing the interchange were losing time from participating in more meaningful activities, and besides, arguments between staff and children decrease rather than increase adult authority over the children. The child was simply removed from the situation by being asked to "Come with me." Authority comes with respect, and respect is earned by fairness, firmness, structure, and commitment, not by engaging in arguments with individual children. Once this concept is accepted by staff, working together becomes natural, and burnout is prevented. It will never be accepted, however, if clinical staff members aren't actively involved in managing aggressive behaviors themselves. If they sit in their offices and pontificate, clinical thinking will never be accepted, and the environment will rapidly become antitherapeutic.

SIGNS OF IMPROVEMENT

When children begin to develop internal controls, they begin to check with adults before they do things ("Is this right?" or "Can I . . . ?"). Their ability to delay their action marks the first step in the development of control. It reflects their desire to please rather than their fear of punishment. When they lose their temper, it will be less violent. They will be more focused on others and will use possessives: "My friend . . . ," "My teacher . . . ," "My counselor. . . ."

Sometimes adults are frustrated at this stage because the children act like babies one moment and tough guys the next. It is difficult to baby a tough guy. Caregivers should not respond to babyish behavior with sarcasm. In fact, an adult's use of sarcasm is a sign that the adult needs support to better manage retaliation desires because sarcasm is one way of expressing retaliation. Extensive use of sarcasm is a sign of burnout and should be addressed by management. Babyish behavior by children in this stage should be allowed and even encouraged. Caregiver commitment will be tested; the children will demand that caregivers stay with them, guide them, and tolerate their moodiness. If educational and child-care staff members are supported to stick to their guns and to ensure that the ten needs listed earlier in this chapter are being met, the children will begin to concentrate longer, take pleasure in activities, and control themselves to please cared-for adults. Remember, most have never pleased anyone before.

As the children begin to trust staff, a more mature conscience will develop, and the control of impulses will increase. With control comes satisfying involvement in activities and investment in learning. The children begin to feel they "want to do" what the caring adult requests. They develop trust in their good impulses and in their ability to control or mitigate their aggressive urges. Throughout this process staff need to be reminded that every setback is difficult for the children. Since they expect failure, they see every new activity as a threat. Staff should be encouraged to reflect these feelings and encourage growth:

> ADULT: It's really hard for you to try new things because you will feel bad if you fail. But you need to try. I'll stick with you no matter what.

Working with extremely defiant youngsters is time consuming and emotionally draining, but even small successes make it worthwhile.

THE POSITIVE EFFECTS OF SUPPORT

On numerous occasions, both of us have been asked by teachers to make classroom observations of children the teacher feels need placement in a more restrictive setting. Following our observation, we have been genuinely impressed with the child's progress under the teacher's instruction. When we communicated this to teachers, their response was often, "Yes, I agree, the child has come a long way," seemingly forgetting that they asked for the observation because they thought they were "failing" with the child. Teachers and other direct-care staff need constant feedback about the progress a child is making, progress they fail to see because they are too close to the situation. If a child gets into conflict with other children at least twenty times a day, and later the conflicts are reduced to fifteen, most staff members will not notice the difference and will begin to question their effectiveness. Children's progress, especially the progress of children in gorilla suits, occurs in barely perceptible steps. Someone, and often it is the child's therapist, needs to notice these small changes and continually point them out to others.

A fine line exists between hope and despair, and the clinician's job is to facilitate hope (Elliot 2002). The clinician needs to "bear despair when others cannot cope and to convey hope when everything seems lost" (Mak-Pearce 2002, p. 9). This quote applies to staff working with children as well as to the children themselves. We discuss the topic of facilitating hope in children in chapter 13. Teachers and other direct-care staff, constantly bombarded by aggressive onslaughts day after day, often begin to distance from the children. They become "burned out" and can even look depressed. The opportunity to verbalize their frustrations, however, often results in their finding new energy to continue their heroic efforts.

CONCLUSION

In this chapter we have suggested approaches to meeting ten treatment needs of children in gorilla suits that professionals, as well as others, including parents, should find helpful. Unfortunately, there will be children for whom none of the approaches seem to have a significant effect. Some children live in areas of such intolerable poverty and social deprivation that their resulting defiance and aggression behaviors render even the most skilled helper powerless to effect change. Sometimes a professional can do everything right, and it is still not enough. We are reminded of the story titled "Ciske, the Rat." In it, a teacher visits a jail in which a pupil to whom he has devoted much attention is imprisoned. The boy had murdered his mother:

> I saw Ciske sitting on a wooden bench. He was swinging his legs, exactly like a boy who is momentarily bored during vacation. Here he was, my pupil. I had given my whole heart to the boy and had been unable to prevent fate from striking him down. (Bakker 1958)

//

Developing Mature Defenses and Calming Skills

This chapter illustrates milieu techniques to develop and enhance the functioning of defense mechanisms in children who lack adequate defenses against anxiety and whose primitive defenses get them into considerable trouble. The defenses used by children are presented in detail. Treatment requires reinforcing rather than confronting existing defenses, minimizing frustrations, selecting emotionally appropriate leisure time activities to reduce frustration, verbalizing alternative defenses, encouraging and reinforcing the child's use of more mature defenses, developing mechanisms of restraint, and acknowledging progress. A discussion of the therapeutic use of projective communications and the development of calming techniques concludes the chapter.

After introductory psychology, the first course Dr. Mordock took as an undergraduate psychology major was Psychology of Adjustment. It was a two-credit course recommended for students majoring in other fields, but the author took it anyway. The course had more effect on his clinical thinking than any course he took in the field. He doubts if the course is still offered at his alma mater, however, or in any college, for that matter. The course was devoted to examining mechanisms that led to healthy adjustment. Interest in healthy behavior was neglected by psychologists for many years until the recent upsurge of interest in resiliency. With the explosion in social science knowledge, the course was preempted by courses in neuropsychology, behavioral genetics, operant conditioning, social learning, culture and personality, and others.

One section of the adjustment course examined ways in which humans manage the stress in their lives—the ways anxiety is kept from overwhelming us and rendering us helpless. We all use mechanisms psychoanalytic theorists call "mechanisms of defense" (Freud and Sandler 1985) and which are listed and defined in the American Psychiatric Association's (1994) *Diagnostic and Statistical Manual.* Since defense mechanisms were first defined by psychoanalytic theorists, whose findings were rejected in many academic circles because they resulted from clinical observation rather than from experimental manipulation, discussion of them behind hallowed walls faded. The mechanisms of defense were never mentioned in any other psychology courses, at the undergraduate or graduate level, that Dr. Mordock took. Nevertheless, the "man on the street" has observational skill and has discovered for himself how his peers handle anxiety. He will accuse them of *rationalizing*, of *displacing* feelings onto others, of *projecting* blame, of *denying* real feelings, of *minimizing* culpability, of *isolating* feelings, of *overcompensating* for inferiority, of *avoiding* involvement, and so on.

Psychoanalytic psychotherapists noticed that when clients experienced something that made them anxious, they found ways to exclude the experience from conscious awareness should it be experienced again. The process has been called selective inattention, dissociation, or repression. This mechanism helps us avoid situations that make us unduly anxious. No one thinks clearly when anxious, and the discomfort anxiety causes is avoided whenever possible. Unfortunately, it is not possible to avoid many experiences, particularly inner experiences. We can't avoid our own unacceptable impulses. Consequently, we develop inner strategies to avoid anxiety stimulated both from within and from without. These strategies are the defense mechanisms that most of us have come to accept as real rather than as the imaginary creations of psychotherapists.

Frequently, we hear one person say to another before a confrontation, "Now don't get defensive, but you hurt my feelings with that remark." When the offender simply says "I feel bad. I really blew it making that tactless remark. I realize now that it hurt," the person is not being defensive. He or she feels bad that the friend was hurt, but what is done is done. If the offender says "That's not how I intended that remark; you misinterpreted what I said," he or she is being defensive. The friend was hurt, and the offender is denying a role in the hurt. If the offender says "I didn't mean to hurt you. What I meant was . . . ," the offender is now trying to minimize his or her role in the friend's pain. The offender could combine minimizing with blaming by suggesting that the friend is "too sensitive" or that others would not have been hurt by the remark. Or the offender could negate the experience, claiming that "this is unlike him or her" because he or she has never done anything like this before.

Dr. Crenshaw recalls stopping to help a woman whose car was in a ditch. Although two of the wheels were spinning while suspended in air, the hysterical woman kept pumping the gas, crying "This isn't me. I can't be stuck. I don't run cars off the road." It took more than ten minutes to calm the anxious woman down and get her to leave the car, largely by emphasizing that the road must have been extra slippery (it wasn't) and that it wasn't her fault (which, of course, it was).

Suppose the insensitive offender presented above takes every opportunity to compliment the hurt friend during the rest of the evening. The offender is now trying to undo the effects of the tactless remark. The anxiety experienced is decreased by undoing efforts. Or the offender could explain to the friend that he or she recently became aware of his or her tactless behavior and that corrective action was being taken through a planned series of readings on proper etiquette. The offender is now using intellectualization as a defense. Anxious feelings are controlled by thinking about them instead of experiencing them.

The offender could rationalize that friendship with this individual is not that important. "So who cares if I hurt his feelings!" In the future, the offender could avoid situations in which the friend might be encountered and the embarrassment caused by the tactless remark reexperienced. Or a combination of defenses could be used. Initially, the offender could minimize the offensive remark and avoid the friend in the future. But suppose the offender felt nauseous all evening, could not eat, felt tired, or got a headache. Now somatization has been used as a defense. The painful affect has been converted into bodily sensations.

All of us behave insensitively and make mistakes. But if we never admit to ourselves any wrongdoing because we cannot tolerate the anxiety of being imperfect, we would be viewed as being very defensive and possibly as maladjusted. But if we had no defenses, and each time we got anxious we became overwhelmed and could not function, we would also be maladjusted. Well-adjusted persons use defenses sparingly when faced with low levels of anxiety. When faced with high anxiety, they use them initially and then gradually drop their use as the anxiety state becomes more manageable. When a child dies, a parent's first reaction is denial. Only with time does the parent accept the finality of the child's death, and even then the child's room may remain unchanged for a long period.

Most of us are defensive when our anxiety is high, but after the passage of time we reevaluate our behavior and give up our defensive posture. Later we admit our mistake to ourselves and resolve not to repeat it. This fact is very important. Rarely will individuals whose defenses are made clear to them during treatment give up their defenses at that time. Each time the therapist points out how a client has used a defense to avoid experiencing a feeling, the client will resist accepting this fact. He or she most likely will increase the use of the defense for a time because anxiety has increased following the interpretation. Only with time and repeated revelations will the client begin to accept that certain defenses are used to contain anxiety.

Through a gradual process, the client comes to accept certain truths about how he or she deals with anxiety. Therapists call this gradual process of acceptance *working through*. The client comes to accept truths about how he or she deals with anxiety, truths whose acceptance has been resisted. After a time, the client will also learn the reason he or she becomes anxious in the first place. Sometimes unacknowledged wishes, which one part of ourselves finds unacceptable, cause anxiety. Other times anxiety results from reminders of repressed traumatic experiences. In addition, the client needs time to replace maladaptive defenses with more appropriate ones. Should the tactless individual discussed above become a client, he or she might want to know why mistakes cause so much anxiety or why so many tactless remarks are made to friends.

We need to emphasize that defenses are adaptive responses to anxiety. We all need defenses to keep anxiety from overwhelming us and disrupting our functioning. At times it is helpful to deny anxiety. A mother's initial denial of her newborn's diagnosed disability helps her maintain the maternal behavior necessary to ensure bonding with her child. But if she continues to deny her child's disability and pushes the child to excel beyond his ability, then her denial is maladaptive. Similarly, the mother who, six months after her child's death, still hopes that her child will return to the unchanged nursery is now pathologically denying her child's death.

Because of their upbringing, children in gorilla suits use relatively few defense mechanisms to protect themselves against anxiety. Those few they do use, such as denial, displacement, blaming, and negation, get them into considerable trouble. In fact, their fragile defenses break down quickly, leaving them with only the two most primitive defenses, those displayed by all creatures, flight or fight, the former of which may often be at least more adaptive than the latter. It most cases it is better to flee from adults, or even peers, than to hit them. When frustrated and anxious, the children hit peers and run away from authority figures. A major treatment goal with children in gorilla suits is to help them employ defenses against anxiety that get them into less trouble with society. Instead of locking horns with others when they get anxious, they need to learn to manage their anxiety in noncombative ways.

THE MECHANISMS OF DEFENSE

In order to help children develop more adaptive defenses against anxiety, staff members working with them need to be clear about the defense mechanisms employed by children. We now turn to a detailed presentation of the mechanisms of defense.

Table 1 below, also presented in *A Handbook of Play Therapy with Aggressive Children*, lists the major defense mechanisms used by children, cate-

Table 11.1. Ego Defenses of Children

Primitive	Mature
Introjection	Somatization
Denial	Avoidance
Minimizing	Inhibition
Blaming	Restriction
Negation	Distancing (Autistic Fantasy)
Splitting	Reversal
Binding and Compartmentalization	Isolation of Affect
Dissociation	Turning Feelings Inward
Grandiosity or Omnipotence	Self-Hate, Self-Love
Externalization	Undoing
Projective Identification	Overcompensation
Projection	Reaction Formation
Identification with the Aggressor	Sublimation
Provocative Behavior	Rationalization
Displacement	Devaluation
Regression	Anticipation
Negativism	

gorized for both developmental and heuristic purposes into primitive and mature.

The Primitive Defenses

Introjection When a child's response to the mother's departure is anxiety, an inner image of her is created in the mind to soothe the child; the child introjects, "takes in," or incorporates parts of the mother. A child's introjections can be witnessed in immature behavior and play; when a doll is fed or spanked, the child has introjected the mother's caring or punishing behaviors.

Denial Denial is directed against acknowledgment of frightening or objectionable impulses, feelings, or preoccupations. It is a common defense of young children: "I didn't do it." "I'm not afraid." "I'm not angry" (minimizing). "It was his fault I did it" (blaming). Denial is not lying, although it can appear so to onlookers, particularly when children deny an act they have just been caught doing. Sometimes the denial results from earlier blaming. "I didn't take the cookies" is the child's statement, but in the back of the child's mind is the unexpressed feeling that "I deserved them." The child can deny in words, in acts, or in fantasy. More sophisticated denial in fantasy appears when the child's fantasies are the complete reversal of the real situation. The child who is frightened of the lion becomes the lion tamer. The child also transforms anxiety-provoking objects into friendly beings who either protect or obey the child. This defense should not be confused with reaction formation, a more mature defense. Denial characterizes the behavior of gorilla-suit wearers. But, in some cases, denial is necessary for survival. Children who deny being rejected by their parents are doing so to avoid being overwhelmed by fears for their own safety. Denial is necessary for survival!

Negation   When a two-year-old is embarrassed by soiling, this unacceptable part of the self can be denied by making another child (or doll) the one who lacks toilet-training skill: "This is not like me." The child may not only negate unacceptable parts of the self but may split off these parts so that they are never integrated into the sense of self. This is called splitting.

Splitting   The anxiety-arousing aspect of what is repressed becomes "split off" from the child's conscious image of self. But when repression fails and anxiety is generated, the child's feeling is not that "I feel this emotion" but that "something alien to me operates within me!" "The 'bad me' made me do it." Splitting also applies to the play actions the child displays. The play figure who kills or messes is not the child; as a result, the child is free from guilt or shame since the child does not feel responsible for the action of the play figures.

Binding and Compartmentalization   Both of these are aspects of splitting. Children made anxious by a specific stimulus tightly restrict their behavior to master the feared stimulus—they "bind the anxiety" associated with that stimulus. They also split the stimulus off, or separate it, into a detached "compartment." Children who momentarily close their eyes, tighten their muscles, and continue ongoing activities when faced with fear, rather than fleeing from it, are using binding to manage anxiety. Those who split off the images associated with the trauma, "file" them in a "drawer in their personality," and continue functioning minus the psychic energy it takes to keep the drawer closed and frightening images safely inside are compartmentalizing the images associated with a traumatic experience. They function reasonably well as long as they can avoid situations that might evoke the frightening images.

For example, a child who was seriously hurt in a dark alley on a rainy night might store the images connected with this abusive experience until faced with a reminder of the situation. Anxiety may occur when hiking and a dark canyon has to be negotiated. With considerable energy, however, the hiker might be able to bind the anxiety and continue along. But should it rain or should night approach, the hiker may become numb and be retraumatized. If too many traumatic experiences are compartmentalized, the individual has little energy left to function well. Each compartmentalized experience must be faced and integrated into the personality in order for the person to feel whole again and function normally.

Extreme splitting combined with the defense of turning feelings inward can produce omnipotence or grandiosity. The child attributes strengths to the self that enable the domination of enemies and the protection of those worthy of rescue. The child fabricates an exaggerated sense of self and self-attributes, believing the self to possess superior traits, such as cunning, secret knowledge, deceit, artful craftiness, hidden physical strength, and more. Grandiosity can shield the child from feeling helpless and abandoned. The defense masks the impotence that results from feeling alone and unwanted. The defense is also employed to mask feeling depreciated and worthless. Grandiosity is activated to increase the sense of self-value. The child devalues others, especially care-giving adults, since self-worth is measured only in comparison with another.

Although grandiosity is a defense against anxiety, some of the superior traits the child attributes to the self can be better developed than other traits. Alfred Adler, father of the child guidance movement, saw creative abilities behind all distorted behaviors. The child may actually be stronger or more cunning than others his age. And the child may actually cultivate these traits. Sometimes the traits can be the hidden strengths that the staff members look for when attempting to foster a more realistic self-concept. Extreme splitting has been linked to multiple personality disorder and has been called dissociation (see the "Glossary of Specific Defense Mechanisms and Coping Styles," American Psychiatric Association, 1994, p. 755).

Negativism   To ward off anxiety (either present or anticipated), fears of passive surrender, loss of identity, or fear of merging, a child may become actively defiant and oppositional. Remember, however, that some negativism is necessary for self-differentiation; this phase-appropriate negativism must be differentiated from negativism as a defensive maneuver.

Externalization   When the child attributes to someone else the denied bad parts of the self, the child has externalized them. Many children externalize their unacceptable parts onto adults, who then become the stupid or the retarded ones and are bombarded with insults.

Projection   A child is projecting when he or she attributes to another person unacceptable wishes or impulses. The child can then blame another for possessing these impulses. The angry child often sees others as more angry than they are because the child has projected retaliating anger onto them. Externalization involves negation of self while projection involves denial of felt impulses. For example, a group of children in playgroup therapy are cutting out pictures from magazines to make a group collage. Jim comes across a picture of a woman's bra and hits Phil for no apparent reason. The therapist asks Jim why he did that, and he replies, "Philip said a nasty thing." The group therapist heard no such comment from Phil. Later the therapist hypothesized that Jim was sexually stimulated by the bra advertisement and projected these feelings to Phil, whom he then punished for having them. Projections abound in children who display fantasy. The king is the one with the angry bad impulses, not the good knight who slays him to free the people from tyranny.

A more involved defense is one called projective identification, a situation in which one or more individuals are the repeated targets of the child's externalizations and projections. We will discuss the therapeutic use of projective identifications later in the chapter.

Identification with the Aggressor   Children can also introject the threatening, critical features of the parent. Being the threatener is less anxiety producing than being the person threatened. At the same time, however, the child feels worthless because external criticism has become self-criticism. The child now develops a method to handle this double-edged sword. The child becomes protected from self-criticism by both externalizing the negative self-image and projecting the unacceptable impulses onto others. In the playroom, a three-year-old girl immediately hit a baby doll with a drumstick, saying, "The baby is not going to bed, she needs a whipping." Then, dissatisfied with the drumstick, she asked the therapist for his belt so she could beat the bad baby. Then she wanted to leave the room and take the doll with her and hit the therapist when he went to retrieve it from her.

Provocative Behavior   When a child expresses hostility against another by inducing the other to attack first, the hostility appears as a self-defense and can be expressed without internal conflict. Provocative behavior may also occur as a defense against guilt. By getting another to inflict punishment first, the child can reduce or eliminate guilt feelings without becoming conscious of their nature.

Displacement   Expressing an emotion toward a substitute object is displacement. John attacks Sally when he really has been angered by Bill (who is larger). Displacement abounds in children who fantasize. The wicked witch stands for the mother, the evil king for the father, and the wolf for the child. All are called masking symbols and are discussed in *A Handbook of Play Therapy with Aggressive Children*. One dramatic example of displacement occurred during a family session that included two parents involved in a bitter divorce in which acrimony, feuding, and court battles were never ending. The couple had three children, but their seven-year-old girl, Suzie, was the most vulnerable. She had spent a year at a renowned psychiatric teaching hospital and had been diagnosed as psychotic because she reported seeing images of the clown in the movie *It* (1986), based on Stephen King's novel. She was considered to be hallucinating, and because the images were persistent, she remained in the psychiatric hospital for an entire year before being referred for residential treatment, where she was treated by Dr. Crenshaw and his cotherapist Chris Foreacre. Before a family therapy session, Dr. Crenshaw and his cotherapist were advised by a consultant, Andrew Fussner, to view the alleged "hallucination of the clown" as a metaphor for the child's hostility. The therapists entered the room with the family and began the session:

THERAPIST: We have been thinking a lot about Suzie's image of the clown and how she can't get the image out of her mind. We have talked it over extensively with the family therapy team, and we think we understand what it means. [*Long pause; both the parents and Suzie rivet their attention on the therapists.*] Suzie is a very sensitive and loyal child, so we don't think she'd be able, without guilt, to directly express her feeling to you. She would want to protect you and not upset you. We think she views her parents as "clowns," as phonies, pretending to be parents, but in fact poisoning the family atmosphere by constant fighting and feuding, and she doesn't think it will ever end, no matter what you say.

There was a long, pregnant silence. Nothing more was said but, to our knowledge, the symptom of the "hallucination of the clown" never troubled Suzie again.

Regression   When a child reverts to earlier, less mature patterns of behavior when overcome by anxiety, the child is regressing in an effort to use previously successful coping strategies. Regression occurs in therapy when the child wants to mess the finger paints or be pushed in a wagon, curls up on the therapist's chair, or sucks his thumb. With aggressive, macho children, such behavior may signal progress in developing trust. They have stopped inhibiting their needs for affection.

The More Mature Defenses

The more mature defenses are those defenses whose use results in less resistance to socialization and educational practices. For example, the child who converts anxious feelings into stomach aches may feel physically stressed and could develop an ulcerated condition. Nevertheless, the child will elicit more caring feelings from adults than would be elicited if projection and displacement characterized his or her functioning.

Somatization   When children convert anxious feelings into bodily symptoms, they are doing what is called *somatization* or *conversion*. Somatization is a widely used defense against anxiety, even by aggressive children, and attention to their bodily symptoms is a good way of getting rapport with them. King (1975), who worked with aggressive adolescents in prison settings, emphasized administering to their somatic complaints no matter how trivial they may seem to the observer.

Avoidance   The child can avoid talking about painful feelings or facing painful situations. If afraid of the dark, the child may act up at bedtime, trying to avoid sleeping alone. Avoidance can be subdivided into inhibitions, restrictions, and distancing. The child inhibits the expression of forbidden impulses and thereby constricts functioning or limits activities thought to cause anxiety.

Children also avoid activities in which failures have produced humiliation and resulting anxiety, most often academic activities or new activities they are encouraged to try.

In one type of avoidance, inhibition, the child avoids painful feelings from within, while in another type, restriction, painful feelings stimulated by outside sources are avoided. Children who distance from anxiety are those who make use of masking symbols to put what is feared in faraway places. While they are supposed to be concentrating on academic or recreational pursuits, instead they are fantasizing about being in far-off places. Extreme distancing has been called autistic fantasy. In between autistic fantasy and the normal use of distancing is pathological use of the defense. The children use the monsters as the personification and receptacle of all their bad impulses, which enables them to establish distance from those impulses and deny them as their own. The children also put the monsters out in some distant space, far away from them. The undesirable, unconscious, forbidden, and repressed are sent far away. Anxiety is avoided by distance.

> CHILD: Here's a witch killing people, cowboys eating people up! [*The child becomes anxious, loses distance, remarks*] It's just a story.
> CHILD: [*An anxious child, asked to tell a story, introduces her task by immediately distancing.*] I don't know any stories, but I'll tell one that isn't true.

Dragons and monsters have always been the basis of early conscience development; the small child experiences the parent as threatening and punitive and as magically omnipotent and giving. Normally the child's early images become modified and synthesized into developing moral structures. As the internalization of values and identification with parents proceed, the archaic, distorted features recede. In contrast, the disturbed child is unable to synthesize the good and bad parental images and, thus remains with only the primitive precursors of a conscience, derived from a period in development in which love and hate are fused rather than synthesized. The child's fantasies reflect this integrative failure. Such children suffer from certain integrative deficits. Their personalities are composed of disconnected and fragmented parts (split-off parts of themselves). Some children distance from their problems by maintaining a strong, though not total, commitment to a self-centered, illusory world of pleasure. Yet even these fantasies, on close inspection, actually reflect terrors being denied.

Reversal   When the child attempts to mask anxious feelings by displaying behaviors seemingly incompatible with anxiety, the child is using reversal. The child may laugh or joke when hurt or punished or may profess love when the feeling is hate. Reversal masks anxious feelings, and reaction formation (discussed below) masks unacceptable impulses. Reversal can also involve isolation of affect: conflict or stress is dealt with by separation of the feelings from the ideas originally associated with them. The child can discuss the cognitive component of a traumatic event but cannot get in touch with the feelings.

Turning Feelings Inward   Instead of expressing anger or hatred against another, the hatred is turned inward, taking the form of self-hate and self-accusation. Similarly, the feeling of love for another can be withdrawn and turned into self-love or narcissism. Children who are accident prone may be displaying this defense, as well as children who bang their heads against the wall when angry.

Undoing   When a child attempts to recant or undo the possible effects of an anxiety-producing thought or act, the defense is called undoing. This defense is most often employed when the child feels both anger and affection or hate and fear for the same person. A child may hide the toy guns in the therapy room to undo the hostility felt in seeing them as objects to express aggression against the therapist. A child may destroy parental figures in play and then rescue them. (Ritualized undoing is displayed by individuals with obsessive-compulsive behaviors and by some psychotics as a defense against intrusive thoughts.)

Overcompensation   When the child makes use of an acceptable attitude to cover up an unacceptable one, overcompensation is the defense. Pity may cover up unconscious cruelty. Shyness can serve as a defense against exhibitionism or boastful conceit against feelings of inferiority.

Reaction Formation   The child substitutes an acceptable impulse for an unacceptable one. The anxiety aroused by the thought of expressing an unacceptable impulse is managed by displaying behaviors incompatible with the expression of that impulse. The older sibling displays solicitous behavior toward the younger sibling to avoid expressing the anger actually felt toward the sibling, who is seen as taking away much of the mother's love. Angry feelings toward the therapist are repressed and solicitous behavior takes its place. Children whose play behavior when they were younger suggested they were fascinated with bodily functions or who talked endlessly about "poopies, snot, and pee-pee" now vehemently profess disgust with such talk.

Sublimation   In sublimation, the unacceptable impulse attains a certain amount of direct expression in a socially acceptable manner. The girl who desires to show off her body finds an outlet for these needs in dance or drama. The sexually curious child now wants to read about sex with the therapist instead of trying to touch her.

Rationalization   The child made anxious by failing to accomplish a task or to please another person now reinterprets the situation to excuse unacceptable behavior. "The task was stupid anyway." A child whose anxiety follows a

failed effort may deny his initial interest in an accomplishment. "What would
I do with the cheap ribbon anyway?"

Devaluation   The child displays a derogatory attitude toward relationships
and activities that others seek. By devaluing relationships or activities, the child
avoids the anxiety that participating in them might arouse. Devaluation is a
form of rationalization. The "cheap ribbon" comment above devalues the reward that was sought.

Anticipation   Very mature children anticipate what will make them anxious and plan accordingly. If they are made anxious by the thought of being
alone, they will manipulate events so that they have company. This is the one
defense that is consciously employed. Most conduct-disordered children are
excellent anticipators, but instead of planning an appropriate action to handle
their anxiety, they either avoid the feared situation or lash out in an aggressive
manner.

SUPPORTING RATHER THAN CONFRONTING DEFENSES

Using the defenses listed in the left-hand column of the table of defenses earlier in this chapter typically gets a child into trouble with others. Denial, blaming, externalization, and so forth, while helpful to the child in containing anxiety, are socially unacceptable behaviors often leading to displays of aggression,
particularly when these defenses are confronted by others. The child who employs the defenses in the right-hand column in the table gets into less trouble
with others. For example, formal studies of children reveal that those who rely
on what we have called primitive defenses report higher levels of self-rated social anxiety and depression and are rated higher by parents on conduct problems. In contrast, those making more use of more mature defenses exhibit
higher scores on perceived competence in social, academic, conduct, athletic,
and global adjustment domains (Sandstrom and Cramer 2003).

When most children enter treatment, they use their fragile defenses when
anxious, and they become anxious often because placement in a treatment center is of itself an anxiety-producing situation. Children are asked to relate to
new teachers and new peers, the latter being as defensive and aggressive as they
are. Displacement, projection, blaming, and negativism will abound, and if these
defenses are not respected, flight or fight will follow. Respecting a child's defenses has a very important and specific meaning in this context. In our experience, without specific training to honor each child's defenses, no matter how
maladaptive, until the child is able to replace them with more adaptive ones,
educational and direct-care staff will confront them, leaving the child no

choice but to use the defenses more or to regress to even more primitive ones, such as flight or fight.

Many adults in caregiving or instructional relationships with aggressive children attribute motives to children's behaviors, making "dynamic interpretations" when annoyed by them.

> BOY: [*Strikes out in a baseball game, angrily throws the bat, and storms off the field.*]
> ADULT: [*Yells at the departing boy*] Every time you feel defeated, you storm off the field and refuse to play. Grow up and accept defeat like a man.

This admonishment is actually a confrontation of the child's use of a defense. The boy was disappointed, perhaps because he expected to hit the ball and win admiration. His disappointment, and the self-disparagement that followed it, raised his anxiety. He instantly, and unconsciously, masked the anxiety with anger first, followed by flight (leaving the game). Such confrontational comments are never helpful. If the boy knew how to handle disappointment better, he would not behave in this fashion. Pointing out the defensive behavior adds insult to injury. Adults working with children should not "take away" a child's defense until the child has been taught to use better ones. Otherwise the child will replace the defense used, in this case "flight," with an even more primitive one, such as "fight." The boy may throw the baseball bat at the supervising adult or at another child. Stripping the child of his or her defense is one reason adult-child interchanges can escalate into aggression. After flight, fighting is the most primitive defense against anxiety, and children often are forced to use it when mishandled.

Respecting the boy's defenses and treating him empathetically, the adult would have responded as follows.

> SUPERVISING ADULT: Bill, I'm sorry you didn't get a hit. I know you wanted to hit one bad. You're swinging well; maybe next time you'll hit one. When you calm down, you can rejoin us. I'm glad you left the game instead of hitting someone [*acknowledgment of the child's use of a better defense—better because it is less destructive*].
> BILL: F—— you, I'm not coming back.
> SUPERVISING ADULT: That's how you feel now. If you change your mind, let us know. We'd like to have you back.

Children who are somewhat more developed may blame their failures on others or on the equipment being used. They may yell angrily at the pitcher for not getting the ball over the plate. If the pitcher is an adult (as it should be in a treatment center), a child's blaming should not be confronted by remarks such as the following: "Stop blaming me for your own mistakes. The other children have no trouble hitting the balls I pitch." Instead, the adult should accept the blame and make the following remark:

> SUPERVISING ADULT: I'm sorry you can't hit my pitches, but I'm glad you told me instead of throwing the bat at me or leaving the game like you used to do [*acknowledgment of the child's use of a better defense—blaming—instead of the child's past use of flight or fight*]. Here, I'll move closer to be sure that I get the ball over the plate.

Educators should handle blaming in the same manner.

> CHILD: These problems you gave me are too hard. [*The problems are similar to ones the child successfully completed earlier in the week, but troubled children's functioning is variable and mood dependent.*]
>
> TEACHER: I'm sorry. I'm glad you told me instead of ripping up the paper, as you used to do [*acknowledgment of the child's use of a more mature defense, blaming rather than angry destructiveness*]. Here's another five. Pick those you think you can do and leave the rest. [*The child is given five easier problems instead of the ten previously given.*]

We can't tell you how many discussions, if not downright arguments, we have had with educators and child-care workers who equate treatment with constant confrontation. They insist that it is "lying" to accept the child's displacement, blaming, or negativism. "The child needs to 'face the reality' of his or her defensive behavior." For us, that amounts to saying "A two-year-old should stop being a two-year-old and act ten years old." Children will not automatically use a more mature defense when the ones they customarily use are stripped from them. Instead, they will regress to using more primitive ones. Time, instruction, and patience are required before children will replace old behaviors with new ones. To deny this truth is akin to claiming "A patient who has lost a leg should be able to use a new prosthesis without practice."

Ross Greene (2003), in a presentation, emphasized that rewards and punishments work only when the desired positive behavior is well established in a child's repertoire. He also reminds us,

> Any child will do well if the child can. If the behavior has not been consistently mastered and is, therefore, unavailable to the child on a consistent basis, all the rewards and punishments in the world will be of little use. It would be like placing a neophyte basketball player on a basketball court and consistently expecting the player to hit a thirty-foot jump shot. No matter how richly rewarded for success or severely punished for failure, performance would not improve.

Lots of practice is required to achieve most skills, and a supportive environment is needed to practice them in. Formal studies demonstrate that more adaptive defenses increase over time in therapeutic relationships (Drapeau, DeRoten, Perry et al. 2003), and therapeutic environments, by their very nature, are supportive.

In *A Handbook of Play Therapy with Aggressive Children*, chapters 7, 8, and 9, we present examples of ways play therapists can help children to use defenses more adaptively and to develop new defenses. Clinicians can translate these examples into the fields of child care, education, and recreation and help staff respond similarly to the child's behavior, including play behavior, outside of therapy. For example, instead of simply being punished for hurting another child, the perpetrator can assist the nurse or staff member in administering to the victim's hurts. Simply handing the victim a bandage can help the perpetrator develop the defense of undoing.

Staff can reward more adaptive defensive behaviors with the following approach: If a child fails at a task and runs away from the group, the child-care worker can respond with "Good. You left the group when you were angry instead of hitting another child. Let's think about what you could do the next time you are upset instead of leaving." When child-care workers perform life space interviews, instead of confronting children's defenses when they are upset, or probing into what made them upset, the worker can ask, "What will make you less upset?" or "What will help you to feel calmer?" Child-care staff modeling more appropriate defenses can carry the approach further. They can do this, first of all, by remaining calm and in control themselves in the face of the child's upset. Secondly, they can suggest some additional ways of feeling less upset (less angry, less afraid, etc.), drawing from their own experiences to supplement whatever the child produces. "When I'm upset, I try to think of my favorite food, or about things that I like to do, and it makes me feel better." Staff members can model rationalization by communicating about disappointments in their owns lives with statements such as "I really didn't want to go to that party anyway."

A child-care worker who observes a boy playing that a toy house is on fire but who suddenly stops his play in response to anxiety elicited by the breakthrough of aggressive impulses (burning a house down) can respond with "Wait a minute, Tony, let's put that fire out! The fire truck is over here. Let's call the fire department." By remaining within the metaphor of the play, the worker models the defense of undoing, a defense that may help the child deal with the anxiety raised by his own aggressive themes.

Classroom teachers can assess the current defenses children might use from the stories they write or dictate to the teacher. Defenses are revealed in their stories because the thoughts that enter their head and that they write down or dictate first often raise their anxiety, and they manage the anxiety by introducing a defensive action to continue or complete the story. Stories told by three different children appear below.

I.

The little rabbit went into the lady's garden to eat her food. He took it into the woods to eat it. He chews the lettuce all up. He doesn't eat any more lettuce at all. He goes home to bed. He sleeps. He goes out to play.

II.

Once the bear had a fire. And he got burned in the fire and had to go to the hospital. And he got better and had a new house. There was no flames in it. There was no burner burning. There were no stoves working. There was no heat coming out of the radiator. There were no rats in the basement. The end.

III.

A cowboy road a bucking house and the horse ate the saddle. So the boy gave his horse to some Indians because Indians ride bareback.

In the first story, the child attempts to deny the basic oral needs of the rabbit, while in the second, the child denies the initially frightening image of damage by fire. The second story is even more revealing because the child had just learned about an upcoming move to a new home. The third story reveals rationalization, a defense not often seen in gorilla-suit wearers. Should the teacher bring this story to a treatment-team meeting, staff may learn that the child has more potential than was revealed by surface behavior.

Sometimes it is even appropriate to support an immature defense, such as regression. James Garbarino (1999), in *Lost Boys*, tells the story of interviewing in prison a tough, macho youth who had committed forty-eight armed robberies, had been stabbed in the chest, and after a carefully planned attempt at revenge had shot the person who stabbed him. After telling the story of his violent escapades to Garbarino, the youth leaned back in his chair and began to rock and to suck his thumb. Perhaps this fawn in a gorilla suit was taking a small step toward trusting enough to begin to show a small part of his vulnerability.

REWARDING MATURE DEFENSES

When children start using more mature defenses, the key adults in their lives should actively comment on their improvement. Troubled children can become extremely pessimistic about their ability to change. They need reassurance when others see change. Improvements come in steps so small that often neither the children nor other adults notice them. If the child first uses "fight," praise should be given for the use of "flight," with comments like "It's more grown-up to leave the room than to hit me." When attempts to hit a staff member are displaced onto objects, the child must be restrained, but at the same time the staff member should comment, "Throwing the toy against the wall is not permitted, but it's more grown-up to do that than to hit me." Notice the skill in the following interchange between a nurse and a boy who uses somatization.

> NURSE: Hi, Jackson. Are you not feeling well this morning?
> JACKSON: My neck and shoulders are stiff and sore. I can't sleep.
> NURSE: Let me have a look. [*She begins to rub his shoulders and back of the neck.*] I can see how tight and stiff these muscles are. No wonder they give you pain and you're having trouble sleeping. I will massage them gently and then put some lotion on them, and you will feel better.

The nurse at no point tries to connect Jackson's physical aches and pains to the anxieties he defends against by somatization. She knows that he would feel unmasked and exposed. Rather, she administers tender, loving care to his aches and pains. By her accepting his current defense, Jackson may accept care and nurture that ordinarily he would reject. In time, following a period of receptivity to loving care, Jackson's major anxieties may diminish, and he may no longer manage those that remain with this particular defense.

Sometimes improvement is viewed as regression rather than as progress. Staff can confuse the development of a defense with resistance to an activity. A boy who used to get very anxious, agitated, and disruptive every time he was asked to participate in a particular activity started going to a corner of the room and playing actively with some toys when the activity was offered. Sometimes he openly stated, "I don't want to do that!" The boy has initiated avoidance to handle his anxiety, a sign of progress rather than of resistance. A child's use of a more mature defense should be rewarded with comments something like the following:

> CHILD-CARE WORKER: You feel really nervous taking your turn right now.
> CHILD: I just don't want to!
> THERAPIST: So pulling back helps you not to feel so anxious. That's good! Is there anything else you are doing right now to prevent you from feeling anxious?

Children progressing to higher developmental levels can sometimes look worse than before. Because the use of a more mature defense may not at first appear as progress, child-care, recreational, and teaching staff need to be familiar with concepts of developmental change. Sexually provocative behavior, for example, can be more troublesome for staff than other provocations. It is important for progress notes to include material on the child's defenses and to save all the drawings, artwork, and written stories a child produces in school, art therapy, or play therapy. Saving and examining each child's productions enable staff, and each child, to see concrete demonstrations of progress. Periodically referring to these materials also helps children develop a continuity of self and a past they can relate to their present.

MINIMIZING FRUSTRATIONS: A PREREQUISITE FOR DEVELOPMENTAL ADVANCEMENT

Contrary to the belief of some individuals, treatment centers are not supposed to represent reality. They are supposed to temporarily shelter children from it. Treatment centers are supposed to design and maintain milieus that will meet the emotional, not the chronological age–appropriate, needs of children in gorilla suits, most of whom were not sheltered by parents in their early development. In several other published works, Dr. Mordock has presented a milieu design that successfully treats children in gorilla suits (Mordock 2002a, 2002b). Dr. Crenshaw has discussed a milieu approach to managing sexual acting out (Crenshaw 1988). None of that material will be repeated here. In chapter 10, we list children's needs that, if met by a thoughtful milieu design, foster the development of children in gorilla suits, and in the next chapter we discuss milieu modifications for sexually traumatized children. In this chapter, we focus on two needs: to develop more appropriate defenses against anxiety and to develop calming behaviors.

One of the sheltering conditions necessary to achieve both tasks is an environment where frustrations are kept to a minimum. If continually frustrated, children will continue to use their maladaptive defenses. Only when frustrations are kept to a minimum will new defenses be adopted. This is true for all new learning (and it should go without saying because it was identified more than fifty years ago; see Beres 1952). If the child is constantly frustrated, frustrations will continue to be managed by flight or fight. The child will be so busy fleeing or fighting that no time will be available to learn the more adaptive defenses. Consequently, the therapeutic environment cannot be a duplication of the "real world" because the child has already failed in such a world. Academic demands should be kept to a minimum and gradually increased as the child makes progress. Competitive games, such as baseball, dodgeball, basketball, or capture the flag, should not be played by children in the early stages of treatment. Instead these gross motor activities should be replaced with tumbling, aerobic exercises, nature hikes, group swims, camping, dance, and physical education activities appropriate for much younger children. Clinicians unfamiliar with emotionally appropriate activities can examine a book on physical education for young children, such as Pangrazi's (2004) *Lesson Plans for Dynamic Physical Education for Elementary School Children*, and compare the activities listed for developmental level one with those the child-care workers or recreational staff are using.

In a therapeutic milieu, the frustration experienced by the reluctant batter presented earlier would not occur because baseball would not be played until the child had better frustration tolerance and more adaptive defenses. Competitive games require children to learn or display skills that require frustration tolerance, which they lack. Consequently, they become anxious and mobilize their primitive defenses to manage ongoing frustrations. Even when tolerance for frustration improves, the rules of competitive games should be modified. For example, baseball can be played by the hitter batting a large softball propped up on a stand or kicking a rolled soccer ball (with unlimited strikes); children can run between two bases, as in cricket, instead of four, making it easier for fielders to know where to throw; and so on. Only children nearly ready for discharge should play competitive games.

Children with minimal self-control should have pleasurable activities with minimal frustration, any frustrations that are experienced should be made into objective issues rather than confronted, relationship aspects of recreational activities should predominate, and recreational activities should never be contingent on acceptable behavior. Initial activities should be those that require the development of simple skills, such as CD playing, simple board games, well-known table games, crayoning, and storytelling. The activities should be ones in which children need no extra help or support, waiting and taking turns are minimized, there is no element of danger, and the need for impulse control is minimal. Food and rhythm should be involved whenever possible. Activities to be avoided include those involving frustration tolerance, such as treasure or scavenger hunts; those involving impulse control and concentration, such as relay races; or highly competitive and potentially hurtful activities, such as dodgeball or even hide-and-seek. And children should never be deprived of recreational activities because of disruptive or aggressive behavior; time-outs from recreation, if necessary at all, should be minimal.

Most child-care workers in residential treatment centers dread rainy and bitterly cold days. They dread being cooped up inside with children who prefer gross motor and outdoor activities. Many children, particularly those who have been severely and repeatedly traumatized, display very little make-believe play. Rarely do they engage in cooperative make-believe play with other children, even failing at parallel play (typical of children between the ages of two and three years, who play side by side without interaction) because such play requires imagination. Sometimes they can play at being space monsters, evil emperors, and warriors, but such play quickly regresses into open conflicts with peers. Rarely can the children be left alone to play cooperatively with one another without the watchful eye of a staff member. As a result, even leisure time activities have to be structured by child-care or recreational staff. Nevertheless, the very skills they lack are the ones they need to learn.

Most children in gorilla suits lack not only social play skills but also skills at self-calming. Indoor and outdoor recreational activities can teach them both skills. Child-care workers lacking knowledge of nature; arts and crafts; rhythm, dance, music; and camping procedures should be quickly trained in these skills. Some of the best times reported by both staff and children have been rainy days when the children decorated bottles with colored waxes, decorated wreaths, created collages, cut out and pasted pictures into scrap books, glued leaves previously collected outdoors into nature albums, colored in "sophisticated" coloring books, wrapped and decorated boxes with magic markers, sorted and polished rock collections, made and decorated gingerbread cookies, and on and on.

While many child-care workers believe that children should be "run ragged" during the day so they will sleep at night, children actually sleep better when their minds are free from thought-provoking images. Children can compulsively relive humiliations and create fantasies of revenge all night long while trying to fall asleep, one reason so many have sleep-related difficulties. Participation in noncompetitive activities, especially mood-altering activities, such as nature hikes, fishing, arts and crafts, music, and dance, results in less conflict with others, which creates periods of calm leading to sleep-filled nights. And when the children do go to the gym on rainy days, they should tumble, perform aerobic exercises, or play games played by younger children, such as leap frog, ponies in the stable, or run and assume shapes, and games with high-powered "It" roles, such as "red light-green light," "Simon says," or "statues," in which the child can experience mastery rather than frustration and humiliation.

ENCOURAGING SUBLIMATION AND REACTION FORMATION

A large portion of recreation time with children in gorilla suits should be spent in helping them sublimate impulses and substitute acceptable for unacceptable impulses. Instead of being disorganized and messy in the uninhibited expression of impulses, children are encouraged to be orderly. The normal child in latency is a collector and organizer of collections. Stamps, coins, or baseball cards are organized and reorganized. These obsessive-compulsive activities, or reaction formations, keep the child from experiencing and acting on destructive impulses. Sarnoff (1987) grouped the defenses of reaction formation, undoing, sublimation, and rationalization as "mechanisms of restraint," all activities that assist in repression and in symbol and fantasy formation. Without mechanisms of restraint, children have little energy to meet developmental challenges. They cannot move to Erikson's (1963) stage of initiative, in which a relatively calm, impulse-free state is needed to initiate and complete the tasks required to become industrious children, the next stage of development in Erikson's schema.

Child-care staff should encourage children to collect rocks, baseball cards, coins, and stamps and to play repetitive, meaningless games like organizing dominoes so that they fall down in sequence. Children can collect lollipop sticks and, on rainy days, glue them onto cardboard. They can cut out pictures of athletic figures, and so forth. They can draw and color geometric forms, with all the forms of one shape colored black, those of another shape colored red, and so on. Children also can be encouraged to sublimate their unacceptable impulses through engaging in activities that are symbolic equivalents of their wishes. Staff can encourage aggressive children to collect miniature war toys or war pictures or to make war scrapbooks, the purpose being to develop intellectualization as a defense, with the hope that the child will feel less anxious when more is known about war and defense.

Games also can be used to develop mechanisms of restraint. The games should be simple, repetitive ones like Candy Land, Chutes and Ladders, and occasionally checkers. Games help to develop a sense of organization and adherence to regulations in a manner that can be pleasurable (Sarnoff 1987). Even better than games are the partially absorbing miniature "puzzles" that many children play, such as getting all the little balls in the holes on plastic-enclosed frames. Pick-Up Sticks was modified by McDowell (1994) so that the colors of the sticks are paired with different feelings of the child, and whenever a stick is successfully picked up, the player tells of a time when he or she felt that emotion. The game is also helpful in teaching restraint, especially with the action-oriented, impulsive, aggressive child.

CALMING TECHNIQUES

In addition to utilizing more adaptive defense mechanisms and developing mechanisms of restraint, children need to employ self-calming activities when they feel anxious. One calming technique children can use when they become overly upset when frustrated is to remember activities they enjoyed doing with a significant other and to think about, or in some cases to perform, these activities. Recently, such efforts have been referred to as mood-repair strategies, and recollection of parental images has been related to the restoration of positive moods (Cohen 1998). Unfortunately, because of parental abuse, children in gorilla suits can experience difficulty recalling positive events, but because memory for positive emotional events is better than for negative emotional events (Lindsay et al. 2004), especially in clients with acute stress disorders (Moulds and Bryant 2002), with help and encouragement, children can usually remember some time spent with a parent or other caregiver that was emotionally satisfying, and these memories can be used to calm themselves. But for others, it can be thinking about going to a ball game with a friend, remembering a meaningful family gathering, coloring with a brightly colored crayon, perhaps a reminder of a positive early experience with a cared-for adult, or recalling their "safe place" (see *A Handbook of Play Therapy with Aggressive Children*, chapters 9 and 13). Each child should be helped to find and utilize his or her own calming procedures.

For some, it will be images; for others it will be actions. For children requiring actions, efforts should be made to find symbolic equivalents. These efforts can take place following crisis intervention or at another time. The child who is calmed only by eating can be encouraged to draw foods and to color the drawings. Children can be encouraged to keep a picture of a preferred adult on their person and look at it when they are about to lose control. This procedure has been used with handicapped preschoolers with separation difficulties (Mordock 1979).

THERAPEUTIC USE OF THE CHILD'S DEFENSES

Contrary to popular opinion, countertransference is not always inappropriate. Based on the work of many prominent therapists (for example, see Borowitz 1970; Colm 1966; Ehrenberg 1992; Ekstein, Wallerstein, and Mandelbaum 1992; Gill 1982; Hoffman 1998; or Rinsley 1980), we believe that many reactions to aggressive children's behaviors are the result of projective communications. In other words, not all personal reactions are unhealthy contaminants contributed by the staff's own issues. By the creative use of self as a healing instrument, the reactions that arise in staff during the course of therapeutic interactions can provide a window into the child's inner world and past experience.

McCready (1987) presents examples of a way the collective countertransference of staff can be used therapeutically. When staff members feel impotent, hopeless, and defeated, they should be asked, "Is this how the child feels, only much more intensely? Paraphrasing Walter Bonime, whom we quote in chapter 2 of *A Handbook of Play Therapy with Aggressive Children*, no matter how frustrated, hopeless, impotent, or miserable staff may feel in the midst of a treatment process fraught with obstacles and setbacks, these feelings cannot begin to match the intensity of the feelings experienced by the client (Bonime 1982).

Children often display projective identifications with staff members. Unacceptable parts of the self are externalized onto others, and unacceptable emotions are projected onto staff, followed by the child's identifying with this "unreal" image of the staff member. Children externalize their negative self-image by berating direct-care staff, calling them "stupid," "dumb," or "ugly." They fail to see the workers' real traits because they have turned the workers into the undesirable aspects of themselves. Children also project their anger onto staff and, as a result, believe that the staff members are always angry, and so the children become fearful of them. When children attribute hostile intent to a staff member, there is often a "degree of fit" between the projection and reality. The children may hang the projection on some real event, such as a denied request, a hurried remark, or an elevated voice level. Often a worker is busy with another child or distracted by some other event and may express annoyance, or even anger, when the child interrupts to make a request. As a result, the staff member is feared because he or she has "been made into" an undesirable and rejecting tyrant.

> Martha was a nine-year-old girl who was irascible but also withdrawn and who elicited much ridicule from her peers, whom she taunted and teased in retaliation. She continually belittled the young female child-care worker in charge of her living unit. She included "stupid" and "ugly" among her various insults. Martha's behaviors could be her attempts to ward off anticipated insults from the worker, who occasionally regressed with a sarcastic rebuttal to Martha's insults. Martha's affect suggests that she identified with her powerful, arrogant mother, who felt humiliated by her daughter's placement in treatment and humiliated her in return. In response, Martha externalized the "Little Martha" who was laughed at, criticized, and often ignored.

With consultation from Martha's therapist, the young child-care worker began to respond to Martha's outpourings of criticisms by verbalizing how she was being viewed by Martha, how she was being seen and treated as a stupid little girl, and how it feels to be treated in this manner.

CHILD-CARE WORKER: You talk to me this way because you have been called "stupid" and "ugly," and it's very painful to be called these things. Sometimes I think you even believe these insults. It's hard living in this place and not thinking you're dumb, or even crazy. Just because you have a quick temper and cannot concentrate in school doesn't mean you're not a worthwhile, lovable person. I enjoy you when you're not insulting me.

Because Martha frequently experienced insulting attacks from her mother, she expected such attacks from adult staff. Following the principle of turning what is passively experienced into what is actively managed, she insulted the young worker, perhaps because she was the staff member who reminded Martha most of her mother. Consequently, this worker, rather than other staff, became the target of projected anger. Martha's anxiety about her worker's "anger" was revealed in her nonverbal behavior. She was always the last to get ready for activities, and when she finally came to an activity, she sat far away from the worker, often shouting angry insults at her from a distance, which disrupted the group and angered the worker. The worker's anger unknowingly frightened the child, and the cycle was repeated.

Martha would accuse the worker of disliking her, citing such evidence as past denials of legitimate requests. The worker did not contradict Martha's view of these events, accepting them as possible, but suggested that what Martha feared more than the worker's dislike or inconsiderateness was that the worker might wish to harm her in retaliation for all her insults. In some sense, Martha externalized her harsh and severe conscience onto the worker, as well as projecting her own anger. After Martha admitted to this fear, the worker attempted to show her that the wish to harm the worker, who stood for all adults who had hurt Martha, was actually Martha's wish to retaliate for hurts inflicted on her by others.

CHILD-CARE WORKER: Simply because you wish to harm me doesn't mean that I wish to harm you. Often you think that your wishes will come true, but wishes are just wishes. I know that you are angry at me, but I'll never harm you, even when I get angry. You've seen me angry at you lots of time, but I have never harmed you. I may yell loudly at you at times, perhaps embarrassing you in front of the other children, for which I apologize, but I would never hit you.

Readers will note that the child-care worker's responses to Martha's projective identifications are similar to those made to Gloria, a child discussed in chapter 11 of *A Handbook of Play Therapy with Aggressive Children*, by her female therapist when she became the object of Gloria's identification with an arrogant father. Most children in gorilla suits make extensive use of externalization and projection. Direct-care staff are constantly confronted with children who greet them with hostility. Understanding that externalization and projective identification are two defenses children use to handle their anxiety helps direct-care staff distance from this hostility and maintain objectivity.

CONCLUSION

Understanding the defenses each child employs is the first step in designing a treatment plan that will support the child's ego development. Milieu staff can then direct their efforts toward helping the child use each defense more efficiently and develop those defenses that will elicit more positive responses from caregivers, including the child's parents. In most situations, milieu staff members need to actively select leisure time materials that will contribute to defensive development, model defensive play behavior, reinforce the child's developing play, and accept and praise the child's use of defenses that are more mature than those the child typically employs. As children gradually develop more mature defenses, they may be able to discuss events associated with earlier traumas. Some, however, because of the degree of their trauma, may never be strong enough to do this very painful work while in residential treatment.

12

Creating a Therapeutic Milieu for Traumatized Children

An ego-strengthening approach for treatment of traumatized children, with special emphasis on treating sexually abused children, requires a particular milieu. The functional elements deemed especially critical for treating traumatized children are (1) creating empowerment, (2) respecting privacy, (3) providing a safe haven, (4) building genuine self-esteem, and (5) facilitating constructive reenactment of trauma.

*M*ultiply traumatized children make up a large portion of those placed in residential treatment centers because the symptoms that result from their traumatic experiences and the gorilla suits they put on to defend themselves from pain make their treatment in the community difficult. Abused when young, they lack the capacity to integrate the overwhelming feelings that accompanied their abuse, and the result is markedly underdeveloped ego capacities, particularly regulation of impulses and affects, and a fragmented sense of self. These children's fragmented memories and associated feelings often result in their being continually traumatized by intrusive thoughts. In addition, posttraumatic stress disorder symptoms, such as frequent nightmares, sleep loss, and somatic complaints, are usually present (Clum, Nishith, and Resick 2001). Many are easily overwhelmed by painful emotions, and spurious events often trigger memories of a traumatic event, as was demonstrated by the two case vignettes presented in chapter 3.

In chapter 11, we discuss creating a therapeutic milieu to help children use more adaptive defenses against anxiety and to employ self-calming activities when upset. In chapter 10, we discuss creating a treatment environment to meet ten significant needs. The purpose of this chapter is to discuss five additional therapeutic tasks that, if accomplished in conjunction with the tasks discussed in chapters 9, 10, and 11, contribute to successful residential treatment of abused children, especially those who have been traumatized by sexual abuse.

ELEMENTS OF AN EGO-STRENGTHENING APPROACH

Community-based children seen in outpatient clinics following suspected sexual abuse are usually encouraged to communicate the details of the abusive incidents. They are helped to describe, in words, drawings, or play with anatomical dolls, what has happened to them. While evidence suggests that children are unable to reveal many aspects of their abuse because they lack both the language skills and the concepts to do so (Sjoberg and Lindblad 2002), revelation of any details is deemed helpful. In addition to the therapeutic value of verbalizing or playing out traumatic experiences, as well as sharing the accompanying feelings, therapeutic interviews help validate that sexual abuse has taken place, and the material elicited may be used as evidence to prosecute the offender. In fact, research by Dr. Mordock suggests that when the therapist does not specifically structure sessions so that sexual material is elicited, the children almost never bring up the topic (Mordock 1996b). He also stresses the difficulty of interviewing many abused children in outpatient settings (Mordock 2001), but the focus is still on eliciting details of the abuse.

Children in residential treatment must be handled differently. Most often, their sexual abuse took place years earlier, and the experiences are buried in their memories, even though they act out daily the effects of these abusive experiences. Often their abuse has been ongoing, and they need a period of quiet reintegration before being able to discuss it openly. They need a period of therapy on the coping track, a track we introduce in chapter 5 of *A Handbook of Play Therapy with Aggressive Children* and discuss throughout that volume, and they need staff sensitive to issues related to their traumatic experiences.

Most sexually abused children have experienced additional traumas, including neglect; frequent losses and separations, accompanied by abandonment anxiety; and chronic academic failure. Issues related to these traumas usually preoccupy them more than their abuse. Nevertheless, much of their inappropriate behavior stems from their early abusive experiences. Many blame themselves not only for their abuse but also for their parents' problems, such as substance abuse or depression. Instead of experiencing a discrete or isolated trauma, they lead lives characterized by multiple and ongoing stresses.

As a consequence, the treatment of repeatedly abused children requires an ego-strengthening approach (a coping approach) before abusive experiences can be worked on openly (Crenshaw and Mordock 2004). The children need an individualized milieu treatment plan that includes intensive individual therapy, speech and language development, expressive art therapy, and staff working closely together to accomplish a number of specific tasks. In fact, some writers think that an integrated treatment system is the essence of milieu therapy (Whitewell 1998). While integration of treatment components is essential, a specific milieu attitude is more important.

Fortunately, the field of residential treatment has become increasingly sensitive to the needs of traumatized children. In psychiatric hospitals serving adults who have been abused as children, staff can feel overwhelmed, numbed, even shell shocked after listening to patients describing traumatic events; staff members even report feeling shaken about their own safety (Lyons 1993). On the other hand, staff members in child-care settings, bombarded with negative provocations, need to be particularly sensitive to the children's traumas; otherwise the staff's counteraggression will further traumatize the children. Staff in living units, constantly facing aggressive behavior, can as a group regress in functioning and mirror the children's functioning (McCready 1987).

In the past five years, several models of milieu treatment directed to the needs of traumatized children have been described in the professional literature, and others have built on the special components of past milieu treatment designs to address the needs of traumatized youth. Gunderson (1978) has identified five components of a milieu that are therapeutic: containment, structure, support, involvement, and validation. Containment provides the child with a sense of security, structure with predictability, support with the development of self-esteem, involvement with ways to integrate social distance with social intimacy, and validation with the ability to separate thinking and feeling.

Clinicians in some residential settings have introduced procedures into their milieus to help traumatized children with validation, one of which will be presented later in the chapter. Others have focused on making the milieu more empathic (McCready 2002), fostering relationships (Chop 2003), and understanding and making therapeutic use of projective identifications, a defense we discuss in chapter 11. Bloom and her colleagues are developing and refining a model of milieu treatment for youth focused on trauma recovery, which they call the Sanctuary Model (Abramovitz and Bloom 2003; Bloom et al. 2003; Bloom and Bills 2000; Rivine et al. 2003). An acronym for one aspect of the model is S.A.G.E., or a focus on safety, affect management, grieving, and emancipation. In addition to Gunderson's five components, the milieu environment we will discuss embraces the concepts of the models mentioned above. We emphasize concentrating on five tasks: helping the children to feel empowered, respecting their need for privacy, making them feel safe and creating safety nets, building true self-esteem, and helping them cope with trauma reenactment.

HELPING CHILDREN TO FEEL EMPOWERED

Multiply traumatized children experience little meaningful control over their lives. They may have exerted control by being absent from home for long periods, hiding from caregivers, and resisting routines, but the cost of such control is failure to develop emotionally. Unable to avoid abuse from caregivers, in spite of efforts to do so, they have felt helpless and powerless. Because they feel so controlled, they have a strong need to control others. But their controlling behavior and their active resistance to being controlled (experienced as defiance by adults) retard normal development, get them into repeated difficulties, and eventually get them referred for treatment. Given the histories of such children, their controlling and defiant behaviors should be considered adaptive responses. Treatment planning efforts should focus on helping each child gain control over his or her life while in residential treatment, itself a very controlling situation that initially elicits noncompliance.

Staff efforts should focus on reinforcing each child's sense of personal control. The early focus of treatment is to help children learn, not only that choices are possible, but how to make choices, a decision-making process denied them by past caregivers. Structuring individual therapy to accomplish this purpose is discussed in *A Handbook of Play Therapy with Aggressive Children*. In the larger milieu, children should be encouraged to make choices when they can do so without conflict, a topic for treatment-team discussion and individualized treatment planning. For example, the teacher might place several tasks on a child's desk and allow the child to choose which task to tackle first. The child might be given ten math problems and asked to choose five to complete. When a girl has mastered several rudimentary arts-and-crafts skills, she can choose which arts-and-crafts activities to work on. When a boy is asked to brush his teeth and wash his face, he can choose which he wants to do first. In the living group, if the children clean their rooms on Saturday mornings, following a staff-generated list of chores to complete, each child should be encouraged to choose from the list the chores he or she wants to do first. When chores involve another child, the two should be helped to work together to choose those to do first. If a child shows anxiety about decision making, the choices to be made are simplified by the supervising adult. The more that children can make choices that affect their lives, the less they will resist the routines of the treatment center.

RESPECTING THEIR NEED FOR PRIVACY

Children who have been repeatedly sexually violated lack a sense of personal boundaries and of private zones. Immediately on admission, each child's rights for privacy should be respected and special emphasis placed on each having private spaces. Private storage areas for each child should be created in the classroom and living group, and the consequences of violating another's privacy should be made clear. Many children will need to learn the concept of privacy because the concept was never taught in their homes. The bigger and stronger children always took whatever they wanted from their younger or weaker siblings, who secretly took and hid things from their bullying siblings. And they will behave accordingly in the treatment center until they learn to respect, as well as to enjoy, the right to privacy.

Staff should clarify that no one has a right to violate personal boundaries, including touching others in a way that is secret or makes them uncomfortable. In individual therapy, the therapist emphasizes that each child is entitled to his or her private thoughts and does not have to share thoughts or worries. It is helpful if a folder is created for each child, which is kept in a locked cabinet, with the child's name on it, in which material such as the child's drawings or paintings made in art or play therapy can be kept private from others. The child can add things to the private folder at any time and is told that its contents never have to be shared with anyone unless the child wants to.

Once children understand that their right to privacy is respected, they gradually realize the benefits of sharing their thoughts, particularly their most sensitive and intimate feelings. Sometimes they share them at night with the child-care worker, other times with a teacher whom they especially like, and other times with the therapist.

MAKING THE CHILDREN FEEL SAFE AND CREATING SAFETY NETS

Traumatized children, instead of feeling safer among adult caregivers, can feel more threatened (Zimrin 1991). This threat can dramatically increase when they see an adult out of control. And yet abused children typically push adults beyond endurable limits. They are masters at upsetting others, knowing exactly how to provoke even patient and reflective adults. Nevertheless, caregivers, while experiencing verbal abuse and even physical assault, must find ways to set firm, nonpunitive limits. The art of setting limits includes the ability to state the rule or the boundary in a matter-of-fact manner without being drawn into a battle of wills with the child. The staff member simply states the rule and the consequences of breaking the rule and allows the natural or logical consequences built into the system to have the desired effect, even though the impact will be gradual.

Both authors have worked with many highly skilled child-care workers and teachers who set boundaries and limits for kids without losing control of their own emotions. Their modulated behavior enabled children in their care to feel safe and protected, secure in their knowledge of the boundaries and confident they will be dealt with fairly should they exceed them. Unfortunately, we have also worked with caregivers who, like the child's parents, lacked the ability to control their own emotions. In those cases, their ability to handle children was hampered by the children's not feeling safe in their care. A milieu cannot be truly therapeutic unless this issue is addressed and appropriate training and support for staff provided. Responses to the provocations of children should not include those resulting from personalizing the situation. This statement, while an obvious truth, needs to be stated. Each staff member's greatest challenge is controlling his or her emotions when faced with the highly provocative behavior displayed by children who experience compliance as overcontrol and overcontrol as a precursor to abuse.

The aggressive child anticipates counteraggression from caregivers, which, in turn, reinforces the view that adults are abusive and not to be trusted and that rage against them is justified. When staff members refuse to respond in kind, the child must reexamine his or her beliefs in a new light. Only when caregivers consistently respond with firm, nonpunitive limits can the child's destructive and repetitive sequence of inappropriate behavior be broken. Every residential worker knows the difficulties in meeting this challenge.

When children grow up in families in which they feel nurtured and protected, they take their safety for granted. In marked contrast, if they grow up in an abusive, violent environment, safety is their predominant concern. The children experience terror when situations activate memories of their abusive past. When they act out, lose self-control, or engage in self-destructive behavior, often they are responding to feelings that their safety net has been removed.

When the child is exposed to angry adults or to peers fighting, violent memories can be triggered. Or the sexually abused child may feel threatened by adults who are especially nice since "nice adults" have often been their abusers. The world becomes a frightening place when childhood innocence is shattered by sexual assault. Marked feelings of vulnerability are reflected in the following symbolic play of Miguel, age six.

MIGUEL: [*Playing with puppets*] The people in the town brought their pets to the store to be sold. Instead the pets were killed. [*This scenario became repetitive.*]

THERAPIST: Let's get the Animal Rights people involved to protect the animals.

MIGUEL: [*Miguel agreed, but when the Animal Rights people showed up to take the animals, Miguel stated*] They would only permit the babies to go. The babies are scared by being loaded onto the truck. They don't trust the Animal Rights people. [*Miguel then drove the truck down a hill and turned it over on its side. He had the driver load the baby animals onto a chute with a conveyor belt that went to the bottom of a pit.*] They were chopped and ground into little pieces.

Miguel's mother prostituted him in exchange for money and drugs. He lost forever, not only the innocence typically associated with childhood, but also the belief that adults protect children from harm.

A child's acting out may be triggered by perceived, rather than actual, threats to safety. Having a history of exploitation by adults, the child is constantly vigilant for signs of danger, particularly those associated with mood swings in adult caregivers and tensions among them. Sometimes external stimuli trigger a sense of danger, but often the trigger is a bad dream or a memory associated with a past trauma. Internal warnings can be followed by misbehavior without staff having any clue about what caused the child's reaction. In addition, the child is usually unwilling, but more often unable, to talk about the situation. However, awareness of this pattern enables staff to respond more patiently and with more support. The best direct-care staff are those especially attuned to this issue, observe when it occurs, and bring it up with clinical staff so that a plan to create a safety net can be developed.

For example, a group of children is watching television, and one boy suddenly hits another. The hurt child yells out, "I didn't do nothin'!'" The child who hit him looks confused. Some child-care workers handle such situations by physically separating the two children and taking no further action. Others attempt to interview both children, either together or separately, to find out what actually transpired. Still others, particularly when other children in the group loudly proclaim that the victim was hit for no reason, may punish the assailant. It is the rare worker who first finds out what the boy saw on television that might have upset him and caused him to handle his upset by attacking another child and then, keeping this knowledge in mind, monitors future television viewing. Yet this astute worker will be the most helpful to abused children, whose overwhelming feelings get them into trouble and who need a safety net when such trouble occurs. Workers who share such observations at treatment-team meetings will develop a more meaningful role in the meetings, and better treatment plans for children will result.

Sometimes simply viewing television commercials for women's products can trigger maladaptive responses from sexually abused children who have become sexualized and, therefore, easily stimulated. The child above may have seen such a commercial, handled his feelings by displacing or projecting them onto a peer, and then punished the peer for having such feelings.

Abused children need to feel safe, not only in their environment, but in relationship to specific staff members. Many sexually abused children, feeling ashamed, equate intimacy and attention with sexual seduction associated with loss of control and masochistic excitement (Wursmer 1981). As a result they avoid intimacy and hide self-expression. Zimrin (1991) suggests that child-care workers should place real or metaphorical barriers between themselves and sensitive children, allowing the children to control the degree of intimacy they want with adults. Sometimes the physical characteristics of a staff member can trigger an exaggerated fear reaction, if not an outright phobia. The example below illustrates one way in which a worker modified his behavior, in keeping with Zimrin's suggestions, to help with containment.

> Henry, age six, was terrified when a particular child-care supervisor, who was a huge man, came into his cottage. He would cower in a corner or run out the back door. The supervisor handled Henry's re-actions to him sensitively. Knowing that Henry's father physically and sexually abused the boy, and that the father was also a very tall and muscular man, the supervisor made his visits to the cottage as brief as possible and never approached Henry directly. Henry observed how much the other boys liked and admired this staff member, how friendly he was, and that he had a good sense of humor. Over time, the supervisor's visits gradually increased in frequency and length. Henry seemed less visibly shaken and would usually stay in the room with him. Nevertheless, the supervisor was extremely patient and did not approach Henry. Eventually, Henry joined the others when the supervisor engaged them in conversation or in a game. The supervisor always allowed Henry to initiate interaction between them and to lead the direction of their developing relationship. After a year, Henry regarded the supervisor as one of his favorite adults and looked forward to his visits to the cottage.

Besides physical features, some staff members will exhibit personality traits, habits, interests, or specific behaviors that resemble the feared and abusive adult or adults. And whenever they raise their voices, a situation that cannot always be avoided, the children will experience anxiety, followed, not necessarily immediately, by maladaptive behavior. Verbalizing to a child that the worker is not the feared person is rarely helpful; the child needs to learn this truth over time.

BUILDING TRUE SELF-ESTEEM

Children who have been traumatized by sexual abuse often view themselves with the same contempt displayed by their abusers. Consequently, caregivers should identify and highlight each child's strengths, interests, and positive qualities, some of which might not seem so positive to others, such as an interest in famous criminals and spies, card tricks, or escape artists. Self-esteem is a term bandied about by everyone engaged in treating disturbed youth. Most treatment centers claim their programs are directed toward this task, but our observations suggest that most could do a much better job. Helping children to identify strengths involves more than just observing their functioning. The effort to identify strengths should be a collaborative one. Shifron and Bettner (2003) help youth to recall early memories that assist them in developing what the two authors call the Crucial Cs: to connect, to feel capable, to feel as if "I count," and to have courage. Often the early memories are of positive relationships with others and situations the child handled competently.

Structuring a milieu for success requires that teachers and child-care workers have a realistic understanding of each child's emotional rather than physical development and that expectations are established in keeping with emotional development. Many caregivers fail to capitalize on each child's efforts to raise self-esteem because they mistakenly view the child's current efforts as maladaptive and in need of extinction. When discussing strength-oriented treatment planning in chapter 9, we mention that a child who sings in class should be encouraged to sing at other, more appropriate times and acknowledged for an interest in music rather than scolded for "rude" or "disruptive" behavior. We emphasize that the boy who copies drawings and claims them as his own should be praised for an interest in drawing and encouraged in art rather than confronted with his counterfeit productions. The girl who displays disorganized behavior in the morning but who works better in the afternoon should be praised for her afternoon control rather than punished for her morning disorganization. And the girl's treatment plan should focus more on maximizing her afternoon opportunities than on managing her disruptive mornings.

False praise, or flattery, usually backfires because abused children are masters at sensing insincerity. After all, how many times have they been praised into performing sexual favors? Praise that is too generous (for example, the frequent use of superlatives) can be experienced as oppressive because living up to inflated estimates of ability can elicit anxiety.

All caregivers will do well to practice "catching children doing things right." When a caregiver is alert to things a child does that can be praised, and then praises the observed behavior, the child's self-esteem can be enhanced. This statement should go without saying. Nevertheless, observation of direct-care staff reveals that most remarks directed at children are reprimands rather than praise. If reprimands worked, the children would not have been referred for residential treatment. Praising the children who stand correctly in line should be the caregiver's initial response to the children who are standing incorrectly. We would emphasize, however, that many accomplished people have low self-esteem and that many others evaluate themselves by their accomplishments. When their skills diminish, their self-esteem suffers. The children in care need to be admired for themselves and not just for their accomplishments. Urie Bronfenbrenner, a noted child psychologist, once included in a lecture the statement that "every child needs someone in its life that is irrational about it." When an audience member asked for clarification, he replied, "Crazy in love with it." Because of this need, we not only encouraged child-care workers to spend more time with their favorite children; we institutionalized the process in the agency where both of us worked (Mordock 2002a).

HELPING WITH TRAUMA REENACTMENT

Many sexually or physically abused children tend to repeat, or reenact, their traumas in an effort to gain mastery over the strong feelings they arouse. When abuse occurs, the feelings aroused are rarely processed afterwards and, therefore, are never integrated into the child's psyche. The children never "understand" what exactly happened to them or why it happened and often create their own reasons for the abusing events, blaming themselves or internalizing the accusations of blame directed at them by the abuser. Some of them think things like, "If I hadn't spilled my cereal, I wouldn't have been hit" or "If I had been stronger, my brother wouldn't have molested me." Others avoid thinking about the events because the thoughts aroused are too painful.

When children reenact a traumatic experience in the larger world, or in the *macrosphere*, as Erik Erikson (1963) calls it, they recreate the situation, or parts of the situation, that originally traumatized them (Terr 1981, 1983), often attempting to provoke the original abuse (Arata 2002). Some sexually abused children respond to adults in a seductive or flirtatious manner and try to provoke caregivers into responding to them like the original abuser. Several dynamics underlie reenactment. In part, the child attempts to gain mastery through desensitization; that is, by repeated exposure to the originally overwhelming experience, the child unconsciously hopes to assimilate and integrate it into existing explanations of reality. A reenactment can be an attempt to make the original trauma turn out differently. Utilizing the defense of undoing, combined with magical thinking, the child hopes the reenactment will change the original outcome.

Reenactments also can stem from underlying rage, expressed by efforts to degrade caregivers, to get them to behave like their former abusers. If the caregivers do, then their authority is discredited. "I don't have to listen to you anymore because you're like my past abusers." Some abused children also abuse other children. The child repeats the trauma by exposing others to the same traumatic experience. A major worry of direct-care staff is that abused children will abuse others in their care, and sexual abuse is tolerated less by staff, and by society at large, than physical abuse. The child attempts to master early abuse experiences by identifying with the aggressor, by becoming the controlling figure, the abuser, rather than the passive, helpless victim. Many sexually abused children, overstimulated sexually, are easily aroused by sexual stimuli, and sexual misbehavior is triggered.

Other children act out their abuse on themselves, or in the *autosphere.* Physically abused children may hurl themselves against the wall, hit themselves, or experience many injuries. Staff often describe them as accident prone, but when a girl thrusts objects up her vagina or a young boy excessively masturbates, then most trained staff recognize the behavior as a symptom of sexual abuse. Sometimes trauma replay is triggered by memory fragments of the original trauma, activated by external stimuli, such as another child being sexually provocative, or from internal stimuli, such as intrusion of memories related to being raped. The activation of memory fragments is less apparent, but staff should watch for them. The vignettes below illustrate this phenomenon.

A boy who had been locked in the closet for long periods felt compelled to turn doorknobs after being reprimanded, a compulsion he tried to hide from others.

Witnessing the reprimands of another, a girl reclined on the floor in a tightly curled-up position, perhaps an early effort to avoid being sexually molested.

A girl, without apparent reason, would suddenly fall to the floor, turn on her back, and scream hysterically. Her teacher felt she was being manipulative, trying to avoid her lessons. Her therapist, in conflict with her teacher over the reasons for this seemingly bizarre behavior, called the team psychiatrist during one of her "fits." The psychiatrist explained that she was having a dissociative reaction and had probably been raped by a relative.

A boy repeatedly tried to jump out of the agency van when his group went on trips, necessitating that other workers take him under their care while his group went on trips. Later it was discovered that he had been brutalized in a small bus. When the therapist made clear to him the relationship between his abuse and his current behavior, the boy no longer felt the compulsion and could travel with his peers in the van.

Direct-care staff should interrupt all reenactments. Each child's efforts to draw adults into their reenactments are best handled by ignoring and redirection. If children try to touch adults inappropriately, they should be reminded about respect for privacy. If the child is seductive, he or she should be directed back to the ongoing task. Some children, however, need simple instructions on how to behave appropriately. For example, "Young ladies don't sit like that. Sit up, put your skirt over your knees, keep your knees together, and continue your schoolwork." While children observing the exchange might giggle at such frankness, they eventually appreciate the clarity of the limits.

Reenactments involving other children should be handled with firm limits, followed by emphasizing that violation of one's personal or private space is forbidden. Consequences of various kinds, such as loss of privileges, may be tied to such actions but should be kept to a minimum. Dr. Crenshaw discusses the topic of managing sexual acting out in more detail elsewhere (Crenshaw 1988). In addition to sensitive responses by caregivers, play therapy, or expressive art therapy, should be available to children who display trauma replay. Therapy is a safe and controlled place where the child can work constructively on his or her difficulties. When the child reenacts the abusive experience in the *microsphere* (the realm of make-believe play), the reenactment can be utilized therapeutically. The trauma is reenacted in a symbolic form, such as through doll or puppet play, in the therapy room. Properly managed, this play can gradually dilute the effects of the original trauma. *A Handbook of Play Therapy with Aggressive Children* is devoted entirely to presenting play therapy techniques useful with traumatized children.

Trained child-care workers also can help children better manage traumatic experiences, which elicits validation, one component of milieu treatment. Once staff members become sensitive to a client's traumatic history, they often want to help instead of creating a facilitating environment and letting the situation play itself out (Lyons 1993). One technique, which helps them do both, is autogenic storytelling within the metaphor, after Davis (1990). Its use is suggested at bedtime (Lawson 1998), but because it can arouse strong emotions, we recommend setting time aside for the activity in the late afternoon. It also requires that a worker be available to spend time alone with the child, making its implementation difficult in settings with single coverage in a living unit. The child-care worker starts a story by identifying the main character and then stops in midstream and signals the child to pick up the story line. For example,

> There was a coyote who lived in the deep forests. The coyote especially liked exploring dark places where other coyotes rarely ventured. One day . . .

The child and the staff member alternate turns until the actions reach a positive resolution. The story is given a title to synthesize themes and emphasize pertinent aspects. The storytelling atmosphere allows the child an opportunity to explore the meaning of traumatic events metaphorically, separated from action, to process anxiety-related experiences without the associated emotional distress (Hartman and Burgess 1988). In addition, milieu staff are alerted to the emerging themes in the stories so they can reinforce messages of love, power, and healing. In chapter 6 of *A Handbook of Play Therapy with Aggressive Children*, we discuss the major themes revealed in the play and stories of children in gorilla suits.

CONCLUSION

In summary, an ego-enhancing approach for traumatized children features creating a milieu environment that adds to its basic structure the following five tasks: empowering the children, respecting their need for privacy, helping them feel safe and creating safety nets for them, building their self-esteem, and helping them with trauma reenactment. The order in which the tasks are presented is important because the children's responses to some tasks predict their responses to others. Children who feel neither safe nor empowered will struggle with these two issues throughout their placement and never make true developmental advancements. Consequently, we believe that the first several tasks in the list are the most important to accomplish. When children fail to improve following their initial treatment plans, staff should examine whether they feel safe and empowered. If not, these are the issues that should be addressed in treatment plan revisions.

13

Fostering Hope and Resilience

Children in gorilla suits have suffered so many defeats that they quickly become demoralized and lose hope with each subsequent loss and setback. Hope is a key factor in studies of resilience in children, and this chapter focuses on ways to foster hope and resilient traits in these children.

A growing chorus of refreshing voices advocates for mental health services directed at reinforcing competency and developing the strengths of clients, challenging therapists to move from an excessive interest and investment in pathology to a greater interest in resiliency (Richardson 2002). Brooks (2003), Greene (2003), Hardy (2003), and Waters and Lawrence (1993) from the field of family therapy, and Levine (2002) are prominent members of the chorus. Brooks talks about finding the "islands of competence" in each child. Greene reminds us that "any child will do well if he or she can." Levine looks for "buried treasure" in children.

A young lad and his parents met with Dr. Crenshaw for an initial interview. The boy was extremely sullen, sad, angry, withdrawn, and uncommunicative. The boy acted as if he was in the principal's office at school, where he spent considerable time. He expected to be punished and admonished by three adults. His parents had become weary of his argumentativeness and of the constant battles and power struggles that followed, both at home and at school. He was unwilling to accept authority unless persuaded by overwhelming evidence that the adult in charge was right. And he was a tough taskmaster; few could ever prove their case. His parents and his teachers were exhausted by endless confrontations with him. Something needed to be done to interrupt these unproductive interchanges between the child and his superiors and the futile sequences that always followed.

The boy was invited to accompany Dr. Crenshaw to explore the therapy room. He showed no interest in drawing, but he was attracted to the puppets.

He was asked if he wanted to put on a puppet show, and he nodded affirmatively. He chose Alligator, who immediately attacked Monkey, then Parrot, and finally Dog.

> THERAPIST: Are Monkey and Parrot friends?
> CHARLIE: Nope.
> THERAPIST: How about Dog? Is he friends with anyone?
> CHARLIE: Nope.
> THERAPIST: So no one gets along with anyone. Could one of the other puppets teach them how to be friends?
> CHARLIE: Nope. [*Begins to put the puppets away and asks if there are any army men.*]
> THERAPIST: Sure. [*Shows him where the soldiers and tanks are kept.*]

Charlie began to set up the opposing armies and explained that one side is almost sure to win. The Green Army had a tank and outnumbered the Camouflaged Army by at least three to one. It looked very much one sided. Perhaps this was how Charlie felt just before we came to the therapy room. The grownups outnumbered him (three to one), and they had the heavy artillery—or so it seemed to him. Feeling little control over his life, he defended his scant turf and argued endlessly over each small matter because he couldn't afford to cede any more ground. His argumentative skills and ability to split hairs were world class. At age eight, he probably could hold his own with a good trial lawyer.

As he began to play out the war, the green soldiers quickly and decisively advanced, and within seconds only one camouflaged soldier remained alive. He courageously stood his ground, battling alone against the odds in a clever manner. He outmaneuvered and outsmarted the Green Army with endless tricks he pulled from up his sleeve. Toward the end of the play session, the lone soldier still held his ground, and the battle was far from over. Dr. Crenshaw decided to share his ideas with Charlie and his parents about what he thought was going on.

> THERAPIST: You know, that camouflaged soldier makes me think of you. You also seem to be fighting a lonely battle. That brave soldier doesn't give up, and he really believes he can take on a whole Green Army by himself and fight to the bitter end. I get the feeling that you are just as determined as that soldier. Like him, you don't like to leave the battlefield unless you are the clear victor over the adults in your life. You will not let your will be crushed! No matter what the odds, no matter the heavy artillery on the other side, you will fight to the end if you believe you are right! Not many children would have the courage of their convictions, as you and that lone soldier on the battlefield do. I have two

questions I want you and your parents to think about between now and your next visit with me. I will be curious to hear your answer and also that of your parents. My first question is this: "Do you think the war will ever be over?" And my second question is "How will you decide that the war is over?"

Neither Charlie nor his parents ever answered these questions, but the lonely soldier relentlessly fighting a battle that couldn't be won became a key metaphor in the treatment.

RESIST THE PULL INTO HOPELESSNESS

To help children wearing gorilla suits to maintain hope, the therapist must avoid becoming engulfed in hopelessness. The children's horrid life stories amply supply the therapist with reasons to despair. The severity of their abuse, the traumas they experienced, the domestic violence to which they have been exposed, and the horrors they have witnessed on the streets can be difficult to endure. The children and their families struggle every day, if not for physical survival, then for survival of their hope and spirit. If the therapist recoils because their struggles are too painful to hear, the message is sent that their lives are beyond repair. In addition, many come from impoverished backgrounds and have suffered economic, racial, or gender oppression. Most dare not dream or hope because they believe dreams and hopes to be exercises in futility.

HOPES AND DREAMS AND EFFORTS TO SURVIVE

Hardy (1999) describes the survival orientation typical of low-income families. Their goal is to get through today—to find their next meal. They have little time to plan for the next day, let alone for the future. Hopefulness can be dangerous for those who have suffered much. Realistic hopes leave them open to the crippling impact of additional defeat, another loss. Typically, their hopes are unrealistic. Some play the lottery or even bet with bookies. Single mothers dream of finding the perfect man. Their children also long for impossible events, such as being given a sports car or becoming a professional basketball player. They know such hopes are unrealistic, but they study automobile and sports magazines and swoon over the pictures. These senseless preoccupations keep them from hoping for things that they should have but don't—the love and admiration of others. Many display sustaining fictions, fantasies about their lives that aren't true but help to keep them sane. In *A Handbook of Play Therapy with*

Aggressive Children, we stress ignoring these fictions. Clients with numerous sustaining fictions and who frequently daydream have fewer positive coping behaviors (Greenwald and Harden 1997), but when a child develops coping skills, the fictions usually disappear.

To destroy a person's soul, one needs only to take away the person's dreams. This is the paradox a therapist must wrestle with when treating children in gorilla suits and their families. Both the children and their parents need to more realistically appraise their possibilities yet at the same time not be stripped of hopes and dreams. Nor should they be given false hopes because such hopes can be followed by devastating setbacks. Therapists cannot change the conditions of their wretched lives, and if the conditions are too oppressive, they can offset the efforts of the most skilled and dedicated helpers.

Reassurance is of little or no help. Real help and real hope come only after locating, identifying, facilitating, and reinforcing assets, talents, and resources within individual family members. Clients can't rely on the therapist's strength. They need to identify their hidden strengths, talents, and assets and find ways to amplify and expand on them. Therapists are sometimes more heavily invested in change than the child or family is. Such rescuing behavior almost always leads to sorrow.

THE FIGHT TO MAINTAIN HOPE AMID
THE STRUGGLE TO SURVIVE

Remember that children and families who are seen by mental health professionals have traveled far over rough roads and have survived. It is possible that part of their spirit remains uncrushed. Straus (2003), emphasizing that kids who still fight still believe there is something left in them worth fighting for, gives us an uplifting way of looking at what others consider pathological actions. Straus adds that children who have given up, who have no fight left in them, are the ones she worries about the most.

When treating low income families, therapists must respect the spiritual beliefs and faith that are central to their lives. Many families take pride in the suffering they have endured (Hardy 1999), while others attribute their survival to their religious convictions. They do not enjoy suffering, but the knowledge that they have survived in spite of it sustains them as they travel the rough and dusty roads in their lives. "If I can handle that, I can handle anything that comes along." "The Lord looks after me!" In the latter case, it is tempting to emphasize that it is their own strength that has pulled them through, but they may need their faith more than they need to appreciate their own strengths. Hope can be a powerful ally in the healing process, no matter its source. Studies of children identified as high risks reveal that regular church attendance was related to less aggression in late adolescence (Herrenkohl et al. 2003). Religion can give individuals a sense of coherence, which is a disposition to see the world as comprehendible, manageable, and meaningful, and the sense of coherence has been linked to greater stress resistance and better health (Amirkhan and Greaves 2003). Religious activities can also produce positive emotions, and positive emotions buffer against depression and promote thriving (Fredrickson et al. 2003). Nevertheless, therapists must not be glib or make sweeping assurances that life can get better; often it won't.

When Dr. Mordock was new to the field, he held out the possibility of a foster home to an abandoned, overweight girl he was treating in a residential center. Her mother was a gay drug addict who provided inconsistent care. Constantly teased for her mother's sexual orientation and for her own "butch" behavior, she saw no future for herself until the author suggested that, when her behavior improved, she would be eligible for a foster home. The girl made rather remarkable progress when the agency found a childless single woman who saw past her boorish demeanor and looked forward to being her foster mother. Right before the girl's discharge to the foster home, however, her mother showed up and, over the girl's objections, took her back. It wasn't long before the girl was placed in a neighboring treatment center for substance-abusing adolescents. Never again did Dr. Mordock discuss with children where they could go when they improved. The message was changed to communicate that the children must improve for their own sake and not because they might be adopted or placed in a foster home. Dr. Mordock left the task of planning for their future to the social work staff.

Nevertheless, there are ways to hold out hope rather than to give in to the hopelessness and despair that threaten to overpower both the child and therapist. These ways are presented in the remainder of this chapter.

VALIDATE THEIR STRENGTHS, TALENTS, AND REDEEMING QUALITIES

Children in out-of-home placement often have medical records thick enough to break a toe if dropped on one. They contain numerous reports, evaluations, and summaries, most of which address damage and pathology. Few of those records devote much space or attention to the children's talents, strengths, positive qualities, ways they have helped or contributed to others, or resilient features that have enabled them to survive an arduous life journey. Yet most therapists recognize that far more leverage is gained by pursuing and building on strengths than by pouncing on pathology (Crenshaw 1990a). Brooks (1993) reminds us that every child has an "island of competence" that can be found if we can look beyond the pathology in which we have been trained. Katz (1997) emphasizes that a sense of mastery is important to all children, but more so to those who are traumatized. "Learning to feel good about yourself is probably the single most important way that you can overcome trauma" (van der Kolk, 1994). Waters and Lawrence (1993) remind us that all pathology contains seeds for strengths. We often don't notice or, more accurately, don't search for the positive polarities that exist. An unbelievably stubborn, oppositional, and strong-willed child may be difficult, if not impossible, to live with, but the child can also be a self-determined, independent thinker who perseveres, at all costs, in the pursuit of a goal.

The purpose of social skills training, discussed more fully in *A Handbook of Play Therapy with Aggressive Children*, chapter 14, is to help the child develop a repertoire of socially appropriate assertion skills. The goal is to make the child more competent in everyday social situations. Immediate feedback, coaching, encouragement, and reinforcement follow each skill-building session. Prosocial behaviors, such as "friendly behavior," should also be practiced. (As someone has put it, "Smiles win more attention than frowns, and children should practice smiling.") Simple tasks that can win others over, such as friendly interest in others and outgoing behavior, often get overlooked, but they should be in every therapist's toolbox.

Some of the more advanced role-playing scenarios that can help a child become more appropriately assertive may provoke considerable anxiety. This happens because the children's lack of assertiveness, their numbness that causes inaction and later inappropriate rage, results from earlier traumas and therefore involves powerful themes such as loss, abandonment, and betrayal, which we describe in *A Handbook of Play Therapy with Aggressive Children*, chapter 6. Such themes, if not properly timed, can trigger a rage reaction that appears out of nowhere but in fact comes from the very roots of the child's aggression.

SEEING VIRTUE IN CHILDREN AT THEIR WORST MOMENTS

A powerful point is made when the therapist sees something good in children at their worst moments and conveys it to them. Their defenses are down, but they shore them up and brace themselves for confrontation. They never expect anyone to see good in them at their worst. And their surprise can be healing. Lenny, treated by Dr. Crenshaw, serves as an example. Lenny once ran off the grounds of a residential treatment center after a fight with another child. It was starting to get dark and cold on a wintry night. Dr. Crenshaw caught up with Lenny and said he would prefer to go with Lenny since he didn't want Lenny to be out there alone on a cold night. Lenny kept walking at a brisk pace.

THERAPIST: Where are we headed?

LENNY: To California.

THERAPIST: Why California?

LENNY: That's where my Dad lives, stupid!

THERAPIST: Oh, you're going home! Do you think he will be surprised to see you?

LENNY: I can't believe how stupid you are! Of course he will be surprised.

THERAPIST: I guess he will be even more surprised when I show up too!

LENNY: You're nothing but a dumb shit! You're not going! Oh, this whole thing is ruined. No fun at all! Let's go back.

THERAPIST: Are you sure? I'm not tired. I'll go as far as you want. I just don't want you to be out here all alone.

LENNY: No, damn it—I want to go back!

THERAPIST: Whatever you say.

[*Lenny and the therapist walked quietly for a while, and the dialogue resumed.*]

THERAPIST: By the way, Lenny, even though we are turning back, I do think you took some steps tonight that bring you a little closer to actually returning home.

LENNY: Man, are you weird! What the hell are you talking about?

THERAPIST: Well, when you had that fight with Gene tonight, you walked away after one punch and took off so you wouldn't hurt him. Not hitting—pulling back—that's progress. And the last time you ran away, we walked halfway to Poughkeepsie before you were ready to turn around. Tonight, it was more like a mile.

LENNY: Like hell, it was more like two miles.

THERAPIST: Maybe, but it was less than half the distance we walked last time. By the way, I noticed something else.

LENNY: What now?

THERAPIST: You only called me stupid twice, and a dumb shit once, and you didn't call me a dumb f— once! You've got to admit that's big progress!

LENNY: Dr. Dave, I can't believe you! [*and we both laughed heartily*].

Dr. Crenshaw received a very cool reception back at campus when Lenny showed up laughing and in a good mood. The staff felt that punishment was called for and that clinicians are too easily manipulated by the kids. While there may be some truth in the latter criticism, neither of us agreed that punishment was in order (our beliefs about punishment have been presented in earlier chapters). Hardy (2000) emphasizes that our society has become so punishment oriented that teachers are more interested in "correction" than in "connection." He challenges us to ask whether we want to assume the role of jailer or healer in our work with kids. If sympathies are aligned with the jailer, then clinicians will end up meting out punishments, and their emphasis will be on correction. If identifying with the healer, clinicians will find ways to make a connection with the disconnected children who populate our treatment centers.

Identifying with healers doesn't mean there are no consequences for inappropriate actions. Limits are always necessary, but note that the limit setting we describe in *A Handbook of Play Therapy with Aggressive Children*, chapters 3 and 4, involves no punishment. Limit setting in the larger environment shouldn't either. For years, learning theorists have demonstrated that punishment only suppresses behavior, and only in the presence of the one administering the punishment. Yet we ignore these findings and continue to punish our children. Instead, we need to find ways to engage children in dialogue that has significant healing potential and eventually to address the invisible wounds that underlie the many and varied forms of acting out.

CONVEYING PROFOUND RESPECT

Unless profound respect for family strengths is conveyed to the children and their families, treatment efforts will be futile. One subtle form of disrespect, but never missed by the child, is the "adoption fantasy"—the assumption that therapists, and other caregiving adults, can do a better job raising the child than the family can. Yet most children remain loyal to the original family, even children who have been abused and maligned.

John Allen Muhammad, the sniper who terrorized the District of Columbia and nearby Virginia, received endearing letters from his children after he was jailed (Associated Press 2003). His ten-year-old child sent a message saying "I miss you sooooooo much." Later she asked, "Why did you do all of these shootings?" Yet Muhammad had threatened to kill their mother, and the child was fearful he might carry out the threat. He had not seen his children in three years, and his parenting deteriorated after he returned from the Gulf War in 1991. The result was that two of his children had never received good fathering from him, and the oldest had for only two years. Nevertheless, all three children wrote him loving letters. His son wrote, "I love you so much and nothing will change that."

When other adults walk into the children's lives and assume they can be the "good parent" and supplant the natural family, they convey both disrespect and naïveté. Caregivers need to gain a multicultural perspective in order to be sensitive to the ethnic, class, racial, and cultural identifications that are crucially important to each child. Children of color should not be burdened by having to teach caregivers what it is like to be a member of a minority group in our society. Caregivers from the dominant culture should constantly strive for self-improvement by challenging their own cultural ignorance and insensitivity and seeking out supervision, consultation, and training to fill these gaps in their knowledge, understanding, and sensitivity. Obviously the successful recruitment of more caregivers and healers of color would be a great advantage. Since children in gorilla suits have typically suffered a deep sense of shame, degradation, and humiliation throughout their lives, they demand respect out of urgent necessity. They lack reserves of positive self-regard to draw on. One more failure, one more humiliation, one more disrespectful incident and they are prepared to die, if necessary, to preserve a modicum of pride. In view of the power inherent in this issue, it can be helpful to make it explicit. To an angry, challenging youngster, the therapist can say, "Look, I'm going to treat you with respect, and I expect the same from you." That statement lets the child know you speak the same language. It conveys the message that you know how important this issue is, and it lays the groundwork for mutual respect. Children who have suffered repeated assaults on their dignity as human beings will benefit enormously when teachers or caregivers take them aside and talk with them privately about a problem rather than dressing them down in front of their peers. They need to be spared, whenever possible, from further degradation because they already have had more than they can tolerate. Failure to respect the children's need to maintain their fragile sense of dignity and self-respect frequently triggers aggressive episodes.

PUNCTUATE THEIR GIVING

Hardy (2003) urges caregivers to emphasize how the children can contribute to others. Doing so elevates the children's spirits. Simply knowing that the therapist looks forward to seeing them is helpful. Conversely, to feel one has nothing to give punctures the spirit. Helping others through a crisis helps the helper survive the same crisis (Katz 1997). Focusing on what the child can contribute enhances the child's sense of virtue. Jerome Kagan (1998) notes that all children need a sense of virtue, a sense that there is something basically good in them. In order to experience oneself as having value and worth, one needs to feel that one contributes to others. Privileged children in our culture do not struggle with this issue the same way that children of color and of economic deprivation do. Many more opportunities to demonstrate one's value are provided to the privileged; very few are provided to the economically disadvantaged. They lack the stage and audience of privileged children, and therefore helpers must look diligently. Finding the "buried treasure in these kids" can be a turning point in their treatment.

Dr. Crenshaw conducted a number of informal interviews with adults who had spent one or more years of their childhood at a residential treatment center. When they recounted their stories, they often mentioned one particular staff member who made an unusual and extraordinary effort to make a connection with them at a time when they felt extremely disconnected. They described how one particular staff member refused to give up on them, even when they had given up on themselves. Frequently, someone discovered a hidden talent or gift in them, either in art, music, math, or sports, and encouraged and supported them to develop the talent further. When such accounts are listened to carefully, we learn that a significant relationship with even one person can make a difference in clients' lives. Someone who believed in them and really cared about them jump-started the healing process.

When a therapist's caseload contains a number of aggressive children, particularly those with bland affect who are closed off and unfeeling, yet at the same time demanding, looking forward to seeing each one of them is a difficult task. Dr. Mordock had considerable difficultly getting himself emotionally ready to see one girl who never stopped demanding goodies from him, never sat still for a minute, and treated him no differently than she treated all people—they existed only to met her needs, and when they did not, she pestered and tormented them. But her most offending trait was her shallowness and insincerity. Truly empty children are the most difficult to relate to. They are like shadows in the night.

Knowing that the healing process is facilitated by the therapist's conveying real pleasure in being with the child, Dr. Mordock realized that his negative attitude hampered her treatment. Consequently, he decided to transfer her to another therapist. Never having invested even a small part of herself in Dr. Mordock, she wouldn't experience a transfer as a rejection but as an opportunity to manipulate another well-meaning adult. When he checked with other therapists, he learned that not one was the least bit attracted to her. In fact, all the clinical staff and most of the direct-care staff disliked her.

Finally, one child-care worker was found who actually enjoyed the girl, who the worker said reminded her of herself when she was younger. Since Dr. Mordock was quite fond of this particular worker, he began to see the child in a different light. While he still never looked forward to seeing her, he was no longer cowed at the thought of doing so. He also began to verbalize his dislike for her in the following manner:

> THERAPIST: Marlene, you must know that I don't really look forward to seeing you. All you ever do is try to break the rules and get me to give you things and then pretend to be angry with me when I don't. You don't even allow yourself to feel real anger at me. I'd rather feel your anger than

experience the mocking smile that hides your real feelings from me and, perhaps, from yourself as well. You have done a great job getting me to dislike you. Now we need to find out why it was important for you to do so because I have discovered one person who works here that likes you.

MARLENE: Who?

THERAPIST: I'm not going to tell you because then you'll make an effort to get that person to dislike you, and that wouldn't be good for you. Everyone needs to be liked by someone, and you're no exception, even though you try to be. In our early sessions, you certainly did a good job getting me not to like you. Nevertheless, you haven't been completely successful because I now find I'm challenged by being with you even though I don't look forward to it. My challenge is to try my hardest to discover one good thing about you!

WHAT CAN BE LEARNED FROM STUDIES ON RESILIENCE?

Children who have overcome the odds, who have faced unusual adversity and yet managed not only to survive but, in some cases, even to thrive, are good sources to guide our efforts to help others faced with formidable obstacles. The study of resilient children has received considerable attention in recent decades, and therapists can make use of the findings in treatment planning (see Anthony 1985; Brooks 1993; Garbarino 1995; Garmezy 1991; Katz 1997; Rutter 1979, 1990; Werner and Smith 1992; Wolin and Wolin 1993).

SPIRITUAL FAITH AND POSITIVE PHILOSOPHY OF LIFE

A strong spiritual faith or a sustaining positive philosophy of life can be a protective factor when one is facing extreme adversity (Pelcovitz 1999). James (1989) emphasizes that a positive outlook is especially critical for children traumatized by abuse and neglect and urges clinicians to communicate that some things can never be taken from the child, such as the spiritual faith that sustains both the child and the family in the worst of times or the child's love of animals, art, music, or sports. What they deeply value, whatever it is, and the essence of who they are can never be stripped away. The song, "All My Trials," contains a verse that expresses this poetically:

> The river of Jordan is chilly and cold,
> It chills the body but not the soul,
> All my trials, Lord, soon be over.

Over the years, both of us have been intensely curious about the factors that enable some children to survive. And by survival, we mean literally to remain alive. Both of us have treated a number of children who were killed in the prime of their lives. Sister Mary Teressa, one of the Daughters of Charity, who worked at the center where both of us once worked, always cried when the children put on plays during the holidays. When asked why she did so, she replied, "I cry because I'm both happy and sad for them. For some of them, this will be the best period of their lives. Nothing in their futures will equal the care they received here." While Dr. Mordock never became tearful or even sad while working with the children, tears flowed every year during the United Way fund-raising campaign when films were shown about troubled children. It was a good outlet for pent-up feelings. If he allowed himself to feel such sadness while working with the children, he couldn't treat them effectively. If they witnessed his sadness, they would be overwhelmed by their own.

Some of the children seen by both of us were killed within several years of their discharge. One died in a knife fight, another was run over by a train, another was shot in a drive-by shooting, another was pushed from a building, and so on. And some, although surprisingly few, spend time in jail. We marvel at the times when the children do quite well. On a playground or ball field they can hold their own with any child in the community. And when they smile and laugh, their joy often exceeds that displayed by the normal child in similar circumstances. Cautiously and gradually, most learn to trust and make attachments. How is that possible given their life experience? We remain in awe of the human spirit to survive!

One inspiring child was Anne Frank, who hid in an attic awaiting capture and almost certain death in a concentration camp. Yet this teenager retained a positive outlook on life and a belief in the basic goodness of people. She cited her love of nature as a source of strength that she drew on when in need (Frank and Pressler 1991). Her revelations suggest that child therapists should vigorously pursue the sustaining forces in the child's life; make the child, and others, more mindful of these forces; and build on them at every opportunity. Therapists need to pursue health, strength, and virtue as aggressively as they identify pathology (Bonime 1987).

FACILITATE POSITIVE THINKING, MOOD, AND MEANING

The literature on resilience repeatedly emphasizes that children who exhibit positive temperaments, who maintain an optimistic outlook, and who display a predominantly positive mood buffer themselves better from the hardships of life than do those holding a basically pessimistic outlook and manifesting negative moods. Children can be taught to think more optimistically. Seligman (2003), in his research on explanatory style, has discovered that some children view adverse events as temporary setbacks and do not generalize or personalize the negative aspects. He labels them as children with an "optimistic style of thinking." Conversely, those who personalize adverse events and see them as having pervasive meaning are said to exhibit a "pessimistic explanatory style."

Children with these two opposite explanatory styles can differ dramatically in their responses to highly stressful events. Studies after the terrorist attacks on the United States on September 11, 2001, indicated that college students who expressed some positive outcomes of these horrifying and devastating attacks, such as "It brought the country together," "It made our family closer," or "I reexamined my priorities in life," made a better adjustment than did those who found no positives in the horrible events (Fredrickson et al. 2003). The child therapist must help children find some positives in the worst of events, using the respectful and sensitive manner illustrated below:

> THERAPIST: Johnny, I know how badly you feel about the murder of your brother. It was so senseless, so tragic to have your brother, so young, someone you loved so much, die for no reason. I was wondering, though, if you can think of anything that is even a little bit good that might have come from this awful thing that happened to your family.
>
> JOHNNY: I don't know. I don't think so.
>
> THERAPIST: Believe me, Johnny, in no way am I saying that this was a good thing that happened. It was a horrible thing! But sometimes when an awful thing happens, people can see something come from it that is good.
>
> JOHNNY: Well, Mom and Dad are not fighting as much, and I saw Dad give Mom a big hug, and they were both crying. My other brothers are spending more time with me and looking out for me. I like that because I'm still really scared!

In addition to facilitating an optimistic explanatory style using some of the techniques developed by cognitive-behavioral therapists, and besides searching for positive meaning in the aftermath of disasters, therapists can teach children to modify their mood (Linehan 1993; Dolan 1991; Straus 1999). Dr. Mordock discovered this fact when he asked a child who had initially given violent responses to the Thematic Apperception Test cards to look at the cards a second time and to tell only positive stories about them. The child returned to class in an excellent mood, and the teacher reported that the child had his best day in school. From this serendipitous finding, techniques were developed to help children calm themselves when in crisis (Mordock 1999c). It is also clear, from a growing body of clinical and research literature, that we can teach children to better manage their moods, such as increasing their tolerance for distress and learning techniques to distract and shift themselves from oppressive moods. Since a predominance of positive mood has emerged as a protective factor in studies of resilient children, learning mood-changing skills is crucial to the well-being of children.

> THERAPIST: Whenever you get upset, do you ever think about some of the good things that have happened to you or that you enjoy?
> CHILD: Like what?
> THERAPIST: What do you like best to do?
> CHILD: Go to the ball park with my grandpa.
> THERAPIST: The next time you get upset, why don't you sit down and think about being at a ball park with your grandpa.
> CHILD: Why? That's stupid. I'm not at a game!
> THERAPIST: Yes, but imagining it may make you calm and less angry. Wouldn't you rather sit down and think about being at the park with your grandpa than being interrogated by a staff member about what upset you so much?
> CHILD: Yeah! They always ask me what got me so upset, and when I think about it, I just get upset again.
> THERAPIST: If I can get staff to stop asking you that question when you get upset, will you agree to think about being at the ball park with Grandpa the next time you get angry and upset? In fact, with some practice, maybe you could learn to think about Grandpa, or other pleasant and joyful experiences, when you begin to feel upset rather than when you are already upset.

Below we present a therapeutic dialogue with a fourteen-year-old girl who has responded to her bleak and oppressive moods by inflicting harm on herself. Instead of getting into a power struggle with her over this issue, the therapist focused on expanding her range of coping behaviors to deal with her emotional distress. Challenging children or adolescents to delay their destructive urges, even if only for ten seconds, is a way to exercise a degree of control, and this control can be built on. Once the child demonstrates the ability to delay impulses for ten seconds, the step to twenty seconds seems shorter, and the power of their destructive urges seems less.

> THERAPIST: Can you tell me what you were going through inside just before you started cutting yourself?
> JANEY: I was miserable, angry, hurt, pissed off! I just didn't want to feel any more pain.
> THERAPIST: Was cutting helpful to you?
> JANEY: Yeah, it hurt, but not that bad, and I was no longer thinking about the fact that my friends have no time for me!

THERAPIST: Would you recommend it to others who have similar feelings?
JANEY: I don't know. It works for me.
THERAPIST: What else would you have been thinking about if you hadn't cut yourself when you did?
JANEY: My grandfather dying.
THERAPIST: What other options do you have when you are feeling this badly and you can't stand the pain?
JANEY: I don't know—I guess I never really gave it much thought.
THERAPIST: Suppose you try to think of at least three other choices that might distract you, or soothe you, or numb the pain, but that do not harm you. You may still decide to cut yourself, but at least you will be aware of other choices you can make.

Zimrin (1986) reports that people who have actually overcome an abusive childhood display a strong sense of personal control. Nonsurvivors hold a defeatist view, feeling their lives were determined by destiny and their efforts didn't really matter, so there was no use in trying. Whenever children become more mindful of the choices they make and take responsibility for them, the more they experience a sense of personal control over their lives.

Children need to understand that hopelessness leads to decreased efforts and that their situation actually becomes hopeless when they see it that way. They need to understand that feeling hopeless is a conscious decision and only one of several choices available to them. Goleman (1995) found that the most successful prevention and wellness programs emphasized helping children to better identify, understand, express, and manage their emotions. Goleman points out that our "emotional intelligence," more often than our intellectual strengths, determines our outcome and the quality of our life.

Trauma in middle childhood alters the assumption a child has made about life. The child's view of the world shifts to one of distrust. Therapeutic efforts must be directed at helping the child see the world in a better light so that a future in it can be planned (Everly and Lating 2004). Several chapters in *A Handbook of Play Therapy with Aggressive Children* present some practical tools to help children become more self-aware—more capable of identifying, expressing, and managing their emotional life.

CHILDREN ARE NOT DOOMED BY THEIR EARLY EXPERIENCES

Jerome Kagan (1998) challenges the widely held belief of infantile determinism—the view that our early life experiences determine our functioning over the rest of our lifetime. Kagan points out that the evidence for this popular concept is simply not compelling. Studies reveal that about one-third of persons who are abused or neglected as children will abuse their own children. Two-thirds do not! (Katz 1997). Studies of girls raised in group homes in England found that the majority were adjusting well (Rutter et al. 1990). So were most of the children followed up by Dr. Mordock (Mordock 1978). A supportive spouse also tended to offset adversity in childhood (Rutter et al. 1990). A study of adults abused as children revealed that the following factors differentiated between those who were doing well and those showing signs of serious disturbance (Zimrin 1986):

1. They had a much greater sense of control and influence over their destiny.
2. They had a more positive self-image.
3. They maintained a sense of hope.
4. They had a relationship with a supportive adult in their life who proved to be a stable resource over a long period of time.
5. They took responsibility for helping someone else.

Janoff-Bulman (1992), in her extensive studies of those who overcame traumatic life events, found three factors critical to the healing process:

1. The ability to tolerate strong and distressing emotions.
2. The ability to see their experiences from a new perspective.
3. The availability of support from others.

These findings point to the importance of a trusting, supportive, sincere, and stable relationship over time. Teaching pro-social skills, especially the ability to empathize with the feelings of others, is an essential ingredient for developing the stable relationships from which trauma survivors can draw support. The positive impact of helping others in meaningful ways, of taking responsibility for them, needs major emphasis in treatment programs. Children, especially those who have been repeatedly devalued and forced to live on the margins of society, have had very few opportunities to help or give to others. Their capacity to give is not appreciated because society becomes so focused on the disquieting surface behavior of aggression. Finding opportunities for the children to help others is a treatment goal that can easily be accomplished and does not require revamping of programs or additional funds. The help needs to be meaningful. They might participate in a park cleanup in the community, rake leaves for elderly residents in the neighborhood, put on a bake sale or car wash for charity, or read to a younger child.

DEVELOPING A SENSE OF A POSITIVE FUTURE

"One terrible result of a life absorbed with sustaining oneself in the face of external stressors and uncertainty is that there is little vision about the future, little idea of what might be, or what can be" (Dowling et al. 2003, p. 197). Studies of resilient individuals highlight the crucial role of being able to emotionally process traumatic events and assign them new meanings so that the individuals can look to the future. Traumatized children need help to put into perspective the horrifying events of their lives. They need to learn that these events do not define who they are or determine the rest of their lives. One way for them to gain a sense of perspective is the use of a time line.

By graphically picturing the events of their life across the entire life span, children can appreciate that traumatic events were confined to a relatively brief and encapsulated period of their childhood. Two cautions must be considered when using this technique. The first is that we must not convey the impression that we take lightly, or trivialize, the horrific experiences the children have experienced. While the goal of creating hope is a worthy one, it must be done in a sensitive and carefully timed manner. The child must experience our efforts to impart hope, to give new meanings to past experiences, or to place experiences in a different perspective as not just another "pull yourself up by your bootstraps" message. That kind of message, so often sent by society, is not helpful (Hardy 1998).

The second caution is that many children in gorilla suits have not experienced recognized or discrete traumas confined to brief periods of their childhood. Consequently, a time-line depiction of these events emphasizes that they occurred over a significant portion of their childhood. Repeated exposure to trauma and violence is usual. In addition, their traumatic experiences are complicated by economic hardship, if not abject poverty. Further, devaluation is experienced as a result of being poor, a child of color, or a female in a society that grants white males more privileges. Finally, their lives are complicated by repeated losses, both tangible and acknowledged and intangible and unacknowledged. If caregivers suggest that such obstacles can be overcome, but don't show a corresponding appreciation for the difficulty of the obstacles, legitimate struggles will be devalued.

Yet when climbing their mountain of troubles, many children are forced, or indirectly choose, to climb the roughest and steepest side of the mountain. They need help to find easier routes to the top, to learn that friends are needed to help them climb, and to learn that friends are acquired by being friendly rather than hostile. To push them to undertake a perilous climb without the proper equipment and helping hands needed disrespects their courageous efforts to date.

Time Line

Write in memories along your time line. Use color to show feelings you had during different times in your life and fill in the color key with the colors you chose.

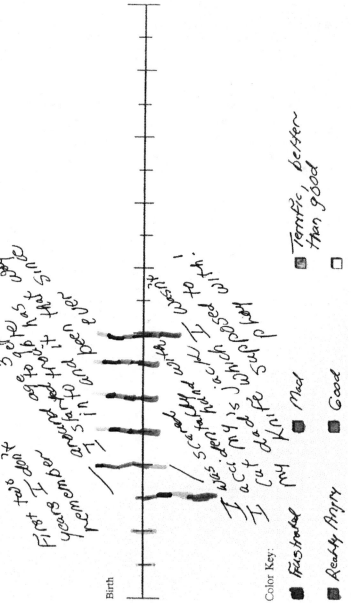

Birth

First tooß
years I don't
remember

3 gesters
age to Job has
arrived and that I, that 5,000
I sin to and been ever

was at.

I scaulled with
was dental hand which I to
I acci my is which posed with
I cut dads knife so much how

Color Key:

■ Frustrated

■ Really Angry

■ Mad

■ Good

■ Terrific, better
than good

□

Figure 3.1.

Without a set of social skills, the children will continue to climb the most diffi-cult, treacherous, and steepest side of the mountain. Yet even when they possess good social skills, many will have to climb the mountain alone. Most profession-als who extend a helping hand rarely appreciate the perilous and dangerous path the children must follow when no longer in treatment.

Because Dr. Crenshaw was once an avid mountain climber, the metaphor of climbing a mountain seems a good one for understanding the treatment process. With children who terminate their treatment in collaboration with their therapist, we sometimes used a story written by Dr. Crenshaw and his col-leagues called "Jose and Pete on the Mountain" (Crenshaw et al. 1983) to assist in working through the process of termination (see *A Handbook of Play Therapy with Aggressive Children*, chapter 21). Hardy (1999) speaks about children from low-income families and children of color and their efforts to ascend the moun-tain, often having to climb the rough side even with improved skills. Karen Hor-ney (1942) used the metaphor of climbing a mountain in explaining the process of psychoanalysis to new patients. She explained that she had climbed many mountains, could serve as a guide, and was considered by some to be an expert climber. She told each patient, however, that "I've never been up this mountain before, and in order to make the climb, we will have to do it together."

Dr. Crenshaw has used this analogy repeatedly in his clinical work, believ-ing that the proper attitude of therapists is that mountains must be climbed but that each mountain is uniquely different. In order to reach the top of each client's mountain, the therapist must discover what makes each client's mountain chal-lenging but also rewarding. If time is not taken to make the effort to learn each crevice, each steep, rocky, and slippery slope, each sudden drop-off, general knowledge about climbing mountains is of little value. Furthermore, such lack of care shows a lack of respect for the mountain. Experienced mountain climbers know that when climbers do not properly prepare, understand, and take the time to get to know the nuances of the mountain, tragedy is certain to follow.

Keeping in mind these cautions, one can introduce the possibility of a better future, even if the child or family has difficulty envisioning it. At the very least, introducing the possibility puts it on clients' "radar screens." Even if their entire childhood was characterized by pain and suffering, different choices can be made, different steps taken, and changes sought that at least offer the possi-bility of something better.

A LETTER FROM THE FUTURE

One way older children can explore the possibility of a more hopeful future is by writing a letter from the future (Dolan 1991). The child is asked to imagine a time in the future when life might be better. Children are told to try to visualize a healthy and satisfying life at some point in the future (too big a leap for some children in gorilla suits) and to write a letter describing their life at that point. It could be five or ten years later or after they are grown up, employed, or married. It can be any reference point that makes sense to them. They are encouraged to use their imaginations to describe in the letter what they are doing, what people are in their life at that point, who they feel close to, and what things are important to them.

It takes courage to hope and dream about a meaningful future. Many gorilla-suit wearers dare not entertain the possibility of hope. Sammy, age eight, a child in residential treatment, is an example of a child without hopefulness who constantly battles with his murderous thoughts. His mother died of lung cancer when he was four, and his disinterested father was in jail. He had been freed for adoption, but not adopted, and hadn't seen any family member since the age of four. Hope could threaten Sammy's will to survive; he clings to life by keeping expectations low. If he were to risk hoping that, for example, an adoptive family would come along and be the family he used to long for, he would become extremely vulnerable to pain. Should the hoped-for family never appear, it could be more than he could bear. It might sever the thin lifeline that keeps him going. Daring to hope when circumstances are bleak requires remarkable courage! Here is Sammy's "Letter from the Future," with a few spelling and punctuation errors corrected.

> Dear Dr. Dave:
>
> I'm now twenty-three years old. I gave up on finding a family and decided to make the people who have cared about me my family. That includes all the people at Astor. Things are better now. When I left Astor I went to live with a foster family, but that didn't work out; I guess I was not meant to live in a family so I went to an adolescent program (name of program deleted). I stayed there until I was eighteen. Some of the staff there are my family too. I have learned to control my temper better and I don't get into much trouble.
>
> I live in an apartment with two guys who were in the same program (name deleted) as myself near (name of city deleted). I did get my GED and I have a job at a factory that puts together electronic parts. It is not a high paying job, but I'm able to pay my part of rent. I don't have a girlfriend, but I wish I did. I get kind of lonely. There is a woman at my job who seems to like me. I hope I work my courage up to asking her to go to a movie.
>
> Well, I have to go now, but you can see I have made it. I'm living on my own. I have an apartment with my roommates and I have a job. And I soon hope to have a girlfriend. I will let you know when it happens. Thank you for never giving up on me and seeing something good in me

Figure 3.2. Drawing of a positive future

when I could only see the bad. Please thank all the Astor staff for what
they did for me.
    Bye for now,
    Sammy

Many children will find writing a "Letter from the Future" too difficult
because of poor language or writing skills, or they may simply prefer an artis-
tic creation. Such children can be asked, instead, to picture in their mind a time
in the future when they can imagine their life being better and to draw a picture or make a collage of what that time would look like. Other children may
prefer to describe it to the therapist. Regardless of the modality selected, if they
can articulate a vision of a more positive future, it is an encouraging sign and
another testament to their strength and courage. Such courage is illustrated in
figure 3.2 in the drawing of a positive future made by a girl who had experienced significant traumas. She drew it when she was seven, depicting herself
playing the violin at age nineteen, when she hoped all the troubles in her life
would be gone, but she hastened to add, "I can't be sure about that."

CONCLUSION

Treatment staff are strongly advised never to underestimate the healthy forces
in children. Sometimes staff can slide into a deep pit of hopelessness, set low
expectations for clients, and develop a pessimistic outlook about their lives. Often the children, and their families, surprise us in their ability to rise above obstacles. At the end of each school year in the residential treatment center where
both of us worked, a ceremony called Awards Day is held. Every year, Dr.
Crenshaw, although no longer employed in the center, presents an award, in
memory of his brother, to the student and staff member best exemplifying the
spirit of the center—caring, compassion, courage, and resilience. The child
who received the award in 2003 was a youngster who at one time engaged in
very serious self-injurious behavior, and staff felt pessimistic about his future.
The author was totally amazed when presented with the name of the child to
receive the award, and his selection is a great credit to him, his family, and the
Astor staff. Some children, even with all the help and best efforts of family,
committed teachers, caregivers, and child and family therapists, will never make
it to the top of the mountain. But regardless of the distance they climb, whatever represents the peak for them, we find it a privilege to accompany them!

14

Past and Present Prevention and Intervention Services and Some Suggested Modifications

In the year 2000, it was estimated that 199,000 adolescent homicides occurred globally or about 565 adolescents died each day, due to interpersonal violence (Merrick, Kandel, and Vardi 2003). In 1996, the World Health Assembly declared violence a leading public health issue (Merrick, Kandel, and Vardi). A host of biological, psychosocial, and environmental factors have been found to be predictive of adult aggression and antisocial behavior. Violence prevention requires a comprehensive approach that takes into account these multiple developmental pathways.

The research reviewed in this volume attributes violence and aggression to neglect, rejection, and abuse, accompanied by living in violent communities on the margins of society, and emphasizes the hyperaroused alarm state that contributes to the continued expression of aggression. Violence disrupts homes, schools, neighborhoods, and entire communities. Although national rates of youth violence have declined in recent years, an unacceptably large number of young people still remain both victims and perpetrators of violence (Flannery et al. 2003; Dahlberg 1998; Mercy and Potter 1996; Sickmund, Snyder, and Poe-Yamagata 1997; Snyder and Sickmund 1999). A plethora of studies reveal that violent behavior occurs along a developmental continuum of behavioral severity (see, for example, Tolan, Guerra, and Kendall 1995; Tremblay et al. 1992).

Because the cycle of violence begins early (Olson, Ceballo, and Park 2002), a number of prevention and early intervention programs have sprung up across the country. These programs range from preventing date violence (Wekerle and Wolfe 1999; Wolfe, Wekerle, and Scott 1997) to anger management training for high-risk elementary school students (Larson and Lochman 2002). In between are relationship-based prenatal services to pregnant adolescents (Rogers, Peoples-Sheps, and Suchindran 1996); home visiting programs for mothers of high-risk infants (Affleck et al. 1989; Barrera, Rosenbaum, and Cunningham 1986; Olds et al. 1998); training programs for parents of children enrolled in Head Start (Webster-Stratton, Reid, and Hammond 2001; Zigler, Taussig, and Black 1992); school-based violence prevention (Embry 2003; Farrell et al. 2001); comprehensive youth programs (Furlong, Paige, and Osher 2003), including after-school activities (Epstein and Sheldon 2002; Grossman et al. 2002; Munoz 2002; Whetten 2002); modification of school climates (Peterson and Skiba 2001); comprehensive community initiatives (Berlin, Brooks-Gunn, and Aber 2001; McNeelly 1999; Telleen and Mak-Pearce 2002); wellness centers in schools (Guerra and Williams 2003); and mental health services linked to schools or delivered in school settings (Kirst 1994; Weist et al. 2003).

The prevention programs concentrate on helping pregnant mothers feel worthwhile, training new mothers in proper infant care, and training mothers of preschool children to use less harsh disciplinary techniques and to encourage and reward their children's pro-social behaviors. Aronen and Kurkela (1996) and Olds, Eckenrode, and Henderson (1997) report on the long-term effects of home visitation programs, the American Psychological Association (2003) and Durlak (1997) review the effects of primary mental health prevention programs, Feldman (2003) reviews the effects of early intervention programs throughout the United Kingdom, and Nixon (2002) reviews the outcome studies of preschool interventions, perhaps the most popular form of early intervention.

A recent literature review reveals that young children who hit, kick, verbally insult, and threaten others are more likely to display more serious violence in adolescence (Flannery et al. 2003). These early aggressive behaviors are targeted in early intervention programs because they escalate interpersonal conflict into violence (Flannery et al.). With aggressive toddlers, particularly those enrolled in programs such as Head Start, in which outreach efforts are a key program component, parent training programs help reduce the aggressive behavior of some identified children (Webster-Stratton, Reid, and Hammond 2001), especially when attention is directed at helping mothers provide more structure, anticipate the child's point of view, exert modulated and respectful control, and reinforce pro-social behaviors (Cavell 2001).

Efforts with the children concentrate on helping children achieve better impulse control, manage anger more appropriately, develop pro-social behaviors and interpersonal skills, and enhance self-esteem. In chapter 4, we mention three early prevention programs emphasizing developing greater empathy for others, as well as the Roots of Empathy, the Second Step, and the Dina Dinosaur programs. Others operating in preschools, realizing that success in the preschool years provides the foundation for later success in school, emphasize autonomy, problem solving, social competence, and sense of purpose. Children's use of positive thinking, acceptance, and distraction is associated with fewer symptoms resulting from living with depressed parents (Langrock et al. 2002), all skills emphasized in early intervention programs.

WHAT WE LEARNED FROM
EARLIER EFFORTS AT PREVENTION

Unfortunately, we learned several decades ago from follow-up studies that gains associated with carefully planned and well-executed preschool and early elementary school prevention and intervention programs cannot be maintained unless subsequent educational endeavors are equally well planned and executed. Lucco (1972) notes that a child will be at a cognitive disadvantage when individuals in the home environment function at a lower level of conceptualization than is required of the child in school. This conclusion can be applied equally to pro-social, empathy, and self-monitoring skills. Consequently, intervention programs with aggressive children need to direct equal efforts at helping parents take an active role in the cognitive and social development of their child.

Social skills training alone, especially if narrowly focused (e.g., anger management training), does not address the complex emotional underpinnings of aggression and violence in youth (Hardy and Lazaloff 2004; Skarlew et al. 2002), although Patrick and Rich (2004) have attempted to make the training more meaningful by embedding it in the internal world of the client. Social skills training, however, can enhance a child's prospects for successful adjustment. The research on resilience suggests that the availability of at least one trusting relationship can buffer against depression and stress-related mental health disorders. Children with better social skills have a greater chance of forming such a relationship. The development of pro-social skills, especially the ability to empathize, is crucial in efforts to interrupt the cycle of violence (Fraiberg, Adelson, and Shapiro 1965; Hardy and Lazaloff in press). Problem-solving ability is another crucial skill. Individuals who survive traumas relatively unscathed use problem-solving coping strategies rather than anxiety-management coping strategies when faced with traumatic situations (Ness and Macaskill 2003).

A number of cognitive-behavioral programs have been developed to teach social skills and have been widely used in both individual and group formats. A number of these programs are cited in chapter 5, when discussing the coping approach to treating traumatized children.

Studies suggest that aggressive behavior can be reduced by altering the social environment at school (Dahlberg 1998; Englander-Golden et al. 1989; Flannery et al. 2003; Reid et al. 1999; Stoolmiller, Eddy, and Reid 2000; Tremblay, McCord, Boileau et al. 1991), especially by emphasizing rewards for and praise of pro-social behavior (Walker, Colvin, and Ramsey 1995) and by facilitating social competence (Hawkins et al. 1999).

PREVENTION AND EARLY INTERVENTIONS NEED TO BE BROAD BASED

Zigler and his colleagues (Zigler, Taussig, and Black 1992) stress that the risk factors that make a child prone to delinquency involve many systems, including the individual, the family, and the community network. Consequently, isolated treatment methods will be ineffective. This view is consistent with a recent review of school-based violence-prevention programs. The review concluded that elementary school interventions focusing on the broader school environment appeared more successful in changing violence-related behavior than discrete services for high-risk children (Howard, Flora, and Griffin 1999). Longitudinal studies of several early childhood intervention programs that did not directly target disruptive behaviors suggest that, in addition to demonstrating academic gains, participants were less involved in delinquent acts in adolescence (Zigler, Taussig, and Black). These early childhood programs are broad based and attempt to promote overall social competence at an early age. One example of a comprehensive early intervention program is the Perry Preschool Program.

THE PERRY PRESCHOOL PROGRAM

The Perry Preschool Program was developed by Weikart (1967) in an effort to encourage the language development of disadvantaged African American children. This program was initiated in 1962, and longitudinal data about participants has been gathered each succeeding year. Several different curricula were employed over the years, including one based on a language mastery program and the work of Piaget, which emphasizes skills of classification, seriation, numbering, spatial reasoning, and temporal reasoning, as well as the use of symbols, a skill lacking in many children wearing gorilla suits and discussed in *A Handbook of Play Therapy with Aggressive Children*, chapter 2. In addition, weekly home visits are made to encourage parent participation in the child's education.

During the first three years, children experienced an instructional method that Weikart described as "verbal bombardment." The teacher attempted to draw the children's attention to important stimuli through a constant series of questions and comments. Weikart thought this method would make the children more aware of various uses of language, another skill deficient in gorilla-suit wearers and addressed in *A Handbook of Play Therapy with Aggressive Children*, chapter 16. In later years, based on research demonstrating that highly programmed, skill-focused programs sacrifice later learning potential for immediate outcome (Miller et al. 1971; Weikart 1971), Weikart shifted the emphasis from language to cognition, implementing one program emphasizing concept formation and a second based on the concepts of Piaget.

The Perry Preschool Program continues to provide high-quality, early education programs to economically disadvantaged children and their parents. Interestingly, the program was never designed to reduce delinquency. No direct efforts were made to help the children develop self-esteem or to curb their aggressive behaviors. Yet a serendipitous finding occurred: when the participants reached adolescence, they were less involved in delinquent acts than were youth in the comparison group, highlighting the connection between quality preschool education and later reductions in delinquency rates (Berrueta-Clement et al. 1987; Greenwood et al. 1996; Schweinhart, Barnes, and Weikart 1993). Following the participants until most reached the age of 19 revealed the following achievements compared with nonparticipants:

- improved scholastic achievement during the school years
- decreased delinquency and crime rates
- less reliance on welfare assistance
- less incidence of teenage pregnancy
- increased rates of high school graduation and postsecondary program enrollment
- higher rates of employment, pay, and greater job satisfaction

The program has been designated by the Center for the Study and Prevention of Violence as a Blueprints Promising Program and is now sponsored by the National Crime Prevention Council. More information about the program can be found at www.highscope.org/Research/PerryProject/perrymain.htm.

CENTER FOR THE STUDY AND PREVENTION OF VIOLENCE (CSPV)

Founded in 1992 with a grant from the Carnegie Corporation, the Center for the Study and Prevention of Violence (CSPV) was established to assist groups dedicated to understanding and preventing violence. The original focus of the center was on preventing adolescent violence, but its mission has expanded to include understanding and preventing violence across the life span. The center sponsors research within the Institute of Behavioral Science at the University of Colorado, Boulder. One of the center's initiatives has been to identify programs that successfully reduce aggression and violence. Those identified are called Blueprints for Violence Prevention. More information about the program can be found at www.colorado.edu/cspv/blueprints/. The Blueprints Model Programs, of which there are currently eleven, meet strict scientific standards of program effectiveness in reducing aggression, delinquency, substance abuse, and violent crimes. Twenty-one other programs, selected from 600 violence-prevention programs, are designated Blueprints Promising Programs. The federal Office of Juvenile Justice and Delinquency Prevention provides funding to CSPV to replicate Blueprints programs in various locations across the United States. We describe five Blueprints Model Programs and then several Blueprints Promising Programs.

Nurse-Family Partnership

This Blueprints Model Program involves ongoing home visits by nurses to low-income parents, both during pregnancy and after birth. The program was initiated in Elmira, New York, and has been replicated in Denver, Colorado. The program is grounded in theories of self-efficacy (Bandura 1973, 1977, 1997), human attachment (Bowlby 1969), and human ecology (Bronfenbrenner 1970, 1977). The program's specific intervention strategies are targeted to address risk factors and to promote adaptive behaviors that will reduce these risks. Each family is assigned a nurse, who visits the family twice monthly during the pregnancy and the first two years of the child's life. The nurse provides guidance, support, coaching, and teaching of important parenting skills to ensure effective physical and emotional care of the child.

The program targets specific parental behaviors and modifiable environmental conditions that research has associated with adverse outcomes. Whenever possible, the same nurse remains with the family throughout the project because program effectiveness tends to decline when families are served by more than one nurse over the course of the program. Evidence of the program's effectiveness for low-income women and their children is summarized below:

- reduction of pregnancy complications, such as hypertensive disorders and kidney infections;
- improved women's prenatal health-related behaviors (improved diet and reduction in cigarette smoking);

- reduction in harm to children, reflected in a 79 percent reduction in reports of child abuse and neglect and fewer injuries to children revealed in their medical records;
- improved personal development in the mothers, indicated by declining rates of subsequent pregnancy (a 31 percent drop in subsequent births), an increase in the spacing between first and second children, a reduction in welfare reliance, and reductions in behavioral problems related to maternal substance abuse and criminal behavior (a 9 percent decline in maternal arrests) of mothers from low-income households and unmarried at registration during pregnancy;
- reduction in criminal and antisocial behavior by the fifteen-year-old children, as revealed by fewer arrests, fewer days consuming alcohol, and fewer convictions and violations of probation.

Unfortunately, recent reanalysis of the fifteen-year follow-up in Elmira, New York, showed that the program's effects on child abuse and neglect were lost on families that reported high rates of domestic violence (defined as more than twenty-eight incidents since the birth of the study child). When the program was replicated in Denver, its directors added a partner communication component, which referred families experiencing domestic violence to more intensive programs to interrupt this pattern.

Remarkably, the costs of this program are recovered by the time the children reach four years of age. In fact, over a child's lifetime, the cost savings to government and society are more than four times the cost of the program. (Olds et al. 1998). More information about the program can be found at www .nccfc.org/nurseFamilyPartnership.cfm/.

The Bullying Prevention Program

In a survey of more than 6,000 middle school students in rural South Carolina, 23 percent reported that they had been bullied by other students "several times" or more during the past three months. Boys are more likely to bully others physically than are girls, and a relatively high percentage of girls report being bullied mainly by boys. When girls bully, they make less use of physical aggression and more use of verbal harassment and exclusion, specifically slandering, spreading rumors, intentionally excluding others from a group, and manipulating friendship relationships. While teachers usually interrupt physical bullying behaviors, they rarely respond to verbal forms of bullying (Yoon and Kerber 2003).

In terms of victims, younger and weaker students are more often exposed to bullying, although those with fewer friends and those less assertive and with fewer pro-social behaviors are also bullied more than others (Schwartz et al. 1997, 2000; Schwartz, Chang, and Farver 2001). Children who are less appropriately assertive and who lack pro-social behaviors are often those who later put on gorilla suits and become bullies themselves. At age twenty-three, children who were bullied in grades six to nine tended to be more depressed and had lower self-esteem than their nonvictimized peers. Persistent bullying can leave the invisible wounds and scars discussed in chapter 2. As for the bullies themselves, approximately 60 percent of boys characterized as bullies in grades six to nine are convicted of at least one officially recorded crime by the age of twenty-four, compared with 23 percent of boys who were characterized as nonbullies. Furthermore, as many as 35 to 40 percent of the former bullies had three or more convictions by this age, while only 10 percent of the control-group boys had multiple convictions. Because of the negative impact of bullying on others and because of the future adjustment problems of the bullies themselves, a number of school-based programs have targeted bullying as a behavior to reduce.

The Bullying Prevention Program was developed in Norway after three adolescent boys committed suicide attributed to severe bullying by peers. In response, Dan Olweus, a professor at the University of Bergen in Norway, was commissioned in 1983 to develop and evaluate an intervention program directed at bullies and their victims. The result was the Olweus Bullying Prevention Program, which has been refined over the intervening years. The program, which has been adopted and studied in other cultures, including England, parts of Germany, and the southeastern United States, was developed and researched in the Scandinavian countries, particularly Sweden and Norway (Olweus 1993). The program makes an effort to create a school culture that is positive and caring, with firm limits for hostile and bullying behaviors and in which adults act as authorities and positive role models. The Scandinavian version is a multilevel, multicomponent school-based program designed to prevent or reduce bullying in elementary, middle, and junior high schools. The program is geared to restructure the school environment to reduce both opportunities and rewards for bullying. School staff members are responsible for introducing, implementing, and evaluating the program. The goal is to improve peer relationships and make the school a safe and positive place for students to learn.

Interventions are undertaken at three levels: schoolwide interventions, classroom-level interventions, and individual-level interventions. The schoolwide interventions entail administration of the Olweus Bully/Victim Questionnaire about bullying, filled out anonymously by students. Staff training is provided, and a Bullying Prevention Coordinating Committee is formed. Schoolwide rules against bullying are established. Finally, a coordinated system of supervision during break periods is provided to staff. On the classroom level, regular classroom meetings about bullying and peer relations are conducted, and class-parent meetings are held to address the topic. All students participate in the first two phases of the program, while in the third phase, individual-level interventions, the bullies and those victimized by them receive additional services. The services include individual meetings with children who bully and who are targets of bullying. Meetings with parents of the children involved are also held.

A comprehensive study of 2,500 student-participants in Norway reported dramatic reductions in student reporting of bullying or being bullied by other program participants. Reductions also occurred in other antisocial behaviors, including vandalism, fighting, theft, and truancy. Evaluations of programs in the United States, Germany, and Norway have produced similar but somewhat more modest positive findings. More information can be found at www .clemson.edu/olweus/index.htm.

Functional Family Therapy (FFT)

This Blueprints Model Program is a prevention-intervention program for at-risk youth between eleven and eighteen presenting with oppositional defiant disorder, substance abuse, disruptive behavior disorders, or conduct disorder. The program was developed in 1969 by researchers at the University of Utah's Psychology Department Family Clinic. The FFT program is offered in phases that build on each other. The key phases are (1) engagement, (2) motivation, (3) assessment, (4) behavior change, and (5) generalization (Alexander et al. 1998). More information can be found at www.fftinc.com/.

This family intervention program serves clients from a variety of ethnic and cultural groups. The clients are served in both outpatient clinics and their own homes. Considerable emphasis is placed on protective factors that reduce risk (Sexton and Alexander 2000). Although commonly used as an intervention, the program is also an effective prevention program for at-risk adolescents and their families. Services include PINS (person in need of supervision) diversion (a program that provides clinical intervention to divert a child from an antisocial path), probation, alternatives to incarceration, and reentry programs for youth returning to the community from high-security, severely restrictive institutional settings. The emphasis is on short-term interventions that include, on average, eight to twelve sessions for mild cases and up to thirty hours of direct service for more difficult cases. In most cases, sessions are spread over a three-month period. As a core value, the program emphasizes the importance of respecting family members and using their strengths to develop treatment plans (a strength-based family approach).

Sexton and Alexander (2000) describe the basic philosophy of the program as motivating families to change by uncovering family members' unique strengths in ways that enhance self-respect and by offering families specific ways to improve. The program has evolved over thirty years into a clinical intervention model that includes training and supervision to agencies that replicate the model. It also includes process and outcome assessment components to improve the delivery of the program in local communities. Outcomes have been highly favorable and include the following:

- Reducing the need for more restrictive, more expensive services
- Preventing younger children from entering a more restrictive placement within the foster care or juvenile justice system
- Preventing adolescents from entering the adult criminal justice system
- Lowering the proportion of treated youths who were arrested after the program (60 percent of treated youth versus 93 percent of controls in one study; 11 percent versus 67 percent in another)

One replication of the program is the Family Project, a partnership between the University of Nevada at Las Vegas and the Clark County, Utah, Department of Family and Youth Services. The Family Project, the largest replication site in the country, is located in one of the nation's fastest growing and most culturally and ethnically diverse urban areas and one recently troubled by the development of large teenage street gangs. Services are provided to at-risk youth referred by the juvenile probation program. Of the youth treated in a two-year period at a university training center, 80 percent completed treatment services, a high rate for juvenile justice interventions. Only 19.8 percent of treatment completers committed an offense during the year following completion, compared with 36 percent of the treatment-as-usual comparison group. The program has been successfully used in various treatment contexts and with culturally diverse populations.

The Functional Family Therapy model is quite similar to the Homebuilder's Model (Bath and Haapala 1993; Kinney et al. 1977; Kinney, Haapala, and Bath 1991), a widely used, intensive, home-based intervention program designed to prevent out-of-home placements of children. The program, first used to prevent foster home placements, was adapted by Dr. Mordock and his staff (Mordock 1997a) to prevent psychiatric hospitalizations of extremely disruptive and suicidal youth. Initially, four social workers served a caseload of only two clients (later a third case was added to each worker and a worker was reassigned to another program); the workers were available to serve families twenty-four hours a day for up to six weeks.

During the first five years of the program, an average of sixty-two hospitalizations were prevented each year. Furthermore, less than 5 percent of referred children needed hospitalization during service delivery and none needed it who completed treatment, suggesting that the service impact was not just a short-term one. Family members learned skills that reduced the impact of future problems, making emergency mental health services unnecessary.

The program thrived when the county Department of Mental Hygiene operated the psychiatric emergency services. When the county turned over emergency services to the local hospitals, children were referred to the diversion service only when no hospital beds were available in any of the surrounding hospitals. Hospital staff would call other hospitals to look for a bed before they would call the diversion service. In addition, only one managed care organization was willing to contract with the program for diversion services. Hospitals, unable to keep the beds full in their psychiatric units because of the diversion program and unwilling to shrink the size of their units, reduced their average length of stay to create a cost that was less than the cost of the home-based diversion service (Mordock 2002b). In an effort to compete, the diversion program's social workers each took on four cases (the original Homebuilders Model called for only two cases per worker). In response, the hospitals again reduced their patients' length of stay.

The hospital diversion program continues to operate on a small scale through funds provided by the state Department of Mental Health, but its main source of funding is through contracts with social services to prevent foster home placements of children in high-risk families.

Multisystemic Therapy (MST)

This Blueprints Model Program is an intensive family- and community-based treatment program that addresses the complex network of interconnected systems, including family, peers, school, and neighborhood, that are determinants in serious antisocial behavior (Henggeler et al. 1998). The program targets both male and female repeat juvenile offenders ages twelve to seventeen who have been chronic, violent, and/or substance abusers and who are at high risk for out-of-home placement. More information may be found at www.mstservices.com.

The program uses a strength-based and family-based approach, and it has a major goal of empowering youth to handle family, peer, and neighborhood stressors in nonviolent and non-self-destructive ways. The program includes family support and emphasizes skill building for all family members. Parents are helped to place developmentally appropriate demands on their adolescent children and to responsibly manage their behavior. The program features a home-based model of service delivery (Mordock 1997a).

Service length is determined by each family's unique needs, but the usual time devoted to each family is approximately sixty hours, spread over a four-month period. The family-based treatment approach is more intensive than traditional family therapies and typically involves several hours of treatment per week versus the typical weekly fifty-minute sessions offered by most outpatient clinics, and which few parents attend regularly (Mordock 1996a). Intervention strategies are organized around a social-ecological framework that takes into account family, community, and cultural influences. Intervention strategies include a range of modalities, such as strategic and structural family therapy, behaviorally based parent training, and cognitive-behavioral therapy. Program evaluation results have demonstrated that the chronic juvenile offenders who participate, in comparison to the control group, have

- 47 to 64 percent fewer out-of-home placements;
- decreased mental health problems;
- 25 to 70 percent fewer rearrests (after 2.4 years, treated youths were half as likely as control youths to have been arrested);
- significant improvements in family functioning;
- an average of seventy-three fewer days incarcerated in justice system facilities and reduced aggression toward peers.

Outcome studies have demonstrated favorable outcomes across the adolescent age range, for both boys and girls, and for both African American and Caucasian youth. Of intervention programs evaluated to date, it is the most cost-effective program geared to serious juvenile offenders.

Multidimensional Treatment Foster Care (MTFC)

The Oregon Social Learning Center Multidimensional Treatment Foster Care was developed to prevent institutional, residential, and group care placement for high-risk teens with histories of chronic and severe criminal behavior. This Blueprints Model Program is located in Eugene, Oregon, and is based on social-learning theory principles (Chamberlain 2003). More information can be found at www.oslc.org. Participants are placed with specially selected families in the community. The foster parents, considered *professional parents*, are extensively trained and closely supervised to provide clear and consistent limits, consistent consequences for disruptive behavior, and positive reinforcement for pro-social behaviors. The program emphasizes adult mentoring and separation from the negative influences of delinquent peers. Family therapy is provided to the natural or adoptive family; the ultimate goal is to return the child to the home. Program evaluations (Chamberlain and Mihalic 1998) demonstrate that in comparison with a control group, participants

- had significantly fewer subsequent arrests
- used hard drugs significantly less in the twelve-month follow-up
- were incarcerated 60 percent fewer days during the follow-up period
- ran away from their programs, on average, three times less often
- received quicker placement in the community from more restrictive settings (e.g., hospital, detention)
- (in the case of boys) reported significantly fewer criminal activities (general delinquency, index offenses, and felony assaults)

The Fast Track Prevention Program

The Fast Track prevention program, a Blueprints Promising Program, is a multisite, multicomponent preventive program for high-risk children selected in kindergarten for participation. Based on a comprehensive developmental model, intervention includes a universal-level classroom program, social skills training, academic tutoring, parent training, and home visiting, all designed to improve competencies and reduce behavioral problems. At the end of the first grade, participants showed moderate gains on measures of social, emotional, and academic skill, positive peer interactions, and social status, and they displayed fewer conduct problems and less use of special education services. Parents reported decreased use of physical discipline, increased parental satisfaction, and more comfortable parenting, and they employed more appropriate and more consistent discipline, displayed more warmth and positive involvement, and collaborated more with the school. A two-year intervention program starting in kindergarten, called Early Risers, includes program components for both parents and children. Interestingly, children whose parents participated showed no greater gains on outcome measures than did children whose parents did not participate (August et al. 2003). (We would argue that either the outcome measures need revision or the parent component needs to be made more meaningful.)

We have emphasized throughout our two volumes on children in gorilla suits that there are no shortcuts or quick fixes to the complex problem of youth aggression and violence. The model programs reviewed are intensive and broad based in scope, and some even address the sociocultural determinants of violence. The roles of trauma, profound loss, and disenfranchised grief, however, have received relatively little attention in prevention and early intervention programs. Two projects that do address these issues are discussed next.

The Center for Children, Families, and Trauma

The Center for Children, Families, and Trauma, a project of the Eikenberg Institute for Relationships in New York City, is under the direction of Kenneth V. Hardy, cited frequently throughout our two volumes. The center addresses the role of loss and trauma in human life, developing intervention strategies to improve the lives of both victims and perpetrators of violence who are still in their youth. In particular, center staff members focus on how profound losses play a pivotal role in the lives of dislocated children, those who share common difficulties as a result of adoption, foster care, migration, immigration, and homelessness. While foster care makes a positive impact on the lives of many children, the majority still score outside the 95th percentile confidence intervals on measures of well-being, especially on measures of conduct disorder (Barber and Delfabbro 2003). A study in Texas revealed that many homeless men had been raised in the state's foster care system (Penzerro 2003). In addition, center staff are exploring sociocultural trauma to understand and develop treatment programs for those whose lives have been adversely affected by societal forces such as poverty and racial oppression.

One innovative program already under way at the Center for Children, Families, and Trauma is called Bullies-to-Buddies. This violence prevention and anti-intolerance program presupposes that addressing early signs of bullying can deter youth aggression. The program has been implemented at all grade levels and in both public and private schools. One of the program's central tenets is that some pro-social and adaptive skills coexist with, but are overshadowed by, a bully's antisocial behavior. The Bullies-to-Buddies program is focused on developing pro-social skills to transform bullies, whose social relationships are based on domination and ridicule, to buddies, whose peer relationships are founded on mutual respect and affiliation.

The families of participating children, along with the children, are involved in a minimum of ten family therapy sessions, and the children attend biweekly group sessions led by a family therapy team. Both the family and group sessions address the psychological roots of bullying. Evaluation of the program is currently in progress.

When Dr. Mordock was in third grade, a bully forced him every morning to stick his head in the school bathroom toilet. If he did not, he would be beaten in a way that left no marks. To Dr. Mordock's surprise, and over his protests, his father invited the bully to Dr. Mordock's next birthday party. The father knew something Dr. Mordock didn't. After the boy attended the party, he not only stopped bullying Dr. Mordock; he became Dr. Mordock's protector throughout his elementary school experience.

The School-Based Mourning Project

The School-Based Mourning Project: A Preventive Intervention in the Cycle of Inner-City Violence, operated by the Georgetown University Medical Center, is a program designed to help children ages seven to fifteen deal with multiple losses and trauma and to promote the work of mourning (Skarlew et al. 2002). The project takes into account how difficult it is for inner-city children to grieve their profound losses. Living in chaotic and impoverished environments and witnessing and enduring violence leaves one little time to grieve. The children, emotionally vulnerable and developmentally impaired, are unable to cope with the feelings of helplessness and hopelessness, the pain of grief, their own violent fantasies, and their ongoing guilt. The result can be underlying depression that youth attempt to avoid by aggressive acting out or by destructive behavior. Children resist grieving, especially those who have experienced trauma or multiple losses. They fear being overwhelmed and engulfed in their grief. They will sometimes state, "If I ever let myself cry, I will not ever stop." The clinical teams at the School-Based Mourning Project have developed techniques similar to the ones we have described in *A Handbook of Play Therapy with Aggressive Children* to enable children in group sessions to unburden and tolerate feelings of loss, if only for brief periods. They use a variety of projective methods, drawings, clay, games, stories, and musical instruments to structure the therapeutic context and make it safe for children to acknowledge and express their grief. We discuss helping children to grieve in play therapy in *A Handbook of Play Therapy with Aggressive Children*, chapters 18 and 19.

On a larger scale, the School-Based Mourning Project is designed to address through a group format the reluctant grief of children who have experienced abundant losses.

> The children were gradually able to bear and voice uncomfortable thoughts and feelings about their losses. Many of them evidenced an increased capacity for empathy and compassion. Parents reported that their children showed an increased ability for concentration and decreased tendency to act out aggressive impulses. (Skarlew et al. 2002, p. 327)

The project started with a focus on adolescents. Later, the project directors switched their focus to children and preadolescents because "once children reach adolescence, they are more likely to deal with the overwhelming and unbearable emptiness and threatening abyss of helplessness and depression by acting out sexually, aggressively, or by self-medicating with drugs" (Skarlew et al. 2002, p. 320). The directors also wanted to counter at an earlier age the developmental arrest that accompanies exposure to multiple traumas and unmourned losses. The clinical team recognizes the depth of children's wounds and hopes to extend its work with the children through their elementary school years (kindergarten to grade six) and to keep up with them through high school.

In the early stages of the project, when the clinicians were interviewing recalcitrant acting-out adolescents, some of the teenagers spontaneously began talking about fatal shootings of their peers. The clinicians recognized that adolescents can talk more easily about peer losses than about earlier losses of parents or siblings, but the intensity of these adolescents' affect hinted at pain from earlier losses. Working with inner-city children in the war zones of high-crime neighborhoods requires addressing the underlying sense of hopelessness and depression experienced by children who have been exposed to repeated losses. The project directors note that 60 percent of inner-city children say they do not expect to reach old age and that some adolescents were planning their funerals in minute detail.

Most of the children treated at the Astor Home for Children, the residential treatment center where both of us worked, were from the inner city, particularly the Bronx. Some of the children who returned to their homes were shot and killed in the streets or knifed to death on the subway. Living in constant danger can be appreciated only if it has been experienced firsthand. Like veterans of combat, the children cannot fully convey the effects of "constant shelling on consecutive days." Only those who were there and survived can fully appreciate the terror of such bombardments.

Dr. Crenshaw remembers being deeply moved by a display of writing and pictures in the hallway of the school at the Astor Home, the Astor Learning Center, shortly before his retirement from Astor. The children were involved in a project requiring them to write and draw their wishes and dreams for the world we all live in. A number of the drawings were quite touching, showing children feeling safe, the world at peace, and a world where children do not go hungry. One picture, a drawing of a home, was captioned, "All children need a home." We should all strive for a world where basic needs for food and shelter are met and where we feel safe and cared for in a place called home. Sadly, there are far too many children who can only dream of such a place. These children need more than problem-solving practice, social skills training, and anger management training. While such efforts are important, greater attention needs to be paid to wounds that have made their young lives a nightmare of greater horror than most of us will experience in a lifetime.

THE NEED FOR EMPATHY TRAINING IN EARLY INTERVENTION PROGRAMS

A longitudinal study of 296 young men and women disclosed that childhood exposure to marital violence predicted aggression toward peers for all ages of youth. Empathic youth, however, were less likely to engage in peer aggression and dating aggression (McCloskey and Lichter 2003). The study's authors recommended that empathy building be emphasized in prevention and intervention programs for youth. We illustrate some empathy building exercises in chapter 14 of *A Handbook of Play Therapy with Aggressive Children.*

A growing body of research supports the pivotal role played by empathy in decreasing externalizing disorders (Hastings et al. 2000; Chandler and Moran 1990; Cohen and Strayer 1996). Evolutionists emphasize how empathic ability has contributed to human adaptability. The skill allows humans to predict each other's behaviors; helps to cement altruistic, helpful, and cooperative acts; and facilitates the development of lasting bonds of trust and reciprocity within social groups (Neese 1991; Sober and Wilson 1998).

In general, girls show more concern for others than do boys, from the second year of life through adolescence (Eisenberg and Fabes 1998; Grusec, Goodnow, and Cohen 1996; Zahn-Waxler et al. 1992). Girls' greater orientation toward the needs of others may be the key link in their decreased risk for the development of disruptive behavior disorders (Hastings et al. 2000). The lack of empathy in many antisocial adolescents has been clearly established (Chandler and Moran 1990; Cohen and Strayer 1996; Ellis 1982). The negative effects of the lack of empathy begin early: children who were disobedient as toddlers are less likely, six to eight years later, to report pro-social responses to vignettes depicting transgressions against others than are children who were less disobedient as toddlers (Kochanska 1991).

The association between lack of empathy and aggressive, or disruptive, behavior is detectable in the early elementary school years (Tremblay et al. 1992), suggesting that the inverse relation between concern for others and antisocial behavior increases with age (Miller and Eisenberg 1988). Hastings and colleagues (Hastings et al. 2000) state,

> The empathic deficits of aggressive individuals emerge over time, either through arrested development of concern at a relatively immature stage or an actual decrease from earlier levels. In addition, antisocial children may not only lack concern but may also actively disregard or be callous toward others in need. (p. 532)

Parents who relate to their children warmly, who are responsive and supportive, who establish guidelines for behavior, and who use reasoning in conjunction with controlled discipline produce preschool children with pro-social behaviors (Baumrind 1967; Robinson, Zahn-Waxler, and Emde 1994; Zahn-Waxler et al. 1995; Krevans and Gibbs 1996), a relationship between parenting behaviors and child attributes that occurs across cultures (Dekovic and Janssens 1992; Janssens and Dekovic 1997). In contrast, parents who are overly strict and

harshly punitive, who fail to reason with their children, who fail to establish
reasonable and consistent rules, and who display frequent anger and disappointment toward their children impede pro-social development (Hastings et
al. 2000). This association is particularly strong with children who display externalizing disorders. The deficit in empathy displayed by children with significant levels of behavior problems becomes increasingly pronounced after the
preschool years, although some differences in children's concerns for others are
detected as early as the preschool years.

    This research has major clinical implications for those working with go-
rilla-suit wearers and their parents, as well as for social policy. Comprehensive
prevention and intervention programs should include parent services that address their own personal histories of harsh life circumstances, overwhelming
current stressors, misguided ideas about parenting and child development, and
lack of expressed empathy for their children's troubles. We emphasize "expressed empathy" as we have found that some parents repress empathic feelings
because feeling empathy brings their own traumas and misfortunes to mind.
Others fail to show empathy because they are at war with their children. Parents of high-risk children need services to support their efforts to provide the
kind of parenting that will have a major influence on the development of their
children's empathy and on other pro-social behaviors.

    Prevention and early intervention programs should provide comprehen-
sive broad-based approaches that include teaching, modeling, and reinforcing
pro-social skills, with special emphasis on empathy. When adults show warmth,
interest, and concern for the emotional well-being of their children, it is far
more likely that the children will develop the capacity to show this same concern for others. To paraphrase Alfred Adler, show me a child who is well socialized and I will show you an adult who has actualized the self to the benefit of society. Show me a poorly socialized child and I will show you an adult
who has strived to be superior at the expense of society.

    We believe that a program that operated in the mid- to late-1960s and
early 1970s should be revived and revised to include training in pro-social skills,
including empathy. The program was called the Mother-Child Home Program
and was developed by the Family Service Association of Nassau County, New
York (Levenstein, Kochman, and Roth 1973). The program consisted of regular home visits by interviewers called toy demonstrators. These visits began
when the child was two years old and continued on a semiweekly basis until
the child was four. The main activity of the home sessions was a structured yet
fun-oriented "curriculum" of verbalized play with the child, designed to foster
the child's verbal and conceptual development (and at the same time the
mother's). The goal of the toy demonstrator was to involve the mother in each
play session with the child and thereby transfer the main responsibility for pro-

moting verbal interaction from the toy demonstrator to the mother. The interviewers were called toy demonstrators to de-emphasize the didactic aspects of their interaction with mothers since direct teaching of the mother can be perceived as demeaning (Hess 1969).

Children who participated in the Mother-Child Home Program demonstrated an average IQ gain of about seventeen points after two years in the program. Unfortunately, other behaviors were not evaluated as only cognitive gains, the stated goal of the program, were evaluated. Initial gains in IQ, however, are less important than the possibility that parents who participate in this program come to view themselves as "educators" of their children. In a similar program, Radin (1972) reported that parental involvement in a preschool program appeared to have no effect on the child's intellectual performance if IQ changes were examined immediately following the preschool experience. However, if tested one year later, children of participating parents had higher IQ scores than those whose parents did not participate.

Building on the concept that interventions should be fun and nonblaming, Catherine Cwiakala developed the puppet-storytelling intervention program for substance-abusing mothers and their children that we mention in chapter 9 (Cwiakala and Mordock 1997).

PRINCIPLES OF EFFECTIVE FAMILY-FOCUSED INTERVENTIONS

In the appendix to their article on family strengthening approaches for the prevention of youth problems, Kumpfer and Alvarado (2003) conclude from their review of the research the following points (source citations have been omitted):

1. Comprehensive multi-component interventions are more effective in modifying a broader range of risk or protective factors and processes in children than single-component programs.
2. Family-focused programs are generally more effective for families with relationship problems than either child-focused or parent-focused programs, particularly if they emphasize family strengths, resilience, and protective processes rather than deficits.
3. Effective parent and family programs include . . . strategies for improving family relations, communication, and parental monitoring.
4. Family programs are most enduring in effectiveness if they produce cognitive, affective, and behavioral changes in the ongoing family dynamics and environment.
5. Increased dosage or intensity (25–50 hours) of the intervention is needed with higher risk families with more risk factors and fewer protective

factors and processes than low-risk universal families who need only about five to 24 hours of intervention.

6. Family programs should be age and developmentally appropriate with new versions taken by parents as their children mature.

7. Addressing developmentally appropriate risk and protective factors or processes at specific times of family need when participants are receptive to change is important.

8. If parents are very dysfunctional, interventions beginning early in the life cycle (i.e., prenatally or early childhood) are more effective.

9. Tailoring the intervention to the cultural traditions of the families improves recruitment, retention, and sometimes outcome effectiveness.

10. High rates of family recruitment and retention (in the range of 80 percent to 85 percent) are possible with the use of incentives, including food, child care, transportation, rewards for homework completion or attendance, and graduation.

11. The effectiveness of the program is highly tied to the trainer's personal efficacy and confidence, affective characteristics of genuineness, warmth, humor, and empathy, and ability to structure sessions and be directive.

12. Interactive skills training methods (e.g., role plays, active modeling, family practice sessions, homework practice, and videos/CDs of effective and ineffective parenting skills, etc.) versus didactic lecturing increase program effectiveness and client satisfaction particularly with low socioeconomic level parents.

13. Developing a collaborative process whereby clients are empowered to identify their own solutions is also important in developing a supportive relationship and reducing parent resistance and dropout. (p. 465)

WHY PUBLIC SCHOOLS EXPERIENCE DIFFICULTY DEVELOPING INTERVENTION PROGRAMS

To adequately serve the needs of children in gorilla suits, major shifts in public school policy and programming would be needed. Because the needs of gorilla-suit wearers are diverse, no one child-serving agency can program adequately for them. The educational system was designed to meet self-actualization needs (Maslow 1954), and the system needs to join forces with agencies addressing more basic needs before gorilla-suit wearers can make maximal use of educational services. Maeroff (1998), speaking about the needs of economically disadvantaged students, emphasizes that disadvantaged students need the kind of support apparatus, referred to as social capital, that builds networks and norms and "engenders the trust that promotes academic success" (p. ix). He writes that enhancement programs for disadvantaged youth, a group with a disproportionate number of gorilla-suit wearers, should share four basic objectives. They should strive to create a sense of connectedness, a sense of well-being, a sense of academic initiative, and a sense of knowing, objectives actually larger than those of most intervention programs designed to help children in gorilla suits.

Public schools also cannot effectively program for gorilla-suit wearers because traditional public school programs are not structured in a manner (nor should they be) that can impose limits on the students' aggressive and delinquent behaviors. Unless these behaviors are limited and suit wearers learn how to respond differently to conflict and stress, they will continue to display maladaptive behavior. Both in-school and out-of-school suspensions are the typical public school response to aggressive and delinquent acts (Rose 1988), a disciplinary strategy used more often with people of color than with other groups, both in the United States (Children's Defense Fund 1975; Nieto 1999; Sonia 1998) and in Great Britain, where African Caribbean children are suspended more often than others (Osler and Hill 1999). Suspensions will not alter maladaptive behaviors and usually make them worse because such practices further alienate the already alienated and disenfranchised child.

Later in this chapter, we present an example of a modest effort by an elementary school to program differently for a small group of children. Such efforts are often described in the literature, but when we have written the school for a copy of their program, we receive either no reply or a brief letter informing us of the program's demise. The same is true of federally funded projects. Dr. Mordock once wrote to more than forty centers receiving federal funds to develop special programs. He received program material from only four, two of which sent him their initial project proposal, suggesting they never completed a final report for the funding agency! Initiating special programs usually requires several "program champions," and if these individuals leave the school system, the programs usually end, some dying a slow death and others killed abruptly.

Interestingly, surveys and observations of special education teachers suggest that many of their ideas about education are related more to control and discipline and to students' social behaviors than to academic achievement (Knitzer, Steinberg, and Fleish 1990). Rios (1996) found these same concerns in surveys of regular classrooms of teachers of color. Assigning students of color to special education classes not only fails to change these teachers' attitudes but may even make them stronger. And those who teach teachers of the emotionally disturbed seem overly preoccupied with the development and refinement of social skills training programs, a deficit approach to service delivery as opposed to the strength-oriented approaches we favor. Designers seem surprised when such services are ineffective and, instead of abandoning them for other models, emphasize improving them (Gresham 1998; Mathur and Rutherford 1996).

INTERVENTION PROGRAMS ANYONE CAN OFFER

The Blueprints Programs, as well as the other programs we have reviewed, are closely associated with major universities or research and training centers and are funded by external sources. Rarely, however, do such innovative programs get replicated elsewhere unless grants become available, and when the grants terminate, the programs usually terminate. In addition, comprehensive early intervention programs are rarely replicated in the public schools. The typical public school usually does not have enough well-trained and supervised teachers to provide highly individualized and specifically structured interventions, a research staff, special equipment, and a commitment to a particular philosophical or theoretical approach. When schools implement programs on a small scale, it is difficult to determine if the actual program produced the changes observed. Hall and Mery (1970) remark,

> Anyone who has taught for long periods of time knows that there is wide variation in attending behavior within and between classes. When there are only one or two teachers involved in the intervention being evaluated, it may well be that the teacher's ability to elicit attending behavior is more important than the treatment itself. (p. 36)

Perhaps a more important question is whether some programs should be replicated. Years ago, researchers demonstrated that a little intervention is not significantly beneficial; programs must be "total push" programs, taking place throughout the day over a four- or five-year period (Karnes 1969). In addition, the larger society, like many professionals who work with troubled children, seems to be caught up in the "adoption syndrome" we discussed in an earlier chapter. More interventions are designed for children than for their parents. Yet the children's parents didn't choose the "culture of poverty"; it was forced on them. We favor prevention and intervention programs designed for the whole family.

A number of successful early interventions, such as the toy demonstrators, no longer operate, either because of funding issues or the departure of "program champions." Innovative services often disappear because new hires have new, but not necessarily better, ideas (Mordock 2002b; Rogers 1983). Nevertheless, without additional funding, motivated communities can modify existing programs or public school climates and work cooperatively together to implement comprehensive community initiatives (Stagner and Duran 1997). A community project in the City of Boston is a good example.

BOSTON'S OPERATION CEASEFIRE

We were totally unprepared for the gang wars and the emergence of crack cocaine. And our cities just became war zones in many respects. And Boston was no different. We would have as many as five and six shootings a night and we were racing from one shooting to another and being totally reactive. (Mediarights 2000, pp. 1–2)

In 1992, a funeral was being held for a young man who had been killed in a gang-related shooting. During that funeral, another fellow came in, and ended up being attacked by a group that was there. He was stabbed several times, but fortunately survived. A gun was shot off in the church, and it created complete chaos. And . . . it led to something like 400 mourners stampeding out of the church. (p. 5)

Operation Ceasefire was a problem-oriented policing intervention aimed at reducing youth homicide and youth firearms violence in Boston (Braga et al. 2001; Winship 2002). The project started in 1995 in response to the number of youth killing other youth in Boston in the early 1990s. One aim of the project was to track down and arrest illegal gun suppliers who provided the youths with guns. The project also focused the attention of the criminal justice system on a small number of chronic offenders, typically gang-involved youth who were responsible for a disproportional number of youth homicides. The goal was to generate a strong deterrent to gang violence. Since the program's initiation, significant reductions in youth homicides, "shot-fired" calls for emergency services, and gun assault incidents have been documented.

Specifically, the implementation of Operation Ceasefire was associated with

- a 63 percent decrease in youth homicides per month;
- a 32 percent decrease in shots-fired calls for service per month,
- a 25 percent decrease in gun assaults per month; and
- a 44 percent decrease in the number of youth gun assaults per month in the highest risk district (Kennedy et al. 2001).

All of the kids thought they were going to die, they were going to be targets, that if they lived to tomorrow, it was a good thing." (Mediarights 2000, p. 1)

The remarkable success of this program was attributed to the unique partnership composed of the Boston Police Department; the Ten Point Coalition, a partnership of inner-city African American ministers formed to deal with the problem of youth violence after a child was shot at church during a memorial service for a youngster killed in a street shooting; state and federal prosecutors; probation and parole; the Department of Youth Services; federal enforcement agencies; gang-outreach street workers; and Harvard researchers (Kennedy 2002). Its success was also attributed to a concerted effort to develop a cooperative relationship between the police and the African American community although that alliance was shaky at best, as can be seen in the following example.

> There was one detective in particular, Detective Waggett, who said, "Last night I sat in a car with a kid I've arrested twice for assault with intent to murder. He's the type of kid you wouldn't be afraid to take him home to dinner with your family. He just needs hope. I talked to him about giving up drug dealing, and he says to me, 'What are you going to do for me? You going to get me a job?'" (Mediarights 2000, p. 12)

Unfortunately, the very success of this program, according to Kennedy, was its undoing. "Ceasefire is dead and has been for several years. Why? The explosion of outside attention was draining. Ceasefire participants were soon spending as much time, or more, going to the White House, Congress, other cities, and handling press as they were fighting crime" (Kennedy 2002).

MENTAL HEALTH PROFESSIONALS IN CLINICS

Therapists in mental health clinics can make an impact on a larger number of children by getting out of the office and into the community rather than simply seeing children and families at the clinic. Funding of off-site services is available through Medicaid and most managed care organizations, and sliding-scale fees can be set for the remainder of clients (Mordock 1990; Weist et al. 2003). A remarkable example of clinicians leaving their offices to make an impact in a much wider community is Kenneth Hardy (Waters 2004) who has traveled from the East Coast monthly in recent years to Des Moines, Iowa, to help alleviate social and racial tensions among eighty adults and hundreds of teenagers who have been brought together by local religious congregations. Hardy has for years led such gatherings with the goal of creating dialogue among groups in conflict, a process that he refers to as "social healing." Hardy believes, "It is the shared experience of suffering that provides a bridge between people separated by differences, and opens up the possibility for the deepest compassion" (Waters 2004, p. 39). Services can be offered at shelters for battered women, Head Start centers, the Family Court, schools, and other community agencies. Older children are more likely to be seen regularly at a school-based clinic than at an outpatient clinic, not only because parental commitment can wane, especially among African American clients (Mordock 1996a), but also because a child can be seen in an office in the guidance department without other children's knowing that mental health services are being received. Parents also can be seen in the evening, especially in "community schools."

Once clinicians get involved in these settings, innovations often follow. For example, at the Center for Domestic Violence in San Mateo, clinicians established an art therapy program, and at the Minnesota Coalition for Battered Women, clinicians helped develop a domestic violence prevention program in local elementary schools that focused on helping children develop personal safety plans (Jones 1991). Expressing trauma-related themes through art, like verbal or written disclosure (Pennebacker and Stone 2004; Hemenover 2003), allows a traumatized child to remember and organize events in a more coherent manner while integrating feelings and thoughts and making them more manageable. The process can increase positive self-perception, decrease stress, and provide a sense of predictability and control over life. Clinicians in family or domestic court settings can offer immediate mediation in domestic disputes. At a Head Start, clinicians developed a twelve-week universal intervention program delivered by the Head Start teachers (Serna et al. 2003).

Based at the University of Pennsylvania's Department of Education, Howard Stevenson Jr. works with African American youth during their martial arts classes and pick-up basketball games. He observes their movements, activities, and reactions to frustration and makes immediate interventions designed to help them express anger more appropriately. In addition, he runs parent empowerment groups for their parents (Stevenson 2002).

ON A MUCH SMALLER SCALE

Dr. Crenshaw interviewed Aviva Kafka, principal of the Violet Avenue Elementary School in Hyde Park, Dutchess County, New York, about a school-initiated pilot program involving close collaboration with parents. The author was immediately impressed with Ms. Kafka's infectious enthusiasm and her love of children and affection for their families, as well as with the dedicated staff of this culturally diverse school. Ms. Kafka noted that all public schools have their share of children who fail to respond to typical interventions and who are so aggressive and violent that ultimately they cannot remain in the school without endangering themselves or others. Dr. William Robelee, the school psychologist assigned to the school, designed, with the support and encouragement of Ms. Kafka, a project for six children already identified as so aggressive or disruptive that they were frequently removed from their classrooms and sometimes sent home.

In this collaborative school-family project, Dr. Robelee meets biweekly with the parents of these six students, the special education teacher, and the principal, writing and updating behavior plans together and working with the parents and teachers to develop consequences that are consistently applied both at home and at school. Dr. Robelee explains that the process is unique because of the ongoing communication between the parents and involved school personnel. The frequency of meetings between parents and program staff far exceeds what is typical in educational settings. The parents and staff also schedule follow-up meetings, with specific dates and times set for each session. This close communication allows for three distinct advantages: (1) a collaborative relationship with parents; (2) ongoing assessment of the possible functions of specific maladaptive behaviors and evaluation of outcomes; and (3) consistency in implementing interventions (treatment fidelity). At midyear one of the six students no longer needed a special behavior plan. Four of the students rely on the plan to maintain appropriate behaviors but no longer require removal from the classroom. One student, seemingly making no progress at first, later showed significant positive change, and the school team attributes the gains to the increased involvement of the student's parents. (In the beginning of the year, the parents were less engaged than the parents of the other five children.)

Ms. Kafka and Dr. Robelee stressed the success rate was due to the school-family partnership. The importance of parental involvement in programming was also illustrated in the education of a high-risk kindergarten child. The child had been classified as disabled by a countywide preschool committee on special education and placed in a special education preschool program, where extremely loud outbursts of screaming and crying were regular daily occurrences. When enrolled in kindergarten, he was in the process of being adopted by a very loving couple.

The preadoptive parents shared with the school the details of the boy's tragic early life with his birth mother. They told the project team that the boy did not behave this way at home because expectations are high and consequences are made consistent and clear. As a result, the school took a chance and declassified the child. The school and parents worked together to develop a plan for communication between home and school, rewards for appropriate behavior, and logical consequences for inappropriate behavior.

Ms. Kafka noted that the boy began the year displaying between four and ten outbursts each day compared with the later status of no outbursts at all during a one month period! He still required special accommodations in the classroom, but his teacher had become an expert in understanding his moods and giving him choices in keeping with this understanding. His principal, Ms. Kafka, went to his home for his adoption party. She explained that the boy's progress resulted from a supportive home environment, his changing life circumstances, the school-family collaboration, and the consistent responses to his behavior.

CONCLUSION

In 1966, Helena Devereux, an educator who started the world-renowned Devereux Schools, made the following remark during staff orientation, "While mental health staff play an important role in the school, I rarely appoint one to run a treatment unit because they put too much emphasis on pathology and not enough on health." Similarly, the best teachers at the Astor Home for Children, the residential treatment center where both Dr. Crenshaw and Dr. Mordock worked, concentrated on teaching residents academic material and responded to their disruptive behaviors by changing academic activities. They did establish firm limits and separated antagonists, but none established formal behavior modification programs. Rarely did children need removal from their classrooms as a result of misbehavior. The teachers believed that when the child "learned" that he or she could learn, disruptions would stop. Follow-up of the children revealed that those closest to grade level at discharge, regardless of the level of emotional disturbance, made the best long-term adjustments in the community (Mordock 1978).

The same general findings were true for children enrolled in the Perry Preschool Program. Recently, kindergarten students at risk for emotional disturbance were given an intensive supplemental reading intervention, and significant academic gains were reported by participants (Trout et al. 2003). Inappropriate behaviors were not studied, but the academic gains noted suggest more on-task behavior by the children.

The acquisition of concrete skills that contribute to future academic success, so important to children, should be included in all prevention and intervention programs for children. If a child cannot read, and this inability causes anxiety and defensive behavior, all the mental health treatment in the world will not help the child read. But if the child is chronically absent from school as a result of health or domestic problems, remedial reading cannot be provided. And if children are fearful in school, they will have little energy available to profit from any type of intervention, even those emphasizing personal safety. A child cannot "walk away," "ignore," or "talk and seek help," the focus of peer victimization interventions, if too fearful. Obviously, comprehensive prevention and intervention programs are needed to enhance the functioning of children in gorilla suits, a point made throughout both of our volumes.

Sadly, there may be some social environments, as Garbarino (1999) notes, that may be too toxic for even good parenting, prevention, and intervention efforts to overcome. Nor should we expect all children, in our rush to embrace the hopeful concept of resilience, to rise above their harsh and adverse environments. If we do so, we will end up, in a subtle way, heaping blame on the victim.

Bibliography

Abramovitz, R., and S. L. Bloom. 2003. Creating sanctuary in residential treatment for youth: From the "well-ordered" to a living-learning environment. *Psychiatric Quarterly* 74:119–35.

Abrams, S. 1990. Orienting perspectives on shame and self-esteem. *Psychoanalytic Study of the Child* 45:411–36.

Ackerman, N. W., and P. B. Neubauer. 1948. Failures in the psychotherapy of children. In P. Hoch (ed.), *Failures in psychiatric treatment*, 85–102. New York: Grune and Stratton.

Affleck, G., H. Tennen, J. Rowe, et al. 1989. Effects of formal support on mothers' adaptation to the hospital-to-home transition of high-risk infants: The benefits and costs of helping. *Child Development* 60:488–501.

Aguilar, B., A. Sroufe, B. Egeland, et al. 2000. Distinguishing the early-onset persistent and adolescent-onset antisocial behavior types: From birth to 16 years. *Development and Psychopathology* 12:109–32.

Alderman, T. 1997. *The scarred soul: Understanding and ending self-inflicted violence.* Oakland, CA: New Harbinger.

Aldwin, C. 1994. *Stress, coping, and development.* New York: Guilford.

Alexander, J., C. Barton, D. Gordon, et al. 1998. *Blueprints for violence prevention,* Book 3: *Functional family therapy.* Boulder, CO: Center for the Study and Prevention of Violence.

Allan, J. 1988. *Inscapes of the child's world: Jungian counseling in schools and clinics.* Dallas: Spring Publications.

American Psychiatric Association. 1994. *Diagnostic and statistical manual of mental disorders.* 4th ed.. Washington, DC: Authors.

———. 1998. Psychiatric effects of television viewing. APA fact sheet series, APA Online Public Information: http://www.psytch.org/public_info/media_violence.html.

American Psychological Association. 1996. *Violence and the family: Report of the American presidential task force on violence and the family.* Washington, DC: Authors.

———. 2003. Prevention that works for children. Special issue, *American Psychologist* 58.

———, Commission on Violence and Youth. 1993. *Violence and youth: Psychology's response.* Washington, DC: Public Interest Directorate, American Psychological Association.

Amirkhan, J. H., and H. Greaves. 2003. Sense of coherence and stress: The mechanics of a healthy disposition. *Psychology and Health* 18:31–62.

Anderson, C. A., and K. E. Dill. 2000. Video games and aggressive thoughts, feelings, and behavior in the laboratory and in life. *Journal of Personality and Social Psychology,* 78:72–90.

Anderson, M. A., P. M. Gillig, M. Sitaker, et al. 2003. Why doesn't she just leave?: A descriptive study of victim-reported impediments to safety. *Journal of Family Violence* 18:151–155.

Angyal, A. 1965. *Neurosis and treatment: A holistic theory.* New York: John Wiley and Sons.

Anthony, J. 1985. Resilience in children. *The Psychiatric Times* 2:13–14.

Appelstein, C. 2003. Personal communication at the Astor Home for Children. Rhinebeck, New York.

Arata, C. M. 2002. Child sexual abuse and sexual revictimization. *Clinical Psychology: Science and Practice* 9:135–64.

Aronen, E. T., and Kurkela. 1996. Long-term effects of an early home-based intervention. *Journal of the American Academy of Child and Adolescent Psychiatry* 35:1665–72.

Associated Press. 2003. Muhammad's ex-wife reads kids' letters to dad. *Poughkeepsie Journal,* November 20.

———. 2004. Parents demand warning of antidepressant suicide risk. *Poughkeepsie Journal,* February 3, 5A.

Attar, B. K., N. G. Guerra, and P. H. Tolan. 1994. Neighborhood disadvantage, stressful life events, and adjustment in urban elementary school children. *Journal of Clinical Child Psychology* 23:391–400.

August, G., S. S. Lee, M. L. Bloomquist, et al. 2003. Dissemination of an evidence-based prevention innovation for aggressive children living in culturally diverse neighborhoods: The early risers effectiveness study. *Prevention Science* 4:271–86.

Bader, M. J. 2003. Who is hurting the children?: The political psychology of pedophelia in American society. *Tikkun* 18:66–69.

Bakker, P. 1958. *Ciske the rat.* Trans. C. Wieniewska and P. Janson-Smith. Garden City, NY: Doubleday.

Bandura, A. 1973. *Aggression: A social learning analysis.* Oxford, England: Prentice-Hall.

———. 1977. *Social learning theory.* Oxford, England: Prentice-Hall.

———. 1997. *Self-efficacy: The exercise of control.* New York: Henry Holt.

Barber, B. K., ed. 2002. *Intrusive parenting: How psychological control affects children and adolescents.* Washington, DC: American Psychological Association.

Barber, J., and P. H. Delfabbro. 2003. The first four months of foster placement: Psychosocial adjustment, parental contact, and placement disruption. *Journal of Sociology and Social Work* 30:69–85.

Barrera. M. E., P. L. Rosenbaum, and C. E. Cunningham. 1986. Early home intervention with low birth-weight infants and their parents. *Child Development* 57:20–33.

Bath, H. I., and D. A. Haapala. 1993. Intensive family preservation services with abused and neglected children: An examination of group differences. *Child Abuse and Neglect* 17:213–226.

Baumrind, D. 1967. Child-care practices associated with three patterns of preschool behavior. *Genetic Psychology Monographs* 75:43–88.

Bell, H. 2003. Strength and secondary trauma in family violence work. *Social Work* 48:513–22.

Benjamin, J. A. 1994. What angel would hear me?: The erotics of transference. *Psychoanalytic Quarterly* 14:535–57.

Beres, D. 1952. Clinical notes on aggression in children. *Psychoanalytic Study of the Child* 7:241–63.

Bergmann, M. S., and M. E. Jucovy, eds. 1982. *Generations of the holocaust.* New York: Basic Books.

Berkowitz, D. A. 1977. On the reclaiming of denied affects in family therapy. *Family Process* 16:495–501.

Berlin, L. J., J. Brooks-Gunn, and J. L. Aber. 2001. Promoting early childhood development through comprehensive community initiatives. *Children's Services: Social Policy, Research, and Practice* 4:1–24.

Bernard, B. 1991. Fostering resiliency in kids: Protecting factors in the family. Portland, OR: *National Research Association.*

Berrueta-Clement, J. R., L. J. Schweinhart, W. S. Barnett, et al. 1987. The effects of early educational intervention on crime and delinquency in adolescence and early adulthood. In J. D. Burchard and S. N. Burchard (eds.), *Primary prevention of psychopathology.* Vol. 10, *Prevention of delinquent behavior,* 220–40. Newbury Park, CA: Sage.

Blair, R. J. 2003. Neurobiological basis of psychopathy. *British Journal of Psychiatry* 18:5–7.

———, D. G. Mitchell, S. Kelly, et al. 2002. Turning a deaf ear to fear: Impaired recognition of vocal affect in psychopathic individuals. *Journal of Abnormal Psychology* 111:682–6.

Blatt, S. J., and R. B. Blass. 1990. Attachment and separateness: A dialectic model of the products and processes of development throughout the life cycle. *Psychoanalytic Study of the Child* 45:107–127.

Bloom, S. L., M. Bennington-Davis, B. Farragher, et al. 2003. Multiple opportunities for creating sanctuary. *Psychiatric Quarterly* 74:173–90.

———, and L. J. Bills. 2000. Trying out sanctuary the hard way. *Therapeutic Communities. International Journal for Therapeutic and Supportive Organizations* 21:119–31.

Bloomquist, M. L., and S. V. Schnell. 2002. *Helping children with aggression and conduct problems: Best practices for intervention.* New York: Guilford.

Bonanno, G. A. 2004. Loss, trauma, and human resilience: Have we underestimated the human capacity to thrive after extremely adverse events? *American Psychologist* 59:20–28.

Bonime, W. 1982–1987. Private supervision sessions with David A. Crenshaw.

Borgman, R. 1984. Problems of sexually abused girls and their treatment. *Social Casework: Journal of Contemporary Social Work* 65:182–6.

Borowitz, G. H. 1970. The therapeutic utilization of emotions and attitudes evoked in caretakers of disturbed children. *British Journal of Medical Psychology* 43:129–39.

Bowen, M. 1978. *Family therapy in clinical practice.* New York: Jason Aronson.

Bowlby, J. 1969. *Attachment and loss.* New York: Basic Books.

Bowman, E. S., S. Blix, and P. M. Coons. 1985. Multiple personality in adolescence: Relationship to incestual experiences. *Journal of the American Academy of Child and Adolescent psychiatry* 24:109–14.

Braga, A. A., D. M. Kennedy, E. J. Waring, et al. 2001. Problem-oriented policing, deterrence, and youth violence: An evaluation of Boston's operation ceasefire. *Journal of Research in Crime and Delinquency* 38:195–225.

Brandwein, R. A., ed. 1999. *Battered women, children, and welfare reform.* Thousand Oaks, CA: Sage.

Bremmer, J. D., M. Vythilingam, G. Anderson, et al. 2003. Hypothalamic-pituitary-adrenal axis of a 24-hour diurnal period in response to neuroendocrine challenges in women with and without childhood sexual abuse and post-traumatic stress disorders. *Biological Psychiatry* 54:710–8.

———, M. Vythilingam, E. Vermetten, et al. 2003. Cortisol response to cognitive stress challenge in post-traumatic stress disorder (PTSD) related to childhood abuse. *Psychoneuroendocrinology* 28:733–50.

Brent, D. 2002. Clinical practice: Adolescent depression. *New England Journal of Medicine* 347:667–71.

Bronfenbrenner, U. 1970. *Two worlds of childhood: U.S. and U.S.S.R.* New York: Russell Sage Foundation.

———. 1977. Toward an experimental ecology of human development. *American Psychologist* 32:513–31.

Brook, F., and J. Cassidy. 2003. Reconstructive memory related to adolescent-parent conflict interactions: The influence of attachment-related representations on immediate perceptions and changes in perceptions over time. *Journal of Personality and Social Psychology* 85:944–55.

Brooks, R. 1993. *Fostering the self-esteem of children with ADD: The search for islands of competence.* Presentation at the Fifth Annual Conference of CHADD (Children and Adults with Attention Deficit Disorder). San Diego, CA.

———. 2003. *Facilitating hope and resilience in children.* Keynote presentation at the Fiftieth Anniversary Conference of the Astor Home for Children. Fishkill, NY.

Bryant, R. A., and P. Panasetis. 2001. Panic symptoms during trauma and acute stress disorder. *Behavior Research and Therapy* 39:961–6.

Buka, S. L., T. L. Stichick, I. Birdthistle, et al. 2001. Youth exposure to violence: Prevalence, risks and consequences. *American Journal of Orthopsychiatry* 71:298–310.

Burke, A., D. A. Crenshaw, J. Green, et al. 1986. The influence of verbal ability on the expression of aggression in physically abused children. *Journal of the American Academy of Child and Adolescent Psychiatry* 28:215–8.

Cahn, D. D., and S. A. Lloyd, eds. 1996. *Family violence from a communication perspective.* Thousand Oaks, CA: Sage.

Carlson, B. E. 1984. Children's observations of interparental violence. In A.R. Roberts (ed.), *Battered women and their families,* 147–67. New York: Springer.

Carr, A. 2002. *Depression and attempted suicide in adolescents.* United Kingdom: Blackwell.

Cassidy, J., and J. J. Mohr. 2001. Unsolvable fear, trauma, and psychotherapy: Theory, research, and clinical considerations related to disorganized attachment across the life span. *Clinical Psychology: Science and Practice* 8:275–98.

Cavell, T. A. 2001. Updating our approach to parent training. I: The case against targeting noncompliance. *Clinical Psychology: Science and Practice* 8:299–318.

Centers for Disease Control and Prevention. 1996. *National summary of injury mortality data, 1987–1994.* Atlanta, GA: U. S. Department of Health and Human Services, National Center for Injury Prevention and Control.

Chalk, R., and P. A. King, eds. 1998. *Violence in families.* Washington, DC: National Academy Press.

Chamberlain, P. 2003. *Treating chronic juvenile offenders: Advances made through the Oregon multidimensional treatment foster care model.* Washington, DC: American Psychological Association.

———, and S. F. Mihalic. 1998. *Blueprints for violence prevention,* Book 8: *Multidimensional treatment foster care.* Boulder, CO: Center for the Study and Prevention of Violence.

Chandler, M., and T. Moran. 1990. Psychopathology and moral development: A comparative study of delinquent and nondelinquent youth. *Development and Psychopathlogy* 2:227–46.

Chang, L., D. Schwartz, K. A. Dodge, et al. 2003. Harsh parenting in relation to child emotion regulation and aggression. *Journal of Family Psychology* 17:598–606.

Chartrand, T. L., and J. A. Bargh. 1999. The chameleon effect: The perception-behavior link and social interaction. *Journal of Personality and Social Psychology* 76:893–910.

Children's Defense Fund. 1975. *School suspensions: Are they helping children?* Cambridge, MA: Washington Research Project.

Chop, S. M. 2003. Relationship therapy with child victims of sexual abuse placed in residential care. *Child and Adolescent Social World Journal* 20:297–301.

Cialdini, R. B., S. L. Brown, B. P. Lewis, et al. 1997. Reinterpreting the empathy-altruism relationship: When one into one equals oneness. *Journal of Personality and Social Psychology* 73:481–94.

Cicchetti, D., and M. Lynch. 1993. Toward an ecological/transactional model of community violence and child maltreatment: Consequences for children's development. *Psychiatry* 56:96–118.

Clarizio, H. F., and G. F. McCoy. 1983. *Behavior disorders in children.* New York: Harper and Row.

Clum, G. A., P. Nishith, and P. A. Resick. 2001. Trauma-related sleep disturbances and self-reported physical health symptoms in treatment-seeking female rape victims. *Journal of Nervous and Mental Disease* 189:618–22.

Coco, E. L. 1998. Identifying and evaluating critical components of therapeutic foster care related to child outcomes. *Dissertation Abstracts International, Section A: Humanities and Social Sciences* 59(3-A), 0956.

Cohen, D. A. 1998. The impact of motivation on people's recollection of their parents. *Dissertation Abstracts International, Section B: Science and Engineering* 58(12–B), 6384.

Cohen, D., and J. Strayer. 1996. Empathy in conduct-disordered and comparison youth. *Develpmental Psychology* 32:988–98.

Colm, H. 1966. *The existential approach to psychotherapy with adults and children.* New York: Grune and Stratton.

Columbia World of Quotations. 1996a. #62117. Mark Twain [Samuel Clemens] (1835–1910). New York: Columbia University Press.

———. 1996b. #16421. Emily Dickinson (1830–1886). New York: Columbia University Press.

Conner, K. R., C. Cox, P. R. Duberstein, et al. 2001. Violence, alcohol, and completed suicide: A case-control study. *American Journal of Psychiatry* 158:1701–5.

Connor, D. F. 2002. *Aggression and antisocial behavior in children and adolescents: Research and treatment.* New York: Guilford.

Constantine, L. L. 1987. Adolescent process and family organization: A model of development as a function of family paradigm. *Journal of Adolescent Research* 2:349–66.

Conterio, K., and W. Lader. 1998. *Bodily harm: The breakthrough healing program for self-injurers.* New York: Hyperion Books.

Cooley-Quille, M. R., S. M. Turner, and D. C. Beidel. 1995. Emotional impact of children's exposure to community violence: A preliminary study. *Journal of the American Academy of Child and Adolescent Psychiatry* 34:1362–8.

Cordilla, A. 1985. Alcohol and property crime: Exploring the causal nexus. *Journal of the Studies on Alcohol* 46:161–71.

Corsen, A. S., and J. R. Furnell. 1992. What do foster parents think of natural parents: A comparative study. *Child Care, Health and Development* 18:670–80.

Crenshaw, D. A.. 1988. Responding to sexual acting out. In C. E. Schaefer and A. J. Swanson (eds.), *Children in residential care: Critical issues in treatment,* 50–76. New York: Van Nostrand Reinhold.

———. 1990a. An ego-supportive approach to children in residential treatment. *Perceptions* 26:5–7.

———. 1990b. *Bereavement: Counseling the grieving throughout the life cycle.* New York: Continuum. Soft cover edition, 1991; reprinted 2002, Eugene, OR: Wipf and Stock.

———. 1992. Reluctant grievers: Children of multiple loss and trauma. *The Forum* 18:6–7.

———. 1994. Death and dying. In J. L. Ronch, W. Van Ornum, and N. C. Stilwell (eds.), *The counseling sourcebook: A practical reference on contemporary issues,* 510–18. New York: Crossroad.

———. 1995. The crisis of connection: Children of multiple loss and trauma. *Grief Work* 1:16–21.

———. 2002. The disenfranchised grief of children. In K. J. Doka (ed.), *Disenfranchised grief: New directions, challenges and strategies for practice,* 293–306. Champaign, IL: Research Press.

———, J. Boswell, R. Guare, et al. 1986. Intensive psychotherapy of repeatedly and severely traumatized children. *Residential Group Care and Treatment* 3:17–36.

———, and C. Foreacre. 2001. Play therapy in a residential treatment center. In A. A. Drewes, L. J. Carey, and C. E. Schaefer (eds.), *School-based play therapy,* 139–62. New York: Wiley.

———, and P. Garritt. 2004. *A child therapy activity workbook: Facilitation of affect recognition, empathy and genuine self-esteem.* Unpublished manuscript. Rhinebeck, NY: Rhinebeck Child and Family Center Publications.

———, and K. V. Hardy. In press. Fawns in gorilla suits: Understanding and treating the aggression and violence of children. In N. C. Boyd (ed.), *Helping traumatized children and youth in child welfare: Perspectives of mental health and children's services practitioners.* New York: Guilford.

———, A. Holden, J. Kittredge, J. McGuirk. 1983. Therapeutic techniques to facilitate termination in child psychotherapy. Unpublished manuscript. Rhinebeck, NY: The Astor Home for Children.

———, and J. B. Mordock. 2004. An ego-strengthening approach with multiply traumatized children. *Special Reference to the Sexually Abused* 21:1–18.

———, and J. B. Mordock. In press. *A handbook of play therapy with aggressive children.* New York: Jason Aronson.

———, C. Rudy, D. Triemer, et al. 1986. Psychotherapy with abused children: Breaking the silent bond. *Residential Group Care and Treatment* 3:25–38.

Crick, N. R. 1997. Engagement in gender normative versus gender non-normative forms of aggression: Links to social-psychological adjustment. *Developmental Psychology* 33:610–17.

———, and M. A. Bigbee. 1998. Relational and overt forms of peer victimization: A multi-informant approach. *Journal of Consulting and Clinical Psychology* 66:337–47.

———, and N. E. Werner. 1998. Response decision processes in relational and overt aggression. *Child Development* 69:1630–9.

Crimmins, S. M., S. D. Clearly, H. H. Brownstein, et al. 2000. Trauma, drugs and violence among juvenile offenders. *Journal of Psychoactive Drugs* 32:43–54.

Crowell, J. A., E. Waters, D. Treboux, et al. 1996. Discriminant validity of the adult attachment interview. *Child Development* 67:2584–99.

Cwiakala, C., and J. B. Mordock. 1996. Let's discover health and happiness play groups: A model for psychoeducation of young children in addiction recovery. *Journal of Child and Adolescent Group Therapy* 6:147–62.

———, and J. B. Mordock. 1997. The use of multi-family play groups for families with a parent in addiction recovery. *Alcoholism Treatment Quarterly* 15:15–28.

Dahlberg, L. L. 1998. Youth violence in the United States: Major trends, risk factors, and prevention approaches. *American Journal of Preventive Medicine* 14:259–72.

Dalenberg, C. J. 2000. Therapy as a unique human interaction: Management of boundaries and sexual countertransference. In C. J. Dalenberg, *Countertransference and the treatment of trauma,* 199–239. Washington, DC: American Psychological Association.

Dallas, C., T. Wilson, and V. Salgado. 2000. Gender differences in teen parents' perceptions of parental responsibilities. *Public Health Nursing* 17:423–33.

Davis, M. H. 1983. Measuring individual differences in empathy: Evidence for a multidimensional approach. *Journal of Personality and Social Psychology* 44:113–26.

Davis, N. 1990. *Once upon a time . . . : Therapeutic stories to heal the abused children.* Oxon Hill, MD: Psychological Associates.

Deater-Deckard, K., K. A. Dodge, J. E. Bates, et al. 1996. Physical discipline among African American and European American mothers: Links to children's externalizing behaviors. *Developmental Psychology* 32:1065–72.

258   Bibliography

DeBellis, M. D., A. S. Baum, B. Birmaher, et al. 1999. Developmental traumatology. Part I: Biological stress symptoms. *Biological Psychiatry* 45:1259–70.

———, M. S. Keshavan, D. B. Clark, et al. 1999. Developmental traumatology. Part II: Brain development. *Biological Psychiatry* 45:1271–84.

Dekovic, M., and J. M. Janssens. 1992. Parents' child-rearing style and child's sociometric status. *Developmental Psychology* 28:925–32.

Della, R. 2003. When the bough breaks . . . : Examining intergenerational parent-child relational patterns among street-level sex workers. *Applied Developmental Science* 7:216–28.

DeVries, A. C., E. K. Glasper, and C. E. Detellion. 2003. The social modulation of stress responses. *Physiology of Behavior* 79:399–407.

Dieperink, M., J. Leskela, P. B. Thuras, et al. 2001. Attachment-style classification and post-traumatic stress disorder in former prisoners of war. *American Journal of Orthopsychiatry* 71:374–8.

DiGuiseppe, R., and R. C. Tafrate. 2003. Anger treatment for adults: A meta-analytic review. *Clinical Psychology: Science and Practice* 10:70–84.

Dill, K. E., and J. C. Dill. 1998. Video game violence: A review of the empirical literature. *Aggression and Violent Behavior* 3:407–28.

Dodge, K. A. 1993. Social-cognitive mechanisms in the development of conduct disorder and aggression. *Annual Review of Psychology* 44:559–84.

Doka, K. J., ed. 1989. *Disenfranchised grief: Recognizing hidden sorrow.* Lexington, MA: Lexington Books.

Dolan, Y. M. 1991. *Resolving sexual abuse: Solution-focused therapy and Ericksonian hypnosis for adult survivors.* New York: Norton.

Dowling, E. M., S. Gestsdottir, P. M. Anderson, et al. 2003. Spirituality, religiosity, and thriving among adolescents: Identification and confirmation of factor structures. *Applied Developmental Science* 7:253–60.

Drapeau, M., Y. De Roten, J. C. Perry, et al. 2003. A study of stability and change in defense mechanisms during a brief psychodynamic investigation. *Journal of Nervous and Mental Disease* 191:496–502.

Dubrow, N. F., and J. Garbarino. 1989. Living in the war zone: Mothers and young children in a public housing development. *Child Welfare* 68:3–20.

Duhig, A. M., V. Phares, and R. W. Birkeland. 2002. Involvement of fathers in treatment: A survey of clinicians. *Professional Psychology: Research and Practice* 33:389–95.

Duncan, A., and C. Miller. 2002. The impact of an abusive family context on childhood animal cruelty and adult violence. *Aggression and Violent Behavior* 7:365–83.

Duncan, D. F. 1996. Growing up under the gun: Children and adolescents coping with violent neighborhoods. *Journal of Primary Prevention* 16:343–56.

Durlak, J. A. 1997. Primary prevention mental health programs for children and adolescents: A meta-analytic view. *American Journal of Community Psychology* 25:115–54.

Dyregrov, A. 1997. The process in psychological debriefings. *Journal of Traumatic Stress* 10:589–605.

Ecklwich, J., and A. Brodsky. 1980. *Burnout: Stages of disillusionment in the helping professions.* New York: Human Sciences Press.

Edleson, J. L. 1999a. Children witnessing of adult domestic violence. *Journal of Interpersonal Violence* 14:134–54.

———. 1999b. The overlap between child maltreatment and battering. *Violence Against Women* 5:134–53.

Egeland, B. 1997. Mediators of the effects of child maltreatment on developmental adaptation in adolescents. In D. Cicchetti and S. Trouth (eds.), *Perspectives on trauma: Theory, research, and intervention. Rochester Symposium on Developmental Psychology*, Vol 8, 403–34. Rochester, New York: University of Rochester Press.

———, M. Breitenbucher, and D. Rosenberg. 1980. Prospective study of the significance of stress in the etiology of child abuse. *Journal of Consulting and Clinical Psychology* 48:195–205.

———, A. Sroufe, and M. Erickson. 1983. The developmental consequences of different patterns of maltreatment. *Child Abuse and Neglect* 7:459–69.

———, T. Yates, K. Appleyard, et al. 2002. The long-term consequences of maltreatment in the early years: A developmental pathway model to antisocial behavior. *Children's Services: Social Policy, Research, and Practice* 5:249–66.

Ehrenberg, D. B. 1992. *The intimate edge: Extending the reach of psychoanalytic interaction.* New York, London: Norton.

Ehrensaft, M. K., P. Cohen, J. Brown, et al. 2003. Intergenerational transmission of partner violence: A 20-year prospective study. *Journal of Consulting and Clinical Psychology* 71:741–53.

Eisenberg, N., and R. A. Fabes. 1998. Prosocial development. In W. Damon (Series ed.) and N. Eisenberg (Vol. ed.), *Handbook of child psychology: Vol 3, Social, emotional and personality development*, 701–78. 5th ed. New York: Wiley.

Ekstein, R., J. S. Wallerstein, and Mandelbaum. 1992. Countertransference in the residential treatment of children. In J. R. Brandell (ed.), *Countertransference in psychotherapy with children and adolescents.* Northvale, NJ: Aronson.

Elliot, L. 2002. A fine line between hope and despair. In J. Berke and M. Fagan (eds.), *Beyond madness: Psychosocial interventions in psychosis. Therapeutic communities*, 178–87. Philadelphia: Jessica Kingsley Publishers.

Ellis, P. L. 1982. Empathy: A factor in antisocial behavior. *Journal of Abnormal Child Psychology* 10:123–34.

Embry, D. 2003. Initial behavior outcomes for the peace builders universal school-based violence prevention program. *Developmental Psychology* 39:292–308.

Emery, R. E., and L. Laumann-Billings. 1998. An overview of the nature, causes, and consequences of abusive family relationships. *American Psychologist* 53:121–35.

Englander-Golden, P., J. E. Jackson, K. Crane, et al. 1989. Communication skills and self-esteem in prevention of destructive behaviors. *Adolescence* 24:481–502.

English, D. 1998. The extent and consequences of child maltreatment. *The Future of Children* 8:39–53.

Epley, N., K. Savitsky, and T. Gilovich. 2002. Empathy neglect: Reconciling the spotlight effect and the correspondence bias. *Journal of Personality and Social Psychology* 83:300–12.

Epstein, J. L., and S. B. Sheldon. 2002. Present and accounted for: Improving school attendance through family and community involvement. *Journal of Educational Research* 95:308–18.

Erikson, E. 1963. *Childhood and society*. 2nd ed. New York: Norton.
———. 1968. *Identity:Youth in crisis*. New York: Norton.
———. 1982. *The life cycle completed:A review*. New York: Norton.
Evans, B., E. Gonzales, R. Heringa, and B. Torres. 2003. *Parent panel: Building ultimate partnerships with families*, moderated by Joan DiBlasi. The Fiftieth Anniversary Conference of the Astor Home for Children. Fishkill, NY.
Evans, G. D., and J. Rey. 2001. In the echoes of gunfire: Practicing psychologists' responses to school violence. *Professional Psychology: Research and Practice* 32:157–64.
Everly, G. S., Jr., and J. M. Lating. 2004. From the therapeutic alliance to trauma resolution: Restoring assumptive world views and integrating the trauma event. In G. S. Everly and J. M. Lating (eds.), *Personality-guided therapy for post-traumatic stress disorder*, 177–95. Washington, DC: American Psychological Association.
Fairbairn, W. R. 1962. Synopsis of an object-relations theory of the personality. *International Journal of Psychoanalysis* 44:224–5.
Fantuzzo, J., R. Boruch, A. Beriama, et al. 1997. Domestic violence and children: Prevalence and risk in five major U.S. cities. *Journal of the American Academy of Child and Adolescent Psychiatry* 36:116–22.
Farrell, A. D., A. L. Meyer, E. M. Kung, et al. 2001. Development and evaluation of a school-based violence prevention program. *Journal of Clinical Child Psychology* 30:207–30.
Feldman, M. 2003. *Early intervention*. United Kingdom: Blackwell.
Felthous, A. R., and S. R. Kellert. 1987. Childhood cruelty to animals and later aggression against people: A review. *American Journal of Psychiatry* 144:710–17.
Feshbach, N. 1978. Studies of empathic behavior in children. In B. A. Mahler (ed.), *Progress in experimental personality research*. Vol. 8, 1–47. New York: Academic Press.
Fick, A. C., J. D. Osofsky, and M. L. Lewis. 1997. Perceptions of violence: Children, parents, and police officers. In J. D. Osofsky (ed.), *Children in a violent society*, 261–76. New York: Guilford.
Figley, C. R. 2002. Compassion fatigue: Psychotherapists' chronic lack of self-care. *Journal of Clinical Psychology* 58:1433–42.
Fitzpatrick, K. M., and J. P. Boldizar. 1993. The prevalence and consequences of exposure to violence among African American youth. *Journal of the American Academy of Child and Adolescent Psychiatry* 32:424–30.
Flannery, D. J., A. K. Liu, K. E. Powell, et al. 2003. Initial behavior outcomes for the peace builders universal school-based violence prevention program. *Developmental Psychology* 39:292–308.
Florian, V., M. Mikulincer, and O. Taubman. 1995. Does hardiness contribute to mental health during a stressful real-life situation?: The role of appraisal and coping. *Journal of Personality and Social Psychology* 68:687–95.
Flour, E., and A. Budman. 2003. The role of mother involvement and father involvement in adolescent bullying behavior. *Journal of Interpersonal Violence* 18:634–49.
Flynn, C. P. 1999. Exploring the link between corporal punishment and children's cruelty to animals. *Journal of Marriage and the Family* 61:971–81.
Foa, E. B., L. A. Zoellner, N. V. Feeny, et al. 2002. Does imaginal exposure exacerbate PTSD symptoms? *Journal of Consulting and Clinical Psychology* 70:1022–28.

Forehand, R., and D. J. Jones. 2003. Neighborhood violence and coparent conflict: Interactive influence on child psychosocial adjustment. *Journal of Applied Psychology* 31:591–604.

Fox, R., and L. A. Carey. 1999. Therapist collusion with the resistance of rape survivors. *Clinical Social Work* 27:185–92.

Fraiberg, S., E. Adelson, and V. Shapiro. 1965. Ghosts in the nursery. *Journal of the American Academy of Child Psychiatry* 14:387–424.

Frances, A., and J. F. Clarkin. 1981. No treatment as the prescription of choice. *Archives of General Psychiatry* 39:542–6.

Frank, O. H., and M. Pressler, eds. 1991. *Anne Frank: The diary of a young girl.* New York: Doubleday.

Fredrickson, B. L., M. M. Tugdale, C. E. Waugh, et al. 2003. What good are positive emotions in crisis?: A prospective study of resilience and emotions following the terrorist attacks on the United States on September 11th, 2001. *Journal of Personality and Social Psychology* 84:365–76.

Freud, A., and J. Sandler. 1985. *The analysis of defense: The ego and the mechanism of defense revisited.* New York: International Universities Press.

Frey, K. S., M. K. Hirschstein, and B. Guzzo. 2000. A second step: Preventing aggression by promoting social competence. *Journal of Emotional and Behavioral Disorders* 8:102–12.

Friedrich, W. N., and J. A. Boriskin. 1976. The role of the child in abuse: A review of the literature. *American Journal of Orthopsychiatry* 46:580–90.

Furlong, M., L. Z. Paige, and D. Osher. 2003. The safe schools/healthy students (SS/HR) initiative: Lessons learned from implementing comprehensive youth development programs. *Psychology in the Schools* 40:447–56.

Gabbard, G. O. 1996. Lessons learned from the study of sexual boundary violations. *American Journal of Psychiatry* 50:321–2.

———, and L. P. Lester. 1995. *The early history of boundary violations in psychoanalysis.* Washington, DC: American Psychiatric Publications.

Galdston, R. 1971. Violence begins at home. *Journal of the Academy of Child Psychiatry* 10:336–50.

———. 1975. Preventing the abuse of little children. *American Journal of Orthopsychiatry* 45:372–81.

———. 1981. The domestic dimensions of violence. *Psychoanalytic Study of the Child* 36:391–414.

Galley, M. 2003. Student self-harm: Silent school crisis. *Education Week* 23:1, 14–15.

Garbarino, J. 1995. *Raising children in socially toxic environments.* San Francisco: Jossey-Bass.

———. 1999. *Lost boys: Why our sons turn violent and how we can save them.* New York: Anchor Books.

———, and V. Bedard. 2001. *Parents under siege.* New York: Free Press.

Garmezy, N. 1991. Resiliency and vulnerability to adverse developmental outcomes associated with poverty. *American Behavioral Scientist* 34:416–30.

Gaurilovie, J., D. Lecic-Tosevski, S. Dimie, et al. 2003. Coping strategies in civilians during air attacks. *Social Psychiatry and Psychiatric Epidemiology* 38:128–33.

Gaylord, N. K., and K. L. Kitzman. 2003. Internalizing, externalizing, and peer rejection. *Journal of Child and Family Studies* 12:201–13.

Gelles, R. H., and M. A. Straus. 1988. *Intimate violence.* New York: Simon and Schuster.

George, C., and M. Main. 1979. Social interactions of young abused children: Approach, avoidance and aggression. *Child Development* 50:306–18.

Gerra, G., D. Monti, and A. E. Panerai. 2003. Long-term immune-endocrine effects on bereavement: Relationships with anxiety and levels of mood. *Psychiatry Research* 121:145–58.

Ghent, E. 1992. Paradox and progress. *Psychoanalytic Dialogues* 2:135–59.

Gil, E. 1995. *The healing power of play with abused children.* Presentation at the Second Annual Play Therapy Conference, cosponsored by the Astor Home for Children and Dutchess Community College. Poughkeepsie, NY.

Gill, M. M. 1982. *Analysis of transference,* Vol. I: *Theory and technique.* New York: International Universities Press.

Gilligan, J. 1996. *Reflections on a national epidemic: Violence.* New York: Vintage Books.

Goleman, D. 1995. *Emotional intelligence.* New York: Bantam.

Goodman, S. H., and I. H. Gotleib, eds. 2002. *Children of depressed parents: Mechanisms of risk and implications for treatment.* Washington, DC: American Psychological Association.

Goodwin, J., M. Simms, and R. Bergman. 1979. Hysterical seizures: A sequel to incest. *American Journal of Orthopsychiatry* 49:698–703.

Gorman-Smith, D., and P. Tolan. 1998. The role of exposure to community violence and developmental problems among inner-city youth. *Development and Psychopathology* 10:99–114.

Grant, C. L., and L. R. Vartanian. 2003. Experiences with parental aggression during childhood and self-concept in adulthood. *Journal of Family Violence* 18:361–7.

Grantz, K. L. 2003. Patterns of avoidant coping in individuals with early childhood exposure to trauma. *Dissertation Abstracts International, Section B: Sciences and Engineering,* 64(1-B), 419.

Gratz, L. L. 2003. Risk factors for and functions of deliberate self-harm: An empirical and conceptual review. *Clinical Psychology: Science and Practice* 10:192–205.

Green, A. H. 1979. Child-abusing fathers. *Journal of the American Academy of Child Psychiatry* 18:270–82.

Greenberg, L., and W. Malcolm. 2002. Resolving unfinished business: Relating process to outcome. *Journal of Consulting and Clinical Psychology* 70:406–16.

Greene, R. W. 2003. *Collaborative problem solving.* Keynote presentation at the Fiftieth Anniversary Conference of the Astor Home for Children. Fishkill, NY.

———, J. Biederman, S. Zerwas, et al. 2002. Psychiatric comorbidity, family dysfunction, and social impairment in referred youth with oppositional defiant disorder. *American Journal of Psychiatry* 159:1214–24.

Greenwald, D. F., and D. W. Harden. 1997. Fantasies, coping behavior, and psychopathology. *Journal of Clinical Psychology* 53:91–97.

Greenwood, P. W., K. E. Model, C. P. Rydell, et al. 1996. *Diverting children from a life of crime: Measuring costs and benefits.* Santa Monica, CA: Rand.

Gresham, F. A. 1998. Social skills training: Should we raze, remodel, or rebuild? *Behavioral Disorders* 24:19–25.

Grossman, J. D., M. L. Price, V. Fellerath, et al. 2002. Multiple choices after school: Findings from extended-service schools. Philadelphia, PA: Public/Private Ventures (www.ppv.org).

Gruber, C. 1987. Repairing ego deficits in children with developmental disorders. *Child and Adolescent Social Work* 4:50–63.

Grusec, J. E., J. J. Goodnow, and L. Cohen. 1996. Household work and the development of concern for others. *Developmental Psychology* 32:999–1007.

Guerra, N. G., and K. R. Williams. 2003. Implementation of school-based wellness centers. *Psychology in the Schools* 40:473–87.

Gunderson, J. G. 1978. Defining the therapeutic process in psychiatric milieus. *Psychiatry* 41:327–35.

Haight, W. L., J. D. Kagle, and J. E. Black. 2003. Understanding and supporting parent-child relationships during foster care visits: Attachment theory and research. *Social Work* 48:195–207.

Hall, V. C., and M. Mery. 1970. *Language intervention research: Rationale, results, and recommendations.* Unpublished paper, Syracuse Center for Research and Development in Early Childhood Education. Syracuse, New York.

Hallern, L. H. 2002. Overview of child forensic psychiatry. *Child and Adolescent Psychiatric Clinics of North America* 11:685–8.

Halperin, J. M., J. H. Newcorn, K. Matier, et al. 1995. Impulsivity and the initiation of fights in children with disruptive behavioral disorders. *Journal of Child Psychology and Psychiatry* 36:1199–211.

Hardy, K. V. 1998. *Overcoming learned voicelessness.* Presentation at the Family Therapy Network Symposium. Washington, DC.

———. 1999. *Voices from the margins: Therapy with low-income clients.* Presentation at the Family Therapy Network Symposium. Washington, DC.

———. 2000. *Are we jailers or healers?* A Keynote presentation at the Family Therapy Networker Symposium. Washington, DC.

———. 2003. *Working with aggressive and violent youth.* Presentation at the Psychotherapy Networker Symposium. Washington, DC.

———, and T. Lazaloff. In press. *Teens who hurt: Clinical interventions for breaking the circle of violence.* New York: Guilford.

Harper, K., and J. Steadman. 2003. Therapeutic boundary issues in working with childhood sexual abuse survivors. *American Journal of Psychotherapy* 57:64–79.

Hartman, C. R., and A. W. Burgess. 1988. Information processing of trauma: Case application of a model. *Journal of Interpersonal Violence* 3:443–57.

Hastings, P. D., C. Zahn-Waxler, B. Usher, et al. 2000. The development of concern for others in children with behavior problems. *Developmental Psychology* 36:531–46.

Haugaard, J. J. 1992. Sexually abused children's opposition to psychotherapy. *Journal of Child Sexual Abuse* 1:1–16.

———, and N. D. Repucci. 1988. *The sexual abuse of children.* San Francisco: Jossey Bass.

Havens, L. 1989. *A safe place: Laying the groundwork for psychotherapy.* Cambridge, MA: Harvard University Press.

Hawkins, J. D., R. F. Catalono, R. M. Kosterman, et al. 1999. Preventing adolescent health-risk behaviors by strengthening protection during childhood. *Archives of Pediatrics and Adolescent Medicine* 153:226–34.

Hemenover, S. H. 2003. The good, the bad, and the healthy: Impacts of emotional disclosure of trauma on resilient self-concept and psychological distress. *Personality and Social Psychology Bulletin* 29:1236–44.

Henderlong, J., and M. R. Lepper. 2002. The effects of praise on children's intrinsic motivation: A review and synthesis. *Psychological Bulletin* 128:774–95.

Henggeler, S. W., S. F. Mihalic, L. Rone, et al. 1998. *Blueprints for violence prevention.* Book 6, *Multisystemic therapy.* Boulder, CO: Center for the Study and Prevention of Violence.

Henry, G. 1983. Difficulties about thinking and learning. In M. Boston and R. Szur (eds.), *Psychotherapy with severely deprived children,* 82–88. London: Routledge and Kegan Paul.

Herrenkohl, E. C., and R. C. Herrenkohl. 1979. A comparison of abused children and their nonabused siblings. *Journal of the American Academy of Child Psychiatry* 18:266–69.

———, R. C. Herrenkohl, L. Toedter, et al. 1984. Parent-child interactions in abusive and nonabusive families. *Journal of the American Academy of Child Psychiatry* 23:641–8.

Herrenkohl, T. I., K. G. Hill, J. Ick-Joang, et al. 2003. Protective factors against serious violent behavior in adolescence: A prospective study. *Social Work Research* 27:179–91.

Hess, R. D. 1969. Parental behavior and children's school achievement: Implications for Head Start. In E. Grothman (ed.), *Critical issues in research related to disadvantaged children,* 1–76. Princeton, NJ: Educational Testing Service.

Heyman, R. E., and P. H. Neidig. 1997. Physical aggression couples treatment. In W. K. Halford and J. H. Markman (eds.), *Clinical handbook of marriage and couples intervention,* 589–617. Chichester, England: John Wiley and Sons.

Hickey, E. 1991. *Serial murderers and their victims.* Belmont, CA: Wadsworth.

Hill, J., and B. Maughan, eds. 2001. *Cambridge child and adolescent psychiatry: Conduct disorders in childhood and adolescence.* New York: Cambridge University Press.

Hindman, J. 1987. *Step by step: Sixteen steps toward legally sound sexual abuse investigations.* Ontaria, OR: Alexandra Associates.

Hocutt, A. M., and J. Y. Alberg. 1994–1995. Case studies of the application of categorical and noncategorical special education. *Exceptionality* 5:199–221.

Hoffman, I. Z. 1998. *Ritual and spontaneity in the psychoanalytic process.* Hillsdale, NJ: Analytic Press.

Hoffman, M. L. 2000. *Empathy and moral development.* New York: Cambridge University Press.

Holden, G. W., R. A. Geffner, and E. N. Jouriles. 1998. *Children exposed to marital violence: Theory, research, and applied issues.* Washington, DC: American Psychiatric Association Press.

Horney, K. 1942. *Self-analysis.* New York: Norton.

Howard, K. A., J. Flora, and M. Griffin. 1999. Violence-prevention programs in schools: State of the science and implications for future research. *Applied and Preventative Psychology* 8:197–215.

Hoxter, S. 1983. Some feelings aroused in working with severely deprived children. In M. Boston and R. Szur (eds.), *Psychotherapy with severely deprived children,* 125–32. London: Routledge and Kegan Paul.

Hunter, R. S., and N. Kilstrom. 1979. Breaking the cycle in abusive families. *American Journal of Psychiatry* 136:1320–22.

Huston, A. C., and J. V. Wright. 1998. Mass media and children's development. In I. E. Sigel and K. A. Renninger (eds.), *Handbook of child psychology*. 5th ed., Vol. 4, 999–1058. New York: Wiley and Sons.

Hyman, J. D., M. V. Stochmal, and R. Paley. 2003. Did bullying or a mother's neglect drive a 12-year-old boy to suicide? *People* 60:117–19.

Jacobsen, L. K., S. M. Southwick, and T. R. Kosten. 2001. Substance use disorders in patients with post-traumatic stress disorder: A review of the literature. *American Journal of Psychiatry* 158:1184–90.

Jaffe, P. G., D. A. Wolfe, and S. K. Wilson. 1990. *Children of battered women.* Newbury Park, CA: Sage.

James, B. 1989. *Treating traumatized children: New insights and creative interventions.* Lexington, MA: Lexington Books.

Janoff-Bulman, R. 1992. *Shattered assumptions: Toward a new psychology of trauma.* New York: Free Press.

Janssens, J., and M. Dekovic. 1997. Child rearing, prosocial moral reasoning, and prosocial behavior. *International Journal of Behavioral Development* 20:509–27.

Jenkins, E. J. 1995. Violence exposure, psychiatric distress and risk behaviors in a sample of inner-city youth. In R. Block and C. Block (eds.), *Trends, risks, and interventions: Proceedings of the Third Annual Spring Symposium of the Homicide Research Working Group*, 287–98. Washington, DC: U.S. Department of Justice.

———, and C .C. Bell. 1997. Exposure and response to community violence among children and adolescents. In J. D. Osofsky (Ed.), *Children in a violent society*, 9–31. New York: Guilford.

Johnson, J. G., P. Cohen, M. S. Gould, et al. 2002. Childhood adversities, interpersonal difficulties, and risk for suicide attempts during late adolescence and early adulthood. *Archives of General Psychiatry* 59:741–9.

Johnson, T. H., ed. 1960. *The complete poems of Emily Dickinson.* New York: Little, Brown.

Jones, D. P. 1986. Individual psychotherapy for the sexually abused child. *Child Abuse and Neglect* 10:377–85.

Jones, J. D., and I. H. Gehman. 1971. The taboo of virginity: Resistances of male therapists and early adolescent girl patients to treatment. *Journal of the American Academy of Child Psychiatry* 10:351–57.

Jones, L. 1991. *The Minnesota school curriculum project: A statewide domestic violence prevention project in the secondary schools.* Minneapolis, MN: Minnesota Coalition for Battered Women.

Joshi, P. T., and D. A. O'Donnell. 2003. Consequences of child exposure to war and terrorism. *Clinical Child and Family Psychology Review* 6:275–92.

Jouriles, E. N. 2004. Documenting the prevalence of children's exposure to domestic violence: Issues and controversies. In S.A. Graham-Bermann and J. L. Edleson (eds.), *Intimate violence in the lives of children: The future of research, intervention and social policy*, 12–34. Washington, DC: American Psychological Association.

Justice, B., and R. Justice. 1976. *The abusing family.* New York: Human Sciences Press.

Kagan, J. 1998. *How we become who we are.* A presentation at the Family Therapy Networker Symposium. Washington, DC.

―――. 2000. *Life matters*, with Norman Swan: Interview with Jerome Kagan, July 1: www.abc.net.au/rn/talks/lm/stories/s29331/htm.

Kalmus, D. S., and P. B. Namerov. 1994. Subsequent childbearing among teenage mothers: The determinants of stress of a closely spaced second child. *Family Planning Perspectives* 26:149–53, 159.

Karnes. M. B. 1969. *Research and development program on preschool disadvantaged children.* Vol 1. Urbana IL: Institute for Research on Exceptional Children.

Karr-Morse, R., and M. S. Wiley. 1997. *Ghosts from the Nursery.* New York: Grove/Atlantic.

Katz, M. 1997. *On playing a poor hand well.* New York: Norton.

Kaufman, G., and P. Uhlenberg. 1998. Effects of life course transitions on the quality of relationships between adult children and their parents. *Journal of Marriage and Family* 60:924–38.

Kellert, S. R., and A. R. Felthous. 1985. Childhood cruelty toward animals among criminals and noncriminals. *Human Relations* 38:1113–29.

Kendall-Tucker, K. R., L. M. Williams, and D. Finkelhor. 1993. Impact of sexual abuse on children: A review and synthesis of empirical studies. *Psychological Bulletin* 113:164–80.

Kenemore, T. K., and S. Peterson. 1987. Therapist abandonment experience in work with families disrupted by protective intervention. *Child and Adolescent Social Work* 4:195–209.

Kennedy, D. M. 2002. We can make Boston safe again. *Op-ed, Boston Globe,* July 15, 2002.

―――, A. A. Braga, A. M. Piehl, et al. 2001. *Reducing gun violence: The Boston gun project's operation ceasefire.* Washington, DC: U.S. Department of Justice, Office of Justice Programs, National Institute of Justice.

Kent, D, and D. Pepler. 2002. The aggressive child as an expert in cohesive family process. In L. Kuczynski (ed.), *Handbook of dynamics in parent-child relations.* Thousand Oaks, CA: Sage.

Keown, L. J., and L. J. Woodward. 2002. Early parent-child relations and family functioning of preschool boys with pervasive hyperactivity. *Journal of Child Abnormal Psychology* 30:541–54.

Kernberg, O. F. 2000. The influence of gender on patient and analyst in the psychoanalytic relationship. *Journal of the American Psychoanalytic Association* 58:859–83.

Kestenbaum, J. D. 1984. Expectations for therapeutic growth: One factor of burnout. *Social Casework: The Journal of Contemporary Social Work* 65:374–7.

King, C. H. 1975. The ego and the integration of violence in homicidal youth. *American Journal of Orthopsychiatry* 45:34–45.

King, R. A., M. Schwab-Stone, A. J. Flisher, et al. 2001. Psychosocial and risk behavior correlates of youth suicide attempts and suicidal ideation. *Journal of the American Academy of Child and Adolescent Psychiatry* 40:837–46.

King, S. 1986. *It.* New York: Viking Books.

Kinney, J. M., D. Haapala, and H. I. Bath. 1991. *Keeping families together: The homebuilders model.* New York: Aldine de Gruyter.

―――, B. Madsen, T. Fleming, et al. 1977. Homebuilders: Keeping families together. *Journal of Consulting and Clinical Psychology* 45:667–73.

Kinzie, J. D. 2001. Psychotherapy for the massively traumatized refugees: The therapist variable. *American Journal of Psychotherapy* 55:475–90.

Kirst, M. W. 1994. School-linked services: Pitfalls and potentials. *Spectrum: Journal of State Government* 67:15–24.

Klein, M. 1957. *Envy and gratitude*. London: Tavistock Publications.

Knitzer, J., Z. Steinberg, and B. Fleish. 1990. *At the schoolhouse door: An examination of programs and policies for children with behavioral and emotional problems*. NY: Bank Street College of Education.

Kobasa, S. C., S. R. Maddi, and S. Kahn. 1982. Hardiness and health: A prospective study. *Journal of Personality and Social Psychology* 42:168–77.

Kochanska, G. 1991. Socialization and temperament in the development of guilt and conscience. *Child Development* 62:1379–92.

Kohut, H. 1971. *The analysis of the self*. New York: International Universities Press.

———. 1977. *The restoration of the self*. New York: International Universities Press.

———. 1982. Introspection, empathy, and the semi-circle of mental health. *International Journal of Psychoanalysis* 63:395–407.

Koltler, J. A. 1991. *The complete therapist*. San Francisco: Jossey-Bass.

Koop, C. E., and G. Lundberg. 1992. Violence in America: A public health emergency. *Journal of the American Medical Association* 22:3075–6.

Kraft, R. 1990. Incest and subsequent revictimization: The case of the therapist-patient sexual exploitation, with a description of the sitting duck syndrome. In R. Kluft (ed.), *Incestual related syndromes of adult psychopathology*, 263–87. Washington, DC: American Psychiatric Press.

Kranzler, E. M., D. Schaffer, G. Wasserman, et al. 1990. Early childhood bereavement. *American Academy of Child and Adolescent Psychiatry* 29:513–20.

Krevans, J. and J. C. Gibbs. 1996. Parents' use of inductive discipline: Relations to children's empathy and prosocial behavior. *Child Development* 67:3263–77.

Krueger, D. W. 1978. Psychotherapy of adult patients with problems of parental loss in childhood. *Current Concepts in Psychiatry* 4:173–9.

Kumpfer, L. L., and R. Alvarado. 2003. Family-strengthening approaches for the prevention of youth problem behaviors. *American Psychologist* 58:457–65.

L'Abate, L. 1975. Pathogenic role rigidity in fathers: Some observations. *Journal of Marriage and Family Counseling* 1:69–79.

Lamb, H. R. 1980. Therapist-case managers: More than brokers of services. *Hospital and Community Psychiatry* 31:762–4.

LaMothe, R. 2001. Freud's unfortunates: Reflections on haunted beings who know the disaster of severe trauma. *American Journal of Psychotherapy* 55:543–63.

Lane, K. L., J. Wehby, H. M. Menzies, et al. 2003. Social skills instruction for students at risk for antisocial behavior: The effects of small-group instruction. *Behavioral Disorders* 28:229–48.

Langrock, A. M., B. E. Compas, G. Keller, et al. 2002. Coping with the stress of parental depression: Parents' reports of children's coping, emotional, and behavioral problems. *Journal of Clinical Child and Adolescent Psychology* 31:312–24.

Larson, J., and J. E. Lochman. 2002. *Helping schoolchildren cope with anger: A cognitive-behavioral intervention*. New York: Guilford.

Lauder, J. M. 1988. Neurotransmitters as morphogens. *Progress in Brain Research* 73:365–88.

Lawson, L. 1998. Milieu management of traumatized youngsters. *Journal of Child and Adolescent Psychiatric Nursing* 11:99–106.

Leary, M. R., R. M. Kowalski, S. Smith, et al. 2003. Teasing, rejection and violence: Case studies of the school shootings. *Aggressive Behavior* 29:202–14.

LeDoux, J. 1996. *The emotional brain: The mysterious underpinnings of emotional life.* New York: Simon and Schuster.

———. 1998. Fear and the brain: Where have we been and where are we going? *Biological Psychiatry* 44:1229–38.

Levenkron, S. 1998. *Cutting: Understanding and overcoming self-mutilation.* New York: Norton.

Levenstein, P., A. Kochman, and H. A. Roth. 1973. From laboratory to real world: Service delivery of the mother-child home program. *American Journal of Orthopsychiatry* 43:73–8.

Levine, M. 2002. *A mind at a time.* New York: Simon and Schuster.

Lewis, C. S. 1960. *The four loves.* New York: Harcourt, Brace, Jovanovich.

Lewis, D. O., C. Mallough, and V. Webb. 1989. Child abuse, delinquency, and violent criminality. In D. Chiccetti and V. Carlson (eds.), *Child maltreatment: Theory and research on the causes and consequences of child abuse and neglect.* Cambridge, UK: Cambridge University Press.

Lewis, M. 1996. Truama reverberates: Psychosocial evaluation of the care-giving environments of young children exposed to violence and traumatic loss. *Zero to Three* 16:21–8.

Lindqvist, P. 1986. Criminal homicide in northern Sweden, 1970–1981: Alcohol intoxication, alcohol abuse and mental disease. *International Journal of Law and Psychiatry* 8:19–37.

Lindsay, D. S., A. Wade, M. A. Hunter, et al. 2004. Adult memories of childhood: Affect knowing and remembering. *Memory* 12:27–43.

Linehan, M. 1993. *Cognitive-behavioral treatment of borderline personality disorder.* New York: Guilford.

Loeber, R., P. Wung, K. Keenan, et al. 1993. Developmental pathways in disruptive child behavior. *Development and Psychopathology* 5:103–33.

Long, N. 1991. What Fritz Redl taught me about aggression: Understanding the dynamics of aggression and counteraggression in students and staff. *Residential Treatment for Children and Youth* 4:43–56.

Lucco, A. A. 1972. Cognitive development after age five: A future factor in the failure of early intervention with the urban child. *American Journal of Orthopsychiatry* 42:847–56.

Lucero, M. 2003. Secondary trauma stress disorders in therapists: Factors associated with resilience. *Dissertation Abstracts International, Section B: The Sciences and Engineering* 63(11-B), 5526.

Luk, E. S., P. K. Staiger, L. Wong, et al. 1999. Children who are cruel to animals: A revisit. *Australian and New Zealand Journal of Psychiatry* 33:29–36.

Lynch, M., and D. Cicchetti. 1998. An ecological-transactional analysis of children and contexts: The longitudinal interplay among child maltreatment, community violence, and children's symptomatology. *Development and Psychopathology* 10:235–58.

Lyons, E. 1993. Hospital staff reactions to accounts of survivors of childhood abuse. *American Journal of Orthopsychiatry* 53:410–41.

MacVicar, K. 1979. Psychotherapeutic issues in the treatment of sexually abused girls. *Journal of the American Academy of Child Psychiatry* 18:342–53.

Maeroff, G. I. 1998. *Altered destinies: Making life better for schoolchildren in need.* New York: St. Martin's Press.

Magura, S. 1982. Clients view outcomes of child protection services. *Social Casework: The Journal of Contemporary Social Work* 63:522–31.

Main, M., and C. George. 1985. Responses of abused and disadvantaged toddlers to distress in age-mates: A study in the day care setting. *Developmental Psychology* 21:407–21.

Mak-Pearce, G. 2002. Working with the dread of the future. In J. E. Berke, et al. (eds.), *Beyond madness: Psychosocial interventions in psychosis.* Philadelphia: Jessica Kingsley Publishers.

Mammen, O., D. Kolko, and P. Pilkonis. 2003. Parental cognitions and satisfaction: Relationship to aggressive parental behavior in child physical abuse. *Child Maltreatment* 8:288–393.

Mann, D. 1989. Incest: The father and the male therapist. *British Journal of Psychiatry* 6:145–53.

Margolin, G. 1998. Effects of domestic violence on children. In P. K. Trickett and C. J. Shellenbach (eds.), *Violence against children in the family and the community*, 57–101. Washington, DC: American Psychological Association.

———, and E. B. Gordis. 2003. Co-occurrence of marital aggression and parent's child abuse potential: The impact of cumulative stress. *Violence and Victims* 18:243–58.

Markward, M. J., S. S. Cline, and N. J. Markward. 2001. Group socialization, the internet, and school shootings. *International Journal of Adolescence and Youth* 10:135–46.

Maslow, A. H. 1954. *Motivation and personality.* New York: Harper and Row.

———. 1971. *The farther reaches of human nature.* New York: Viking Press.

Masten, A. 2001. Ordinary magic: Resilience processes in development. *American Psychologist* 56:227–48.

Mathur, S. R., and K. B. Rutherford Jr. 1996. Is social skills training effective for students with emotional and behavioral disorders?: Research issues and needs. *Behavioral Disorders* 22:21–8.

Mattsson, A. 1970. The male therapist and the female adolescent. *Journal of the American Academy of Child Psychiatry* 9:707–21.

Mayes, L. C., and D. J. Cohen. 1993. The social matrix of aggression: Enactments and representations of loving and hating in the first years of life. *Psychoanalytic Study of the Child* 48:145–69.

McAllister, A. K., L. C. Katz, and D. C. Lo. 1999. Neurotrophins and synaptic plasticity. *Annual Review of Neuroscience* 22:295–318.

McCloskey, L. A., and E.L. Lichter. 2003. The contribution of marital violence to adolescent aggression across different relationships. *Journal of Interpersonal Violence* 18:390–412.

McCready, K. F. 1987. Milieu countertransference in treatment of borderline patients. *Psychotherapy: Theory, Research, Practice, Training* 24:720–8.

———. 2002. Creating an empathic environment at the San Joaquin Psychotherapy Center. In P. R. Breggin and G. Breggin (eds.), *Dimensions of empathic therapy*, 67–88. New York: Springer.

McDowell, B. 1994. The pick-up sticks game: Adapted to facilitate affective expression. *Association for Play Therapy Newsletter* (September) 13:1–2.

McGrath, E., and R. L. Repetti. 2002. A longitudinal study of children's depressive symptoms, self-perceptions, and cognitive distortions about the self. *Journal of Abnormal Psychology* 11:77–87.

McKibben, L., E. De Vos, and E. Newberger. 1989. Victimization of mothers of abused children: A controlled study. *Pediatrics* 84:531–5.

McKinney, G. E. 1970. Adapting family therapy to multi-deficit families. *Social Casework: The Journal of Contemporary Social Work* 51:327–33.

McNeal, C., and P. R. Amato. 1989. Parents' marital violence: Long-term consequences for children. *Journal of Family Issues* 19:123–39.

McNeely, J. 1999. Community building. *Journal of Community Psychology* 27:741–50.

Mead, S, and D. Hilton. 2003. Crisis and connection. *Psychiatric Rehabilitation Journal* 27:87–94.

Mediarights. 2000. *Unlikely Alliances*. Video transcript. Cambridge, MA: Boston Strategy to Prevent Youth Violence.

Menninger, K., M. Mayman, and P. Pruyser. 1963. *The vital balance*. New York: Viking Press.

Mercy, J., and L. Potter. 1996. Combining analysis and action to solve the problem of youth violence. *American Journal of Preventive Medicine, Supplement to* 12:1–2.

Merrick, J., I. Kandel, and G. Vardi. 2003. Trends in adolescent violence. *International Journal of Adolescent Medicine and Health* 15:285–287.

Merz-Perez, L., K. M. Heide, and I. J. Silverman. 2001. Childhood cruelty to animals and subsequent violence against humans. *International Journal of Offender Therapy and Comparative Criminology* 45:556–73.

Mikulincer, M., O. Gillath, V. Havevy, et al. 2001. Attachment theory and reactions to others' needs: Evidence that activation of the sense of attachment security promotes empathic responses. *Journal of Personality and Social Psychology* 81:1205–24.

———, and I. Orbach. 1995. Attachment styles and repressive defensiveness: The accessibility and architecture of affective memories. *Journal of Personality and Social Psychology* 68:917–25.

Miller, A. 1997. *The drama of the gifted child: The search for the true self*. Revised edition. New York: Basic Books.

Miller, J. B., and I. P. Stiver. 1997. *The healing connection: How women form relationships in therapy and life*. Boston: Beacon Press.

Miller, L. B., et al. 1971. *Experiential variation of Head Start curricula: A comparison of current approaches*. Progress report no. 9. Unpublished paper. Psychology Department, University of Louisville, Louisville, KY.

Miller, L. S., G. A. Wasserman, R. Neugebauer, et al. 1999. Witnessed community violence and antisocial behavior in high-risk, urban boys. *Journal of Clinical Child Psychology* 28:2–11.

Miller, P. A., and N. Eisenberg. 1988. The relation of empathy to aggressive and externalizing anti-social behavior. *Psychological Bulletin* 103:324–44.

Mills, J. C., and R. J. Crowley. 1986. *Therapeutic metaphors for children and the child within.* New York: Brunner/Mazel.

Minuchin, S., E. Auerswald, C. H. King, et al. 1964. The study and treatment of families who produce multiple acting-out boys. *American Journal of Orthopsychiatry* 34:125–33.

———, and J. Colapinto. 1994. Consultation to the Astor Home for Children. Rhinebeck, NY.

Misch, D. A. 2000. Great expectations: Mistaken beliefs of beginning psychodynamic therapists. *American Journal of Psychotherapy* 54:172–203.

Mitchell, S. A. 1993. *Hope and dread in psychoanalysis.* New York: Basic Books.

Mordock, J. B. 1971. Urban renewal agencies: Guidelines for mental health consultation. *Professional Psychology* 2:155–8.

———. 1978. *Ego-impaired children grow up: Post-discharge adjustment of children in residential treatment.* Monograph celebrating the Twenty-fifth Anniversary of the Astor Home for Children. Rhinebeck, NY: The Astor Home for Children.

———. 1979. The separation-individuation process and developmental disabilities. *Exceptional Children* 46:176–84.

———. 1990. Funding children's mental health services in an underfunded climate: Collaborative efforts. *The Journal of Mental Health Administration* 17:108–14.

———. 1996a. The real world of the child guidance clinic: The population served, the services received, and the outcomes observed. *Administration and Policy in Mental Health* 23:211–30.

———. 1996b. Treatment of sexually abused children: Interview technique, disclosure, and progress in therapy. *Journal of Sexual Abuse* 5:105–21.

———. 1997a. In-home treatments. In J. D. Noshpitz, N. E. Alessi, J. T. Coyle, et al. (eds.), *Handbook of child and adolescent psychiatry.* Vol. 6, *Basic psychiatric science and treatment,* 509–16. New York: Wiley.

———. 1997b. The "Clinician's Illusion": More evidence? *Clinical Child Psychology and Psychiatry* 27:241–54.

———. 1999a. *Selecting treatment interventions: A casebook for clinical practice in child and adolescent managed mental health.* 2nd ed. Providence, RI: Manisses Communications Group.

———. 1999b. Some risk factors in the psychotherapy of children and families: Well-established techniques that can put some clients at risk. *Child Psychiatry and Human Development* 29:229–44.

———. 1999c. The life-space interview revisited: Stages in one professional's struggle to develop calming techniques for children in crisis and problems encountered in their utilization. *Residential Treatment for Children and Youth* 16:1–14.

———. 2001. Interviewing abused and traumatized children. *Clinical Child Psychology and Psychiatry* 6:271–91.

———. 2002a. A model of milieu treatment: Its implementation and factors contributing to "drift" from the model over a 30-year period. Part 1: Implementation of the model. *Residential Treatment for Children and Youth* 19:17–42.

———. 2002b. *Managing for outcomes: A basic guide to the evaluation of best practice in the human services.* Washington, DC: Child Welfare Press.

Morgan, A., III, and A. M. Rasmusson. 2003. Trauma exposure rather than post-traumatic stress disorder is associated with reduced baseline plasma neuropeptide-y levels. *Biological Psychiatry* 54:1087–91.

Morse, W. C., ed. 1991. Crisis intervention in residential treatment: The clinical innovations of Fritz Redl. *Residential Treatment for Children and Youth* 8, no. 4.

Moulds, M. L., and R. A. Bryant. 2002. Directing forgetting in acute stress disorder. *Journal of Abnormal Psychology* 111:175–9.

Mulvey, E. P., and E. Cauffman. 2001. The inherent limits of school violence. *American Psychologist* 56:797–802.

Munoz, M. A. 2002. *Outcome-based community-school partnerships: The impact of after-school programs on nonacademic and academic indicators.* Unpublished paper. Louisville, KY (First Search ERIC Data Base—Accession No. ED468973).

Myers, S. 2003. Relational healing: To be understood and to understand. *Journal of Humanistic Psychology* 43:86–104.

Nadelson, C., D. Polonsky, and M. A. Matthews. 1984. Marriage as a developmental process. In C. C. Nadelson and D. C. Polonsky (eds.), *Marriage and divorce: A contemporary perspective* 117–26. New York: Guilford Press.

National School Safety Center. 2004. School-associated violent deaths. www.nssc1.org/savd/savd.pdf.

Neese, R. M. 1991. Psychiatry. In M. Maxwell (ed.), *The sociobiological imagination: SUNY series in philosophy and biology,* 23–40. Albany: State University of New York Press.

Neimeyer, R. A. 2000. Searching for the meaning of meaning: Grief therapy and the process of reconstruction. *Death Studies* 24:541–58.

Ness, G., and N. Macaskill. 2003. Preventing PTSD: The value of inner resourcefulness in the sense of personal control of a situation: Is it a matter of problem solving or anxiety management: *Behavioral and Cognitive Psychology* 34:463–6.

Neumeister, L. 2003. Details of brutal Nazi experiments still emerge. *Poughkeepsie Journal,* January 27, 3A.

Newberger, C. M., and S. J. Cook. 1983. Parental awareness and child abuse: A cognitive-developmental analysis of urban and rural samples. *American Journal of Orthopsychiatry* 53:512–24.

Newman, M. B., and M. S. Martino. 1973. The child and the seriously disturbed parent. *Journal of the American Academy of Child Psychiatry* 12:162–81.

Nieto, S. 1999. *The light in their eyes: Creating multicultural learning opportunities.* New York: Teachers College Press.

Nixon, R. D. 2002. Treatment of behavior problems in preschoolers: A review of parent training programs. *Clinical Psychology Review* 22:525–46.

Noll, J. G., L. A. Horowitz, and G. A. Bonanno. 2003. Revictimization and self-harm in females who experienced childhood sexual abuse: Results from a prospective study. *Journal of Interpersonal Violence* 18:1452–71.

Northrup, G. 1987. Restraints: An interview with Bruce Bona. *Residential Treatment for Children and Youth* 5:25–49.

Nunno, M. A., M. J. Holden, and B. Leidy. 2003. Evaluating and monitoring the impact of a crisis intervention system in a residential child-care facility. *Children and Youth Services Review* 25:295–315.

Olds, D., J. Eckenrode, and C. T. Henderson. 1997. Long-term effects of home visitation on maternal life course and child abuse and neglect: Fifteen-year follow-up of a randomized trial. *Journal of the American Medical Association* 278:637–43.

————, P. Hill, S. Mihalic, et al. 1998. *Blueprints for violence prevention*, Book 7: *Prenatal and infancy home visitation by nurses*. Boulder, CO: Center for the Study and Prevention of Violence.

O'Leary, V. 1998. Strength in the face of adversity: Individual and social thriving. *Journal of Social Issues* 54:425–46.

Olson, S. L., R. Ceballo, and C. Park. 2002. Early problem behavior among children from low-income, mother-headed families: A multiple risk perspective. *Journal of Clinical Child and Adolescent Psychology* 31:419–30.

Olweus, D. 1993. *Bullying at school: What we know and what we can do*. Oxford, UK: Blackwell.

Ornduff, S. R., R. M. Kelsey, and D. K. O'Leary. 2001. Childhood physical abuse, personality and adult relationship violence: A model of vulnerability to victimization. *American Journal of Orthopsychiatry* 71:322–31.

Osler, A., and J. Hill. 1999. Exclusion from school and racial equality: An examination of governmental proposals in light of recent research findings. *Cambridge Journal of Education* 29:33–62.

Osofsky, J. D. 1995a. Children who witness domestic violence: The invisible victims. *Social Policy Report* 9:1–19.

————. 1995b. The effects of exposure to violence on young children. *American Psychologist* 50:782–8.

————, G. Cohen, and M. Drell. 1995. The effects of trauma on young children: A case of two-year-old twins. *International Journal of Psychoanalysis* 76:595–607.

————, and E. Fenichel, eds. 1993/1994. Caring for infants and toddlers in violent environments: Hurt, healing, and hope. *Zero to Three* 14:1–48.

————, and B. Jackson. 1993/1994. Parenting in violent environments. *Zero to Three* 14:8–11.

Overpeck, M. D., R. A. Brenner, A. C. Trumble, et al. 1998. Risk factors for infant homicide in the United States. *New England Journal of Medicine* 339:1211–16.

Pangrazi, R. P. 2004. *Lesson plans for dynamic physical education for elementary school children*. San Francisco: Benjamin Cummings.

Parks, P. L., and V. L. Smeriglio. 1983. Parenting knowledge of adolescent mothers. *Journal of Adolescent Health* 4:163–7.

Patrick, J., and C. Rich. 2004. Anger management taught to adolescents with an experiential object-relations approach. *Child and Adolescent Social Work* 21:85–100.

Patterson, G. R. 1983. Stress: A change agent for family process. In N. Garmezy and M. Rutter (eds.), *Stress, coping, and development in children*, 235–64. New York: McGraw-Hill.

————, and M. S. Forgatch. 1990. Initiation and maintenance of process-disrupting single-mother families. In G. R. Patterson (ed.), *Depression and aggression in family interaction*, 209–46. Hillside, NJ: Erlbaum.

————, J. B. Reid, and T. J. Dishion. 1992. *A social learning theory approach: 4. Antisocial boys*. Eugene, OR: Castalia.

Pegel, R. A. 2003. The experience of three female mental health clinicians coping with work-related stress treating traumatized children. *Dissertations Abstracts International, Section A: Human and Social Sciences,* 64(2-A), 409.

Pelcovitz, D. 1999. *Child witnesses to domestic violence.* Presentation sponsored by Four Winds Hospital, Astor Home for Children, and Ulster County Mental Health, Kingston, NY.

Pennebacker, J. W., and L. D. Stone. 2004. Translating traumatic experiences into language: Implications for child abuse and long-term health. In L. Koenig and L. S. Doll (eds.), *From child sexual abuse to adult sexual risk: Trauma, revictimization, and intervention,* 201–16. Washington, DC: American Psychological Association.

Penzerro, R. M. 2003. Drift as adaptation: Foster care and homeless centers. *Child and Youth Care Forum* 32:229–44.

Perry, B. D. 1997. Incubated in terror: Neurodevelopmental factors in the "cycle of violence." In J. D. Osofsky (ed.), *Children in a violent society,* 124–49. New York: Guilford.

———. 2001. Bonding and attachment in maltreated children: Consequences of emotional neglect in childhood. *CTA Parent and Caregiver Education Series,* Vol. 1, 4. Houston, TX: Child Trauma Academy Press.

———. 2003. *Aggression and violence: The neurobiology of experience.* http://teacher.scholastic .com/professional/bruceperry/aggression-violence.htm,p.1.

———, R. A. Pollard, W. L. Baker, et al. 1995. Continuous heart-rate monitoring in maltreated children [Abstract]. In *Proceedings, Annual Meeting of the American Academy of Child and Adolescent Psychiatry, New Research* 21:69.

———, R. A. Pollard, T. L. Blakley, et al. 1995. Childhood trauma, the neurobiology of adaptation and use-dependent development of the brain: How states become traits. *Infant Mental Health Journal* 16:271–91.

Peterson, R. L., and K. Skiba. 2001. Creating school climates that prevent school violence. *Social Studies* 92:167–75.

Pitman, G. E. 2003. Evolution but no revolution: The "tend and befriend" theory of stress and coping. *Psychology of Women Quarterly* 27:194–95.

Pittman, F. S., III. 1982. Book review of family violence literature. *Family Process* 21:363–7.

Pizer, S. A. 1992. The negation of paradox in the analytic process. *Psychoanalytic Dialogues* 2:215–40.

Plichta, S. 1992. The effects of women's abuse on health care utilization and health status: A literature review. *Women's Health Issues* 2:154–63.

Polansky, N. A., P. W. Ammons, and J. M. Gaudin Jr. 1985. Loneliness and isolation in child neglect. *Social Casework: The Journal of Contemporary Social Work* 66:38–47.

Prentice-Dunn, S., D. Wilson, and R. Lyman. 1981. Client factors related to outcome in residential and day treatment programs for children. *Journal of Clinical Child Psychology* 19:188–91.

Prevatt, F. F. 2003. The contribution of parent practices on at-risk and resiliency model of children's adjustment. *British Journal of Developmental Psychology* 21:469–80.

Price, J. H., E. A. Merrill, and M. E. Clause. 1992. The depiction of guns on prime-time television. *Journal of School Health* 62:15–18.

Pynoos, R. S., A. M. Steinberg, E. M. Orniytz, et al. 1997. Issues in the developmental neurobiology of traumatic stress. In R. Yehuda and A. C. McFarlane (eds.), *Psychobiology and post-traumatic stress disorder*, 176–93. New York: Academy of Sciences.

Quinsey, V. L., T. K. Skilling, M. L. Lalumiere, et al. 2004. Sex differences in aggression and female delinquency. In V. L. Quinsey, et al. (eds.), *Juvenile delinquency: Understanding the origins of individual differences*, 115–36. Washington, DC: American Psychological Association.

Radin, N. 1972. Three degrees of maternal involvement in preschool programs: Impact on mothers and children. *Child Development* 43:1355–64.

Rand, A. L. 2003. A case of vicarious traumatization. *Annals of the American Psychotherapy Association* 5:31.

Redl, F. 1959. Strategy and techniques of the life-space interview. *American Journal of Orthopsychiatry* 29:1–18. Modified version in Redl, 1966.

———. 1966. *When we deal with children*. New York: Free Press.

Reid, J. B., J. M. Eddy, R. A. Fetrow, et al. 1999. Description and immediate impacts of a preventative intervention for conduct problems. *American Journal of Community Psychology* 27:483–517.

Reid, J. R., G. R. Patterson, and J. J. Snyder, eds. 2002. *Antisocial behavior in children and adolescents*. Washington, DC: American Psychological Association.

Reider, C., and D. Cicchetti. 1989. Organizational perspective on cognitive control functioning and cognitive-affective balance in maltreated children. *Developmental Psychology* 25:382–93.

Repetti, R. L., S. E. Taylor, and T. E. Seeman. 2002. Risk factors: Families' social environments and the mental and physical health of offspring. *Psychological Bulletin* 128:230–66.

Rice, M., and G. T. Harris. 2002. Men who molest their sexually immature daughters: Is a special explanation required? *Journal of Abnormal Psychology* 111:329–39.

Richardson, G. E. 2002. The metatheory of resilience and resiliency. *Journal of Clinical Psychology* 58:307–21.

Rieser, M. 1991. Recantation in child sexual abuse. *Child Welfare* 70:612–21.

Rinsley, D. B. 1980. *Treatment of the seriously disturbed adolescent*. New York, London: Aronson.

Rios, F. A. 1996. Teaching principles of practice for teaching multicultural classrooms. In F. A. Rios (ed.), *Teacher thinking in cultural contests*, 129–48. Albany: State University of New York Press.

Rivine, J. C., S. L. Bloom, R. Abramovitz, et al. 2003. Assessing the implementation and effects of a traumas-focused intervention for youths in residential treatment. *Psychiatric Quarterly* 74:137–54.

Robinson, J., C. Zahn-Waxler, and R. Emde. 1994. Patterns of development in early empathic behavior: Environmental and child constitutional influences. *Social Development* 3:125–45.

Rogers, E. M. 1983. *The diffusion of innovation*. New York: Free Press.

Rogers, M. M., M. D. People-Sheps, and C. Suchindran. 1996. Impact of a social support program in teenage prenatal care use and pregnancy outcomes. *Journal of Adolescent Health* 19:132–40.

Rose, T. L. 1988. Current disciplinary practices with handicapped students: Suspensions and explusions. *Exceptional Children* 35:230–9.

Ross, S. M. 1996. Risk of physical abuse to children of spouse-abusing parents. *Child Abuse and Neglect* 20:589–98.

Ruchala, P. L., and D. C. James. 1997. Social support, knowledge of infant development, and maternal confidence among adolescent and adult mothers. *Journal of Obstetric, Gynecologic, and Neonatal Nursing* 26:685–9.

Rushton, A., D. Mayes, and C. Dance. 2003. Parenting late-placed children: The development of new relationships and the challenge of behavioural problems. *Journal of Child Psychology and Psychiatry* 8:389–400.

Rutter, M. 1979. Protective factors in children's responses to stress and disadvantage. In M. W. Kent and J. E. Rolf (eds.), *Primary prevention of psychopathology*. Vol. 3, 49–74. Hanover, NH: University Press of New England.

———. 1990. Psychosocial resilience and protective mechanisms. In J. Rolf, A. S. Masten, D. Cicchetti, et al. (eds.), *Risk and protective factors in the development of psychopathology*, 181–214. New York: Cambridge University.

———, D. Quinton, and T. Hill. 1990. Adult outcomes of institution-reared children: Males and females compared. In L. Robbins and M. Rutter (eds.), *Straight and deviant paths from childhood to adulthood*, 135–57. Cambridge: Cambridge University.

Sandstrom, M. J., and P. Cramer. 2003. Defense mechanisms and psychological adjustment in childhood. *Journal of Nervous and Mental Disease* 191:478–95.

Sarnoff, C. A. 1987. *Psychotherapeutic strategies in the latency years*. Northvale, NJ: Aronson.

Sauzier, M. 1989. Disclosure of child sexual abuse: For better or for worse. *Psychiatric Clinics of North America* 12:455–49.

Schetky, D. H. 1995. Boundaries in child and adolescent psychiatry. *Child and Adolescent Psychiatric Clinics of North American* 4:769–78.

Schonert-Reichl, K. A., V. Smith, and A. Zaidman-Zait. 2003. *The effects of the roots of empathy program on children's emotional and social competence: Initial research findings and future directions.* Presentation at Harvard University, Oct. 16. Boston, MA.

Schore, A. N. 1996. The experience-dependent maturation of a regulatory system in the orbital prefrontal cortex and the origin of developmental psychopathology. *Development and Psychopathology* 8:59–87.

Schwab-Stone, M. E., T. S. Ayers, W. Kasprow, et al. 1995. No safe haven: A study of violence exposure in an urban community. *Journal of the American Academy of Child and Adolescent Psychiatry* 34:1343–52.

Schwartz, D, C. Chang, and J. M. Farver. 2001. Correlates of victimization in Chinese children's peer groups. *Developmental Psychology* 37:520–32.

———, K. A. Dodge, G. Pettit, et al. 1997. The early socialization of aggressive victims of bullying. *Child Development* 68:665–75.

———, K. A. Dodge, G. Pettit, et al. 2000. Friendships as a moderating factor in the pathway between early harsh home environment and later victimization in the peer group. *Developmental Psychology* 36:646–62.

Schweinhart, L. J., H. V. Barnes, and D. P. Weikart. 1993. *Significant benefits: The High/Scope Perry preschool study through age 27.* Monographs of the High/Scope Educational Research Foundation. Number 10. Ypsilanti, MI: High/Scope Press.

Seligman, M.E. 2003. The science of happiness. Presentation at the Psychotherapy Networker Symposium. Washington, DC.

Seligson, A. G. 1993. The fallacy of victimization in the treatment of sexual abuse. *Journal of Child Sex Abuse* 2:135–40.

Seman-Haynes, C., and J. A. Baumgarten. 1994. *Children speak for themselves: Using the Kempe interactional assessment to evaluate allegations of parent-child sexual abuse.* New York: Brunner/Mazel.

Serbin, L., and J. Karp. 2003. Intergenerational studies of parenting and the transfer of risk from parent to child. *Current Directions in Psychological Science* 12:1138–42.

Serna, L. A., E. Nielsen, N. Matten, and S. R. Forness. 2003. Primary prevention in mental health for Head Start classrooms: Partial replication with teachers as interveners. *Behavioral Disorders* 28:124–9.

Sexton, T. L., and J. F. Alexander. 2000. Functional family therapy. *Juvenile Justice Bulletin.* Washington, DC: U. S. Department of Justice, Office of Justice Programs, Office of Juvenile Justice and Delinquency Prevention.

Shapiro, R. J., and S. H. Budman. 1973. Defection, termination and continuation in family and individual therapy. *Family Process* 12:55–67.

Shaw, D. S., and R. Q. Bell. 1993. Developmental theories of parental contributions to antisocial behavior. *Journal of Clinical Child Psychology* 21:493–8.

Shectman, Z. 2003. Cognitive and affective empathy in aggressive boys: Implications for counseling. *International Journal for the Advancement of Counselling* 24:211–22.

Shengold, L. 1989. *Soul murder: The effects of childhood abuse and deprivation.* New Haven: Yale University Press.

Shenken, L. T. 1964. The implications of ego psychology for a motiveless murder. *Journal of the American Academy of Child Psychiatry* 3:241–57.

Shifron, R., and B. L. Bettner. 2003. Using early memories to emphasize strengths. *Journal of Individual Psychology* 59:334–44.

Shupe, L. M. 1954. Alcohol and crime. *Journal of Criminal Law, Criminology and Police Science* 44:661–4.

Sickmund, M., H. N. Snyder, and E. Poe-Yamagata. 1997. Juvenile offenders and victims: 1997 update on violence. Washington, DC: U. S. Department of Justice, Office of Justice Programs, Office of Justice and Delinquency Prevention.

Siegel, S. J. 1991. *What to do when psychotherapy goes wrong.* Seattle: Stop Abuse by Counselors Publications.

Silverman, D. 1977. First do no more harm: Female rape victims and the male counselor. *American Journal of Orthopsychiatry* 47:91–6.

Simon, R. I. 1989. Sexual exploitation of patients: How it begins before it happens. *Psychiatric Annals* 21:104–11.

Singer, J. 1966. *Daydreaming: An introduction to the experimental study of inner experience.* New York: Random House.

———. 1976. *Daydreaming and fantasy.* London: Allen and Unwin.

Singer, M. T., and J. S. Miller. 1983. *Diagnosis and psychotherapy of personality disorders.* Seminar presented at University of California, Los Angeles Extension.

Sjoberg, R. L., and F. Lindblad. 2002. Limited disclosure of sexual abuse in children whose experiences were documented on videotape. *American Journal of Psychiatry* 159:312–4.

Skarlew, B., J. Krupnick, D. Ward-Zimmer, et al. 2002. The school-based mourning project: A preventative intervention in the cycle of inner-city violence. *Journal of Applied Psychoanalytic Studies* 4:317–30.

Sloan, D. M., M. E. Strauss, and K. L. Wisner. 2001. Diminished response to pleasant stimuli by depressed women. *Journal of Abnormal Psychology* 109:460–72.

Slovack, K., and M. Singer. 2001. Gun-violence exposure and trauma among rural youth. *Violence and Victims* 16:389–400.

Smith, G. 1988. Tyson the timid, Tyson the terrible. *Sports Illustrated*, March, 72–80, 82–83.

Smith, P. L. 2003. Adaptive coping strategies of othermothers: An examination of social support, spirituality, stress and depression. *Dissertation Abstracts International, Section A: Humanities and Social Sciences,* 64(3-A), 1081.

Smith, S. L. 1984. Significant research findings in the etiology of child abuse. *Social Casework: The Journal of Contemporary Social Work* 65:337–46.

Snyder, H. N., and M. Sickmund. 1999. *Juvenile offenders and victims: 1999 national report.* Washington: DC: U.S. Department of Justice, Office of Justice Programs, Office of Juvenile Justice and Delinquency Prevention.

Sober, E., and D. S. Wilson. 1998. *Unto others: The evolution and psychology of unselfish behavior.* Cambridge, MA: Harvard University Press.

Sonia, N. 1998. Facts and fiction: Stories of Puerto Ricans in United States schools. *Harvard Educational Review* 68:133–62.

Spaccarelli, S., I. N. Sandier, and M. Roosa. 1994. History of spouse violence against mothers: Correlated risks and unique effects in child mental health. *Journal of Family Violence* 9:79–98.

Spiegel, D., and J. L. Alpert. 2000. The relationship between shame and rage: Conceptualizing the violence at Columbine High School. *Journal for the Psychoanalysis of Culture and Society* 5:237–45.

Stagner, M. W., and A. Duran. 1997. Comprehensive community initiatives: Principles, practices, and lessons learned. *The Future of Children* 7:132–40.

Stallard, P., and E. Salter. 2003. Psychological debriefing with children and young people following traumatic events. *Clinical Child Psychology and Psychiatry* 8:445–57.

Stanley, B., M. J. Gammeroff, V. Michalsen, et al. 2001. Are suicide attempters who self-mutilate a unique population? *American Journal of Psychiatry* 158:427–32.

Stanton, M. D., and T. C. Todd. 1981. Engaging resistant families in treatment. *Family Process* 20:261–93.

Stark, E., and A. H. Fitcraft. 1988. Women and children at risk: A feminist perspective on child abuse. *International Health Services* 18:97–118.

Steel, M., J. Hodges, J. Kaniuk, et al. 2003. Attachment representations and adoption: Associations between maternal states of mind and emotion narratives in previously maltreated children. *Journal of Child Psychotherapy* 29:187–205.

Steele, B. F. 1975. Abusive parents: A psychiatrist's view. *Children Today* 4:3–5, 44.

Stevenson, H. G., Jr. 2002. Wrestling with destiny: The cultural socialization of anger and healing in African American males. *Journal of Psychology and Christianity* 21:357–64.

St. John, R. 1968. Developing a therapeutic working alliance with an adolescent girl. *Journal of the American Academy of Child Psychiatry* 7:68–78.

Stoolmiller, M., J. M. Eddy, and J. Reid. 2000. Detecting and describing preventative intervention effects in a universal school-based randomized trial targeting delinquent and violent behavior. *Journal of Consulting and Clinical Psychology* 68:297–306.

Strand, P. S. 2002. Treating antisocial behavior: A context for substance abuse prevention. *Clinical Psychology Review* 22:707–28.

Straus, M. A. 1999. *No-talk therapy for children and adolescents.* New York: Norton.

———. 2003. *Working with traumatized children.* A presentation at the Family Therapy Network Symposium. Washington, DC.

———, and R. J. Gelles. 1988. How violent are American families?: Estimates from the national family violence resurvey and other studies. In G. T. Hotaling, D. Finkeher, J. T. Kirkpatrick, et al. (eds.), *Family abuse and its consequences: New directions in research,* 95–112. Newbury Park, CA: Sage.

———, and R. J. Gelles. 1990. *Physical violence in American families: Risk factors and adaptations to violence in 8,145 families.* New Brunswick, NJ: Transactions Publications.

Strupp, H. H. 1994. *When things get worse: The problem of negative effects in psychotherapy.* Northvale, NJ: Aronson, 1994.

Stuart, R. B. 1970. *Trick or treatment: How and when psychotherapy fails.* Champaign, IL: Research Press.

Swartz, D., K. A. Dodge, G. Pettit, et al. 2000. Friendship as a moderating factor in the pathway between early harsh home environments and later victimization in the peer group. *Developmental Psychology* 36:646–62.

———, and A. H. Gorman. 2003. Community violence exposure and children's academic functioning. *Journal of Educational Psychology* 95:163–73.

Swartz, R. S., and J. Olds. 2002. A phenomenology of closeness and its application to sexual boundaries: A framework for therapists in training. *American Journal of Psychotherapy* 56:480–93.

Tangney, J. P., and R. L. Dearing. 2002. *Shame and guilt.* New York: Guilford.

Taylor, L., B. Zuckerman, V. Harik, et al. 1994. Witnessing violence by young children and their mothers. *Journal of Developmental and Behavioral Pediatrics* 15:20–3.

Tedeschi, R., and L. Calhoun. 1996. The posttraumatic growth inventory: Measuring the positive legacy of trauma. *Journal of Traumatic Stress* 9:455–71.

Teicher, M., Y. Ito, C. A. Glod, et al. 1997. Preliminary evidence for abnormal cortical development in physically and sexually abused children using EEG coherence and MRI. In R. M. Yehuda (ed.), *Psychobiology of post-traumatic stress disorder,* 160–75. Vol. 821, *Annals of the New York Academy of Science,* NY.

Telleen, S., and S. Mak-Pearce. 2002. Building community connections for youth to reduce violence. *Psychology in the Schools* 40:549–63.

Terkelsen, K. G. 1980. Toward a theory of the family life cycle. In E. A. Carter and M. McGoldrick (eds.), *The family life cycle: A framework for family therapy.* New York: Gardner Press.

Terr, L. 1981. Forbidden games: Posttraumatic child's play. *Journal of the American Academy of Child and Adolescent Psychiatry* 20:741–60.

———. 1983. Play therapy and psychic trauma: A preliminary report. In C. Schaefer and K. O'Connor (eds.), *Handbook of play therapy,* 308–19. New York: John Wiley.

Thornberry, T., A. Freeman-Gallant, and A. Lizotte. 2003. Linked lives: The intergenerational transition of antisocial behavior. *Journal of Abnormal Child Psychology* 31:171–84.

Tjaden, P., and N. Thoennes. 1998. *Prevalence, incidence and consequences of violence against women: Findings from the national violence against women survey.* Washington, DC: U.S. Department of Justice.

Tolan, P. H. 1996. How resilient is the concept of resilience? *Community Psychologist* 4:12–15.

———, N. G. Guerra, and P. C. Kendall. 1995. A developmental perspective on antisocial behavior in children and adolescents: Toward a unified risk and intervention framework. *Journal of Consulting and Clinical Psychology* 63:579–84.

Tonti, M. 1982. Two steps in the integration of the husband-father in dysfunctional families. *Social Casework: The Journal of Contemporary Social Work* 63:176–79.

Tremblay, R. E., J. McCord, H. Boileau, et al. 1991. Can disruptive boys be helped to become competent? *Psychiatry: Journal for the Study of Interpersonal Processes* 54:148–61.

———, F. Vitaro, C. Gagnon, et al. 1992. A prosocial scale for the preschool behaviour questionaire: Concurrent and predictive correlates. *International Journal of Behavioral Development* 15:227–45.

Trieschman, A. E. 1969. Understanding the stages of a typical temper tantrum. In A. E. Trieschman, J. K. Whittaker, and I. K. Brendtro (eds.), *The other 23 hours: Child care work in a therapeutic milieu,* 170–97. New York: Walter de Gruyten.

Trout, A. L., M. H. Epstein, W. J. Michelson, et al. 2003. Effects of a reading intervention for kindergarten students at risk for emotional disturbance and reading deficits. *Behavioral Disorders* 29:313–26.

Tyson, P. 1980. The gender of the analyst: In relation to transference and countertransference manifestations in prelatency children. *Psychoanalytic Study of the Child* 35:321–38.

Ulman, A., and M. A. Straus. 2003. Violence by children against mothers in relation to violence between parents and corporal punishment by parents. *Journal of Comparative Family Studies* 34:41–60.

van der Kolk, B. A. 1994. *Trauma and development in children* [Video]. New York: Bureau of Psychiatric Services, New York State Department of Mental Health.

———. 1996. The complexity of adaption to trauma: Self-regulation, stimulus, discrimination, and characterological development. In B. A. van der Kolk, A.C. McFarlane, and L. Weisaeth (eds.), *Traumatic stress: The effects of overwhelming experience on mind, body, and society,* 182–213. New York: Guilford.

———. 1999. *Neurobiology of trauma.* Presentation at the Sage/Parsons Fall Conference. Albany, NY.

———. 2003. *The frontiers of trauma treatment.* Presentation at the Psychotherapy Network Symposium. Washington, DC.

Van de Putte, S. J. 1995. A paradigm for working with child survivors of sexual abuse who exhibit sexualized behaviors during play therapy. *International Journal of Play Therapy* 4:27–49.

Van Ornum, W., and J. B. Mordock. 1990. *Crisis counseling of children and adolescents: A guide for the nonprofessional.* Expanded edition. New York: Continuum. Reprinted 2002, Eugene, OR: Wipf and Stock Publishers.

Vukelich, C., and D. S. Kliman. 1985. Mature and teenage mother's infant growth expectations and use of child development information sources. *Family Relations* 34:189–96.

Wagner, B. M., M. A. C. Silverman, and C. E. Martin. 2003. Family factors in youth suicidal behaviors. *American Behavioral Scientist* 46:1171–91.

Wagner, M., R. D'Amico, C. Marder, et al. 1992. *What happens next? Trends in post-school outcomes of youth with disabilities: The second comprehensive report from the national longitudinal transition study of special education students.* SRI International. Washington, DC: U.S. Department of Education, Office of Special Education Programs.

Walker, H. M., G. Colvin, and E. Ramsey. 1995. *Antisocial behavior in schools: Strategies and best practices.* Pacific Grove, CA: Brooks/Cole.

Wallis, V. 2003. Does kindergarten need cops? *Time,* 162(24), 52–3.

Wang, Y. W., M. M. Davidson, O. F. Yakushko, et al. 2003. The scale of ethnocultural empathy: Development, validation, and reliability. *Journal of Consulting Psychology* 50:221–34.

Waters, D. B., and E. C. Lawrence. 1993. *Competence, courage and change: An approach to family therapy.* New York: Norton.

Waters, R. 2004. Making a difference: Five therapists who've taken on the wider world. *Psychotherapy Networker* Nov/Dec: 38–39.

Wax, D. E., and V. G. Haddox. 1974a. Enuresis, fire setting, and animal cruelty: A useful danger signal in predicting vulnerability of adolescent males to assaultive behavior. *Child Psychiatry and Human Development* 4:151–6.

———, and V. G. Haddox. 1974b. Enuresis, fire setting, and animal cruelty in male adolescent delinquents: A triad predictive of violent behavior. *Journal of Psychiatry and Law* 2:45–71.

Webster-Stratton, C. 1985. Comparison of abusive and nonabusive families with conduct-disordered children. *American Journal of Orthopsychiatry* 55:59–69.

———, and M. J. Reid. 2003. Treating conduct problems and strengthening social and emotional competence in young children: The Dina Dinosaur treatment program. *Journal of Emotional and Behavioral Disorders* 11:130–43.

———, M. J. Reid, and M. Hammond. 2001. Preventing conduct problems, promoting social competence: A parent and teacher training program in Head Start. *Journal of Clinical Child Psychology* 30:283–302.

Weems, C. F., K. M. Saltzman, A. L. Reiss, et al. 2003. A prospective test of the association between hyperarousal and emotional numbing in youth with a history of traumatic stress. *Journal of Clinical Child and Adolescent Psychology* 32:166–71.

Weikart, D. P. 1967. *Preliminary results from a longitudinal study of disadvantaged preschool children.* Paper presented at the Annual International Convention of the Council for Exceptional Children. St. Louis, MO.

———. 1971. *Early childhood special education for intellectually subnormal and/or culturally different children.* Paper presented at the National Leadership Institute in Early Childhood Development. Washington, DC.

Weinbach, R. W., and C. R. Curtis. 1986. Making child abuse victims aware of their victimization: A treatment issue. *Child Welfare* 65:337–46.

Weist, M. D., J. Goldstein, S. W. Evans, et al. 2003. Funding a full continuum of mental health promotion and intervention programs in the school. *Journal of Adolescent Health* 32:70–8.

Weitzman, T. 1985. Engaging the severely dysfunctional family in treatment: Basic considerations. *Family Process* 24:473–85.

Wekerle, C., and D. A. Wolfe. 1999. Dating violence in mid-adolescence: Empowering youth to promote heatlhy relationships. *Clinical Psychology Review* 19:435–56.

Werner, E., and R. Smith. 1992. *Overcoming the odds: High-risk children from birth to adulthood.* Ithaca, NY: Cornell University.

Werner, N. E., and R. K. Sibereison. 2003. Family relationship quality and contact with deviant peers as predictors of adolescent problem behaviors: The mediating role of gender. *Journal of Adolescent Research* 18:454–80.

Whetten, C. 2002. It's 3:00: Do you know where your children are?: After-school programs to the rescue. *Community Education Journal* 29 (1 and 2):13–17.

White, S., G. Strom, G. Santilli, et al. 1986. Interviewing young children with anatomically correct dolls. *Child Abuse and Neglect* 10:519–29.

Whitewell, J. 1998. Management issues in milieu therapy: Boundaries and parameters in therapeutic communities. *Journal for Therapeutic and Supportive Organizations* 19:89–105.

Widom, C. S., and J. B. Kuhns. 1996. Childhood victimization and subsequent risk for promiscuity, prostitution, and teenage pregnancy: A prospective study. *American Journal of Public Health* 86:1608–12.

Wilkinson, L. R. 2001. Review of D. Howe, M. Brandon, D. Hillings, et al. 1999. *Attachment theory, child maltreatment and family support.* Hillsdale, NJ: Erlbaum. *Clinical Child Psychology and Psychiatry* 6:326–7.

Wilkinson, S. R. 2001. Developing practice on a ward for adolescents with psychiatric disorders. *Clinical Child Psychology and Psychiatry* 6:151–63.

Williams, S. C., J. E. Lochman, N. C. Phillips, et al. 2003. Aggressive and nonaggressive boys' physiological and cognitive processes in response to peer provocations. *Journal of Clinical Child and Adolescent Psychology* 32:68–576.

Winnicott, D. 1965. *The maturational process and the facilitating environment.* London: Hogarth Press and Institute of Psychoanalysis. Reprinted 1971. New York: International Universities Press.

Winship, C. 2002. *End of a miracle?: Crime, faith, and partnership in Boston in the 1990s.* Unpublished paper. Cambridge, MA: Harvard University.

Wittenberg, K., and J. C. Norcross. 2001. Practitioner perfection: Relationship to ambiguity tolerance and work satisfaction. *Journal of Clinical Psychology* 57:1543–50.

Wolfe, D. A. 1984. Treatment of abusive parents: A reply to the special issue. *Journal of Clinical Child Psychology* 13:192–4.

———, C. Wekerle, and K. Scott. 1997. *Alternatives to violence: Empowering youth to develop healthy relationships.* Thousand Oaks, CA: Sage.

Wolfenstein, M., and G. Kliman, eds. 1965. *Children and the death of a president: Multidisciplinary studies.* Garden City, NY: Doubleday.

Wolin, S. J., and S. W. Wolin. 1993. *The resilient self: How survivors of troubled families rise above adversity.* New York: Villard.

Wood, M. J., and N. J. Long. 1991. *Life-space interventions: Talking with children and youth in crisis.* Austin, TX: Pro-Ed.

Woodhouse, S., L. Z. Schlosser, Y. E. Crook, et al. 2003. Client attachment to therapist: Relations to transference and client recollections of parental caregiving. *Journal of Counseling Psychology* 50:395–408.

Woodward, L. J., and D. M. Fergusson. 1999. Early conduct problems and later risk of teenage pregnancy in girls. *Development and Psychology* 11:127–44.

World Health Organization. 1994. *World health statistics annual*. Geneva, Switzerland: Author.

Wright, J., and C. Hensley. 2003. From animal cruelty to serial murder: Applying the graduation hypothesis. *International Journal of Offender Therapy and Comparative Criminology* 47:71–88.

Wursmer, L. 1981. *The mask of shame*. Baltimore: Johns Hopkins University Press.

Wylie, M. S. 2004. The limits of talk. *Psychotherapy Networker* 28:30–6, 38–41, 67.

Yakin, H. 2003. Odell's dark tail: Convicted murderer tells her story of fear, love, horror. *Times Herald-Record* 48(161):2–3.

Yampolskaya, S., E. C. Brown, and P. E. Greenbaum. 2002. Early pregnancy among adolescent females with serious emotional disturbance: Risk factors and outcomes. *Journal of Emotional and Behavioral Disorders* 10:108–15.

Yates, T. M., B. Egeland, and L. A. Sroufe. 2003. Rethinking resilience: A developmental process perspective. In S. S. Luthar (ed.), *Resilience and vulnerability: Adaptation in the context of childhood adversities*, 243–66. New York: Cambridge University Press.

Yoon, J. S., and K. Kerber. 2003. Bullying: Elementary teachers' altitudes and interventions strategies. *Research in Education* 69:27–35.

York, C., T. Balogh, and P. Cohen. 1990. The development and functioning of the sense of shame. *Psychoanalytic Study of the Child* 45:377–410.

Zahn-Waxler, C., P. M. Cole, J. D. Welsh, et al. 1995. Psychophysiological correlates of empathy and prosocial behaviors in preschool children with behavior problems. *Development and Psychopathology* 1:27–48.

———, and M. Radke-Yarrow. 1990. The origins of empathic concern. *Motivation and Emotion* 14:107–30.

———, M. Radke-Yarrow, E. Wagner, et al. 1992. Development of concern for others. *Developmental Psychology* 28:126–36.

Zeanah, C. Z., and M. Scheeringa. 1996. Evaluation of posttraumatic symptomatology in infants and young children exposed to violence. *Zero to Three* 16:9–14.

Ziegenhain, U., B. Deriksen, and R. Dreisörner. 2003. Young parenthood: Adolescent mothers and their children. *Monatsschrift Kinderheilkunde* 151:608–12.

Zigler, E., C. Taussig, and K. Black. 1992. Early childhood interventions: A promising preventative for juvenile delinquency. *American Psychologist* 47:997–1006.

Zimmerman, D. P. 2003. Is life good enough?: A close race to make it better. *Residential Treatment for Children and Youth* 20:1–24.

Zimrin, H. 1986. A profile of survival. *Child Abuse and Neglect* 10:339–49.

———. 1991. *The black mirror: A treatment technique for the severely traumatized child*. Paper presented at the San Diego Conference on Responding to Child Maltreatment. San Diego, California.

Zoccolillo, M., J. Myers, and S. Assiter. 1997. Conduct disorder, substance dependence, and adolescent motherhood. *American Journal of Orthopsychiatry* 67:152–7.

Index

administration of, 157–58; for trauma survivors, 216
socioeconomic hardship, 203–5, 217, 242–43
somatization, as defense, 165, 171
soul murder, 29
space, giving children, 146–47
special education: behavior disorders and, 22; disciplinary focus of, 243
Spiegel, D., 18
spiritual faith, 211. *See also* religion
splitting, as defense, 85–86, 168–69
St. John, R., 62
staff: behavior modification practices for, 145–46; burnout of, 96; conflicts over treatment among, 57–58; countertransference of, 184–85; emotional control of, 192–93; I-messages from, 141–42; limit setting by, 145; management of, 58; physical interventions by, 143–45; positive reinforcement by, 145–46, 153–54; problem diagnosis by, 150–52; punishment by, limiting of, 142–43; relationships with children of, 139–42, 146–50, 160, 192–95; for sexually abused clients, 190; skill training by, 157–58; strengths of child recognized by, 154–57; support for, 159–61; teachers versus, 152–53; therapist resented by, 138–39; therapist-staff relations, 136–62
Stanley, Janet, 8
Stanton, M. D., 113
Stevenson, Howard, Jr., 247
Stiver, I. P., 29
storytelling, therapy through, 199–200
Straus, M. A., 204
strengths, recognition of children's, 154–57, 205–6
sublimation, 173, 182–83
substance abuse: brain hyperarousal and, 36; emotional emptiness and, 39; parent-child activities concerning, 119

suicide: incidence of, 51; rejection and, 19–20
suspensions, school, 243
sustaining fictions, 25–26, 84, 203–4
symbolic sexual play, 75–76

Tangney, J. P., 17
Taussig, C., 226
teachers. *See* school; staff
teenage mothers, 109–10
testosterone, 35
therapeutic holds, 143–45
therapeutic milieu: aspects of effective, 136–62, 190; for development of defenses, 163–87; reality versus, 180; for sexually abused children, 188–200
therapists: as client's advocate, 136; difficulties of, 56–59; foster child issues for, 95; and hope, 203; male, and female clients, 70–73; overidentification with child by, 76–78, 98; parent relations, 98, 113–35; praise from, 90, 196; and staff-child relations, 136–62; therapy for, 59, 71, 73, 88; and transference, 87–88; ultimatums by, 130–32. *See also* therapeutic milieu
therapy: action-oriented, 40; children's needs in, 137–38; coping approach in, 65; ego-strengthening approach to, 189–90; females and, 39–40; length of, 98; nonclinic sites for, 246–47; staff role in, 136–62; trauma issues in, 40–42; treatment plans, 154–57. *See also* therapeutic milieu; therapists; therapy risks
therapy risks, 60–78; arousal of strong emotions, 61–66; deviant self-image confirmation, 69–70; diversion from pressing problems, 66–67; male therapists and female clients, 70–73; overidentification with child, 76–78; self-blame increase, 67–68; sexualized play, 73–76

About the Authors

David A. Crenshaw, Ph.D., ABPP, RPT-S, is currently in private practice in Rhinebeck, New York, and is director of the Rhinebeck Child and Family Center, LLC, www.rhinebeckcfc.com. He was formerly clinical director at the Rhinebeck Country School and the Astor Home for Children, both residential treatment centers for emotionally disturbed children located in Rhinebeck. For close to twenty years, he was also director of the Astor Home's doctoral-level psychology internship program, which is accredited by the American Psychological Association. He has authored numerous professional publications and book chapters on issues related to grief, abuse, and trauma in children and is the author of *Bereavement: Counseling the Grieving throughout the Life Cycle* and *A Guidebook for Engaging Resistant Children in Therapy: A Projective Drawing and Storytelling Series*. He is registered by the Association of Play Therapy as a play therapist–supervisor and is currently president of the New York Association of Play Therapy.

John B. Mordock, Ph.D., ABPP, was employed by the Astor Home for Children for twenty-eight years. In his last position, he directed the agency's community mental health programs, helping to develop a full continuum of services for emotionally disturbed children and their families. Before that time, he was coordinator of research at the Devereux Foundation in Devon, Pennsylvania. He is the author of twelve books, including a textbook on exceptional children, and has a chapter in *The Handbook of Child and Adolescent Psychiatry*. Dr. Mordock is a fellow of the American Psychological Association. His numerous writings on topics of play therapy and abused and traumatized children have appeared over the past forty years in many highly respected journals.

Both authors are board certified by the American Board of Professional Psychology.

Atmosphere Changer

" Everyone has a past — I dont
want to be defined by mine "

Judging Amy —
New Social Worker

Say Something
like there is always
going to be bumps
in the road —
figure out which ones
to groove & which ones
to flatten